# T-DISTRIBUTION TABLE

Critical Values of *t* For Given Levels of Significance and Degrees of Freedom

α = areas in one tail of curve

## One-Tailed Tests

| df | α = 0.1 | α = 0.05 | α = 0.025 | α = 0.01 | α = 0.001 |
|---|---|---|---|---|---|
| 1 | 3.078 | 6.314 | 12.706 | 31.821 | 318.309 |
| 2 | 1.886 | 2.920 | 4.303 | 6.965 | 22.327 |
| 3 | 1.638 | 2.353 | 3.182 | 4.541 | 10.215 |
| 4 | 1.533 | 2.132 | 2.776 | 3.747 | 7.173 |
| 5 | 1.476 | 2.015 | 2.571 | 3.365 | 5.893 |
| 6 | 1.440 | 1.943 | 2.447 | 3.143 | 5.208 |
| 7 | 1.415 | 1.895 | 2.365 | 2.998 | 4.785 |
| 8 | 1.397 | 1.860 | 2.306 | 2.897 | 4.501 |
| 9 | 1.383 | 1.833 | 2.262 | 2.821 | 4.297 |
| 10 | 1.372 | 1.812 | 2.228 | 2.764 | 4.144 |
| 11 | 1.363 | 1.796 | 2.201 | 2.718 | 4.025 |
| 12 | 1.356 | 1.782 | 2.179 | 2.681 | 3.930 |
| 13 | 1.350 | 1.771 | 2.160 | 2.650 | 3.852 |
| 14 | 1.345 | 1.761 | 2.145 | 2.625 | 3.787 |
| 15 | 1.341 | 1.753 | 2.131 | 2.603 | 3.733 |
| 16 | 1.337 | 1.746 | 2.120 | 2.584 | 3.686 |
| 17 | 1.333 | 1.740 | 2.110 | 2.567 | 3.646 |
| 18 | 1.330 | 1.734 | 2.101 | 2.552 | 3.610 |
| 19 | 1.328 | 1.729 | 2.093 | 2.540 | 3.579 |
| 20 | 1.325 | 1.725 | 2.086 | 2.528 | 3.552 |
| 21 | 1.323 | 1.721 | 2.080 | 2.518 | 3.527 |
| 22 | 1.321 | 1.717 | 2.074 | 2.508 | 3.505 |
| 23 | 1.319 | 1.714 | 2.069 | 2.500 | 3.485 |
| 24 | 1.318 | 1.711 | 2.064 | 2.492 | 3.467 |
| 25 | 1.316 | 1.708 | 2.060 | 2.485 | 3.450 |
| 26 | 1.315 | 1.706 | 2.056 | 2.479 | 3.435 |
| 27 | 1.314 | 1.703 | 2.052 | 2.473 | 3.421 |
| 28 | 1.313 | 1.701 | 2.048 | 2.467 | 3.408 |
| 29 | 1.311 | 1.699 | 2.045 | 2.462 | 3.396 |
| 30 | 1.310 | 1.697 | 2.042 | 2.457 | 3.385 |
| 31 | 1.309 | 1.696 | 2.040 | 2.453 | 3.375 |
| 32 | 1.309 | 1.694 | 2.037 | 2.449 | 3.365 |
| 33 | 1.308 | 1.692 | 2.035 | 2.445 | 3.356 |
| 34 | 1.307 | 1.691 | 2.032 | 2.441 | 3.348 |
| 35 | 1.306 | 1.690 | 2.030 | 2.438 | 3.340 |
| 36 | 1.306 | 1.688 | 2.028 | 2.435 | 3.333 |
| 37 | 1.305 | 1.687 | 2.026 | 2.431 | 3.326 |
| 38 | 1.304 | 1.686 | 2.024 | 2.429 | 3.319 |
| 39 | 1.304 | 1.685 | 2.023 | 2.426 | 3.313 |
| 40 | 1.303 | 1.684 | 2.021 | 2.423 | 3.307 |
| 45 | 1.301 | 1.679 | 2.014 | 2.412 | 3.281 |
| 50 | 1.299 | 1.676 | 2.009 | 2.403 | 3.261 |
| 55 | 1.297 | 1.673 | 2.004 | 2.396 | 3.245 |
| 60 | 1.296 | 1.671 | 2.000 | 2.390 | 3.232 |
| 70 | 1.294 | 1.667 | 1.994 | 2.381 | 3.211 |
| 80 | 1.292 | 1.664 | 1.990 | 2.374 | 3.195 |
| 90 | 1.291 | 1.662 | 1.987 | 2.369 | 3.183 |
| 100 | 1.290 | 1.660 | 1.984 | 2.364 | 3.174 |
| 110 | 1.289 | 1.659 | 1.982 | 2.361 | 3.166 |
| 120 | 1.289 | 1.658 | 1.980 | 2.358 | 3.160 |
| ∞ | 1.282 | 1.645 | 1.960 | 2.326 | 3.096 |

# INTRODUCTION TO
# STATISTICS
## FOR
# SOCIAL SCIENCES
### FIRST EDITION

SCOTT R. COLWELL

EDWARD M. CARTER

McGraw-Hill
Ryerson
*Connect. Learn. Succeed.*

**McGraw-Hill Ryerson**
*Connect. Learn. Succeed.*

**Introduction to Statistics for Social Sciences**
**First Edition**

Statistics Canada information is used with the permission of Statistics Canada. Users are forbidden to copy this material and/or redisseminate the data, in an original or modified form, for commercial purposes, without the expressed permission of Statistics Canada. Information on the availability of the wide range of data from Statistics Canada can be obtained from Statistics Canada's Regional Offices, its World Wide Web site at http://www.statcan.ca and its toll-free access number 1-800-263-1136.

The Internet addresses listed in the text were accurate at the time of publication. The inclusion of a Web site does not indicate an endorsement by the authors or McGraw-Hill Ryerson, and McGraw-Hill Ryerson does not guarantee the accuracy of information presented at these sites.

ISBN 13: 978-0-07-073522-4
ISBN 10: 0-07-073522-0

1 2 3 4 5 6 7 8 9 10 DOC 1 9 8 7 6 5 4 3 2

Printed and bound in the United States of America.

Care has been taken to trace ownership of copyright material contained in this text; however, the publisher will welcome any information that enables them to rectify any reference or credit for subsequent editions.

**Sponsoring Editor:** *Marcia Siekowski*
**Marketing Manager:** *Stacey Metz*
**Developmental Editor:** *Lindsay MacDonald*
**Senior Editorial Associate:** *Stephanie Giles*
**Editorial Associate:** *Erin Catto*
**Supervising Editor:** *Katie McHale*
**Copy Editor:** *Ann Firth/EditWrite*
**Production Coordinator:** *Lena Keating*
**iLearning Sales Specialist:** *Smiljana Orlic*
**Permissions Researcher:** *Allison McDonald*
**Inside Design:** *Aptara®, Inc.*
**Composition:** *Aptara®, Inc.*
**Cover Design:** *Gord Robertson*
**Cover Photo:** *Ray Lego/Getty Images*
**Printer:** *R.R. Donnelley/Crawfordsville (U.S.)*

**Library and Archives Canada Cataloguing in Publication**

Colwell, Scott, 1969–
    Introduction to statistics for social sciences / Scott Colwell, Ed Carter.
    Includes bibliographical references and index.
    ISBN 978-0-07-073522-4

    1. Social sciences—Statistical methods—Textbooks.
    I. Carter, Edward, 1951-  II. Title.
    HA29.C64 2012          300.1'5195                    C2011-907591-1

# About the Authors

## Scott R. Colwell, Ph.D.

Dr. Colwell received his Ph.D. from the University of Bradford in West Yorkshire, United Kingdom in 2003. He is an Associate Professor at the University of Guelph where he has been a faculty member since 2003. While his home department is the Department of Marketing and Consumer Studies, he is also an Adjunct Professor in the Department of Psychology. He has taught statistics to students in the social and behavioural sciences at both the undergraduate and the graduate levels. His research interests include ethical decision making and applied statistics. He enjoys watching and playing hockey (particularly on a PS3) and lives in a small town just outside of the City of Guelph, with his wife Marissa and two daughters, Ahleigha and Alexa.

## Edward M. Carter, Ph.D.

Dr. Carter received his Ph.D. from the University of Toronto in 1975. He has been a faculty member in the department of Mathematics and Statistics at the University of Guelph since 1975, where he is currently a Professor of Statistics. He has taught students at the undergraduate and graduate levels in both the life sciences and social sciences. His research interests include multivariate analysis, applied statistics and biostatistics. He loves computers, soccer, and lives in Guelph with his wife Bianca.

# Brief Contents

# Contents

# Preface

## ABOUT THIS BOOK

Statistics is a really interesting subject to study. The problem is, despite our best intentions and efforts, it is often hard for instructors and authors to put the concepts into everyday language that students understand. So, in writing this book, we decided to ask students to help us with the language. As we wrote the first six chapters, we asked social science students to read the drafts and provide feedback on their readability and relevance. After completing the first draft, we then piloted the entire book in an introductory statistics class, offered to social science students at the University of Guelph, and then asked those students for feedback. The result, we hope, is a book that will break the statistical language barrier between instructors and students.

Aside from wanting a readable textbook, we also found that instructors and students wanted a book that included only the material they require for a one-semester introductory statistics class. Our original thought was to include 12 chapters. However, after receiving extremely helpful comments from our reviewers, we included an additional chapter in order to separate confidence intervals (Chapter 8) and single sample hypothesis testing (Chapter 9). This allowed for more detail in both areas without being overwhelming. Although you may find that one or two of the chapters are not needed for your course, we believe that we have managed to narrow the focus of the book down to what is typically covered in the majority of introductory courses.

Prior to writing this textbook, we examined the literature on student "statistical anxiety" for insights that might help us shape the structure and content. Cruise and Wilkins (1980) found six reasons for student statistical anxiety: (i) not understanding the value and worth of statistics in their field; (ii) fear of not being able to interpret results properly; (iii) worry about tests and classroom exercises; (iv) lack of confidence regarding the use of statistical computer programs; (v) not asking for help for fear of looking stupid; and (vi) a general nervousness around statistical professors. Armed with this information, we set out with the hope of addressing these areas. We detail our approach in Chapter 1, but would like to highlight a few things that we think students may find of value.

1. *Research Examples:* To help students see the relevance of statistics to their chosen field of study, we have included examples of social science research that Canadian researchers have published in peer-reviewed journals. At the end of each chapter, there is a summary of their research, questions about that research that tie into the topics covered in the chapter, and answers to the questions. This will give students the opportunity to see how researchers use the statistical methods.

2. *Frequently Asked Questions:* At the end of each chapter, students will find a list of frequently asked questions (and their answers). Based on student feedback and our own experience, we included some of the most commonly asked questions that students have after reading each chapter. We then provide a detailed response to each.

3. *For Your Information* and *Take a Closer Look:* To provide students with additional information about specific topics we have included "For Your Information" and "Take a Closer Look" sections in each chapter. These are meant to help students become more comfortable with certain topics. For example, in Chapter 5 there is a "For Your Information" section that explains how the normal curve applies to everyday life. In Chapter 8 there is a "Take a Closer Look" section that discusses when students might use a one-sided versus two-sided test.

4. *A Brief History of . . .:* Cruise and Wilkins (1980) found that students often feel nervous around statistics instructors. As such, we wanted to show that famous statisticians of the past were also normal people. To accomplish this, we included a section at the beginning of each chapter called "A Brief History of . . ." section where we profile famous statisticians, such as Florence Nightingale.

5. *Did You Know:* We have also included a "Did You Know" section in each chapter that provides students with lighthearted and interesting tidbits. For example, in Chapter 4 we explain how the Monty Hall Problem works and in Chapter 11 we discuss the Elevator Paradox.

6. *Sample Problems:* As we wrote this text, one thing that students and instructors kept asking for was sample problems. In each chapter there are two types of sample problems: exercises and end-of-chapter problems. The exercises have been placed at key points within the text of each chapter. After students have read a certain amount of the material, they can test themselves using the exercise. The answers to these exercises can then be found at the end of the chapter. The end-of-chapter problems include questions that cover the entire chapter. The answers to these as well as additional practice problems and materials can be found on Connect.

7. *Video Tutorials and Interactive Figures:* This textbook includes a number of online resources. Two that we are particularly fond of are the video tutorials and the demonstration tools. We have created a series of short video tutorials that cover the areas we find students tend to have the most problems with. Students will find these tutorials listed by chapter on Connect. We have also included a series of interactive figures that allow students to visualize specific types of analyses and then manipulate various settings in the demonstration to see the effects on the results. These are also on Connect.

8. *Datasets:* We have often found that instructors want datasets that can be used throughout the entire textbook. We have simulated four datasets, built around fictitious scenarios that contain enough variables to allow the dataset to be used across the entire textbook. Other more topic specific datasets are also available. These are on Connect.

9. *Computer Software Guides and Video Tutorials:* Students will notice that this textbook does not incorporate the SPSS software within each chapter. The reason for this is twofold. First, given that instructors maybe using different versions of SPSS, we did not want to provide information within the text that might not be consistent with a specific version of SPSS. Second, we found that many instructors are using software other than SPSS, so by not including SPSS material in the textbook, we were able to keep the material relevant to more instructors. However, on Connect there are brief written instructions on how to run various types of analysis using SPSS. Students will also find a series of short video tutorials that show them how to use SPSS for various types of analysis.

# RESOURCES

**McGraw-Hill Connect™** is a web-based assignment and assessment platform that gives students the means to better connect with their coursework, with their instructors, and with the important concepts that they will need to know for success now and in the future.

With Connect, instructors can deliver assignments, quizzes and tests online. Nearly all the questions from the text are presented in an auto-gradeable format and tied to the text's learning objectives.

Instructors can edit existing questions and author entirely new problems. Track individual student performance—by question, assignment or in relation to the class overall—with detailed grade reports. Integrate grade reports easily with Learning Management Systems (LMS) such as WebCT and Blackboard.

By choosing Connect, instructors are providing their students with a powerful tool for improving academic performance and truly mastering course material. Connect allows students to practice important skills at their own pace and on their own schedule. Importantly, students' assessment results and instructors' feedback are all saved online—so students can continually review their progress and plot their course to success.

Connect also provides 24/7 online access to an eBook—an online edition of the text—to aid them in successfully completing their work, wherever and whenever they choose.

## Key Features

### Simple Assignment Management

With Connect, creating assignments is easier than ever, so you can spend more time teaching and less time managing.

- Create and deliver assignments easily with selectable end-of-chapter questions and testbank material to assign online.
- Streamline lesson planning, student progress reporting, and assignment grading to make classroom management more efficient than ever.
- Go paperless with the eBook and online submission and grading of student assignments.

### Smart Grading

When it comes to studying, time is precious. Connect helps students learn more efficiently by providing feedback and practice material when they need it, where they need it.

- Automatically score assignments, giving students immediate feedback on their work and side-by-side comparisons with correct answers.
- Access and review each response; manually change grades or leave comments for students to review.
- Reinforce classroom concepts with practice tests and instant quizzes.

### Instructor Library

The Connect Instructor Library is your course creation hub. It provides all the critical resources you'll need to build your course, just how you want to teach it.

- Assign eBook readings and draw from a rich collection of textbook-specific assignments.
- Access instructor resources, including ready-made PowerPoint presentations and media to use in your lectures.
- View assignments and resources created for past sections.
- Post your own resources for students to use.

*eBook*

Connect reinvents the textbook learning experience for the modern student. Every Connect subject area is seamlessly integrated with Connect eBooks, which are designed to keep students focused on the concepts key to their success.

- Provide students with a Connect eBook, allowing for anytime, anywhere access to the textbook.
- Merge media, animation and assessments with the text's narrative to engage students and improve learning and retention.
- Pinpoint and connect key concepts in a snap using the powerful eBook search engine.
- Manage notes, highlights and bookmarks in one place for simple, comprehensive review.

## Course Management

McGraw-Hill Ryerson offers a range of flexible integration solutions for Blackboard, WebCT, Desire2Learn, Moodle, and other leading learning management platforms. Please contact your local McGraw-Hill Ryerson *i*Learning Sales Specialist for details.

## Additional Technology and Learning Solutions

To see the latest technology and Learning Solutions offered by McGraw-Hill Ryerson and their partners, please visit us online.

www.mcgrawhill.ca/he/solutions.

Connect your campus to
our solutions

Customize to meet your
needs

eTextbook options

# Acknowledgements

We have many people that we owe our deepest thanks to for helping us with this book. Starting with the wonderful people at McGraw-Hill we would like to thank our Sponsoring Editor, Marcia Siekowski; our Supervising Editor, Katie McHale; our Developmental Editor, Lindsay MacDonald; our Permissions Editor, Allison McDonald; and our Copy Editor, Ann Firth. We would also like to thank the supplemental and Connect authors David Desjardins (John Abbott College), Scott Schau (University of Guelph), and Thomas Varghese (Athabasca University) and our Technical Checker Jason Greenberg. Furthermore, we would like to thank Kristian Adomait, Patrick Visintini, all of the students who took the introductory statistics course where we piloted this textbook (Jason Alam, Allison Barr, Stephanie Figliomeni, Jessica Laidlaw, Amanda Morris, and Andrea Walters), and our colleagues at the University of Guelph. We also owe a great deal gratitude to the reviewers who spent a lot of their own personal time reading our drafts and providing very detailed and useful feedback.

**John O. Anderson**
*University of Victoria*

**Silvia Bartolic**
*University of British Columbia*

**Tony Christensen**
*Wilfrid Laurier University-Brantford*

**Diane Crocker**
*Saint Mary's University*

**David Desjardins**
*John Abbott College*

**Judy Eaton**
*Wilfrid Laurier University-Brantford*

**James Frideres**
*University of Calgary*

**John Jayachandran**
*Concordia University College of Alberta*

**Alan Law**
*Trent University*

**Renan Levine**
*University of Toronto Scarborough*

**William Marshall**
*University of Western Ontario*

**Amanda McCormick**
*University of the Fraser Valley*

**Andrea Noack**
*Ryerson University*

**Sheldon Ungar**
*University of Toronto Scarborough*

**Thomas Varghese**
*Athabasca University*

**Weiguo Zhang**
*University of Toronto Mississauga*

Finally, we would like to pay a special thank you to our families (Marissa, Ahleigha, and Alexa Colwell, and Bianca, Diana, and Michael Carter) who have put up with our absence over countless nights and weekends and supported us through this entire journey.

# The Role of Statistics in the Social Sciences

# 1

Visit **connect**™
for additional study tools.

**Learning Objectives:**

By the end of this chapter you should be able to:

1. Describe the meaning of the term "statistics."
2. Explain why statistics is important in the social sciences.
3. Explain where statistics fits in the research process.
4. Define the difference between the population and the sample.
5. Describe in general terms the difference between descriptive and inferential statistics.
6. Explain the importance of ethics in statistics.
7. Describe the difference between an independent and a dependent variable.
8. Provide examples of independent and dependent variables.
9. Define the four levels of measurement.
10. Identify the level of measurement of different variables.

# A Brief History of...

## John Graunt (1620–1674)

John Graunt was a men's clothing store owner (haberdasher) and statistician. He is considered by many to be the father of vital statistics, which is the analysis of birth and death data. Graunt published the first "Life Table," which is a table of probabilities, by age, of dying in a given future period. In medieval England, parishes were required to keep "Bills of Mortality" that recorded data on baptisms, deaths, and causes of deaths. Graunt conducted what is quite likely the first vital statistical analysis on these Bills of Mortality. For example, he analyzed the numbers of deaths due to the Plague, as shown in Table 1.1.

Graunt went even further by analyzing different causes of deaths and found differences between gender and rural locations versus the City of London. The most notable publication of his findings was released in print in 1662 and was titled *Natural and Political Observations, Mentioned in a Following Index, and Made Upon the Bills of Mortality*. Most of Graunt's belongings were destroyed in the Great Fire of London in 1666 and he died of jaundice on April 18th, 1674.[1]

**TABLE 1.1**   **Number of Deaths Due to the Plague**

| Year | Number of Deaths |
|------|------------------|
| 1620 | 2 |
| 1621 | 11 |
| 1622 | 16 |
| 1623 | 17 |
| 1624 | 0 |
| 1625 | 35,417 |
| 1626 | 134 |
| 1627 | 4 |

**Source:** Graunt, John. Reflections on the weekly bills of mortality for the cities of London and Westminster, and the places adjacent. London: Printed for Samuel Speed, at the Rainbow in Fleet-Street, 1665. HEW 11.11.1 v.1. Houghton Library, Harvard University, Cambridge, Mass.

## Introduction

Chances are that if you reading this textbook, you are enrolled in some form of statistics course. We are willing to bet that many of you are not terribly interested in statistics and are a bit anxious about taking this course. We are also willing to bet that eight out of every 10 of your classmates are experiencing the same anxiety about studying one of those "evil mathematical subjects." We know this is true because social science researchers have found that approximately 80 percent of students experience "statistics anxiety" when taking a statistics course. In fact, believe it or not, there is actually a scale that researchers use to measure statistics anxiety. Cruise and Wilkins (1980) developed the "Statistical Anxiety Rating Scale," or STARS, for measuring student anxiety toward statistics.

There are plenty of reasons why students experience statistics anxiety. In fact, Cruise and Wilkins found six primary reasons: (i) not understanding the value and worth of statistics in their field; (ii) fear of not being able to interpret results properly; (iii) worry about tests and classroom exercises; (iv) lack of confidence regarding the use of statistical computer programs; (v) not asking for help for fear of looking stupid; and (vi) a general nervousness around statistics professors. So, if you are feeling anxious about your statistics course, you need to know that you are not alone, it's natural. After all, 80 percent of the students in your classroom probably feel the same way. We have designed this textbook in such a way as to address the reasons why students feel statistics anxiety. Here is how we will try to do that.

1. Not understanding the value and worth of statistics in your field of study.

   **Our approach:** We will attempt to convince you of the importance of statistics to the social sciences by providing you with plenty of different examples within each chapter, linking the key learning concepts to these examples. Furthermore, at the end of each chapter, we provide you with a brief explanation of a real research study and provide you with questions and answers that link the key concepts of that particular chapter to that study. This way you can see how the concepts work within real social science research.

2. Fear of not being able to interpret results properly.

   **Our approach:** Each chapter includes examples with easy examples that we will walk you through using plain language. We also include datasets that you can work on with questions and answers.

3. Worry about tests and classroom exercises.

   **Our approach:** Each chapter includes examples with questions and answers that you can work through while reading the chapter. Working through these prior to going to class or prior to tests will help you understand the concepts. The Example Questions and Answers that we have provided are based on our experience with students similar to you.

4. Lack of confidence regarding the use of statistical computer programs.

   **Our approach:** Connect, the textbook's online resource, includes a user guide to the IBM® Statistical Package for the Social Sciences (SPSS®, also known as PAWS®). In each chapter of the user guide that requires you to conduct some analysis in SPSS® or PAWS®, we provide you with a tree diagram to follow for each step of the analysis.

5. Not asking for help for fear of looking stupid.

   **Our approach:** Generally, students still have questions even after they go through the material. Unfortunately, students don't always ask the questions they want to ask. At the end of each chapter we have included a Frequently Asked Questions (FAQs) section. To create this section, we asked undergraduate students in social science programs to read various chapters of this book and develop questions that they felt students would ask. We also included questions that we have found that students commonly ask. Finally, we have also developed a series of short online tutorials. In each tutorial we focus on helping you understand the areas that students tend to have the most difficulty with. While watching these, please keep in mind that we aren't actors.

These features should help you to feel more comfortable with the material. If you still have questions after working through these, you should feel comfortable asking for help at this point. Most material covered in each chapter builds on material from previous chapters, so it is important that you understand each part before moving on. So go ahead and ask your questions. Your professor is there to help—that's what we do—and in our experience, there are no stupid questions if you have read the material and still need additional help.

6. A general nervousness around statistical professors.

**Our approach:** This is a tricky one. Most statistics professors understand why students are a bit nervous around us. Movies that portray "math types" as eccentric and unapproachable definitely do not help. To try to ease some of this nervousness, we included profiles of some of the most famous and interesting statistics professors in history. We also provide you with some interesting statistical issues, problems, and games in a section titled *Did You Know?* We hope that these will help you realize that statistics—and statistics professors—can be interesting and, as a result, you will feel more comfortable when speaking with your statistics professors.

**FIGURE 1.1**
**The Approachable Professor**

**LO1**

# What is Statistics?

**Statistics** is the science and practice of developing human knowledge through the use of empirical data. It is based on statistical theory that uses probability theory to estimate population values.

Believe it or not, there is a lot of confusion about what statistics is. A statistic is simply a numerical value describing something of interest in the population or sample. For example, Statistics Canada reported that in 2005 there were 3,743 suicide-related deaths in Canada.[2] This is a numerical value telling us about suicide in the population of Canada.

**Statistics** (with an "s" on the end), is generally considered to be the science and practice of developing human knowledge through the use of empirical data. It is based on statistical theory, which uses probability theory to estimate population values. This sounds a bit confusing, but once you work through it, it's really quite simple. In the social and natural sciences, we try to understand social and natural phenomena, such as how poverty and criminal activity are related (social), or why the sky is blue (natural). We further our understanding of these phenomena by using the scientific method to create research studies that provide us with quantitative data. We then use various statistical methods to analyze the data and draw conclusions.

There are two different versions of the study of statistics and not clarifying this often makes students who are not fond of mathematics a little bit nervous. **Mathematical statistics** is the study of how to create the statistical methods using mathematical principles. This is the type of statistics that you would study if you wanted to be a statistician or a professor who researches the creation of statistical methods. Take a deep breath and sigh with relief, because this is not what we are doing. Applied statistics is what the large majority of researchers use. So looking back at our general definition, applied statistics is simply taking the statistical methods that the mathematical statisticians have created, and using them to analyze data. This is really what we are dealing with in this book. We won't be dealing with the mathematical proofs of statistical equations in this book. We will simply be using them to analyze data. That's not to say that you won't find equations in this text, because you will, but they will be explained in the applied sense.

So if you like, we can simplify the general definition of statistics as follows. **Applied statistics** is the practice of developing knowledge by using statistical methods to analyze data and make inferences about the population from which the data came.

> **Mathematical statistics** is the study of how to create the statistical methods using mathematical principles.

> **Applied statistics** is the practice of developing knowledge by using statistical methods to analyze data and make inferences about the population from which the data came.

# Why Do We Need Statistics in Social Science?

**LO2**

Social science is a field of study that includes many different disciplines such as sociology, psychology, political science, criminology, economics, education, business, anthropology, social work, geography, and many more. In contrast to the natural sciences, where scientists study nature and natural phenomena, social science includes scientists who study the nature of society and social phenomena. While that may be a bit too general for most people it will do for our purpose, since we are more interested in the role of statistics in the social sciences.

Social scientists try to understand how things in the social world work. During the research process, social scientists form hypotheses, gather data, and then analyze the data to draw conclusions about the validity of their hypotheses. Applied statistics—or to be more technically correct, applied statistical analysis methods—provide the means for analyzing the data. For example:

1. A criminologist, who wants to understand the likelihood that an offender will repeat his or her offenses after undergoing some form of rehabilitation program, may hypothesize that the treatment is effective at reducing recidivism. By gathering data from offenders and analyzing that data using specific

applied statistical methods, the researcher can test the hypothesis and draw inferences about the rehabilitation program.

2. A sociologist studying how social economic status and stereotyping affects elementary school student grades may hypothesize that low social economic status and negative stereotyping is associated with lower grades. The sociologist would then gather data from elementary school students, analyze the data using applied statistical methods, and draw conclusions.

You probably get the point now, but here are some other examples for you to think about. A psychologist investigating how varying levels of exposure to a certain therapy influences a patient's mental health will use applied statistics to analyze the data. A political scientist researching social factors that contribute to minority voter turnout on election day will use applied statistics to analyze the data.

So statistics (often used interchangeably with applied statistical analysis methods) is a vital part of all social science research because it helps us to answer questions we have about the social world. For example, suppose we want to know if there is a difference in labour wages between women with children and women without children. Data gathered and statistically analyzed by Statistics Canada shows that on average females with children earn 12 percent less than females without children.

## Statistics in the Research Process

**LO3**

Statistics plays an important role in the social sciences. As you know from examples in the previous section, social scientists use statistics to answer their research questions. But where in the research process should statistics be considered? Broadly speaking, theory is the basis upon which research questions and hypotheses are developed, while statistics are the tools used to test the hypotheses. Consider the research process shown in Figure 1.2. When conducting research, social scientists follow a rigorous process designed to test their theories of the social world.

First, the theory that underlies the phenomenon of interest is considered. For example, Merton's Anomie Theory is often used to explain deviant behaviour in individuals and in organizations. Theory is what helps to develop the research question to be investigated.

Next, the researcher develops the research question regarding the situation of interest. For example: Do neighbourhood watch programs increase the risk of vigilantism by neighbourhood citizens? At this point researchers need to be clear on how they conceptualize the concepts they want to measure. For example, how should vigilantism be conceptualized? Conceptualizing essentially involves defining what a concept is and is not.

Hypotheses are then developed to test the theory in light of research question. We will cover hypotheses in more detail in chapter 7 but, for example, one might hypothesize that police community presence decreases the risk of vigilantism. From here the research study is designed.

Following hypothesis development, research design involves determining things such as how the concepts will be measured (also referred to as operationalized),

**FIGURE 1.2**
**The Research Process**

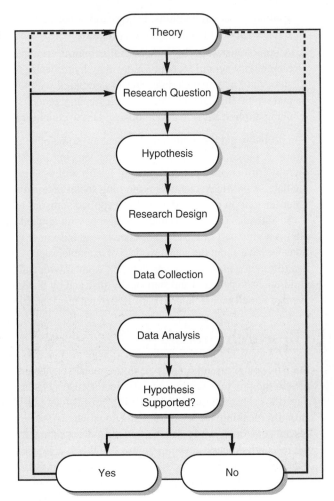

what type of data is needed, how the data will be collected, what sample size is required, and so on. The study must be designed such that it provides the researcher with the ability to test the hypotheses and answer the research question.

After deciding on the design, data collection is completed using a research instrument (e.g., a survey, an interview protocol, unobtrusive observations, etc.) to physically collect the data required to test the hypotheses.

Once the data is collected, data analysis is conducted and the hypotheses are tested. Hypothesis testing is covered in chapters 7 through 13.

Finally, having gathered and analyzed the data, the researcher can draw conclusions about his or her hypotheses and the research question. The researcher then explains the impact the findings may have on the theory considered in the study so that other researchers may replicate and/or build on those results.

So where does statistics come in? Theory is what drives our research questions and hypotheses, and determines the type of research method to be used (i.e., qualitative versus quantitative methods). When quantitative research methods are used, there is a tendency to consider statistics only in the data analysis stage. The reality is that statistics should be considered from the research question development stage through to the results and conclusion stage. Although actual analysis required to test the hypotheses occurs during the data analysis stage, the researchers need to consider the statical analysis throughout the entire process in order to properly test their research questions and hypotheses. Figure 1.3 provides a diagram of the statistical considerations at each stage.

**FIGURE 1.3   Statistical Considerations in the Research Process**

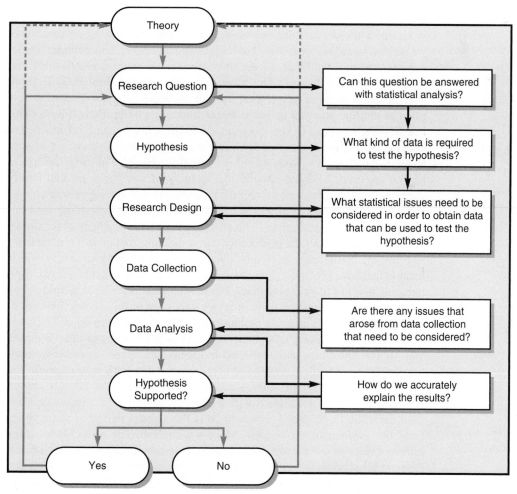

Throughout the text, we will briefly discuss the connection between the data analysis and the research process. However, given that our focus is on statistical analysis and not research methods you may wish to refer to a research methods textbook if you need further clarity regarding research methods issues not discussed in this textbook.

# "Statistically Speaking"—Thinking and Speaking Statistically

Most of us informally use statistics, or at least statistical language, every day without even realizing it. We say things such as "chances are if you drink and drive, you will get arrested, cause a serious accident, or both." We may choose not to play the lottery because "the odds of winning are so small." Or we might convince a nervous friend that flying to a vacation spot is safe because the chances of the plane crashing are so small that it's not worth worrying about.

Granted, these examples are very general and much more informal than we need to be for our purposes, but it gives you an idea of how common statistics are. You will find that the use of statistics does require you to think and speak a little bit differently. Don't worry; we'll walk you through it. To think statistically is to think in a logical manner, in which you can determine how usual or unusual an event is. For example, suppose a lightning bolt were to hit and fatally wound one of your neighbours. To think that because it happened to your neighbour means that it is definitely going to happen to you would be silly and non-statistical. You know that it is unusual for this type of thing to happen, so you are more likely to say that the chances of you being hit and fatally wounded by lightning are low. (Please note that we are not suggesting you ignore warnings during lightning storms.) Thinking about how likely and unlikely or usual and unusual an event is, is thinking statistically. In other words, you are thinking about the probability that something will or will not happen.

Speaking statistically is simply a way of communicating your results in a manner that adds precision. Previously we said that we know it is unusual for a lightning bolt to kill your neighbour. But how unusual is it? We may find out by using statistical techniques (which aren't important at this stage) that it is so unusual that the odds of dying by lightning strike are over 1 in 73,000.[3] That is what we mean by speaking statistically. Let's take another example. Suppose you want to know how many students in grade 5 and 6 classes suffer from attention deficit disorder (ADD) and also have trouble with mathematics. You might survey 10 different schools and find that out of 250 randomly chosen students, 15 fit this description with a standard deviation of 2 (more on standard deviation in chapter 3; basically, it is the amount that each score varies from the average of all scores). Since we can't survey all schools in the province, we can use these numbers to estimate how many grade 5 and 6 students in all schools suffer from ADD and have problems with mathematics. Again, using simple statistical techniques we could say that with 95 percent confidence we believe this number is between 14.75 and 15.25 students. In other words, if we repeat the survey 100 times, we would find that in 95 of the surveys, between 14.75 and 15.25 students would fit our description. That is what we mean when we say talking statistically.

In order to prepare you for the next chapter, we need to cover two basic concepts in statistics: population versus sample, and descriptive statistics versus inferential statistics.

## LO4

## The Population versus the Sample

You have probably heard of or read about research studies where a particular sample of individuals were randomly selected from a particular population or group of people. For example, 10 undergraduate student union presidents were randomly selected from the population of all student union presidents across Canada, or 200 canoeing enthusiasts were randomly selected from the entire membership of the Ontario Recreational Canoeing and Kayaking Association. What these statements are referring to is the difference between a population and a sample. A **population** is the total number of individuals, objects, or items that you are interested in. A **sample** is a subset of the population. Look at Figure 1.4 and imagine that the circle represents a country, or a province, or a specific group of people that you are interested in. These people represent the population. Keep in mind that when we say population, we are not referring to the population of a town or province or country, but rather we are referring to the total number (population) of individuals (or objects, items, etc.) of interest to the research.

Now consider Figure 1.5. Here, 10 individuals (5 males and 5 females) have been randomly selected from the population to be in the sample. These 10 individuals are a subset of the population. When we randomly select individuals from a population, such that each person has an equal chance of being in the sample, we say that the sample is **representative of the population.**

A **population** is the total number of individuals, objects, or items that you are interested in.

A **sample** is a subset of the population.

A sample is considered to be **representative of the population** when those in the sample have been randomly selected from the population such that each individual has an equal chance of being in the sample.

**FIGURE 1.4**
**The Population**

The Population

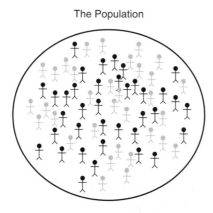

**FIGURE 1.5**
**The Population and the Sample**

The Population

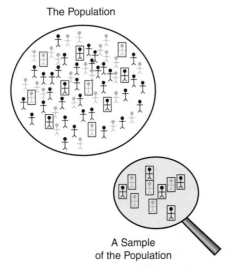

A Sample
of the Population

Recall our previous example regarding the prevalence of ADD in grade 5 and 6 students. Although we are interested in the results for the 250 students in our sample, what we are more interested in is estimating what the results might be for all grade 5 and 6 students across the province. Now imagine that we find there are 150,000 grade 5 and 6 students in the province. Since we can't possibly survey all 150,000 students, we can take a random sample of 250 students that are representative of the population. Therefore, the population of interest is the 150,000 students and our sample is 250 of those 150 000 students (see Figure 1.6). If we do our research and analysis correctly, we can make inferences (i.e., conclusions) about the population of 150,000 students from our sample of 250 students because the sample is representative of the population.

**FIGURE 1.6**
**Example of a Population and Sample**

Population: 150,000 grade 5 and 6 students

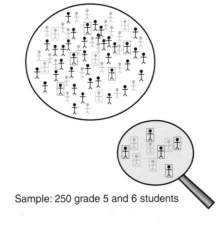

Sample: 250 grade 5 and 6 students

**LO5**

## Descriptive versus Inferential Statistics

There are two different statistical purposes for collecting and analyzing data. The first is for descriptive purposes and the second is for inferential purposes. This textbook teaches you how to conduct and interpret various descriptive and inferential statistical analyses, but at this point, what we are interested in is the basic concept that differentiates the two approaches to statistical analysis.

If we want to describe some phenomenon about society or people, chances are we would use descriptive statistics. For example, suppose you want to know how many books the average Canadian between the ages of 18 and 21 reads per year. In this case, note that the population of interest is all Canadians between the ages of 18 and 21. You might find that after asking 150 people (150 being the sample) you determine that on average they read three books per year. In this case you are describing the average number of books that people read. This is the basic idea behind descriptive statistics. **Descriptive statistics** explains how frequently something of interest occurs in the observations you make. So if you want to describe how often things occur (such as number of premature births, number of alcoholic drinks consumed, number of faulty products) chances are you are going to use descriptive statistics to describe the phenomenon of interest. Example 1.1 provides you with a real example of descriptive statistics. Notice how the focus here is on describing the details (frequency) of the social assistance plan.

**Descriptive statistics** explains how frequently something of interest occurs in the observations you have made.

---

**Example 1.1**

*Social Assistance Statistics*

Statistics Canada reported that the number of people in Ontario receiving social assistance was 709,200 in 2001, 687,600 in 2002, and 673,900 in 2003. These numbers are simply statements of facts about the population of interest. We can calculate various values of interest such as percentage of the population receiving assistance, and then report it in a readable format such as a table.

|  | 2001 | 2002 | 2003 |
|---|---|---|---|
| Number of people receiving assistance | 709,200 | 687,600 | 673,900 |
| Percentage (%) of the population | 6.0 | 5.7 | 5.5 |

Source: Social Assistance Statistics, 2001–2003, adapted from Statistics Canada publication *Canadian Economic Observer*, Catalogue 11-010-XIE2004011, November 2004, http://www.statcan.gc.ca/pub/11-010-x/01104/7614-eng.htm.

---

Now imagine that you are interested in knowing if the number of alcoholic drinks a person consumes per week is somehow connected to a person's overall mental health. Here we are asking if there is a relationship (i.e., are they connected) between the number of alcoholic drinks consumed per week and overall mental health. In this case we use inferential statistics to see if these two are related. **Inferential statistics** are used to help generalize the results found in a sample to the entire population of interest. For example, after randomly surveying 150 people, we discover that overall mental health decreases as the number of alcoholic drinks consumed per week increases. Using the results found in the sample, we can estimate, with a specified amount of accuracy, what may happen in the entire population of interest. An example of inferential statistics is given in Example 1.2.

**Inferential statistics** are used to help generalize the results found in a sample to the entire population of interest.

## For Your Information

We rarely, if ever, know the exact details of a phenomenon in the population. However, if we have information about the phenomenon from a random sample of the population, we can make inferences about the population within a certain degree of accuracy (referred to as error). A good example is the use of political polls. The *Vancouver Sun* (June 26, 2010) reported on a poll conducted by the Gandalf Group, regarding the G8/G20 summits. It stated that "78 percent of respondents wanted Prime Minister Stephen Harper's government to use the summits 'to signal that Canada wants to be a leader in the global fight against climate change' . . . The poll surveyed 1,158 Canadians and is considered accurate within 2.88 percentage points, 19 times out of 20."

Here, the sample consists of 1,158 Canadians. The population (presumably, since we are not given the details) is Canadians who are eligible to vote. The results from the sample found 78 percent of Canadians in favour of the statement. These results can be generalized to the population with the degree of accuracy (error) stated. In the population the result is estimated to be between 75.12 percent and 80.88 percent (78 ± 2.88 percentage points) 19 times out of 20. Meaning if you repeated the poll 20 times with the same sample size, you would obtain these population results 19 of the 20 times. The results would be different 1 out of 20 times.

We will learn more about this in chapter 8.

---

**Example 1.2**

*Problem Gambling*

Marshall and Wynne (2009) studied problem gambling among Canadians. They found that individuals considered to be problem gamblers experienced relationship and monetary problems more frequently than others. They further found that problem gamblers experienced higher degrees of stress, depression, and alcohol abuse than non-problematic gamblers.[4]

Notice that in this study the researchers are making statements about the negative effects of problem gambling on specific relationship, monetary, and physical and mental health issues. Using the results found in their sample, they can infer (or make statements about) the consequences that may be found in the broader population.

Source: "Problem Gambling," adapted from Statistics Canada publication *Canadian Social Trends,* Catalogue 11-008-XIE2004001, No. 73, Summer 2004, http://www.statcan.gc.ca/bsolc/olc-cel/olc-cel?catno=11-008-x&lang=eng.

## Ethics and Statistics

**LO6**

You may have heard the phrase "there are three kinds of lies—lies, damn lies, and statistics."* As is the case with anything you read, you should have a critical perspective when reading and interpreting statistics. There are known cases where individuals and the media have either innocently or purposely misrepresented the results of their data analysis. In fact, there are famous cases in legal studies where judges, lawyers, expert witnesses, and juries have misunderstood statistical results with terrible consequences.

As social scientists, it is imperative that we present our data and findings in an honest and professional manner. In fact, you will find that many professional societies, such as the Canadian Sociological Association, Canadian Economics Association, Canadian Psychological Association, and the Canadian Political Science Association, have codes of ethical conduct dealing with presenting data analysis. One such association, the Statistical Society of Canada (SSC), provides the "four major areas of responsibility that define ethical statistical practice"[5] shown in Figure 1.7.

* This quote is often attributed to British Prime Minister Benjamin Disraeli (1804–1881) but it is also mentioned by Mark Twain (1835–1910) in his autobiography.

**FIGURE 1.7**   **Statistical Society of Canada: Code of Ethical Statistical Practice**

Source: Statistical Society of Canada, *Code of Ethical Statistical Practice*, www.ssc.ca.

---

### A. Responsibility to Society

1. Conform to procedures that protect human rights and dignity. In particular, ensure that the collection and storage of information and the publication of results adhere to relevant privacy laws or privacy standards set out by the SSC or other relevant bodies.
2. Strive to advance public knowledge and understanding of information by the application of appropriate statistical methods and interpretation of results, and by providing assistance in discrediting false or misleading information.
3. Maintain objectivity and strive to avoid procedural or personal bias. The creation of valid data-based information is vital to informed public opinion and policy.
4. Acquire appropriate knowledge and understanding of relevant legislation, regulations and standards in the practitioner's field of application and comply with these requirements.

### B. Responsibility to Employers and Clients

1. Carry out and document work with due care and diligence in accordance with the requirements of the employer or client.
2. Avoid disclosure or authorization to disclose, for personal gain or benefit to a third party, confidential information acquired in the course of professional practice without the prior written permission of the employer or client, or as directed by a court of law.
3. Declare any interest, financial or otherwise, that could be perceived as influencing the outcome of work undertaken for a client or employer.
4. Advise clients or employers of any potential or actual conflict between the ethical standards of statistical practice and the interests of the client or employer.
5. Exercise care to prevent the use of any misleading summary of the data. Strive to ensure that all assumptions and limitations relevant to the data, the analysis and the results are fully disclosed.

### C. Responsibility to Other Statistical Practitioners

1. Uphold the reputation of statistical practice and seek to improve professional standards by participating in their development, use and enforcement. Avoid any action that will adversely affect the good standing of Statistics and Statisticians.
2. Refrain from speaking in the name of the Society without the authorization by the Executive of the Society.
3. Encourage and support fellow statisticians in their professional development and, wherever possible, encourage recruitment and provide opportunities for new entrants to the profession.
4. Act with integrity toward fellow statisticians and other professionals, avoiding any activity that is incompatible with professional standards. Ensure that due credit is ascribed to fellow professionals. While question and debate are encouraged, criticism should be directed toward procedures rather than persons. Avoid publicly casting doubt on the professional competence of others.

### D. Professionalism

1. Adhere to the Guidelines for Professional Development, seeking to upgrade professional knowledge and skills and to be informed of technological developments, procedures and standards relevant to the field of application.
2. Seek to exercise recognized good practice, upholding quality standards and encouraging fellow-practitioners to do likewise.
3. Only undertake work and provide services that are within the limits of professional competence; and do not lay claim to any level of competence not possessed.
4. Accept responsibility for work and give objective and reliable information on procedures in any professional review or assessment.
5. Refuse to enter into, or comply with, any arrangement where financial or other rewards are contingent upon the outcome of a proposed statistical inquiry.

# The Concept of Variables

During the research process we develop a research question and formulate hypotheses. To test these hypotheses, we need to gather data. When we say "gather data" what we really mean is that we are gathering information on variables of interest. A variable is a phenomenon that you are interested in measuring. We call it a variable because the values of the variable may vary across people, place, time, and so on. Table 1.2 provides some examples of variables.

**TABLE 1.2**
**Example of Variables in Social Science Research**

| | | |
|---|---|---|
| Acceptance of new ideas | Heart rate | Number of days |
| Age | Height | Occupation |
| Alcohol consumption | Honesty | Place of birth |
| Anxiety level | Income | Political membership |
| Attitude | Industry type | Product type |
| Car ownership | Intelligence | Rate of recidivism |
| Commitment | Interest rates | Relationship status |
| Depression | Leadership ability | Religion |
| Education | Marital status | Social economics status |
| Ethnicity | Math scores | Student-teacher ratio |
| Friendliness | Moral conviction | Volunteerism |
| Gender | Mortality rates | Voter turnout |
| Happiness | Number of children | Weight |

Perhaps the easiest way to understand the concept of a variable is with an example. Suppose you want to determine the average age of undergraduate students at your school. What you are measuring is the phenomenon called age. Therefore, age is the variable in your study. If you want to determine the rate of recidivism of offenders, then recidivism is the variable in your study. If you want to investigate peoples' religious opinions, then religious opinion is your variable.

Simply put, a **variable** is a phenomenon of interest that can take on different values and can be measured. The values that a variable can have refer to the difference within the variables. For example, gender has two different values (male and female). Number of children may have values ranging from 0 to *n*, with *n* being the maximum number. Sometimes it seems difficult to determine whether something is a variable. For example, a rock is not necessarily a variable by itself, but depending on how the rock is measured, it very well could be. It can be measured by weight as light or heavy (two values), or be measured by kilograms (theoretically an infinite number of values); it can be measured by colour (e.g., red, black, gold, etc.). The way we measure a variable determines the types and number of values a variable may have. Look at the following examples, and see you if can identify the variables.

A **variable** is a phenomenon of interest that can take on different values and can be measured.

1. Number of cigarettes smoked per day.

   *Variable:* Cigarettes smoked.

2. Number of hours spent studying per week.

   *Variable:* Hours spent studying.
3. Number of marital licences issued.

   *Variable:* Marital licences issued.

Quite often we are interested in studying more than one variable. For example, suppose we want to understand the relationship between hours spent studying and grade point average. In this case, we have two variables: hours spent studying and grade point average. Now suppose we want to know if there is a difference between males and females in how many hours they spend studying and their respective grade point averages. In this case, we have three variables: gender (male/female), hours spent studying, and grade point average. Try these research question examples and see if you can identify the variables.

> *Research Question:* Is there a difference between males and females in the number of cigarettes they smoke per day?
> *Variables:* Gender and cigarettes smoked per day.

> *Research Question:* Does voter turnout differ by ethnicity?
> *Variables:* Voter turnout and ethnicity.

> *Research Question:* Do youth social programs reduce the likelihood that a young person will commit a crime?
> *Variables:* Youth social programs and likelihood to commit a crime.

> *Research Question:* Do people who own an iPod Touch (mobile digital device) also own an iPad (mobile digital device)?
> *Variables:* iPod Touch ownership and iPad ownership.

> *Research Question:* Do police community service programs decrease crime rates in Calgary?
> *Variables:* Police community service programs and crime rates.

Notice in the fifth example that location was not included as a variable. The reason for this is that there is only one location in the research question, Calgary. Therefore, Calgary is the population where the sample is drawn from and is not a variable. If the research question included the north west, north east, south west and south east areas of Calgary, then it could be a variable. For example:

> *Research Question:* Does the effect of police community service programs on crime rates differ across the four regions of Calgary?
> *Variables:* Police community service programs, crime rates, and region/location.

Notice that the research question now includes a region/location variable that can be measured. Similarly, suppose we surveyed Calgary, Edmonton, Montreal, Ottawa, Toronto, and Vancouver.

*Research Question:* Does the effect of police community service programs on crime rates differ across Calgary, Edmonton, Montreal, Ottawa, Toronto, and Vancouver?

*Variables:* Police community service programs, crime rates, and city.

In summary, variables represent the phenomenon of interest that we want to measure. To be considered a variable, the phenomenon must have different values and those values must be measureable.

**LO7**

## Independent (Predictor) versus Dependent (Response) Variables

Now that you understand the concept of variables, we need to spend some time discussing the difference between independent variables and dependent variables. When we are interested in studying more than one variable at a time, we usually are also interested in how these variables relate to each other. For example, Lochner (2008)[6] found that "an increase in educational attainment significantly reduces subsequent violent and property crime." Based on the last section, we would say that in this example there are two variables: educational attainment and propensity to commit violent and property crimes.

However, we need to identify which of these variables is proposed to influence the other. In other words, which variable is dependent on the other? Often you will hear the independent variable referred to as the predictor variable and the dependent variable as the response variable. These terms are interchangeable and mean the same thing (see Figure 1.8). An independent (predictor) variable is proposed to influence (or cause) a change in the dependent (response) variable.

A **dependent variable** is a variable that changes as a result of the change in an independent variable.

Looking again at the Lochner example, not only can we say that there are two variables, we can say that "educational attainment" is the independent variable stated to influence the dependent variable "propensity to commit violent and property crimes." Table 1.3 provides some examples of independent and dependent variables found in published research from six different social science disciplines.

**LO8**

An **independent variable** is a variable that is hypothesized to influence the dependent variable.

A **dependent variable** is a variable that changes as a result of the change in an independent variable. In the Lochner example, propensity to commit crimes changes as a result of educational attainment. An **independent variable** is a variable that is hypothesized or suggested to influence the dependent variable. Looking again at the Lochner example, educational attainment is the independent variable since it affects the dependent variable propensity to commit violent and property crimes.

**FIGURE 1.8**
**Independent and Dependent Variables**

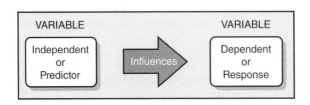

## Take a Closer Look

One way to remember the difference between independent and dependent variables is to picture a horse and buggy ride. The speed of the horse is the independent variable and the speed of the buggy is the dependent variable. A change in the horse's speed changes the buggy's speed; the speed of the horse is independent of the speed of the buggy. That is, the buggy's speed doesn't affect the horse's speed. However, the buggy's speed is dependent on the horse's speed. The faster the horse moves, the faster the buggy moves.

**TABLE 1.3**   **Independent and Dependent Variable Examples**

| | Authors | Findings | Variables |
|---|---|---|---|
| Economics | Ferrara and Missios (2005)[7] | User fees for garbage collection increases household recycling activity of most recyclable material. | Independent Variable: User fees<br>Dependent Variable: Recycling activity |
| Education | Johnson, G. M. (2005)[8] | Student alienation (not feeling involved in the learning process) is associated with lower academic achievement. | Independent Variable: Student alienation<br>Dependent Variable: Academic achievement |
| Criminology | Krahn and Kennedy (1985)[9] | The size of a police force does not influence citizens' fear of crime. | Independent Variable: Police force size<br>Dependent Variable: Fear of crime |
| Management | Tansky, Gallagher, and Wetzel (1997)[10] | When part-time employees feel they are being treated equally, compared to full-time employees, they are more committed to the organization. | Independent Variable: Equitable treatment<br>Dependent Variable: Organizational commitment |
| Political Science | Harell (2010)[11] | Compared to young males, young females are more likely to be tolerant of the civil liberties of multicultural groups. | Independent Variable: Gender<br>Dependent Variable: Multicultural tolerance |
| Sociology | Perkins (2007)[12] | In post-secondary students, individual perception of how many alcoholic drinks students normally consume is positively related to the number of alcoholic drinks the individual consumes. | Independent Variable: Perception of consumption norm<br>Dependent Variable: Personal consumption |

## Did You Know?

In his national bestselling book *Struck by Lightning: The Curious World of Probabilities*, Professor Jeffrey Rosenthal of the University of Toronto estimated the probability of having the single winning ticket for the Lotto 6/49 jackpot, and compared that with the probability of four other interesting outcomes. He states that compared to the probability of holding the single Lotto 6/49 jackpot winning ticket, it is just as likely that a randomly chosen woman will give birth in the next minute and four times more likely that a person chosen at random will become the next prime minister.

**Sources:** J.S. Rosenthal (2005). *Struck by Lightning: The Curious World of Probabilities*. Harper Perennial: Toronto, p. 8; and "Lotto 6-49 jackpot could go even higher than the estimated $41 million," *The Canadian Press*, March 20, 2010, http://www.680news.com/news/local/article/37278—lotto-6-49-jackpot-could-go-even-higher-than-the-estimated-41-million.

Look at the research questions from the previous section, repeated below, and try to identify which variable is the independent variable and which is the dependent variable.

*Research Question:* Is there a difference between males and females in the number of cigarettes they smoke per day?

*Variables:* Gender is the independent variable and cigarettes smoked per day is the dependent variable.

*Research Question:* Does voter turnout differ by ethnicity?

*Variables:* Ethnicity is the independent variable and voter turnout is the dependent variable.

*Research Question:* Do youth social programs reduce the likelihood that a young person will commit a crime?

*Variables:* Youth social programs is the independent variable and likelihood to commit a crime is the dependent variable.

*Research Question:* Do people who own an iPod Touch also own an iPad?

*Variables:* iPod Touch ownership is the independent variable and iPad ownership is the dependent variable.

*Research Question:* Do police community service programs decrease crime rates in Calgary?

*Variables:* Police community service programs is the independent variable and crime rates is the dependent variable.

You've probably already imagined that determining which variable is independent versus dependent can sometimes be difficult. This is where your theory comes in. The theory that you are testing is what determines your research questions, which in turn determines which variable is the independent and which is the dependent. We will cover how we test theories from a statistical point of view in chapter 7.

# Levels of Measurement

We have just learned that a variable is something of interest that we want to measure, but we have yet to cover how we measure (operationalize) a variable. Some variables, such as height or weight, are easy to measure, whereas others are more difficult. We can categorize the different ways we can measure variables. As we will see later in the textbook, how we measure a variable affects the type of analysis we can conduct later, so getting the correct measurement of variables is important.

Think for a moment about how you would measure a participant's height. You can measure in centimetres or inches but you can also measure by the categories of short, medium, or tall. Each way of measuring height has a different level of accuracy to it. Measuring height in centimetres or inches gives you a quantitative sense for how tall someone is. Measuring height using the categories short, medium, or tall, gives you a qualitative sense for how tall someone is. We call the difference in these types of measurement "levels of measurement." We refer to them as levels because they are somewhat hierarchical, in that we can do much more sophisticated types of analysis with the higher levels of measurement than we can with the lower levels of measurement.

In the social sciences, the convention is to categorize the levels of measurement into four levels: nominal, ordinal, interval, and ratio. While they may go by different names in fields of study outside of social science, they are basically all categorized the same. Later on we will talk about how we quantify these variables (i.e., how we assign numbers to them), but for now just focus on understanding what each level of measurement is.

> A variable has a **nominal** level of measurement when the difference within the variable is just a name or symbol.

> A **respondent** is the person being observed in the research study. For example, someone who is completing a survey on his or her political views is a respondent in the study. Often, in experimental research, we refer to respondents as subjects but the meaning is the same.

## Nominal Level of Measurement

The word nominal comes from the Latin word *nomen* meaning "name." In statistics, a variable has a **nominal** level of measurement when the difference within the variable is just a name or symbol. For example, if you take bus #101 to school and your friend takes bus #202, the value 101 versus 202 is meaningful in name only. Bus #202 isn't twice as good as bus #101, the numbers are just a means of identification. We refer to these as qualitative categories. Let's look at some other examples.

### Nominal Example #1

Suppose you want to measure the variable "Gender." Figure 1.9 shows one way you can ask a **respondent** for the information.

**FIGURE 1.9**
**Measuring the Variable "Gender"**

What is your gender:
❑  Female
❑  Male

The terms male and female are qualitative categories (names) we ascribe to the two attributes of gender. There is no quantitative difference in males and females, nor is there any order of importance in gender, it is simply a name.

*Nominal Example #2*

Suppose you want to measure the variable "Political Party Affiliation." The survey question in Figure 1.10 shows an example of how you could gather this information from a respondent. Again, the terms Conservative Party, Green Party, etc., are names assigned to the different political parties. They are attributes or values of the variable "Political Party Affiliation."

**FIGURE 1.10**
**Measuring the Variable "Political Party Affiliation"**

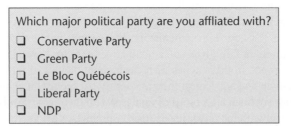

Which major political party are you affliated with?

❏ Conservative Party
❏ Green Party
❏ Le Bloc Québécois
❏ Liberal Party
❏ NDP

At this point it is important to note two criteria required for effectively measuring a concept. The first is that the response categories must be mutually exclusive of one another; that is, there is no overlap between the categories. Suppose the Liberal Party and NDP categories in Figure 1.10 were collapsed into one category that read Liberal Party and NDP. What would respondents answer if they supported one party but not the other? In this case, the category is not mutually exclusive because it combines two potential responses into one response. In order to obtain accurate responses from your respondents, it is important that the categories of potential responses be mutually exclusive of one another. The second criterion is that the response categories are exhaustive; that is, you have included enough categories to represent all possible answers. Consider Figure 1.10 again. What if the scale only included Conservative Party, Liberal Party, and NDP? How would respondents answer the question if they affiliated themselves with the Green Party? In addition to being mutually exclusive, the measurement must also have an exhaustive list of categories. It could be argued that Figure 1.10 is not exhaustive enough in that it does not include some of the lesser known registered parties such as the Libertarian Party of Canada or the Communist Party of Canada. To remedy this situation researchers may decide to include all of the registered parties or to include a category named "Other Registered Party" in order to make the list of categories exhaustive.

A variable has an **ordinal** level of measurement when the answers to the qualitative categories, or attributes, have some order to them.

## Ordinal Level of Measurement

The word ordinal comes from the Latin word *ordinalis* meaning "showing order." A variable has an **ordinal** level of measurement when the qualitative categories, or attributes/values, have some order to them. For example, suppose a respondent is asked the question in Figure 1.11.

**FIGURE 1.11**
**Ordinal Measure of**
**Favourite TV Show**

Rank your favourite TV show from 1 (most favourite) to 5 (least favourite).

| | |
|---|---|
| CSI Miami | 4 |
| Survivor | 5 |
| Vampire Diaries | 1 |
| Bones | 3 |
| Canadian Idol | 2 |

Looking at the answers, we can see the order of the respondent's preference for different TV shows. We can tell that the respondent prefers the TV show Vampire Diaries more than the show Bones. We can see that Canadian Idol is liked more than CSI Miami and so on. While we can see the order of preference, we cannot tell the magnitude of the difference between the preferences. For example, we cannot say that the respondent prefers Vampire Diaries three times more than Bones because the numbers assigned to the order are only meaningful in assigning a rank, it doesn't provide us with the distance between them.

Here's another way of thinking about it. Suppose there are three runners in a race and medals are provided for first, second, and third place based on the time to cross the finish line (see Figure 1.12). Just by looking at the rank of the medals, we cannot say that Jane ran three times faster than Caroline. These medals only provide an order, or rank, of the runners' performance.

**FIGURE 1.12**
**First, Second, and**
**Third Place**

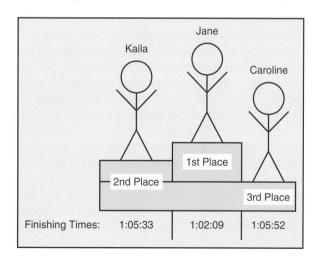

**FIGURE 1.13**
**Measuring the Variable "Social Class"**

Which do you consider to be your social class?

❏  Lower
❏  Lower-Middle
❏  Middle
❏  Upper-Middle
❏  Upper

Figures 1.13 and 1.14 provide additional examples of ordinal variables. In Figure 1.13, we are measuring the variable "Social Class" and in the Figure 1.14 we are measuring the variable "Risk of Recidivism." In both examples we can see the various categories and their ordering, but they do not tell us anything about the magnitude of the difference between them.

**FIGURE 1.14**
**Measuring the Variable "Risk of Recidivism"**

Risk of recidivism for this patient?

❏  Low risk
❏  Medium risk
❏  High risk

## Interval Level of Measurement

Interval and ratio variables are almost identical. Consequently, textbooks often describe them as "interval/ratio" levels. In practice there are only a small number of situations (none covered in this textbook) where the difference matters to the analytical method that you choose to conduct. However, it is still worth understanding the difference between the two. Previously, we used the Latin origins of the words to help explain the meaning of the term (nominal = name, ordinal = ordered), but for interval and ratio we need something other than the etymology.

The word *interval* simply means "a space between things." A variable has an **interval** level of measurement when there is an equal and meaningful difference between the levels of the variable but the variable itself does not have a meaningful absolute zero value. For example, the intelligence quotient (IQ) is considered to be a variable with an interval level of measurement. Modern IQ tests score respondents from 0 to 200. While it may be possible to have an IQ of 0, it does not mean that the individual has no intelligence whatsoever. So in this sense, the zero value does not mean the absence of something. Similarly, someone with an IQ of 140 is not twice as smart someone with an IQ of 70. This, as you will soon see, is where the difference lies between interval and ratio variables. What makes IQ an interval level variable is that the intervals between scores (whether it is one point or 10 points) are the same. A difference in five IQ points means the same thing when comparing two individuals with IQs of 75 and 80 as it does when comparing two other individuals with IQs of 120 and 125. It is the interval between scores that matters.

A variable has an **interval** level of measurement when there is an equal and meaningful difference between the levels of the variable but the variable itself does not have a meaningful absolute zero value.

What is important to remember with interval level variables is that they cannot have a meaningful zero value (the zero value is arbitrary if it is measured) and the intervals between values must be the same so that they may be compared. Here are some examples.

### Interval Example #1

Mental health practitioners (such as psychologists) often use the Yale-Brown Obsessive Compulsive Scale to measure the severity of obsessive compulsive disorder (OCD) in patients. The scale provides a patient score from 0, indicating very mild or not significant symptoms of OCD, to 40, indicating severe OCD symptoms. While it seems possible that a patient can score zero, this doesn't necessarily indicate an absence of symptoms. It simply means that the symptoms are mild enough to be considered insignificant to the patient's daily life. A variable measured with the OCD scale is considered to be an interval level variable because the values between zero and forty are equal and comparable. Although a patient with a score of 30 is not twice as ill as a patient with a score of 15, a five point difference on the scale between two patients that scored 25 and 30 is the same as difference between two patients that scored 10 and 15.

### Interval Example #2

Suppose we want to measure the variable "Academic Ability" and ask students five math questions and five spelling questions. If each correct answer results in one mark, then the values of the variable range from 0 to 10. If a student does not get any of the answers correct and scores zero, that does not mean that he or she has no academic ability. There could be a number of reasons why the student didn't get the right answers, such as being ill that day, distracted by another student, etc. Furthermore, although one student might score 4 and another 8, it doesn't mean that one is twice as smart or has twice the academic ability as the other. It simply means that there is a four point difference between the scores. It is the same four point difference between two students scoring 2 and 6, or 5 and 9. In this case, the zero value is arbitrary in measuring the variable, and the intervals between the scores are equal and comparable.

## Ratio Level of Measurement

A variable has a **ratio** level of measurement when the intervals between the values are equal and comparable and the zero value means the absence of something.

As was previously mentioned, there is not a lot of difference between interval and ratio levels of measurement. The main difference is the meaning of the zero value. With interval level variables the value of zero does not mean the complete absence of the thing you are measuring. With variables that have a **ratio** level of measurement, the zero value means the absence of something. Furthermore, the intervals between the values are also equal and comparable. Given that there is a true zero value, we can create ratios between two values of a variable. For example, age (measured in years and not in categories) is a ratio level variable. If you have two individuals aged 50 and 25, you can create a ratio with the two, such as 50/25 or 25/50, and can say that the first person is twice as old as the second, or the second is half as young as the first.

# Take a Closer Look

## THE LIKERT SCALE: ORDINAL LEVEL TREATED AS INTERVAL LEVEL

In Figure 1.15, we are measuring "Attitude Toward Reinstating Capital Punishment." We can see again that there are categories of answers that provide us with an understanding of the order of level of agreement. However, this example is a bit different. You may have seen this type of question in another class, or on a survey you have completed. This is called a Likert scale (pronounced "Lick-ert"). Technically, this is considered a scale that provides ordinal data. That is, by using a Likert scale to measure this variable, we are creating a variable with an ordinal level of measurement. What makes this one a little bit different is that there is some degree of magnitude inherent in the answers. For example 'strongly disagree' is some degree larger than 'disagree.'

So while technically this is considered an ordinal variable, it is quite often treated as an interval variable during statistical analysis. At this point, you really don't need to be too concerned about this slight

**FIGURE 1.15**   **Example of a Likert-type Scale**

> I think that our country should reinstate capital punishment for first degree murder convictions.
> ❑  Strongly disagree
> ❑  Disagree
> ❑  Neutral
> ❑  Agree
> ❑  Strongly agree

anomaly. Rather, focus on understanding the concept of what makes an ordinal variable ordinal—the variable has categories or attributes that differ in rank or order, but do not tell us anything about the magnitude of difference between them.

Technically this is referred to as a Likert-type scale or Likert response format in order to distinguish it from Likert scaling methods, but in practice it is often referred to as a Likert scale, so we have adopted that term here.

---

Consider the following ratio variable examples. Notice that in these examples, if we had asked the question differently, we would not have had a variable with a ratio level of measurement.

### Ratio Example #1

Suppose you are investigating the frequency of racial prejudice of minority women in the workplace. You can ask respondents to indicate how often they feel they have been subjected to racial prejudice and provide categories of potential answers, such as in Figure 1.16.

**FIGURE 1.16**
**Ordinal Measure of Racial Prejudice in the Workplace**

> In the last year, how often have you been subjected to racial prejudice in your workplace?
> ❑  Never
> ❑  1 to 3 times
> ❑  4 to 6 times
> ❑  7 or more times

By measuring the variable "Racial Prejudice" this way you now have ordered categories, which means this is an ordinal level of measurement. If you ask the question using an open ended response option (see Figure 1.17), the respondent could provide a numerical value. In this case, you would have a variable with a ratio level of measurement because of the meaningful zero value and equal and comparable intervals between values.

**FIGURE 1.17**
**Interval Measure of Racial Prejudice in the Workplace**

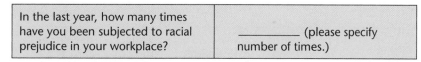

| In the last year, how many times have you been subjected to racial prejudice in your workplace? | _____ (please specify number of times.) |

### Ratio Example #2

In the report *Poverty Profile 2007,* the National Council of Welfare reported that in 2007 there were 637,000 children (less than 18 years of age) living in poverty in Canada. The chart in Figure 1.18 provides the provincial rates.

Again, we can see that number of children living in poverty is measured as a ratio level variable. Zero percent refers to the absence of children in poverty whereas 100 percent indicates that all children live in poverty. This allows us to compare provinces in relation to their respective population size. In this case, British Columbia has the highest rate of child poverty among the provinces. Remember, the main difference between an interval level of measurement and a ratio level of measurement is that latter has a true zero value whereas the former does not.

**FIGURE 1.18**
**Poverty Profile 2007**

Source: "Community: Poverty Profile 2007," National Council of Welfare, http://www.ncw.gc.ca/c.4mm.5n.3ty@-eng.jsp?cmid=3. Reproduced with the permission of the Minister of Public Works and Government Services Canada, 2011.

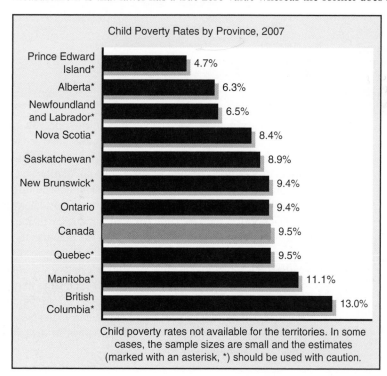

Child Poverty Rates by Province, 2007

| Province | Rate |
|---|---|
| Prince Edward Island* | 4.7% |
| Alberta* | 6.3% |
| Newfoundland and Labrador* | 6.5% |
| Nova Scotia* | 8.4% |
| Saskatchewan* | 8.9% |
| New Brunswick* | 9.4% |
| Ontario | 9.4% |
| Canada | 9.5% |
| Quebec* | 9.5% |
| Manitoba* | 11.1% |
| British Columbia* | 13.0% |

Child poverty rates not available for the territories. In some cases, the sample sizes are small and the estimates (marked with an asterisk, *) should be used with caution.

**EXERCISE 1.1**

Draw the Levels of Measurement Chart in Table 1.4, including only the left column and the column headings. Looking back at the examples of measurement scales provided in the Levels of Measurement section, complete each row of the chart, making sure to take mental note of why it is considered unordered or ordered and so on. For the Example column, try to think of one or two more examples of each level.

**TABLE 1.4**
**Levels of Measurement Chart**

| Level | Ordered or Unordered | Equal Intervals | Meaningful Zero Value | Example |
|-------|----------------------|-----------------|-----------------------|---------|
| Nominal | Unordered | No | No | gender, profession, marital status, political party |
| Ordinal | Ordered | No | No | Letter grades, ranked preferences |
| Interval | Ordered | Yes | No | IQ score, LSAT score, Academic ability score |
| Ratio | Ordered | Yes | Yes | age in years, hours spent studying, money spent of gambling |

## Conclusion

The primary goal of this chapter was to provide you with an understanding of the role of statistics in the social sciences. As social scientists, we are interested in understanding phenomena that occur within society. To research phenomena, we often draw samples of individuals from a population and use variables to measure the phenomenon of interest within the sample. The different levels of measurement we use to gather information about variables determines the type of analysis we can perform with the data. Applied statistics, which incorporates both descriptive and inferential statistical methods, is the practice of developing knowledge by using statistical methods to analyze data. When we want to describe the frequency with which something occurs, we use descriptive statistics. When we want to use the results from our sample data to draw conclusions about the population, we use inferential statistics. Statistics is interwoven through the research process and as such is an important subject for social scientists to study.

In the next chapter, we will look at ways to describe data using frequency tables, cross-tabulations, and graphs.

## Key Chapter Concepts and Terms

Statistics, 5
Mathematical statistics, 6
Applied statistics, 6
Population, 11
Sample, 11

Representative of the population, 11
Descriptive statistics, 13
Inferential statistics, 13
Variable, 16
Dependent variable, 18

Independent variable, 18
Nominal, 21
Respondent, 21
Ordinal, 22
Interval, 24
Ratio, 25

## Frequently Asked Questions

1. How will statistics apply to my life after school?

Statistics is a decision-making tool. Every day we make personal and professional decisions. While many decisions don't require statistical analysis, you'd be surprised at how often you are faced with the need to process statistical information. How do you know if you should trust the information? Quite often, the statistical claims we hear are either misrepresented or complex enough that they may be misunderstood. Some situations are considerably more serious than others. For example, in a 2005 TED Global Conference, Professor Peter Donnelly of the University of Oxford explained how misunderstandings of statistical claims led to an innocent mother being convicted of murdering her children. The point here is that by learning statistics, you will know the right questions to ask when deciding what information to believe. For example, when you hear that four out of five medical doctors recommend product XYZ, you'll know to ask yourself questions such as "What was the sample size?", "Was it a random or non-random sample?", or "What is the confidence interval around this number?" Learning statistics helps you to critically evaluate information that you receive every day.

There are also numerous jobs that require people to analyze and interpret statistics, or even just understand them when they are presented. Learning statistics provides you with the knowledge required to be successful in your career. If you look at job descriptions, they may not explicitly state that you must have a statistics background, but if it requires decision-making capability, you'll want to have an understanding of statistics.

2. How much overlap is there between math and statistics?

Mathematics is the backbone of statistics. We wouldn't have statistics if we didn't have mathematics and mathematicians. Historically, mathematics and statistics were considered to be the same discipline, but now they are seen as being separate. Recall that we distinguished between mathematical statistics and applied statistics. Most social scientists (e.g., sociologists, psychologists, economists) and professionals with a social science background (e.g., teachers, market researchers, lawyers, etc.) deal with applied statistics. Applied statistics uses statistical analysis to evaluate data and make decisions based on the results. Fortunately, there is now an abundant amount of computer software (such as SPSS® and Microsoft® Excel) available to make this task easy.

3. How big is the sample compared to the population?

A population is the total number of individuals, objects, or items that you are interested in. A sample is a subset of the population. In most cases the population is larger (usually much larger) than the sample. Look back at Figure 1.5. There you can see that the population is larger than the sample. How big you make the sample, compared to the size of the population, depends on the study. A population can be quite large and you may only need a small percentage of that population to get accurate results.

4. Can a sample and a population ever be the same thing?

Depending on the study, it is possible that the population and the sample are the same. For example, suppose you want to study the stress and anxiety levels of grade 5 children who have an IQ score greater than 140. It is likely that less than half of one percent (0.038) of children make up this population. If there were 10,000 grade 5 children, then the population of grade 5 children with IQ scores greater than 140 is approximately 380 children. It may be feasible and desirable to include all 380 children in the study. If that were the case, then the sample would be the same as the population.

5. What size of sample do you need for it to be reliable?

There are a few factors that must be considered in creating a reliable sample. At this point, the important part to understand is that a sample comes from the population and is used to make inferences about that population. We will cover sample size, to some extent, in chapters 7 through 13. However, the actual calculation of sample sizes is beyond the scope of this text.

6. When we use statistics, can we be certain of the results?

We can never say that we are 100 percent certain about our results, since we can never know all the possible factors that may influence them. However, we can say, for example, that we are 95 percent or 99 percent confident that these results are accurate within a certain margin of error. We will cover this specifically in chapter 8. Political polls provide a good example; typically, they are reported as, "45 percent of people stated they like the new health bill. These results are accurate to $\pm 2.5$ percent, 19 times out of 20." What this means is that if you conducted the poll 20 times, you would find that 19 of those times, the results would be between 42.5 percent and 47.5 percent. We will cover this topic in more detail later in the textbook.

7. What is the difference between probability and statistics?

Probability deals with predicting how theoretically likely something is to happen. Statistics (or, more appropriate for us, applied statistics) is the analysis of actual data. You can say that statistics rely on probability, in that probability is the basis for all of the statistical analysis discussed in this textbook. We will cover probability in chapter 4.

8. How can I tell the difference between reliable and unreliable statistical claims?

   It is good to be skeptical about all statistical claims that you hear. Some statistics may be completely misinterpreted and others may be correct. Since news and media reports are often limited in space and/or time, sometimes details are left out. So it can be difficult to assess their validity just from that particular source of information. The key is to investigate the claims and determine how rigorous the sampling and analysis was. Was the correct analysis used and was it done correctly? To some extent these are things you will learn as you go through this textbook. More advanced topics may require you to take additional courses in statistics.

9. Do nominal, ordinal, interval, and ratio variables ever flow in to one another? Or, can something be both nominal and ordinal?

   No. By definition, if a variable has a nominal level of measurement, in cannot be ordinal at the same time. This applies to all four levels of measurement.

10. Can there be multiple dependent and independent variables?

    Yes, and in fact, a lot of social science research involves the investigation of multiple independent and dependent variables. This is called multivariate statistics and is usually taught in an advanced level course.

11. Is 'female' considered a variable?

    No. Gender is a variable that has two levels (male and female). If only females were included in the research, then female would be the population/sample, not a variable.

12. If an ordinal variable contains number ranges in the response options, does that make it a quantitative variable? For example, if the variable is age, but the response options are 0–17, 18–25, 26–34, and so on.

    Quite often phenomenon is measured using an ordinal level of measurement. Figure 1.19 provides an example of an ordinal level of measurement. Even though we have numbers in the categories, it is still considered to be qualitative because we have a label describing a range of numbers (1 to 2, 6 or more) rather than an exact quantity. In later chapters you will see how categories are coded as numerical values for the purpose of statistical analysis.

**FIGURE 1.19**
**Example of an Ordinal Level of Measurement**

How many glasses of water do you drink per day?
❑   0
❑   1 to 2
❑   3 to 5
❑   6 or more

13. Which of the levels of measurement are considered categorical by definition and which are quantitative? Can some of these be both?

   Nominal and ordinal levels of measurement are categorical because the response options are categories. Interval and ratio levels of measurement are considered quantitative because they are more than just labels assigned to a specific response. For example, an OCD score of 30 provides a numeric value as opposed to a category. Not all variables are always categorical or always quantitative. Gender is always categorical because there isn't a way to numerically measure it. However, age could be categorical if you asked respondents to provide their answers in categories (i.e., ages 21 to 29) or quantitative if you ask them their exact age or year of birth (i.e., 30 years old). The level of measurement depends on how the question is asked.

14. Is a variable with Yes or No options considered nominal?

   Yes. A nominal variable can have two or more categories. When there are only two, we often refer to it as a dichotomous response.

**Research Example:**

In 2006, Dr. Linda Reutter of the University of Alberta and six of her colleagues published their study "Public Attributions for Poverty in Canada" in the *Canadian Review of Sociology and Anthropology*. They sampled 1,671 Canadians from Edmonton (839) and Toronto (832) and found that most respondents believed that poverty was a result of government policies and unequal opportunities for individual Canadians. Furthermore, the researchers found that wealthier respondents were more likely to believe that children who grew up in poverty were likely to remain in poverty as adults.[13]

**Research Example Questions:**

**Question 1:** What is the population and what is the sample in this study?

**Question 2:** Based on the results in the paragraph describing this research, was the data collected for descriptive purposes (using descriptive statistics) or inferential purposes (using inferential statistics)?

**Question 3:** Some of the variables that Reutter and her colleagues measured were collected using the survey items in Table 1.5. Review these variables and determine the level of measurement for each variable (i.e., nominal, ordinal, interval, or ratio). Refer to Table 1.4 for assistance.

**Research Example Answers:**

**Question 1:** What is the population and what is the sample in this study?

The population in this study was the people of Canada. We know this because they are discussing the beliefs of the Canadian public. The sample in this study was the 1,671 Canadians from Edmonton (839) and Toronto (832).

**TABLE 1.5**
**Sample Survey Items**

| Variable | Survey Item |
|---|---|
| Age | "In what year were you born?"<br>Respondents answered by stating their exact year of birth |
| Gender | "What is your gender?"<br>Respondents answered either Female or Male |
| Education | "What is the highest level of education you have completed?"<br>Respondents answered with one of the following categories:<br><br>Completed elementary school<br>Completed high school<br>Completed community college<br>Completed Bachelor's degree<br>Postgraduate training: MA, MSc, MBA, etc.<br>Postgraduate training: professional degree or PhD* |
| Exposure to poverty | "Have you ever received social assistance or welfare?"<br>Respondents answered either Yes or No** |
| Causes of poverty (Government policies) | "Government policies have caused some people to become poor"<br>Respondents answered using the Likert scale (see below). |
| Causes of poverty (Unequal opportunities) | "Most people are poor because of unequal opportunities in our society."<br>Respondents answered using the Likert scale (see below). |
| Causes of poverty (Intergenerational) | "Most people are poor because they grew up in a poor family."<br>Respondents answered using the Likert scale (see below). |

Likert scale: Strongly agree; Somewhat agree; Neutral; Somewhat disagree; Strongly disagree
* For space purposes, this represents a compressed version of the scale and categories used.
** This is one of six items used to measure this variable.

**Question 2:**  Based on the results in the paragraph describing this research, was the data collected for descriptive purposes (using descriptive statistics) or inferential purposes (using inferential statistics)?

The data was collected for inferential purposes. We know this is the case because inferential statistics are used to help generalize the results found in the sample to the entire population of interest. The authors used the results from the 1,671 Canadians in the sample to make inferences about the Canadian population.

**Question 3:**  Some of the variables that Reutter and colleagues measured were collected using the survey items in Table 1.5. Review these variables and

**TABLE 1.6**
**Variables and Levels**
**of Measurement**

| Variable | Levels of measurement |
|---|---|
| Age | Ratio level of measurement: The respondents are reporting their actual age. Age has order, has equal intervals, and has real zero value. |
| Gender | Nominal level of measurement: The response options "Female" and "Male" are unordered categories. They are names only. |
| Education | Ordinal level of measurement: The response categories for type of education do provide some order but they are not in equal intervals. |
| Exposure to poverty | Nominal level of measurement: The response options "Yes" and "No" are unordered categories. They are names only. |
| Causes of poverty (Government policies) | Interval level of measurement: There are ordered categories with equal intervals, but there is no real zero value. This scale is a special case where technically it is ordinal, but in practice is treated as interval (Likert). |
| Causes of poverty (Unequal opportunities) | Interval level of measurement: There are ordered categories with equal intervals, but there is no real zero value. This scale is a special case where technically it is ordinal, but in practice is treated as interval (Likert). |
| Causes of poverty (Intergenerational) | Interval level of measurement: There are ordered categories with equal intervals, but there is no real zero value. This scale is a special case where technically it is ordinal, but in practice is treated as interval (Likert). |

determine the level of measurement for each variable (i.e., nominal, ordinal, interval, or ratio). Refer to Table 1.4 for assistance.

McGraw-Hill Connect provides you with a powerful tool for improving academic performance and truly mastering course material. You can diagnose your knowledge with pre- and post-tests, identify the areas where you need help, search the entire learning package, including the eBook, for content specific to the topic you're studying, and add these resources to your personalized study plan. Visit  to register.

# Describing Your Data: Frequencies, Cross Tabulations, and Graphs

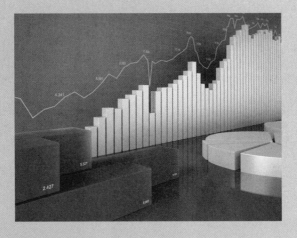

**Learning Objectives:**

By the end of this chapter you should be able to:

1. Define and describe the terms frequency and frequency distribution.
2. Define and describe the terms relative frequency, percentage frequency, and cumulative percentage frequency.
3. Construct frequency tables for nominal and ordinal data.
4. Construct class intervals for interval and ratio data.
5. Construct frequency tables for interval and ratio data.
6. Create cross tabulations.
7. Calculate percentage change, ratios, and rates.
8. Create and interpret pie and bar charts.
9. Create and interpret frequency polygons and cumulative percentage frequency polygons.
10. Create and interpret histograms, stem-and-leaf plots, and boxplots.

### Florence Nightingale (1820–1910)

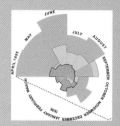

Florence Nightingale, nicknamed "the lady with the lamp," is known for her work in nursing. During the Crimean War (1853–1856), Nightingale sent reports of the conditions and treatment of patients back to Britain. As part of her reports, Nightingale used visual presentations of her data in the form of variations of pie charts. In order to present monthly deaths, she used a more elaborate pie chart that included different forms of death by month. She called these pictures "coxcombs" (see example on the right).

After the war, Nightingale lobbied hard for sanitary reforms in the hospitals. In 1873, while working on the improvement of sanitary conditions in India, Nightingale reported that the mortality rate had dropped from 69 to 18 deaths per 1,000 soldiers.

In 1859, Florence Nightingale became the first female to be elected to the Royal Statistical Society. Shortly after that she became an honorary member of the American Statistical Association.[1]

## Introduction

**Empirical data**
is gathered from objects or participants for a research study.

Researchers use a variety of different methods (such as surveys, interviews, experiments, databases, etc.) to gather **empirical data.** For example, a sociologist gathers data on cultural norms, a political scientist on voting behaviour, an economist on stock fluctuation, and an educational psychologist on gender difference in academic performance. All social science disciplines gather some form of empirical data from the real world. Once gathered, the data needs to be organized and presented in a manner that can provide summary information about the phenomena of interest.

In this chapter we will focus on different ways to present summary information about your data using frequency tables, cross tabulations, and graphs. However, before we do that we need to review how data gets from the collection stage to a dataset that we can work with. Figure 2.1 provides four examples of how variables with different levels of measurement can be measured, coded, and entered in a dataset. Here you can see that the variable "Age," measured at the ordinal level, is given a specific coding and entered in a data analysis program (such as SPSS® or Microsoft® Excel). We code variable responses in order to have numeric information to work with. The coding you use is largely based on what makes the most sense to you. At this stage, it is important to keep notes of which codes match which responses (often called a data dictionary) in order to make the correct interpretations.

**FIGURE 2.1** **Measurement and Coding**

| | Question Example | Coding | Dataset | |
|---|---|---|---|---|
| Nominal (Gender) | **Gender:**<br>❑ Male<br>❑ Female | Male = 1<br>Female = 2 | *n*<br>1<br>2<br>3<br>4<br>5<br>6<br>7<br>8<br>9<br>10 | Gender<br>1<br>2<br>1<br>1<br>2<br>2<br>2<br>1<br>1<br>2 |
| Ordinal (Age) | **Please state your age.**<br>❑ 20 to 25<br>❑ 26 to 35<br>❑ 36 to 45 | 20 to 25 = 1<br>26 to 35 = 2<br>36 to 45 = 3 | *n*<br>1<br>2<br>3<br>4<br>5<br>6<br>7<br>8<br>9<br>10 | Age<br>1<br>2<br>2<br>1<br>3<br>2<br>3<br>1<br>1<br>2 |
| Interval (Satisfied with life) | **I am satisfied with my life:**<br>❑ Strongly Disagree<br>❑ Disagree<br>❑ Neutral<br>❑ Agree<br>❑ Strongly Agree | Strongly disagree = 1<br>Disagree = 2<br>Neutral = 3<br>Agree = 4<br>Strongly Agree = 5 | *n*<br>1<br>2<br>3<br>4<br>5<br>6<br>7<br>8<br>9<br>10 | Life Satisfied<br>4<br>4<br>3<br>2<br>4<br>1<br>5<br>3<br>4<br>2 |
| Ratio (Internet hours) | **How many hours per *week* do you spend on the Internet?** _____ | Record actual number of hours | *n*<br>1<br>2<br>3<br>4<br>5<br>6<br>7<br>8<br>9<br>10 | Internet Hours<br>3<br>15<br>12<br>6<br>9<br>10<br>11<br>0<br>2<br>8 |

*n* = respondent number

**FIGURE 2.2**
**Example of a Dataset**

| n | Gender | Age | Life Satisfied | Internet Hours |
|---|--------|-----|----------------|----------------|
| 1 | 1 | 1 | 4 | 3 |
| 2 | 2 | 2 | 4 | 15 |
| 3 | 1 | 2 | 3 | 12 |
| 4 | 1 | 1 | 2 | 6 |
| 5 | 2 | 3 | 4 | 9 |
| 6 | 2 | 2 | 1 | 10 |
| 7 | 2 | 3 | 5 | 11 |
| 8 | 1 | 1 | 3 | 0 |
| 9 | 1 | 1 | 4 | 2 |
| 10 | 2 | 2 | 2 | 8 |

*n* = respondent number

**FIGURE 2.3**
**Measurement Level and Type of Data**

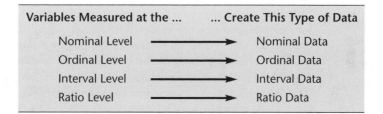

| Variables Measured at the ... | ... Create This Type of Data |
|-------------------------------|------------------------------|
| Nominal Level ⟶ | Nominal Data |
| Ordinal Level ⟶ | Ordinal Data |
| Interval Level ⟶ | Interval Data |
| Ratio Level ⟶ | Ratio Data |

Figure 2.2 provides an example of what the combined data for the examples in Figure 2.1 may look like in a dataset.

One final note about the terminology we use regarding variables. We know that variables can be measured at four different levels: nominal, ordinal, interval, and ratio. When we assess a variable with a specific level of measurement we say that it produces a specific type of data. Figure 2.3 captures this idea. For example, when measuring a variable with an interval level of measurement, we say that it produces interval data. Given this, we often shorten the phrase "a variable with an interval level of measurement" to just "an interval variable." So when you see "ordinal variable," this is referring to a variable that has been measured at the ordinal level, which creates ordinal data.

# Frequency Distributions and Tables

**LO1**

**Frequency** refers to the number of observations of a specific value within a variable. Some textbooks call this absolute frequency but the meaning is the same.

Recall from chapter 1 that a variable is a phenomenon of interest that can take on different values. Furthermore, nominal and ordinal variables have qualitative categories (referred to as just categories) as potential values, whereas interval and ratio variables have quantitative values. Given that a variable can have different values, we can count the **frequency** (also referred to as absolute frequency) of the observed values (categories or quantitative values) of a variable. Consider the following two examples.

**Example 1:** The variable 'Gender' has two possible qualitative categories, male and female. Suppose we collect data on gender by surveying 100 respondents, and observe that 46 are male and 54 are female. In this case, there are two values with differing frequencies.

**Example 2:** Suppose we measure "Student Grade" with a ratio level of measurement, and assume that grades do not include decimals or negative numbers. There are then 101 potential quantitative values, ranging from 0 to 100. Now imagine that we sampled 10 students and observed that three students received a grade of 76, two students received a grade of 79, one student received a grade of 83, and four students received a grade of 86. In this case we observed four potential values with differing frequencies.

Once the data is entered in a software program, we want to get a sense of what the data looks like at a summary level. One way to summarize data into a form that can be easily reviewed is to create a frequency distribution within a table. A **frequency distribution** is the summary of the values of a variable based on the frequencies with which they occur. It is called a frequency distribution because we are looking at how the values of the variable are distributed across all of the cases in the data. When we display the frequency distribution in a table format, we call it a frequency table. As an example, think back to the survey question in Figure 1.10 in chapter 1, which measured the variable "Political Party Affiliation." If we administered the question to 100 respondents, we could calculate the frequency ( $f$ ) with which each category was selected by the respondent and create the frequency table in Table 2.1.

**Frequency distribution** is the summary of the values of a variable based on the frequencies with which they occur.

Often, it is easier to interpret frequency results when they are converted into **relative frequency** ( $f/n$ ). Relative frequency is a comparative measure of the proportion of observed values (category or quantitative value) to the total number of responses within a variable. It provides us with the proportion or fraction of one occurance relative to all occurances. You will often hear this referred to as a proportion.

**LO2**

**Relative frequency** is a comparative measure of the proportion of observed values to the total number of responses within a variable.

The equation for calculating relative frequency ( $f/n$ ) is:

$$\text{relative frequency} = \frac{f}{n} \qquad \qquad \textbf{(2.1)}$$

where: $f$ = frequency of specific responses
$n$ = total number of responses

We use a small "$n$" to represent the size of a sample and a capital "$N$" to represent the size of a population.

**TABLE 2.1**
**Frequency of "Political Party Affiliation"**

| Category | Frequency ($f$) |
|---|---|
| Conservative | 35 |
| Green Party | 10 |
| Le Bloc Québécois | 10 |
| Liberal Party | 33 |
| NDP | 12 |
| Total | 100 |

**TABLE 2.2**

**2009 Statistics Canada Population Estimates of the Northwest Territories**

Source: "2009 Statistics Canada Population Estimates of the Northwest Territories," adapted from Statistics Canada website, http://www40.statcan.ca/l01/cst 01/demo31a-eng.htm, extracted May 18, 2011.

|  | Frequency (f) | Relative Frequency (f/n) |
|---|---|---|
| Males | 22,500 | 0.517 |
| Females | 21,000 | 0.483 |
| Total | 43,500 | 1.00 |

Consider Table 2.2, which provides the 2009 Statistics Canada population estimates for the Northwest Territories. The right column provides the relative frequency of males and females. Given that relative frequencies must add to 1.0, it is generally easier to visualize the comparison of relative frequency than raw numbers. For example, it is likely easier to see the magnitude of difference in 0.517 males versus 0.483 females than it is in 22,500 males versus 21,000 females.

Similar to relative frequency, percentage frequency (%f) also provides a useful way of displaying the frequency of data. A **percentage frequency** (commonly referred to as percentage) is the relative frequency expressed as a percentage value (out of 100) and can be calculated as follows:

A **percentage frequency** is the relative frequency expressed as a percentage value.

$$\%f = \frac{f}{n} \times 100 \qquad \textbf{(2.2)}$$

where: $f$ = frequency of responses

$n$ = total number of responses within the variable

Since relative frequencies are written as a decimal (e.g., 0.10), we can convert them to percentage frequencies by multiplying the relative frequency by 100. For example, 0.10 becomes 10 percent (0.10 × 100). It is also useful to show the cumulative percentage frequency (c.%f) (commonly referred to as cumulative precentage). The **cumulative percentage frequency** gives the percentage of observations up to the end of a specific value. Table 2.3 provides the 2009 Statistics Canada population estimates for the Northwest Territories with the percentage frequency added. Again, we can see that it is easier to see the difference in males versus females when we state that 51.7 percent are male and 48.3 percent are female rather than 22,500 are males versus 21,000 are females.

The **cumulative percentage frequency** gives the percentage of observations up to the end of a specific value.

Now that we have covered some of the basics of frequency tables, we need to focus on how to create frequency tables for nominal, ordinal, interval, and ratio variables. In this section, we will focus two types of frequency tables: simple frequency tables and cross-tabulations.

**TABLE 2.3**

**2009 Statistics Canada Population Estimates of the Northwest Territories**

Source: "2009 Statistics Canada Population Estimates of the Northwest Territories," adapted from Statistics Canada website, http://www40.statcan.ca/l01/ cst01/demo31b-eng.htm, extracted May 18, 2011.

|  | Frequency (f) | Relative Frequency (f/n) | Percentage Frequency (%f) | Cumulative Percentage Frequency (c.%f) |
|---|---|---|---|---|
| Males | 22,500 | 0.517 | 51.7 | 51.7 |
| Females | 21,000 | 0.483 | 48.3 | 100.0 |
| Total | 43,500 | 1.000 | 100.0 |  |

## Take a Closer Look

**Example of Population Estimates by Province**
To show the value of relative frequency and percentage frequency, Table 2.4 provides the Statistics Canada 2009 population estimates by province and territory for individuals 65 years of age or older.

Looking at the relative frequency and percentage frequency, we can see that just over 77 percent of the population age 65 and older live in British Columbia, Ontario, and Quebec.

**TABLE 2.4** **Statistics Canada 2009 Population Estimates**

Source: "Statistics Canada 2009 Population Estimates," adapted from Statistics Canada website, http://www40.statcan.gc.ca/l01/cst01/demo31a-eng.htm, extracted May 18, 2011.

| | Population 65+ (Frequency) | Relative Frequency ($f/n$) | Percentage Frequency (%f) | Cumulative Percentage Frequency (c.%f) |
|---|---|---|---|---|
| Newfoundland and Labrador | 75,200 | 0.0160 | 1.60 | 1.60 |
| Prince Edward Island | 21,600 | 0.0046 | 0.46 | 2.07 |
| Nova Scotia | 147,900 | 0.0316 | 3.16 | 5.22 |
| New Brunswick | 116,400 | 0.0248 | 2.48 | 7.70 |
| Quebec | 1,170,400 | 0.2497 | 24.97 | 32.67 |
| Ontario | 1,787,900 | 0.3814 | 38.14 | 70.82 |
| Manitoba | 168,500 | 0.3590 | 3.59 | 74.41 |
| Saskatchewan | 151,900 | 0.0324 | 3.24 | 77.65 |
| Alberta | 385,200 | 0.0822 | 8.22 | 85.87 |
| British Columbia | 656,300 | 0.1400 | 14.00 | 99.87 |
| Yukon | 2,700 | 0.0006 | 0.06 | 99.93 |
| Northwest Territories | 2,300 | 0.0005 | 0.05 | 99.98 |
| Nunavut | 1,000 | 0.0002 | 0.02 | 100.00 |
| Total | 4,687,300 | 1.0000 | 100.00 | |

## Simple Frequency Tables for Nominal and Ordinal Data

A simple frequency table displays the frequency distribution of one variable at a time. These variables can be nominal, ordinal, interval, or ratio. To create a frequency table, list the possible values the variable can have in one column and record the number of times (frequency) that each value occurs in another column. Figures 2.4 and 2.5 provide examples of frequency tables for nominal and ordinal. These figures provide a diagrammatic view of how data goes from the collection stage (in this case by survey question) to data entry and then to the frequency table.

As you can see it is easy to create frequency tables for nominal and ordinal variables as they have a limited **range** of potential values.

The **range** of the data is the value of the largest observation minus the value of the smallest observation.

## Simple Frequency Tables for Interval and Ratio Data

Creating frequency tables for interval variables can also be fairly straightforward depending on how the variable is measured. In Figure 2.6, "Satisfied With Life" is measured with a Likert scale, making it an interval variable. Since there are only

**FIGURE 2.4**   Nominal Data

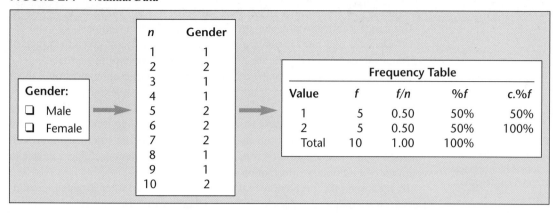

**FIGURE 2.5**   Ordinal Data

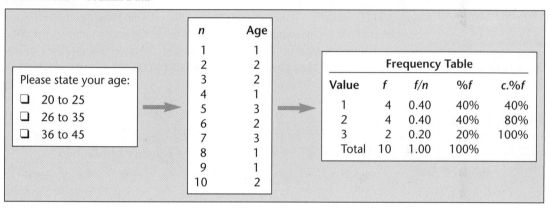

**FIGURE 2.6**   Interval Data

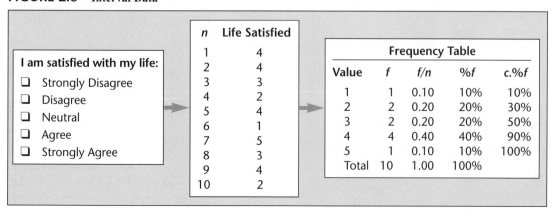

five potential values, the process for creating a frequency table for this variable is the same as that for nominal and ordinal variables.

Creating a frequency table that provides an easy-to-read summary for many interval variables and ratio variables can be a bit more difficult given the range of potential values to include. Figure 2.7 provides an example of this issue.

Here the values range from 0 to 15, but given a large enough sample there are potentially 168 values (24 hours per day × 7 days in a week). Similarly, consider the interval variables "IQ Scores" or the Yale-Brown "Obsessive Compulsive Disorder (OCD) Score." In these cases the values may range from 0 to 200+ and 0 to 40 respectively. The bottom line is that when there are too many values on which to report frequencies, the frequency table become less useful as a device to communicate summary information about the data.

To get around this problem we use class intervals (also called grouped frequencies) to create frequency tables for interval and ratio variables that have a large range of potential values. A **class interval** is a set of values that are combined into a single group for a frequency table. Class intervals have a **class width**, which is the range of each interval, and starting and end values called **class limits**. For class intervals to be meaningful they must following two criteria. First, the class intervals must be exhaustive, meaning that they must include the entire range of the data. Second, class intervals must be mutually exclusive, meaning that the class widths are unique enough that an observed value can only be placed into one class interval.

**Class interval** is a set of values that are combined into a single group for a frequency table.

**Class width** is the range of each class interval.

**Class limits** are actual values in the data that are used as starting and ending values in each class interval

## FIGURE 2.7   Ratio Data

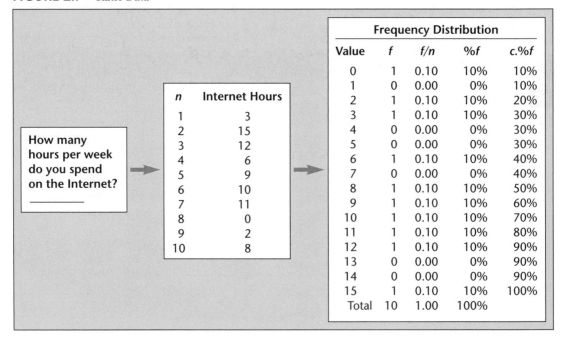

| n | Internet Hours |
|---|---|
| 1 | 3 |
| 2 | 15 |
| 3 | 12 |
| 4 | 6 |
| 5 | 9 |
| 6 | 10 |
| 7 | 11 |
| 8 | 0 |
| 9 | 2 |
| 10 | 8 |

How many hours per week do you spend on the Internet?

**Frequency Distribution**

| Value | f | f/n | %f | c.%f |
|---|---|---|---|---|
| 0 | 1 | 0.10 | 10% | 10% |
| 1 | 0 | 0.00 | 0% | 10% |
| 2 | 1 | 0.10 | 10% | 20% |
| 3 | 1 | 0.10 | 10% | 30% |
| 4 | 0 | 0.00 | 0% | 30% |
| 5 | 0 | 0.00 | 0% | 30% |
| 6 | 1 | 0.10 | 10% | 40% |
| 7 | 0 | 0.00 | 0% | 40% |
| 8 | 1 | 0.10 | 10% | 50% |
| 9 | 1 | 0.10 | 10% | 60% |
| 10 | 1 | 0.10 | 10% | 70% |
| 11 | 1 | 0.10 | 10% | 80% |
| 12 | 1 | 0.10 | 10% | 90% |
| 13 | 0 | 0.00 | 0% | 90% |
| 14 | 0 | 0.00 | 0% | 90% |
| 15 | 1 | 0.10 | 10% | 100% |
| Total | 10 | 1.00 | 100% | |

**FIGURE 2.8**
Comparing
Frequency Tables
With and Without
Class Intervals

| Frequency without Class Intervals | |
|---|---|
| Value | f |
| 0 | 1 |
| 1 | 0 |
| 2 | 1 |
| 3 | 1 |
| 4 | 0 |
| 5 | 0 |
| 6 | 1 |
| 7 | 0 |
| 8 | 1 |
| 9 | 1 |
| 10 | 1 |
| 11 | 1 |
| 12 | 1 |
| 13 | 0 |
| 14 | 0 |
| 15 | 1 |
| Total | 10 |

| Frequency with Class Intervals | |
|---|---|
| Value | f |
| 0 to 3 | 3 |
| 4 to 7 | 1 |
| 8 to 11 | 4 |
| 12 to 15 | 2 |
| Total | 10 |

For example, consider Figure 2.7. We could group the hours spent per week on the Internet into four class intervals with widths of four: 0–3, 4–7, 8–11, and 12–15. It is important to note that in doing this, we are not actually changing the data, we are only creating groups for the purpose of presenting a frequency table that summarizes the data. Figure 2.8 compares the frequency table in Figure 2.7 to one where four class intervals have been created. You can see that although you lose some of the detail when using class intervals, it is easier to read.

LO4

### Creating Class Intervals

Table 2.5 contains the data for the "number of immigrants (in thousands) to Canada" gathered over the course of 20 three-month periods from 2000 to 2004.

Although this example is for a ratio variable, the process that follows is the same for interval variables. Given that the values range from 42 to 73, we need to create class intervals to summarize these numbers into a frequency table. To do so, we need to determine the width and number of class intervals. It is important

**TABLE 2.5**    **Number of Immigrants (in thousands) to Canada From 2000 to 2004**

Source: "Number of Immigrants (in thousands) to Canada from 2000 to 2004," adapted from Statistics Canada, CANSIM Table 051-0006, http://www5.statcan.gc.ca/cansim/a05?lang=eng&id=0510006, extracted May 18, 2011.

| 46 | 58 | 67 | 57 | 58 | 70 | 70 | 52 | 62 | 73 |
|---|---|---|---|---|---|---|---|---|---|
| 53 | 42 | 46 | 59 | 63 | 54 | 55 | 67 | 68 | 48 |

to choose a reasonable number of intervals. One class interval (42 to 73) that includes 20 observations is of little use, as is 20 intervals that include only one observation each. There is no set number of intervals to include, so it is important to consider the audience you are reporting to when creating the number of class intervals. Generally speaking, five to seven intervals are usually sufficient to give a graphical portrayal of the data. The following steps outline how to create class intervals.

### Step 1: Determine the Range of the Data

Since the value of the smallest observation is 46 and the value of the largest is 73, the range is 31 (73 − 42 = 31).

### Step 2: Determine the Width and Number of the Class Intervals

Since we want the width and number of class intervals to incorporate all of the data, we divide the range of the data by the number of class intervals we would like to have and, if necessary, round up to the next value. If we opt for four class intervals, the width of each interval is 7.75 (31 ÷ 4), rounded up to 8. With the width of 8 for each class interval, our intervals are 42–49, 50–57, 58–65, and 66–73. To ensure that the intervals are exclusive of one another, we add 1 to the ending class limit value to create the beginning class limit of the next interval.

Ideally, you want the intervals to be of equal width. However, you may have a situation where the number of desired intervals creates a class interval that falls outside of the range of the data. For example, suppose we opted for five class intervals. Our width would then be 7 (31 ÷ 5 = 6.2, rounded to 7) and our intervals would be 42–48, 49–55, 56–62, 63–69, and 70–76. Since the largest value in our data is 73 it would be misleading to keep the last interval at 76. In this case, we may decide to make the width of the last interval unqual to the rest. For example, we may make the final interval 70–73. The same can be true for the first interval. To summarize then, ideally you want class intervals of equal width. However, if that is not possible given your desired number of class intervals, you can adjust the first or last (or both) interval to be unequal to the others so that your frequency table accurately represents the range of the observed data. When doing so, be sure to keep the remaining intervals at equal widths.

### Step 3: Determine the Class Boundaries

Even though you have class intervals that are exclusive of one another, you still may have observations on the boundary of two classes intervals. For example, if your class intervals were 42–49 and 50–57 where would you put the value 49.5 if it existed in the data? Would it go in the first class interval or the second? You can see that there is a gap between the limits (between 49 and 50). With continuous data (such as that in Table 2.5) having these gaps causes problems when we have values (such as 49.5) that fall between them. To deal with this we create class boundaries that represent the real limits of the class intervals. Class boundaries are numbers that may not necessarily exist in the data but define where the cut-offs are for each class interval. To calculate the class boundary, you subtract 0.50 from the lower class limit and add 0.50 to the upper class limit for each class interval. The boundaries do not have a value separating them, like class intervals do, since they are continuous. Therefore, our class boundaries are 41.5 to less than (<) 49.5, 49.5 to < 57.5, 57.5 to < 65.5, and 65.5 to < 73.5. Thus, the value 49.5 would go in the second class interval, which has the boundaries 49.5 to < 57.5.

### Step 4: Determine Each Class Interval Midpoint

The midpoint is the average value of the class interval. It is often used as a rough estimate of the average case in each interval. It is calculated by adding the lower and upper limits together and dividing by two. Therefore, the midpoints for our intervals are 45.5 [(42 + 49) ÷ 2], 53.5, 61.5, and 69.5.

**LO5**

*Putting the Frequency Table Together*

We can now create a frequency table (Table 2.6), using our four class intervals, by recording the number of observations that fall between the class limits of each interval. Usually frequency tables do not include the values for the class limits, boundaries, or midpoints, but we include them here for explanation. Note that the cumulative percentage frequency gives the percentage of observations up to the end of a class. So the cumulative percentage of the third class is 20 + 25 + 25 = 70. We add up all the percentage relative frequencies of the classes up to and including that class.

Based on this frequency table we can report that 70 percent of the time there were fewer than 65.5 thousand (upper class boundary for class interval 58–65) immigrants to Canada, or that 20 percent of the time there were fewer than 49.5 thousand (upper class boundary for class interval 42–49) immigrants.

**TABLE 2.6   Sample Frequency Table**

| Class Interval | Class Limits | Class Boundaries | Midpoints | Frequency ($f$) | Relative Frequency ($f/n$) | Percentage Frequency (%$f$) | Cumulative Percentage Frequency (c.%$f$) |
|---|---|---|---|---|---|---|---|
| 42–49 | 42, 49 | 41.5 to < 49.5 | 45.5 | 4 | 0.20 | 20 | 20 |
| 50–57 | 50, 57 | 49.5 to < 57.5 | 53.5 | 5 | 0.25 | 25 | 45 |
| 58–65 | 58, 65 | 57.5 to < 65.5 | 61.5 | 5 | 0.25 | 25 | 70 |
| 66–73 | 66, 73 | 65.5 to < 73.5 | 69.5 | 6 | 0.30 | 30 | 100 |
| Total | | | | 20 | 1.00 | 100 | |

# Did You Know?

How many students do you need in a classroom to have a 50 percent probability that at least two of them share the same birthday. The answer may surprise you . . . only 23! Ignoring leap-year birthdays, if you randomly select 23 people there is a 50 percent probability that at least two will have the same birthday. In statistics, more precisely probability theory, this is called the birthday problem.

Here's how it works. Imagine you have an empty classroom that you ask students to enter one at a time, after which you estimate the probability that any two students *do not* share a birthday (it's easier to estimate this way). Student 1 enters the classroom. Since the student is alone, he or she has a 100 percent probability of having a unique birthday (365 days ÷ 365 days). Now student 2 enters the classroom. To have a birthday different than student 1, student 2 must have been born on one of the remaining 364 days. The probability of the two students not sharing a birthday is then (365 ÷ 365) × (364 ÷ 365) ≅ 99.73 percent. Student 3 enters the classroom. To

have a different birthday than student 1 or 2, student 3's birthday must be any of the 363 days remaining. The probability of the three students not sharing a birthday is then (365 ÷ 365) × (364 ÷ 365) × (363 ÷ 365) ≅ 99.73 percent. Add student 4 and the probability ≅ 98.36, student 5 ≅ 97.28 percent, and so on. After 23 students are in the room, the probability that they do not share a birthday is ≅ 49.27 percent. To estimate the probability that they do share a birthday, we just subtract the probability of not sharing a birthday from 100 percent. For example, the probability of sharing a birthday after five students enter the room is 100 − 97.28 ≅ 2.72 percent, and after 23 students is 100 − 49.27 ≅ 50.73 percent.

The graph in Figure 2.9 shows the how the probability of matching birthdays increases as the number of students in the room increases.

**Source:** E. H. Mckinney (1966). Generalized Birthday Problem, *The American Mathematical Monthly, 73 (4),* 385–387.

**FIGURE 2.9** **Probability of Matching Birthdays**

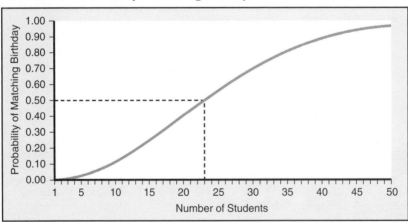

# Cross-Tabulations for Nominal, Ordinal, Interval, and Ratio Data

**LO6**

Whereas frequency tables display a summary of the distribution of a single variable, cross-tabulations (commonly referred to as cross-tabs) display a summary of the distribution of two or more variables. The difference is that cross-tabs allow you to observe how the frequency distribution of one variable relates to that of one or more other variables. It tabulates the frequencies by the categories or class intervals of the variables being compared.

Cross-tabs can include any combination of nominal, ordinal, interval, and ratio variables. Keep in mind that with interval and ratio variables, it may first be necessary to create class intervals as discussed in the previous section. The steps for creating frequency distributions and class intervals from the previous section are the same for cross-tabs, so we won't repeat them here. Following are some examples using data from Statistics Canada's 2004 Canadian Addiction Survey.[2]

**Example 2.1**

*Two Variables— "Gender" and "Drank Alcohol Before" (Nominal Data)*

In this example the nominal variable "Drank Alcohol Before" was measured with the question "Have you ever had a drink?"

**TABLE 2.7    Sample Cross-Tab of Nominal Data**

|  |  | Gender | | |
| --- | --- | --- | --- | --- |
|  |  | Male | Female | Total |
| Drank Alcohol Before | Yes | 806 | 1,392 | 2,198 |
|  | No | 303 | 703 | 1,006 |
| Total |  | 1,109 | 2,095 | 3,204 |

With a simple frequency table we would have seen only one variable with the Yes/No or Male/Female frequencies. With a cross-tab we can see the totals from a simple frequency table plus the breakdown of the numbers by the categories Yes/No and Male/Female.

Looking in the Total row at the bottom of the table, we can see that there were 1,109 Males and 2,095 Females, for a total of 3,204 participants. In the Total column on the right, 2,198 said they have had a drink in the past whereas 1,006 said they had not. Within the table itself, we can see that of those that said they have had a drink in the past, 806 were male and 1,392 were female. Furthermore, 303 males and 703 females said they had not had a drink in the past.

## Example 2.2

*Two Variables— "Gender" and "Drank Alcohol Before" With Percentages (Nominal Data)*

To help interpret a cross-tab, percentages are often included, as seen in Table 2.8. Adding percentages to the cross-tab makes it easier to compare categories within the table. However, they can be a bit difficult to read. Look at the shading added to this table. The percentage within "Drank Alcohol Before" highlighted in light shading shows that of those that stated Yes, 36.7 percent were male and 63.3 percent were female. Since these percentages are within the "Drank Alcohol Before" variable, which runs in a row, it totals 100 at the end of the row. Highlighted in dark shading is the percentage in "Gender." Since "Gender" runs in a column, you need to read the percentages down the column. You can see that of male respondents 72.7 percent said they had drank alcohol before, whereas 27.3 percent said they had not. Similarly, of the female respondents, 66.4 percent said they had drank alcohol versus 33.6 percent who said they had not. The totals for the both Male and Female columns add to 100 percent.

**TABLE 2.8** **Sample Cross-Tab of Nominal Data Including Percentages**

| | | | Gender | | |
| --- | --- | --- | --- | --- | --- |
| | | | Male | Female | Total |
| | Yes | Number | 806 | 1,392 | 2,198 |
| | | % within row (Yes*) | 36.7 | 63.3 | 100 |
| | | % within column (Gender) | 72.7 | 66.4 | 68.6 |
| Drank Alcohol Before | No | Number | 303 | 703 | 1,006 |
| | | % within row (Yes*) | 30.1 | 69.9 | 100 |
| | | % within column (Gender) | 27.3 | 33.6 | 31.4 |
| Total | | Number | 1,109 | 2,095 | 3,204 |
| | | % within row (Yes*) | 34.6 | 65.4 | 100 |
| | | % within column (Gender) | 100 | 100 | 100 |

Yes* = Drank Alcohol Before

## Example 2.3

*Two Variables— "Age" and "Access to Marijuana" (Ordinal Data)*

Table 2.9 provides a cross-tab of an ordinal variable "Access to Marijuana" with an ordinal variable "Age." The variable "Access to Marijuana" was measured with the survey question "How difficult or easy would it be to get marijuana if you wanted some?" In this example, age was originally a ratio variable with 88 different age values. Six class intervals were created using the process outlined in the previous section. Note that in this case, the last interval includes those aged 66+. We can see that 55.1 percent of the respondents indicated that gaining access to marijuana was very easy. The age category with the highest percentage indicating accessing marijuana to be very easy was those in the 15 to 25 age group.

**TABLE 2.9 Sample Cross-Tab of Ordinal Data**

| Access to Marijuana | | | Age | | | | | | |
|---|---|---|---|---|---|---|---|---|---|
| | | | **15 to 25** | **26 to 35** | **36 to 45** | **46 to 55** | **56 to 55** | **66+** | **Total** |
| | Probably impossible | | 12 | 16 | 22 | 26 | 42 | 85 | 203 |
| | | % of Total | 0.3% | 0.4% | 0.5% | 0.6% | 1.0% | 2.0% | 4.8% |
| | Very difficult | | 1.7 | 32 | 37 | 52 | 57 | 63 | 258 |
| | | % of Total | 0.4% | 0.8% | 0.9% | 1.2% | 1.3% | 1.5% | 6.1% |
| | Fairly difficult | | 40 | 57 | 64 | 61 | 39 | 28 | 289 |
| | | % of Total | 0.9% | 1.3% | 1.5% | 1.4% | 0.9% | 0.7% | 6.8% |
| | Fairly easy | | 167 | 222 | 250 | 265 | 153 | 103 | 1160 |
| | | % of Total | 3.9% | 5.2% | 5.9% | 6.2% | 3.6% | 2.4% | 27.3% |
| | Very easy | | 592 | 392 | 476 | 448 | 259 | 174 | 2341 |
| | | % of Total | **13.9%** | 9.2% | 11.2% | 10.5% | 6.1% | 4.1% | **55.1%** |
| | Total | | 828 | 719 | 849 | 852 | 550 | 453 | 4251 |
| | | % of Total | 19.5% | 16.9% | 20.0% | 20.0% | 12.9% | 10.7% | 100.0% |

# Comparing the Distribution of Frequencies

**LO7**

So far we have looked at how to construct and read frequency tables and cross-tabulations. Both are useful when you want to provide a summary of the distribution of responses for one or more variables. However, sometimes researchers want to compare values within variables or compare different variables. For example, suppose we measured the number of females holding executive positions across 100 organizations over the course of five years. How could we determine the percentage change in the number of females in the positions over time? Or, imagine if we collected data on the number of males and females who contracted H1N1 (also called the swine flu). How could we calculate the ratio of illness in males to females? Finally, suppose we collected data on bicycle thefts in three different cities each with different size populations. How could we compare the theft rates across the cities while taking into account the differing sizes of population? For these questions, we need to use percentage change, ratios, and rates. To demonstrate each, a frequency table or cross-tab is provided to assist you in understanding where the numbers are coming from.

## Percentage Change

The **percentage change** is a fraction out of 100 that indicates the relative change in a variable from one time period to another.

In the previous examples, we dealt with situations where we had data from only one time period. However, social scientists are often interested in examining variables across different time periods. When we have data that spans different time periods (e.g., two years), we can calculate the change from one year to another and report this change as a percentage. We call this a **percentage change**.

**TABLE 2.10**
**Number of Marriages**

Source: ****Important: data for 2005 to 2008 is available from Health Statistics Division (hd-ds@statcan.gc.ca) upon request only, as this program is discontinued and data will not be available on CANSIM anymore and neither as Summary Data Table, Marriages by province and territory is discontinued, http://www40.statcan.ca/l01/cst01/famil04-eng.htm.

| Frequency of Marriages (*f*) | |
|---|---|
| 2007 | 148,296 |
| 2008 | 148,831 |

To calculate percentage change from one time period to another, we use the following equation:

$$p = \frac{f_{time_2} - f_{time_1}}{f_{time_1}} \times 100 \qquad (2.3)$$

where: $f_{time_1}$ = frequency of a specific response at time 1

$f_{time_2}$ = frequency of a specific response at time 2

Table 2.10 provides a frequency table of Statistics Canada's estimated number of marriages for 2007 and 2008. The percentage change from 2007 to 2008 is calculated as:

$$\text{Percentage change} = \frac{\# \text{ in } 2008 - \# \text{ in } 2007}{\# \text{ in } 2007} \times 100 \qquad (2.4)$$

$$= \frac{148,831 - 148,296}{148,296} \times 100 = 0.36$$

In this example we can say that there was a slight increase in the number of marriages between 2007 and 2008 of 0.36 percent, which is less than a 1 percent increase. However, according to Statistics Canada the population of Canada was 32,932,000 in 2007 and 33,327,000 in 2008, which means that the percentage change in the population from 2007 to 2008 was 1.19 percent. If the population increased you might ask if the marriage rate really increased. To answer this, we have to calculate the difference using rates. We'll cover this situation in the Rates section of this chapter.

A **ratio** is a comparison of two values of a variable based on their frequency.

## Ratios

A **ratio** is a comparison of two values of a variable based on their frequency. You may have heard of or read reports that include ratios. For example, your school

### For Your Information

Frequencies, proportions, percentages, percentage change, ratios, and rates can be calculated on variables with nominal, ordinal, interval, and ratio levels of measurement. The main difference is the number of values the variable can possibly have. While "Gender" has two, "Weight" may have many differing values. How you measure the variable determines how many potential values the variable may have.

may have a student-to-faculty ratio of 22:1 (22 students for every one faculty member). Or if you make french toast you might decide to use a ratio of 1/3 cups of milk for every one egg. To calculate a ratio comparing two values of a variable, we divide the first value of interest by the second value of interest. The equation is as follows:

$$Ratio = \frac{f_{v1}}{f_{v2}} \qquad (2.5)$$

where: $f_{v1}$ = frequency of the first value to be compared
$f_{v2}$ = frequency of the second value to be compared

For example, consider Table 2.11, which provides the number of motor vehicle accident deaths for 2004 as reported by Statistics Canada.

**TABLE 2.11**

**2004 Motor Vehicle Accident Deaths**

Source: "2004 Motor Vehicle Accident Deaths," adapted from Statistics Canada publication *Health Reports*, Catalogue 82-003-XIE2008003, Vol. 19, No. 3, http://www.statcan.gc.ca/pub/82-003-x/2008003/article/10648-eng.pdf.

|  | Frequency (f) | Relative Frequency (f/n) |
|---|---|---|
| Males | 2,035 | 0.708 |
| Females | 840 | 0.292 |
| Total | 2,875 | 1.00 |

Here we can see that more males are killed in motor vehicle accidents than females. However, how many males does that represent per female? Using equation 2.5 we see that:

$$Ratio = \frac{f_{v1}}{f_{v2}} \qquad (2.6)$$

$$= \frac{\text{\# of male motor vehicle deaths}}{\text{\# of female motor vehicle deaths}}$$

$$= \frac{2,035}{840} = 2.42$$

We can now say that in 2004 there were 2.42 males killed in a motor vehicle accident for every one female killed in a motor vehicle accident (2.42:1). Conversely, if we wanted to know the ratio of females to males, we would just switch the numerator and denominator:

$$\frac{840}{2,035} = 0.41:1$$

Meaning that there were approximately 0.41 females killed in motor vehicle accidents per one male killed in motor vehicle accidents.

**EXERCISE 2.1**

Previously we looked at the cross-tab of the variables "Gender" and "Drank Alcohol Before" from the 2004 Canadian Addiction Survey. This cross-tab is reproduced in Table 2.12. Using equation 2.5 try to determine the following ratios.

**TABLE 2.12**
**Cross Tabulation of "Gender" and "Drank Alcohol Before"**

| | | Gender | | |
| | | Male | Female | Total |
| --- | --- | --- | --- | --- |
| Drank Alcohol Before | Yes | 806 | 1,392 | 2,198 |
| | No | 303 | 703 | 1,006 |
| Total | | 1,109 | 2,095 | 3,204 |

**Question 1:** What is the ratio of those respondents who have previously drank alcohol to those that stated they have not?

Answer 1: There are 2.18 respondents who have previously drank alcohol to every one respondent who has not. (2,198 ÷ 1,006 = 2.18).

**Question 2:** What is the ratio of females who state they have not previously drank alcohol to males who state they have not previously drank alcohol?

Answer 2: There are 2.32 females who state they have not previously drank alcohol to every one male who stated they have not previously drank alcohol.

## Rates

Ratios are useful when the values being compared are in the same units. For example, the number of cars sold by Salesperson A versus Salesperson B; the average heart rate for participants in Group A versus Group B; or the number of speeding tickets for different age groups of drivers. However, if you need to compare values where other factors affect those values, then **rates** are more useful. For example, it wouldn't make a lot of sense to compare the actual number of new housing starts (construction of new homes) in British Columbia to New Brunswick because the population sizes are different. So while these numbers may be useful to a researcher by themselves, comparisons become distorted when we compare regions that have different poulations sizes. To adjust for poulation size we would report the new housing starts per person. That is, we use the ratio of total new housing starts in a region to the population size of that region. In doing so we obtain the rates of new housing starts that can then be used to compare regions of different population sizes. To calculate rates, we use equation 2.7.

A **rate** is the frequency with which a phenomenon occurs relative to a population size or time unit.

Note that "rate" is often referred to as "crude rate" because the rate does not take into consideration the structure of the population (such as age or gender differences in the population). For simplicity, we will just use the term "rate."

$$Rate = \frac{Number\ of\ events\ for\ the\ population\ of\ interest}{Total\ population\ of\ the\ population\ of\ interest} \times 10{,}000 \quad \textbf{(2.7)}$$

**TABLE 2.13**
**2009 Housing Starts and Populations for British Columbia and New Brunswick**

| | Housing Starts | Population |
|---|---|---|
| British Columbia | 16,077 | 4,455,200 |
| New Brunswick | 3,521 | 749,500 |

Sources: Adapted from Statistics Canada website, http://www40.statcan.gc.ca/l01/cst01/demo02a-eng.htm, extracted May 18, 2011, and Canada Mortgage and Housing Corporation (CMHC), Starts and Completions Survey, 2009.

Notice in the equation that we multiple by 10,000. We do this in order to avoid small decimals. For example, a rate of 0.025 car sales per person is a more difficult to interpret than 250 car sales per 10,000 people. You can multiply by whatever number makes sense as long as you report it properly. So mulitplying by 1,000 instead of 10,000 gives you 25 car sales per 1,000 people. Taking the rate without mulitplying by a number (or multiplying by 1) gives you the rate per person. When the rate is per person, you'll often hear it called "per capita."

Continuing with our housing starts example, Table 2.13 provides the 2009 housing starts and populations for British Columbia and New Brunswick, according to Statistics Canada. Looking at the actual numbers it appears that British Columbia is growing more (based on new housing starts) than New Brunswick. However, if we take population into account, and create a rate of new housing starts per 10,000 people, we can equitably compare the two provinces.

British Columbia:

$$rate = \frac{16,077}{4,455,200} \times 10,000 \qquad (2.8)$$
$$= 0.003609 \times 10,000$$
$$= 36.09$$

New Brunswick:

$$rate = \frac{3,521}{749,500} \times 10,000$$
$$= 0.004698 \times 10,000$$
$$= 46.98$$

Based on our calculation in equation 2.8, in 2009, New Brunswick had more new housing starts per person than British Columbia. In fact, New Brunswick had 46.98 new housing starts per 10,000 people whereas British Columbia had 36.09 per 10,000 people.

In our previous example, we compared one phenomenon (new housing starts) in two different populations (British Columbia and New Brunswick). However, with ratios we can compare a phenomonon across a number of different populations. Suppose we want to compare provinces and territories on the volume of wine purchased per person. If we compare only total volume of wine purchased per province and territory we would see that the top three purchasers (by volume) of wine would be Ontario (137,737,000 litres), Quebec (128,614,000 litres), and

**TABLE 2.14**
**Wine Purchased by Per Person Rates**

Source: "Wine Purchased by Per Person Rates," adapted from Statistics Canada CANSIM Database, http://www5.statcan. gc.ca/cansim/home-accueil? lang=eng, CANSIM Table 183-0006, extracted May 18, 2011.

| Region | Volume per Person |
|---|---|
| Newfoundland and Labrador | 6.1 |
| Saskatchewan | 7.3 |
| Northwest Territories and Nunavut | 8.8 |
| Prince Edward Island | 9.0 |
| Manitoba | 9.1 |
| New Brunswick | 9.6 |
| Nova Scotia | 10.1 |
| Ontario | 13.2 |
| Canada | 15.0 |
| Alberta | 15.9 |
| British Columbia | 17.9 |
| Quebec | 20.1 |
| Yukon | 21.0 |

British Columbia (62,805,000 litres). This would make sense because these are the three largest provinces by population. Table 2.14 contains the volume of wine (in litres) purchased per person (15 years of age or older) across the provinces and territories of Canada for the year 2007. Here we can see that when considering per person rate, Yukon, Quebec, and British Columbia are the top three purchasers.

Recall in an earlier section we found that there was a slight increase in the number of marriages between 2007 and 2008 of 0.36 percent, but during the same time the population also increased by 1.19 percent. We left that example wondering if the marriage rate really increased. Now that we understand percentage change and rate, we can combine the two to answer that question. Table 2.15 provides the information regarding numbers of marriages and population per year.

First, we need to estimate the rate of marriages for both 2007 and 2008 so that we can take the difference in population size in to account.

**TABLE 2.15**
**Number of Marriages and Population Per Year**

Source: ****Important: Data for 2005 to 2008 is available from Health Statistics Division (hd-ds@statcan.gc.ca) upon request only, as this program is discontinued and data will not be available on CANSIM anymore and neither as Summary Data Table, Marriages by province and territory is discontinued, http://www40.statcan.ca/l01/ cst01/famil04-eng.htm.

Rate of Marriages per 1,000 people in 2007:

$$rate = \frac{148,296}{32,932,000} \times 1,000 \qquad (2.9)$$
$$= 0.00450 \times 1,000$$
$$= 4.50$$

| Year | Number of Marriages | Population |
|---|---|---|
| 2007 | 148,296 | 32,932,000 |
| 2008 | 148,831 | 33,327,000 |

Rate of Marriages per 1,000 people in 2008:

$$rate = \frac{148{,}831}{32{,}327{,}000} \times 1{,}000$$
$$= 0.00447 \times 1{,}000$$
$$= 4.47$$

We can see that there were 4.50 marriages per 1,000 people in 2007 and 4.47 marriages per 1,000 people in 2008. We can now use equation 2.10 to calculate the percentage change in the rates.

$$percentage\ change = \frac{rate\ in\ 2008 - rate\ in\ 2007}{rate\ in\ 2007} \times 100 \quad \textbf{(2.10)}$$
$$= \frac{4.47 - 4.50}{4.50} \times 100$$
$$= -0.67$$

We can now say that although marriages increased by 0.36 percent from 2007 to 2008, the population also increased during that time by 1.19 percent. As a result, when you take the population change into account, the rate of marriages decreased by 0.67 percent (decreased because the number is negative).

# Graphing Data

A pictorial representation of data efficiently and effectively transmits information. Pie charts, bar charts, frequency polygons, cumulative percentage frequency polygons, and histograms all help present the information contained in the data.

**LO8**

## Pie Charts and Bar Charts, For Nominal and Ordinal Data

Since you have likely already been exposed to pie charts and bar charts during your education, we won't spend a lot of time on them. Pie charts and bar charts are useful for graphically displaying the frequency distribution of nominal and ordinal level data as they can be easily constructed to show the differences in categories within a variable. A **pie chart** displays the distribution of a variable out of 100 percent, where 100 percent represents the entire pie. Either frequency or percentage frequency may be used in constructing the chart. As an example, the pie chart and table in Figure 2.10 displays the frequency of motor vehicle deaths by gender for 2004.

Pie charts are particular useful for nominal and ordinal variables, as the categories are used to separate the pie into the appropriate pieces. While they could be used for interval and ratio level variables using class intervals, frequency polygons and histograms (discussed in the next section) tend to better represent the data.

A **pie chart** displays the distribution of a variable out of 100 percent, where 100 percent represents the entire pie.

## FIGURE 2.10 Example of a Pie Chart

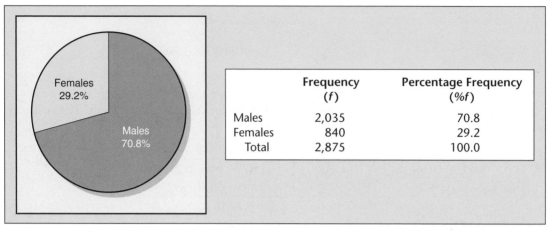

| | Frequency (f) | Percentage Frequency (%f) |
|---|---|---|
| Males | 2,035 | 70.8 |
| Females | 840 | 29.2 |
| Total | 2,875 | 100.0 |

Source: "Example of a Pie Chart—'Motor vehicle accident deaths, 1979 to 2004,'" adapted from Statistics Canada publication *Health Reports,* Catalogue 82-003-XIE, Vol. 19, No. 3, http://www.statcan.gc.ca/pub/82-003-x/2008003/article/10648/5202440-eng.htm.

A **bar chart** displays the frequency of a variable with the variable categories along the *x*-axis and the variable frequencies on the *y*-axis.

Similar to a pie chart, a **bar chart** displays the frequency of a variable with the categories of the variable along the *x*-axis and the frequency of the variable on the *y*-axis. Figure 2.11 displays the same motor vehicle accident data in bar chart format.

As is the case with pie charts, bar charts are best suited to nominal and ordinal data as the categories of the variables can be easily transferred to the *x*-axis of the chart. However, they can sometimes be useful for displaying interval and ratio level variables using class intervals. Figure 2.12 is an example of interval data from a survey item, measured using a 4-point Likert-type scale (four response options), in the 2004 Canadian Addiction Survey. Figure 2.13 provides a ratio example where class intervals are used to categorize age in response to a question about the ease of access to marijuana.

## FIGURE 2.11 Example of a Bar Chart

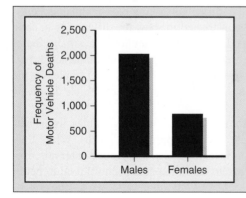

| | Frequency (f) | Percentage Frequency (%f) |
|---|---|---|
| Males | 2,035 | 70.8 |
| Females | 840 | 29.2 |
| Total | 2,875 | 100.0 |

**FIGURE 2.12**
**Example of a Bar Chart For a 4-Point Likert-type Scale**

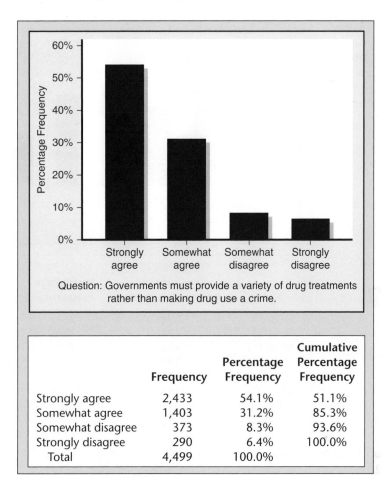

Question: Governments must provide a variety of drug treatments rather than making drug use a crime.

|  | Frequency | Percentage Frequency | Cumulative Percentage Frequency |
|---|---|---|---|
| Strongly agree | 2,433 | 54.1% | 51.1% |
| Somewhat agree | 1,403 | 31.2% | 85.3% |
| Somewhat disagree | 373 | 8.3% | 93.6% |
| Strongly disagree | 290 | 6.4% | 100.0% |
| Total | 4,499 | 100.0% |  |

**LO9**

A **frequency polygon** is a line graph of the frequency of interval or ratio data.

## Frequency Polygon and Cumulative Percentage Frequency Polygon, For Interval and Ratio Level Data

A **frequency polygon** is a line graph of the frequency distribution of interval or ratio data and is constructed by placing the class intervals on the *x*-axis and the frequencies (or percentage frequencies) on the *y*-axis. They are useful for graphically displaying the shape of the frequency distribution. Figure 2.14 is an example of a frequency polygon with its associated frequency table. This data represents a sample of 209 respondents, from Statistics Canada's 2004 Canadian Addiction Survey, from the ages of 11 to 21 who had previously used or continue to use marijuana, cannabis, or hashish. The frequency polygon and table represent the age at which the respondent began using marijuana, cannabis, or hashish. Looking at the frequency polygon, you can see that the largest frequency is age 16 (the highest point in the line).

**FIGURE 2.13**
**Example of a Bar Chart With Class Intervals**

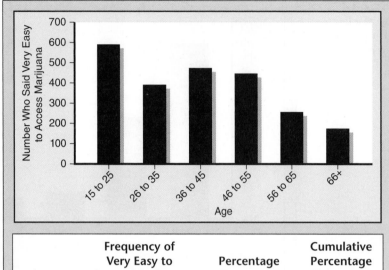

| Age | Frequency of Very Easy to Access Marijuana | Percentage Frequency | Cumulative Percentage Frequency |
|---|---|---|---|
| 15 to 25 | 592 | 25% | 25% |
| 26 to 35 | 392 | 17% | 42% |
| 36 to 44 | 476 | 20% | 62% |
| 46 to 55 | 448 | 19% | 81% |
| 56 to 65 | 259 | 11% | 92% |
| 66+ | 174 | 8% | 100% |
| Total | 2,341 | 100% | |

**FIGURE 2.14**   **Frequency Polygon**

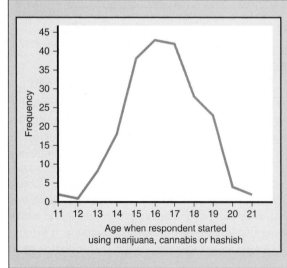

Age when respondent started using marijuana, cannabis or hashish

| Age | Frequency (f) | Percentage Frequency (%f) | Cumulative Percentage Frequency (c.%f) |
|---|---|---|---|
| 11 | 2 | 0.96 | 0.96 |
| 12 | 1 | 0.48 | 1.44 |
| 13 | 8 | 3.83 | 5.26 |
| 14 | 18 | 8.61 | 13.88 |
| 15 | 38 | 18.18 | 32.06 |
| 16 | 43 | 20.57 | 52.63 |
| 17 | 42 | 20.10 | 72.73 |
| 18 | 28 | 13.40 | 86.12 |
| 19 | 23 | 11.00 | 97.13 |
| 20 | 4 | 1.91 | 99.04 |
| 21 | 2 | 0.96 | 100.00 |
| Total | 209 | 100.00 | |

Source: Permission granted by CAS via the Data Liberation Initiative.

**FIGURE 2.15**    **Frequency Polygon by Gender**

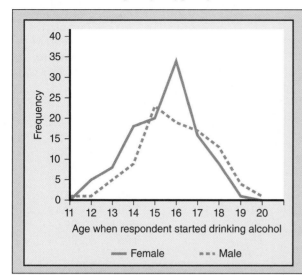

| Age | MALES Frequency (*f*) | FEMALES Frequency (*f*) |
|---|---|---|
| 11 | 1 | 0 |
| 12 | 1 | 5 |
| 13 | 5 | 8 |
| 14 | 9 | 18 |
| 15 | 23 | 20 |
| 16 | 19 | 34 |
| 17 | 17 | 16 |
| 18 | 13 | 9 |
| 19 | 4 | 1 |
| 20 | 1 | 0 |
| Total | 93 | 111 |

Source: Permission granted by CAS via the Data Liberation Initiative.

Frequency polygons can also be used to compare the distribution of a variable across groups of respondents. For example, the 2004 Canadian Addiction Survey asked respondents to indicate at what age they began to drink alcohol (if ever). Using a sample of males and females from the ages of 11 to 20, Figure 2.15 compares the frequency distributions (males versus females) of age in which the respondents stated they began drinking alcohol. You can see from the frequency polygons, and respective frequency tables, that for males the highest age frequency is 15 years of age and for females is 16 years of age.

A **cumulative fre-quency polygon** is a frequency polygon that graphs the cumulative percentage frequency column in a frequency table.

A **cumulative percentage frequency polygon** is a frequency polygon that graphs the cumulative percentage frequency column in a frequency table. Similar to frequency polygons, they can be used for comparing frequencies of a variable across groups. Figure 2.16 provides the cumulative percentage frequency of the example used in Figure 2.14. You can see that approximately 50 percent of the respondents had started using marijuana, cannabis, or hashish by approximately 16 years of age.

The examples in figures 2.14 and 2.16 have class intervals with a width of one year, which makes them a little easier to understand. However, you could have class intervals with greater widths. Say you created the four class intervals 11–13, 14–16, 17–19, and 20+. In this case your *x*-axis would include the numbers from the upper class limit of each interval, 13, 16, 19, and 20+. You would then plot the frequency up to the upper limits of each interval. Therefore, 13 would be 11, 16 would be 99, 19 would be 93, and 20+ would

**FIGURE 2.16** **Cumulative Frequency Polygon**

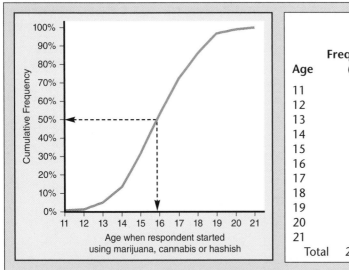

| Age | Frequency (f) | Percentage Frequency (%f) | Cumulative Percentage Frequency (c.%f) |
|---|---|---|---|
| 11 | 2 | 0.96 | 0.96 |
| 12 | 1 | 0.48 | 1.44 |
| 13 | 8 | 3.83 | 5.26 |
| 14 | 18 | 8.61 | 13.88 |
| 15 | 38 | 18.18 | 32.06 |
| 16 | 43 | 20.57 | 52.63 |
| 17 | 42 | 20.10 | 72.73 |
| 18 | 28 | 13.40 | 86.12 |
| 19 | 23 | 11.00 | 97.13 |
| 20 | 4 | 1.91 | 99.04 |
| 21 | 2 | 0.96 | 100.00 |
| Total | 209 | 100.00 | |

Source: Permission granted by CAS via the Data Liberation Initiative.

be 6. The same applies to cumulative frequency polygons, except that you would use the cumulative frequencies.

**LO10**

A **histogram** is a plot of the frequency of interval or ratio data.

## Histograms

A **histogram** is a plot of the frequency of interval or ratio data. Histograms are useful ways of graphically representing interval and ratio variables because they are able to show the continuous nature of the data without necessarily creating class intervals.

Statistics Canada's 2004 Canadian Addiction Survey provides the age that participants stated they had their first alcoholic drink. Figure 2.17 provides two histograms of the variable "Age of First Alcohol Drink." In both histograms, the x-axis represents the ages from 10 to 21. In the histogram on the left, the y-axis provides the frequency with which each age is observed in the data. In this histogram you can see that the most frequently occurring ages are 16 and 18. The histogram on the right provides the same information, only this time y-axis is percentage frequency as opposed to frequency. Again, we can see that the most frequently occurring ages are 16 and 18, but this time we also see that these ages account for approximately 36 percent of the cases (approximately 18 percent each).

Although it is possible to use histograms with class intervals, doing so loses some of the interpretive value of the histogram. Consider the two histograms in Figure 2.18. On the left is a histogram representing the age of 10,060 individuals from the ages of 20 to 60 who participated in Statistics Canada's 2004 Canadian

# For Your Information

A cumulative percentage frequency polygon (line chart) is useful for answering questions, such as "What percentage of participants had their first alcoholic drink at 16 years of age and at 18 years of age?"

To answer this, start at age 16 on the *x*-axis and move upwards (following the red arrow) until you reach the frequency line. Then move across to the *y*-axis to find the percentage. In interpreting this you might say that of those participants who have previously drank alcohol, approximately 52 percent had their first alcoholic drink by the age of 16. Similarly, if you look at the age 18 (green arrow) you might say that of those participants who have previous drank alcohol, approximately 84 percent had their first alcoholic drink by the age of 18. By subtracting the two (84 – 52) we can say that approximately 32 percent had their first alcoholic drink between the ages of 16 and 18.

**Source:** Permission granted by CAS via the Data Liberation Initiative.

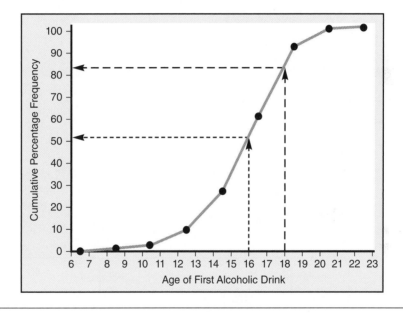

Addiction Survey. In this example, class intervals were constructed to reduce the variable from a ratio level to four classes. On the right is a histogram of age of the same 10,060 individuals, only this time class intervals were not used. You can see immediately that the histogram on the right provides you with a lot more detailed information than the one on the left, even though the same data and same number of cases are included.

A **stem-and-leaf plot** is a plot of the frequency of interval or ratio data similar to the histogram but more informative since it provides actual data values.

## Stem-and-Leaf Plots

A **stem-and-leaf plot** is similar to a histogram in that it provides a graphical representation of the frequency of interval or ratio data. Where it differs from

**FIGURE 2.17**    **Age of First Alcoholic Drink**

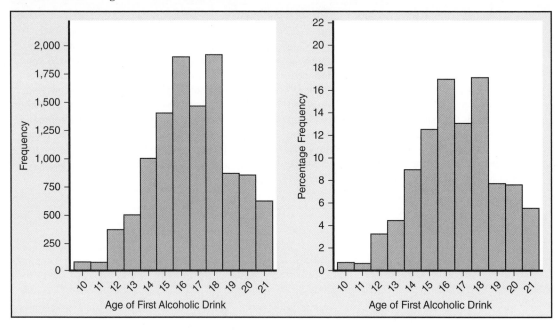

the histogram is that the data within the frequency table is included in the plot. Suppose you randomly select 20 high school students and record the number of text message each individual sends in one day. Table 2.16 represents the number of text messages for one day.

**FIGURE 2.18**
**Histogram With
and Without Class
Intervals**

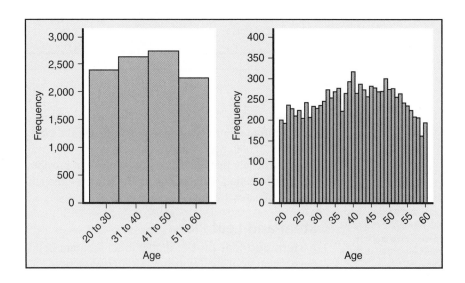

**TABLE 2.16**   **Sample Text Message Data**

| 13 | 21 | 22 | 31 | 35 | 39 | 39 | 42 | 43 | 46 |
|----|----|----|----|----|----|----|----|----|----|
| 46 | 47 | 48 | 50 | 51 | 58 | 60 | 67 | 70 | 79 |

Based on what we know so far, we could create a frequency table with seven class intervals and from there create a histogram (see Figure 2.19). While both the frequency table and histogram are useful ways to display the data, the drawback is that the actual values of the data are not shown. For example, from both the frequency table and the histogram we can see that there are four values in the interval 30 to 39, but without seeing the actual data, we don't know what those values are.

Figure 2.20 provides the stem-and-leaf plot for the same data. The stem represents the value(s) on the left side of each individual number. In this case, the stem represents the tens column of the number. So for the values in the 10 to 19 interval, 1 is the stem, for the values in the 20 to 29 interval, 2 is the stem, and so on. If our values were more than two digits, we could adjust the stem to represent hundreds (as in 1 for 100) or thousands (3 for 3,000). The value you set for the stem is based on your judgment of the best way to present the data.

The leaf represents the value(s) on the right side of each number. In this case, the leaf represents the ones column of the number. For the value 13, 1 is the stem and 3 is the leaf. The place value of the numbers representing the leaf (i.e., ones, tens, hundreds, etc.) depends on the place value you use for the stems.

Looking at Figure 2.20, we can see that the value 35 is shown with 3 in the stem and 5 in the leaf, while 51 is shown with 5 in the stem and 1 in the leaf. All values with the same stem are included on the same line, which is why you see 3 as the stem and 1 5 9 9 in the leaf, representing the values 31, 35, 39, and 39.

**FIGURE 2.19**   **Frequency Table and Histogram of Text Message Data**

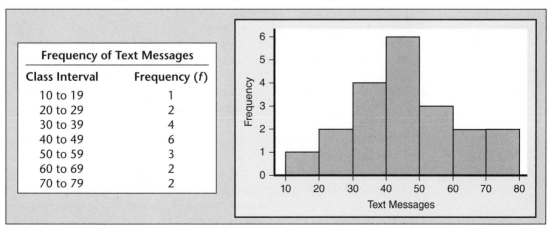

| Frequency of Text Messages | |
|---|---|
| **Class Interval** | **Frequency (*f*)** |
| 10 to 19 | 1 |
| 20 to 29 | 2 |
| 30 to 39 | 4 |
| 40 to 49 | 6 |
| 50 to 59 | 3 |
| 60 to 69 | 2 |
| 70 to 79 | 2 |

**FIGURE 2.20**
**Stem-and-Leaf Plot
of Text Message Data**

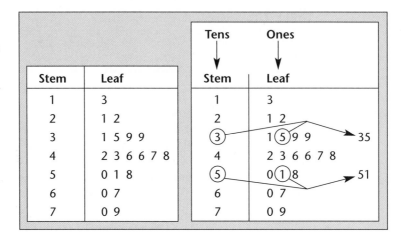

If you look at the histogram and the stem-and-leaf plot you will see that the shape of the leaf corresponds to the shape of the histogram. This is where you can see the value of the stem-and-leaf plot. It is a good way of showing data distribution (like a histogram), but without losing any of the information regarding the values of each number.

**EXERCISE 2.2**

Using the following numbers, create a stem-and-leaf plot.

| 41 | 45 | 50 | 52 | 54 | 54 | 61 | 67 | 67 | 68 |
|----|----|----|----|----|----|----|----|----|----|
| 69 | 71 | 75 | 84 | 86 | 87 | 90 | 91 | 92 | 92 |

## Boxplots

A **boxplot** (also known as a box and whisker plot) is a graphical summary of the data based on percentiles.

A **boxplot** (also known as a box and whisker plot) is a graphical summary of the data based on percentiles. Figure 2.21 is a boxplot of the text messaging data from Table 2.16. The box represents the distribution of the data between the 25th and 75th percentile. The light line in the middle represents the median (50th percentile). The lines coming out of the box (also known as whiskers) extend to the lowest and highest value in the data, which provides you with the range. As we can see in Figure 2.21, the lowest value is 13 and the highest is 79. The 75th percentile sits at 56.25 and the 25th percentile is 36. Finally the median value, which represents the 50th percentile, is 46.

One advantage of boxplots is that you can compare the data distribution of multiple groups. For example, suppose we gathered the number of text messages sent per day from 20 students in School A and 20 students in School B. We could create two boxplots to compare them (Figure 2.22).

**FIGURE 2.21**

**Example of a Boxplot**

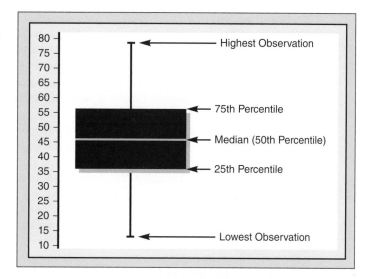

**FIGURE 2.22**

**Example of a Boxplot Comparing Two Groups**

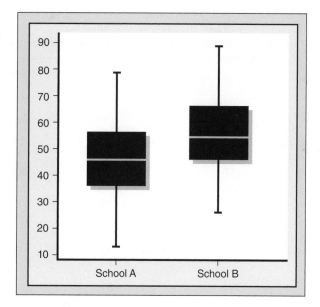

## Conclusion

In this chapter we discussed ways in which you can describe your data using frequencies, cross-tabulations (or cross-tabs), and graphs. Frequency tables are useful in displaying the distribution of scores on a variable and often include relative, percentage, and cumulative frequency information to aid in the interpretation of the data. Frequency tables can be used with variables assessed at all levels of measurement (nominal, ordinal, interval, and ratio data), although keep in mind that with interval and ratio data, you often need to construct class intervals first. Cross-tabs are used when you want to display summary information about two or more variables. They allow you to observe how the distribution of one variable relates to that of another variable. Similar to frequency tables, cross-tabs work with nominal, ordinal, interval, and ratio data.

When you need to compare summary results, using percentage change, ratios, or rates is helpful. Percentage change allows you to see the difference in the variable across different time periods. Ratios allow you to compare two values of a variable based on their frequency. Rates allow you to compare variables where population size or time needs to be accounted for.

Graphical representation of data is also useful. You now know how to present data using pie and bar charts, frequency and cumulative frequency polygons, histograms, stem-and-leaf plots, and boxplots. Each type of graph has a different purpose, and their use depends on the information you need to convey. For example, you could use a frequency polygon to show the dollar amounts of social assistance provided over the course of 10 years, and a pie chart to show percentage of the total amount provided to males versus females.

In the next chapter, we will look at descriptive statistics as another way of describing data. This will provide you with the first look at how the level of measurement influences the types of statistical analysis that can be used.

## Key Chapter Concepts and Terms

| | | |
|---|---|---|
| Empirical data, 37 | Range, 42 | Bar chart, 58 |
| Frequency, 39 | Class interval, 44 | Frequency polygon, 59 |
| Frequency distribution, 40 | Class width, 44 | |
| | Class limits, 44 | Cumulative frequency polygon, 61 |
| Relative frequency, 40 | Percentage change, 51 | Histogram, 62 |
| Percentage frequency, 41 | Ratio, 52 | Stem-and-leaf plot, 63 |
| Cumulative percentage frequency, 41 | Rate, 54 | Boxplot, 66 |
| | Pie chart, 57 | |

## Frequently Asked Questions

1. Does per capita represent a specific number of people? Or does it simply mean proportionately? For example, does per capita automatically mean per 1,000 people or does it vary?

Per capita is translated as 'per head.' So per capita spending is total spending divided by the number of people. However, per capita murders, or even per capita for all crimes, can be a very small number. In those cases the per capita rate is changed to be per 1,000 people or per 10,000 people for ease. So if there are two murders per 1,000 people, we could write 0.002 as the per capita rate, but for many people, 2 per 1,000 is easier to understand.

2. Can you give me an example of the difference between a frequency and relative frequency?

Frequency is the count of observed values in the variable. For example, in the May 2, 2011 federal election, the frequency of seats won by political party was Conservatives 167, NDP 102, Liberals 34, Bloc Québécois 4, and Green Party 1.

Relative frequency is the frequency divided by the total number of observations (308). So the relative frequency is Conservatives 0.5422 (167 ÷ 308), NDP 0.3312 (102 ÷ 308), Liberals 0.1104 (34 ÷ 308), Bloc Québécois 0.0129 (4 ÷ 308), and Green Party 0.0033 (1 ÷ 308).

3. What makes the midpoint of a frequency histogram important to know?

If all we have is a frequency table, then we can use this information to generate approximate values for the sample mean or sample standard deviation. To do so, we assume that the data points are evenly dispersed over an interval and the midpoint represents the average of the values in that interval.

4. When would we use a boxplot instead of a histogram?

A boxplot is useful when you want to provide information about the range and percentiles of your data. It is also useful for comparing the distribution of a variable across groups. When you are asked to display information about the percentiles, boxplots are the best option. When you want to show information about the frequency of observations per class interval, then histograms are the best choice. Remember: boxplots don't provide information about the class intervals.

5. If we have class intervals in a frequency table, why do we need class boundaries?

Class intervals tell you what the start and end points are for groups of data in the frequency. Say you have a class interval for age that ranges from 18 to 25 and 26 to 33. Class boundaries tell you where to put numbers when the values fall on the edge of these limits. For example, what if a participant was 25 years and 2 months old? Where would you put this individual since he or she is not 25 and but not yet 26? The class boundary for the 18 to 25 class interval would likely be 17.5 (17 years and 6 months) to less than 25.5 (25 years and 6 months). So anyone older than or equal to 17 years and 6 months old and younger than 25 years and 6 months old would be placed in the class interval 18 to 25.

**Research Example:**

In 2010, Dr. Carole Orchard, of the University of Western Ontario, and her three colleagues published their paper "Integrated nursing access program: An approach to prepare aboriginal students for nursing careers" in the *International Journal of Nursing Education and Scholarship*. One of the purposes of their paper was to describe the progress of a national program to assist Canadian Aboriginal students in meeting the requirements for admissions to university nursing programs.

As part of the program student participants completed a survey of their readiness to engage in self-directed learning. The survey, with the acronym SLDRS-NNES, consisted of 34 questions measured using a 5-point Likert-type

scale. Dr. Orchard and colleagues detailed the results of the 35 student participants ranging from 34 (low) to 170 (High) in a frequency table similar to the
one below.

| Frequency Table of SLDRS-NNES Scores | | | | |
|---|---|---|---|---|
| Score | f | f/n | %f | c.%f |
| 34–106 | 3 | 0.086 | 8.6 | 8.6 |
| 107–145 | 29 | 0.828 | 82.8 | 91.4 |
| 146–170 | 3 | 0.086 | 8.6 | 100.0 |
| Total | 35 | 1.000 | 100.0 | |

Source: Orchard, Carole A., Paula Didham, Cathy Jong, and June Fry
(2010). "Integrated Nursing Access Program: An Approach to Prepare
Aboriginal Students for Nursing Careers," *International Journal of
Nursing Education Scholarship:* Vol. 7, Iss. 1, Article 10.

**Research Example Questions:**

**Question 1:** What are the class intervals in the frequency table?

**Question 2:** What are the midpoints for each of the class intervals in the frequency table?

**Question 3:** What can be said of the ratio of participants scoring from 107 to 145 compared to all other participant scores?

**Question 4:** Suppose the class intervals and frequencies were as shown in the following table. Complete the frequency table and a histogram using these class intervals with frequency on the *y*-axis.

| Frequency Table for Question 4 | | | | |
|---|---|---|---|---|
| Score | f | f/n | %f | c.%f |
| 34–68 | 1 | | | |
| 69–103 | 2 | | | |
| 104–138 | 25 | | | |
| 139–173 | 7 | | | |
| Total | 35 | | | |

**Research Example Answers:**

**Question 1:** What are the class intervals in the frequency table?
The class intervals are 34 to 106, 107 to 145, and 146 to 170.

**Question 2:** What are the midpoints for each of the class intervals in the frequency table?

The midpoint for the class interval 34–106 is 70 [(34 + 106) ÷ 2].
The midpoint for the class interval 107–145 is 126 [(107 + 145) ÷ 2].
The midpoint for the class interval 146–170 is 158 [(146 + 170) ÷ 2].

**Question 3:** What can be said of the ratio of participants scoring between 107–145 compared to all other participant scores?

$$Ratio = \frac{f_{v_1}}{f_{v_2}} = \frac{\#\text{of scores between } 107 - 145}{\#\text{of scores between } 34 - 106 \text{ and } 146 - 170} = \frac{29}{6} = 4.83 \textbf{ (2.6)}$$

We can say that there were 4.83 scores within the $107 - 145$ interval for every one score outside of that class interval (4.83:1).

**Question 4:** Suppose the class intervals and frequencies were as shown in the following table. Complete the frequency table and a histogram using these class intervals with frequency on the *y*-axis.

| Frequency Table for Question 4 | | | | |
|---|---|---|---|---|
| **Score** | ***f*** | ***f/n*** | **%*f*** | **c.%*f*** |
| 34–68 | 1 | 0.029 | 2.9 | 2.9 |
| 69–103 | 2 | 0.057 | 5.7 | 8.6 |
| 104–138 | 25 | 0.714 | 71.4 | 80.0 |
| 139–173 | 7 | 0.200 | 20.0 | 100 |
| Total | 35 | 1.000 | 100.0 | |

**Histogram for Question 4**

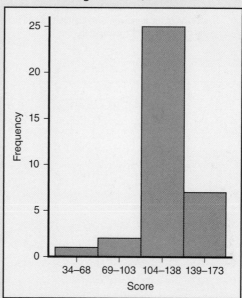

## Problems

Below is a complete list of the grades obtained in a statistics class last semester.

| G | M | G | M | G | M | G | M | G | M |
|---|----|---|----|---|----|---|----|---|----|
| F | 53 | M | 40 | M | 58 | F | 89 | M | 12 |
| M | 6  | M | 27 | F | 65 | M | 79 | F | 70 |
| M | 73 | M | 83 | M | 80 | M | 15 | M | 10 |
| F | 65 | F | 85 | M | 25 | F | 55 | F | 62 |
| M | 56 | M | 77 | F | 54 | F | 43 | M | 49 |

Column headings: G = gender; M = mark
Within rows: M = male; F = female

1. Prepare the grade frequency distribution using class intervals equal to 10.
2. Once completed, include the relative frequency and the cumulative frequency.
3. If 60 percent is considered a passing grade, what proportion of the students passed? Prepare a cross-tabulation with the gender variable in the columns and grade interval in the rows.
4. What percentage of the males passed?
5. What percentage of the females failed?
6. For each grade interval, indicate the ratio of males to females.
7. As a percentage, how many more males are there in the class than females?

# Describing Your Data: Measures of Central Tendency, Dispersion, and Shape

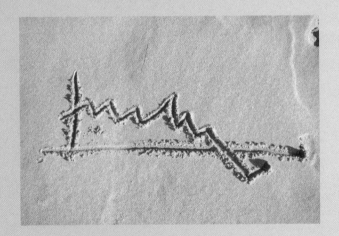

**Learning Objectives:**

By the end of this chapter you should be able to:

1. Explain why central tendency and dispersion are important.
2. Calculate the mean, median, and mode.
3. Explain for which type of variables the mean, median, and mode are most appropriate.
4. Describe what variability is.
5. Calculate range, interquartile range, percentiles, variance, and standard deviation.
6. Define and describe skewness and how it affects the mean.
7. Define and describe kurtosis.

## Sir Francis Galton (1822–1911)

Sir Francis Galton, born in Birmingham, England, in 1857 and a cousin of Charles Darwin, was a well-established researcher in a number of fields including eugenics, meteorology, psychology, and statistics. While studying eugenics, he advanced the conceptual work behind correlation and regression analysis. One of his lesser known contributions to the field of statistics is his invention of The Galton Board,* which was used to graphically illustrate the

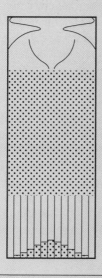

shape of binomial distribution. However, given that the binomial distribution looks a lot like the normal distribution (particularly with larger sample sizes), it is often said that it was used to illustrate the shape of the normal distribution (the normal curve).

The Galton Board, shown to the left, consisted of small balls that were dropped through an opening at the top. The balls would bounce off the pins in the board (the dots) and come to rest at the bottom. When enough balls were dropped, the distribution of the balls formed a normal distribution as seen at the bottom of the board. This remarkably simple experiment is still used today, albeit mostly in computerized simulation versions.[1]

*Also known as the Galton Box, the Galton Quincunx, and the Bean Machine.

**Sources:** Mathworld, http://mathworld.wolfram.com/ GaltonBoard.html; http://galton.org/; Nicholas W. Gillham, *Sir Francis Galton: From African Exploration to the Birth of Eugenics,* New York: Oxford University Press, 2001.

# Introduction

The methods of describing data that we covered in chapter 2 are useful ways of presenting and comparing the distribution of the values of variables. However, social scientists also want information about the location of the central value of the distribution, how spread out it is, and its general shape. In this chapter we will cover some of the more basic elements of statistics. We begin with measures of central tendency as we discuss how to locate the centre of a distribution using the mean, median, and mode. Next, we discuss ways of determining the spread of a distribution using measures of dispersion that include percentiles, range, variance, and standard deviation. Finally, we discuss skewness and kurtosis as measures of the shape of a distribution.

# Measures of Central Tendency

**Central tendency**
is the value at the middle
point of a distribution.

We call the centre value of a distribution the **central tendency**. In other words, we want to know what value tends to lie in the middle (or centre) of a distribution. For example, if you examine the histograms in Figure 2.18 in chapter 2, you can roughly estimate that 40 years of age is the value at the centre of this age distribution, given that the ages range from 20 to 60 and that 40 seems to be the most frequently occurring age. However, we need to be more accurate than that in determining where the centre value lies. Before we examine how we estimate the centre of a distribution, let's first determine why we want to know this information.

Consider this scenario: you just received your midterm examination grade for your Economic and Social Policy course. Regardless of your actual mark, what you want to know is how well you did compared to others in the class. You may have received a grade of 75 percent, which might be disappointing if the average (centre of the grade distribution) was 85 percent. On the other hand, suppose the class average was 65 percent. That being the case, you probably would be quite happy with your grade. Consider another example. You have finally graduated and have just been offered a job with a starting salary of $45,000 per year. Considering just the salary itself (excluding location, promotion potential, etc.) is this a good annual salary? If the distribution of annual salaries ranges from $25,000 to $75,000, you might be tempted to think that $45,000 is somewhere in the middle of that range. However, it could be that 80 percent of the salaries are between $65,000 and $75,000, in which case it's likely that the annual salary that sits in the middle of the distribution is greater than $65,000. So the answer to why it is important to identify the centre of a distribution is that it allows us to make comparisons of values across different samples. Furthermore, in a broad sense, comparing centres of distributions is largely what statistical analysis is about.

Now that we know the importance of determining where the centre of a distribution tends to lie, we need to understand how to calculate it. There are a number of different calculation methods but we will focus on the three most common ones, which we call **measures of central tendency**. These measures are the mean, the median, and the mode. All three provide a different method of determining the centre point in a distribution of values. Furthermore, when they should be used depends on the level of measurement of a variable. We will first discuss the definitions of each measure and how they are calculated. Then we will examine when you should use the mean, the median, and the mode as measures of central tendency for nominal, ordinal, interval, and ratio variables.

While there are no rules that state the order in which to discuss the three measures, we'll start with the easiest measure—the mode—and then work our way through the median and the mean. Chances are you have already covered this material in other courses, so this may be more of a refresher than new information for you.

**Measures of central tendency** are methods to calculate the centre or middle point of a distribution. The most common measures are mean, median, and mode.

## LO2

Mode is the value that occurs with the greatest frequency.

# The Mode

The **mode** is the value that occurs with the greatest frequency. Consider the data in Table 3.1 regarding the dollar amount spent on food per week for a sample of nine households.

**TABLE 3.1** **Sample Dollar Amount Spent on Food Per Week**

| 86 | 96 | 102 | 102 | 106 | 110 | 112 | 114 | 117 |
|----|----|-----|-----|-----|-----|-----|-----|-----|

In this data, the number 102 occurs twice, whereas the other numbers occur once. Therefore, the mode is 102.

The best way to calculate the mode, especially when there is a large number of values, is to create a simple frequency table and look for the value that occurs most frequently. For example, the 2006 Statistics Canada Census data contains 10 visible minority categories. With each category coded in the data set (such as 1 = South Asian, 2 = Chinese, . . ., 10 = Japanese) and considering only the 25 to 44 age group, there are 1,612,330 numbers ranging from 1 to 10 in the data. This is too much data to identify the mode by simply looking at the actual data. However, by constructing a frequency table for this age group (Table 3.2), with the categories in ascending order by frequency, it is easy to see that the mode is South Asian. That is to say that the South Asian category was the most frequently selected category.

**TABLE 3.2**
**Visible Minority\***
**Population**
**(Age 25 to 44)**

Source: Permission granted by CAS via the Data Liberation Initiative.
\*The data also includes the categories "multiple visible minority" and "visible minority (not included elsewhere)", but for simplicity we have not used those two categories.

| Visible Minority Category | Frequency (f) | Relative Frequency (f/n) |
|---|---|---|
| South Asian | 424,850 | 0.26 |
| Chinese | 385,525 | 0.24 |
| Black | 244,805 | 0.15 |
| Filipino | 141,225 | 0.09 |
| Latin American | 114,225 | 0.07 |
| Arab | 96,010 | 0.06 |
| Southeast Asian | 80,410 | 0.05 |
| West Asian | 54,015 | 0.03 |
| Korean | 44,405 | 0.03 |
| Japanese | 26,860 | 0.02 |
| Total | 1,612,330 | 1.00 |

When there is only one mode in the distribution (as in Table 3.2), we say the distribution is uni-modal. However, quite often there may be no mode (no number is repeated) or there may be multiple modes. Consider Table 3.3, which shows the nominal variable "occupation" and four hypothetical frequency tables for the conditions where there is no mode, one mode (uni-modal), two modes (bi-modal), and more than two modes (multi-modal).

**TABLE 3.3**   **Hypothetical Frequency Tables Showing Differing Modes**

| Occupation | No Mode (*f*) | Uni-Modal (*f*) | Bi-Modal (*f*) | Multi-Modal (*f*) |
|---|---|---|---|---|
| Education | 6 | 6 | 1 | 8 |
| Public Safety | 5 | 9 | 7 | 8 |
| Tradesperson | 7 | 7 | 7 | 4 |
| Medical | 3 | 3 | 6 | 4 |
| Government | 8 | 2 | 3 | 3 |
| Transportation | 1 | 3 | 6 | 3 |
| Total | 30 | 30 | 30 | 30 |

## The Median

The **median** is the middle point in the distribution that separates the upper and lower 50 percent of the data.

The **median** is the middle point in the distribution that separates the upper and lower 50 percent of the data. For example, suppose you have a distribution consisting of 10, 21, 34, 42, 56—the number 34 is in the exact centre position and is therefore the median. You'll notice that these numbers are in ascending order. That is because to determine the median, you must first put the numbers in order and then find the middle point. If you need to manually locate the median, there are two methods to keep in mind.

First, if you have an odd number of observations, such as $n = 9$, then the middle observation can be found in position $(n + 1) \div 2$. Remember that $n$ is the symbol for sample size. So when you see $n = 9$ that means that the sample size is 9. To illustrate this, consider the following nine numbers:

42    46    46    48    52    53    54    55    57

There are $n = 9$ numbers, therefore $(9 + 1) \div 2 = 5$. The result (5) indicates that the fifth observation in ascending order is the median; in this case, 52.

## For Your Information

Below is an example of a bi-modal and a multi-modal histogram.

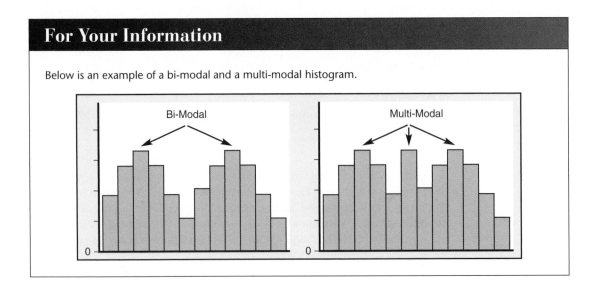

Second, if you have an even number of observations, then the middle point is between two observations. Specifically, it is between the observation found in position $n \div 2$ and the observation found in position $n \div 2 + 1$. To determine the median, take the average of the two middle observations. To illustrate this, consider the following numbers:

| 23 | 42 | 46 | 48 | 52 | 53 | 54 | 55 | 57 | 58 |
| 60 | 62 | 63 | 63 | 67 | 68 | 70 | 70 | 71 | 73 |

There are 20 observations, so the median is between the tenth ($n \div 2 = 20 \div 2 = 10$) position and the eleventh [$(20 \div 2) + 1 = 11$] position. Therefore, the median is between 58 and 60. By averaging the two numbers, $(58 + 60) \div 2$, we find that the median for this distribution is 59.

As another example, suppose you measured the variable "risk of recidivism" with an ordinal level of measurement with the categories Low Risk, Medium Risk, and High Risk. Further suppose that you coded the data for this ordinal variable as 1 = Low Risk, 2 = Medium Risk, and 3 = High Risk. If you had a sample size of $n = 5$, your data might look like the following:

$$1 \quad 1 \quad 2 \quad 3 \quad 3$$

In this case, the median is 2, or the median is "Medium Risk." We might interpret this by saying that 50 percent of the time the cases were below medium risk and 50 percent of the time they were above medium risk. Now suppose you had a sample size of $n = 6$ and the data was:

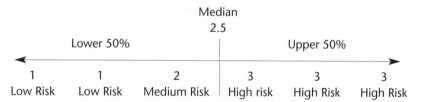

Now, the median is 2.5, which is between "Medium Risk" and "High Risk." We might interpret this by stating that 50 percent of the time the cases were Low and Medium Risk and 50 percent of the time they were High Risk.

## The Mean

The **mean** is the average score in a distribution.

The **mean**, also referred to as the arithmetic mean, is the average score in a distribution. It is calculated as the sum of the numbers in the distribution divided by the total number of numbers. More formally, we write it as:

$$\bar{x} = \frac{\Sigma x}{n} \tag{3.1}$$

where: $\bar{x}$ = mean (pronounced 'x bar')

$\Sigma$ = summation or sum (pronounced 'sigma')

$x$ = the values of $x$

$n$ = the sample size

What this equation is saying is that to obtain the mean score ($\bar{x}$) you add up all of the x scores and divide the total by the sample size (n).

To illustrate this, consider the following numbers:

| 62 | 42 | 46 | 48 | 71 | 53 | 68 | 55 | 57 | 70 |
|----|----|----|----|----|----|----|----|----|----|
| 60 | 23 | 63 | 61 | 67 | 54 | 70 | 58 | 52 | 73 |

Using equation 3.1, we get:

$$\bar{x} = \frac{\begin{pmatrix} 62 + 42 + 46 + 48 + 71 + 53 + 68 + 55 + 57 + 70 + \\ 60 + 23 + 63 + 61 + 67 + 54 + 70 + 58 + 52 + 73 \end{pmatrix}}{20} \qquad (3.2)$$

$$= \frac{1153}{20} = 57.65$$

So the mean value of our data is 57.65.

Let's consider another example. The Statistics Canada data set for the 2004 Canadian Addiction Survey contains a ratio variable labelled "alc11" which was measured with the survey item "What is the largest number of drinks you can recall having in one occasion during the past twelve months?" A subset of eight observations (189 to 196) is presented in Figure 3.1.

Based on just these eight observations, what is the $\bar{x}$ (mean) number of 'greatest number of drinks' consumed by the participants within the last twelve months? Using equation 3.1 for estimating the mean we get:

$$\bar{x} = \frac{(2 + 8 + 2 + 2 + 6 + 15 + 5 + 2)}{8} = \frac{42}{8} = 5.25 \textbf{ (3.3)}$$

Therefore, based on this data, we might interpret that on average, the greatest number of drinks consumed in one occasion (by these eight participants) is 5.25 (or five and a quarter) drinks.

**FIGURE 3.1**
**Subset of Cases From the 2004 Canadian Addiction Survey**

| Observation # | alc11 |
|---------------|-------|
| 189 | 2.00 |
| 190 | 8.00 |
| 191 | 2.00 |
| 192 | 2.00 |
| 193 | 6.00 |
| 194 | 15.00 |
| 195 | 5.00 |
| 196 | 2.00 |

**TABLE 3.4**
**Most Appropriate**
**Measure of Central**
**Tendency By Level**
**of Measurement**

| Level of Measurement | Most Appropriate Measure |
|---|---|
| Nominal | Mode |
| Ordinal | Median |
| Interval | Mean (consider median if data is skewed) |
| Ratio | Mean (consider median if data is skewed) |

**LO3**

# When To Use Mode, Median, and Mean as Measures of Central Tendency

The measure of central tendency that you should use depends on the variable's level of measurement. Table 3.4 provides a quick guide to the most appropriate measures of central tendency by level of measurement. We review each one below.

### Use the Mode for Nominal Data

The mode is the most appropriate measure of central tendency for variables that have a nominal level of measurement (nominal data). The reason for this goes back to the definition of a nominal level of measurement. Recall that the categories in a nominal level of measurement are qualitative labels and as such the differences within the variables are really just a name or symbol, they are not numeric. Therefore, the only measure that makes sense is the one that tells you which is the most commonly occuring qualitative category.

To illustrate why the mean or median is not appropriate, imagine a survey item that requires respondents to provide their occupation by selecting one of the following three categories: "Farmer," "Doctor," and "Plumber," which are then coded as 1, 2, and 3 respectively. Since this is a nominal level of measurement, there is no way of ordering the categories.

For example, the profession Plumber, coded as 3, is not three times better than the profession Farmer, coded as a 1. Given that there is no order in the categories, you cannot calculate the median. Now suppose you had data for three farmers, two doctors, and two plumbers. The resulting data would consist of 1, 1, 1, 2, 2, 3, 3. A mean value of 1.86 would be meaningless since it doesn't make sense to average the Farmer and Doctor categories, which is what a value of 1.86 implies.

### Use the Median for Ordinal Data

For ordinal data, the median is the best measure of central tendency. Since the data for ordinal level variables have some order to them, the value that sits at the centre of the distribution is meaningful. For example, suppose you asked a sample of nine respondents to rank their preference for the three major Canadian federal political parties (Conservative, Liberal, and NDP) as first, second, or third. Examining the Liberal category you may find that five respondents rated them as their first choice (preference), two rated them as their second choice, and two rated them as their third choice. Your data would then be 1, 1, 1, 1, 1, 2, 2, 3, and 3, with a median (middle) value of 1. Here the interpretation of the median makes sense since you are saying the 50 percent of the respondents rated the Liberal Party as their first preference (values to the left of the median). Conversely, 50 percent of respondents rated the Liberal party as either second or third choice (values to the right of the median). While it is possible to use the mode in this case, often with large data sets there will be more than one mode, which makes the interpretation difficult. Finally, the mean (in this case 1.89) is not very useful with ordinal data as the intervals between the categories are not necessarily equal (third place is not three times worse than first place).

## Use the Mean for Interval and Ratio Data

The mean is the most appropriate measure of central tendency for interval and ratio data. This is because the responses have an order to them (e.g., first, second, third) and there are equal intervals between the responses. For example, suppose you had a variable measured with a 1 to 5 Likert scale (treated as interval), where 1 = "strongly disagree" and 5 = "strongly agree." A mean score of 4.25 indicates that the average respondent is somewhere between agree and strongly agree. In other words, they are more than just agreeing with the statement yet they do not strongly agree with it. The mean is also appropriate with ratio data. For example, with a variable such as age measured at the ratio level, an age of 32.5 means approximately 32 years and 6 months.

The median and the mode can also be used with interval and ratio data; however, the mean is considered to be a more accurate measure and is therefore used most often. There is one case when median may be a better measure of central tendency than the mean even with interval or ratio data. That is when the data is denser on one end of the distribution than the other. We call this skewness and discuss this later in the chapter. However, at this stage it is important to recognize how this may influence the decision to use the median or mean. The histogram in Figure 3.2 represents the distribution of personal income (before tax) for the age group 20 to 30, found in the Statistics Canada 2004 Addiction Survey Data. As you can see, although the range of salaries in this histogram varies from $0 to $150,000* most respondents have incomes between $0 and $20,000. As a result, the mean salary of $28,684 is greater than the median salary of $23,000. In this case, $23,000 is likely more representative of respondents' salary as it represents the middle (50 percent) value in the salary distribution. The mean is sensitive to extreme values (also referred to as outliers), such as $150,000, whereas the median is not. This is because the mean uses the actual values in its estimation, whereas the median only counts the number of values. In these situations, it is usually advisable to report both the mean and the median values.

---

* The actual range was $0 to $620,000, but we have cut it off at $150,000 to make the histogram easier to read.

**FIGURE 3.2**
**Personal Income (Before Tax) for the Age Group 20 to 30**

Source: Permission granted by CAS via the Data Liberation Initiative.

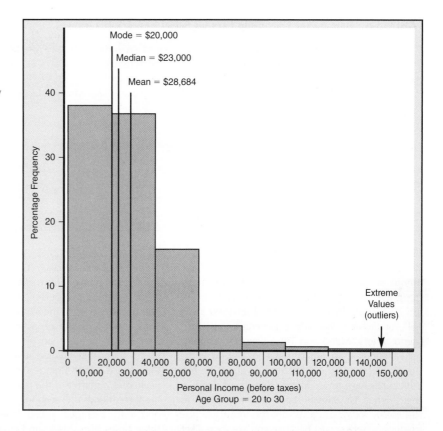

---

## Did You Know?

The "Friendship Paradox" states that on average "most people have fewer friends than their own friends have."[2] In other words, if you count the number of friends you have and compare that to the average number of friends that your friends have, you will find that you have fewer than the average. This paradox was first analyzed in 1991 by sociologist Professor Scott Feld in his *American Journal of Sociology* paper titled "Why your friends have more friends than you do." Figure 3.3, similar to that of Professor Feld's, includes nine individuals and their friendships, while Table 3.5 provides the summary numbers.

**FIGURE 3.3**   **The Friendship Paradox Social Network Diagram**

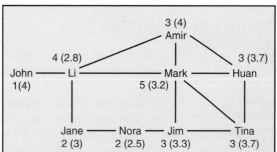

The first number is the number of friends they personally have on Facebook. The number in parantheses is the average number of friends their friends have on Facebook.

**TABLE 3.5** **Data for the Friendship Paradox Social Network Diagram**

| | # of Friends on Facebook | # of Friends of Friends | Mean # of Friends Their Friends Have |
|---|---|---|---|
| Amir | 3 | 12 | 4.0 |
| Huan | 3 | 11 | 3.7 |
| Jane | 2 | 6 | 3.0 |
| Jim | 3 | 10 | 3.3 |
| John | 1 | 4 | 4.0 |
| Li | 4 | 11 | 2.8 |
| Mark | 5 | 16 | 3.2 |
| Nora | 2 | 5 | 2.5 |
| Tina | 3 | 11 | 3.7 |
| Total | 26 | 86 | |

In the diagram, you can see that John has fewer friends on Facebook than his friend Li (one versus four). On average, Nora's two friends Jane and Jim have more friends than she does (two and a half versus two). Similarly, on average Jim's three friends (Nora, Mark, and Tina) have more friends on Facebook than Jim (three and a third versus three). Overall, you can see that seven of the nine individuals have fewer friends than the average of their friends. Dr. Satoshi Kanazawa, who blogs for *Psychology Today,* suggests that this individual phenomenon likely occurs because you are more likely to be friends with someone who has more friends than you than someone who has fewer.

However, that is only part of the paradox, which states that overall the "mean number of friends of friends will always be greater than the mean number of friends of individuals."[3] Looking at Table 3.5 we can see that nine people make up 26 friends, averaging 2.9 friends per person. However, the average number of friends of friends is 3.3 (86 ÷ 26 = 3.3). Thus, it appears that on average an individual will have fewer friends than his or her friends. Given that a friendship involves two people, you might think this is a little strange. The paradox can be explained as a matter of the math. Consider Tina: she has three friends on Facebook, which is counted only once in the average number of friends, but is counted three times (Jim, Mark, and Huan) in the average number of friends of friends. So those with more friends will show up disproportionately more in the average of friends of friends. Therefore, the paradox will always show an individual as having fewer friends than the average.

## Measures of Dispersion

**Measures of dispersion** describe the variability in the data.

**Variability** is the extent to which the data varies from its mean.

In the previous section we discussed the measures of central tendency and how we use them to locate where the centre of the distribution lies. However, when describing our data distribution, we also need to describe how dispersed or spread out the distribution is. **Measures of dispersion** describe the **variability** in the data. Variability is the extent to which the data varies from its mean. That is, variability tells us how spread out the data is across the range of values.

Suppose we asked five respondents to provide us with their monthly income and their responses were:

$500    $500    $500    $500    $500

We would say that there is no variability in monthly salary in this sample because all of the values are the same. Now suppose we asked another five respondents and their answers were:

$400       $500       $600       $700       $800

We would say that there is variability in the data because at least one of the values differs from the others.

There are four common measures (also referred to as the measures of variability) that we can use to describe dispersion. These measures include percentile, range, variance, and standard deviation.

**LO5**

## The Percentile

The percentage frequency and cumulative percentage frequency columns from the frequency table can be used to provide a simple measure of dispersion called percentiles (often referred to as percentile ranks). You may have seen these before with test results. For example, a student may take a test and find out that he or she is in the 80th percentile. What this tells us is that 80 percent of the results fall below that particular student's grade. So **percentiles** are percentages of frequencies indicating the percentage of scores that fall within a given area. You can create percentiles in whatever grouping suits your needs. For example, quartiles (25 percent, 50 percent, etc.) or deciles (10 percent, 20 percent, etc.). Table 3.6 provides the percentiles for full-time tuition fees shown in Figure 3.4. In this sample, we see that 60 percent of student tuition is less than or equal to $4,916. Also, 40 percent of tuition falls between $4,580.20 and $5,615.20 (between the 40th and 80th percentiles).

**Percentiles** are percentage frequencies indicating the percentage of scores that fall within a given area.

**TABLE 3.6**
**Example of Percentiles**

| Percentile | Score at This Percentile | Interpretation |
|---|---|---|
| 20th | $2,928.80 | 20% of tuition is ≤ $2,928.80 |
| 40th | $4,580.20 | 40% of tuition is ≤ $4,580.20 |
| 60th | $4,916.00 | 60% of tuition is ≤ $4,916.00 |
| 80th | $5,615.20 | 80% of tuition is ≤ $5,615.20 |
| 100th | $9,750.00 | 100% of tuition is ≤ $9,750.00 |

### Calculating the Percentile

The following numbers represent the scores (out of 100) for 10 students on an English exam.

65       79       72       76       81       66       91       94       74       89

The first step for calculating percentiles is to place the numbers in order from lowest to highest, then number them in order of their position. For example, the score 74 is in position number 4.

| Scores: | 65 | 66 | 72 | 74 | 76 | 81 | 82 | 89 | 91 | 94 |
|---|---|---|---|---|---|---|---|---|---|---|
| Position: | 1 | 2 | 3 | 4 | 5 | 6 | 7 | 8 | 9 | 10 |

## For Your Information

To understand the concept of variability examine Figure 3.4, which provides a histogram of the 2008/2009 full-time undergraduate tuition fees for the education discipline in Canadian universities and colleges. In this figure you can see the distribution of the data, the mean value, and how the distribution of values varies from the mean to the minimum and maximum values that make up the two ends of the range.

**FIGURE 3.4**  **Tuition and Living Accommodation Costs for Students-2008/2009**

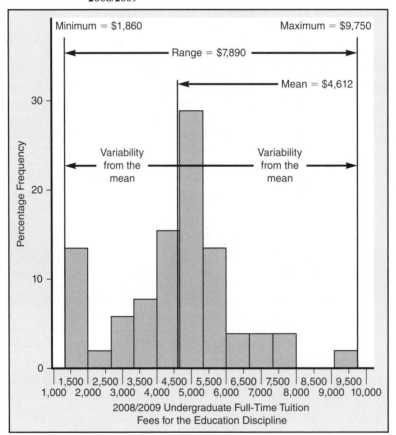

2008/2009 Undergraduate Full-Time Tuition Fees for the Education Discipline

**Data Source:** Adapted from Statistics Canada, Tuition and Living Accommodation Costs for Full-time Students at Canadian Degree-granting Institutions, 2008/2009 [Excel files]: TLAC 2008/2009, Identification Number 81C0049-2008, Statistics Canada, 2008-10-09.

To determine an unknown score for a known (or desired) percentile you multiply the desired percentile by the sample size. Suppose we want to know the score for the 50th percentile. Multiply the desired percentile (0.50) by the sample size (10); $0.50 \times 10 = 5$. The value 5 represents the position of the number for the 50th percentile. From the table of scores you can see that 76 is in the 5th position. Therefore, the score for the 50th percentile is 76.

To determine the percentile for a known score, divide the position number of the known score by the sample size. For example, the score 82 is in the 7th position. Divide the position (7) by the sample size (10); $7 \div 10 = 0.70$. Therefore, 7 is in the 70th percentile.

## The Range

We have already discussed the range in this chapter but as a reminder, the range is the value of the largest observation minus the value of the smallest observation. In Figure 3.4 we see that the range is $7,890 which is $9,750 − $1,860. As you might expect, the range increases as the scores become more disperse from the mean. The range can give a distorted view if most of the values lie close to the mean and only a few are further away. To illustrate, looking at Figure 3.4 you can see that only one value ($9,750) lies in the far right area of the histogram.

**Interquartile range** considers only the middle 50 percent of the data in estimating a range.

In these cases, the **interquartile range** is often a better measure. The interquartile range creates quartiles (25th, 50th, and 75th percentiles) and removes the first and fourth quartile from the calculation of its range, considering only the middle 50 percent of the range (from the 25th percentile to the 75th percentile). It does so in order to remove the extreme values that lie at the beginning and end of the distribution. Figure 3.5 provides an example using the tuition data. You can see the interquartile range is $5,409.25 − $3,494.75 = $1,914.50.

**FIGURE 3.5**   **Interquartile Range Using Tuition Data**

| Percentile | Score at This Percentile |
|---|---|
| 25th | $3,494.75 |
| 50th | $4,713.00 |
| 75th | $5,409.25 |

Note: The median is the value at the 50th percentile ($4,713.00)

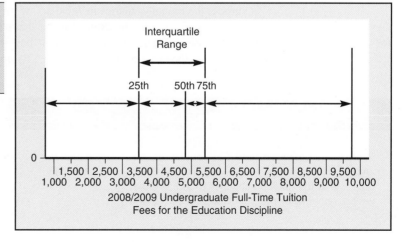

*Calculating the Interquartile Range*

The following represents the number of goals scored (and percentiles) by seven hockey players in the last season.

| Goals: | 6 | 7 | 8 | 9 | 10 | 11 | 12 |
|--------|---|---|---|---|----|----|----|
| Percentile: | | 25th | | 50th | | 75th | |

To calculate the interquartile range, you first need to calculate the 25th and 75th percentiles using the methods discussed earlier. Since the interquartile range only considers the values between the 25th and the 75th percentile, the range can be obtained by subtracting the value in the 25th percentile (7) from the value in the 75th percentile (11). Therefore, the interquartile range is 4.

## The Variance

**Variance** is a measure of the extent to which the data varies from its mean. When referring to a sample, it is called the sample variance. When referring to the population it is called the population variance.

The **variance** is a measure of the extent to which the data varies from its mean. When we refer to the variance in a sample (e.g., the opinion of 150 primary school principals on public funding of after-school programming) we call it the sample variance, represented as $s^2$. When we refer to the variance in a population (e.g., the opinion of *all* primary school principals on public funding of after-school programming) we call it the population variance, represented as $\sigma^2$.

When we want to calculate the sample variance we use the equation

$$s^2 = \frac{\Sigma(x - \bar{x})^2}{(n - 1)} \qquad \textbf{(3.4)}$$

where: $s^2$ = sample variance

$x$ = observation for each respondent

$\bar{x}$ = the mean value of $x$

$n$ = the sample size

The easiest way to understand what is happening in equation 3.4 is to explain it in pieces, starting with the numerator.

Consider the monthly salaries in Table 3.7. If we subtract each observation ($x$) from the mean ($\bar{x}$), we get the **deviation** for that particular observation, meaning how far the observation deviates from its mean. For example, the value $400 deviates by −$200 from the mean, $500 deviates by −$100 from the mean, and so on.

**Deviation** is the distance of an observed score from its mean.

## For Your Information

The equation for estimating the population variance $\sigma^2$ is similar to the sample variance. The difference is that the notation changes to indicate that we are referring to the population mean ($\mu$) and population size ($N$), and the denominator becomes $N$ rather than $n - 1$:

$$\sigma^2 = \frac{\Sigma(x - \mu)^2}{N} \qquad \textbf{(3.5)}$$

**TABLE 3.7**
**Estimating**
**Deviations**

| Monthly Salaries ($x$) | Deviations ($x - \bar{x}$) |
|---|---|
| $400 | $400 − $600 = −200 |
| $500 | $500 − $600 = −100 |
| $600 | $600 − $600 = 0 |
| $700 | $700 − $600 = +100 |
| $800 | $800 − $600 = +200 |
| $n = 5$ | |
| $\bar{x} = \$600$ | |

Now that we know the amount that each value deviates from the mean, you might think that by adding all the deviations we would get the total deviation. However, if we sum the deviations of any values from their mean, we will always get a value of zero because the negative values will cancel out the positive ones. In order to get around this we square each deviation value before we sum them. Building on Table 3.7 we get the values in Table 3.8.

**TABLE 3.8**
**Estimating the Sum**
**of the Squares**

| Monthly Salaries ($x$) | Deviations ($x - \bar{x}$) | Squared Deviations ($x - \bar{x})^2$ |
|---|---|---|
| $400 | $400 − $600 = −200 | $-200^2 = 40,000$ |
| $500 | $500 − $600 = −100 | $-100^2 = 10,000$ |
| $600 | $600 − $600 = 0 | $0^2 = 0$ |
| $700 | $700 − $600 = +100 | $+100^2 = 10,000$ |
| $800 | $800 − $600 = +200 | $+200^2 = 40,000$ |
| $n = 5$ | $\Sigma(x - \bar{x}) = 0$ | $\Sigma(x - \bar{x})^2 = 100,000$ |
| $\bar{x} = \$600$ | | (sum of squares) |

The **sum of squares** represents the total of the squared distance from one end of the range to the other.

By summing the individual squared deviations we get what is called the **sum of squares**, denoted $\Sigma(x - \bar{x})^2$ in Table 3.8. The sum of squares is the numerator in the equation for the variance. It represents the total of the squared distance from one end of the range to the other. Figure 3.6 shows a histogram of the five salaries. As you can see at the bottom, the total of the Sum of Squares is 100,000.

While the sum of squares is a useful statistic, especially for some types of analysis that we will cover in later chapters, it isn't easy to interpret as a measure of dispersion. Although it tells us about the total variability, it doesn't tell us the average variability in the data. Therefore, we need to take it one more step and divide the sums of squares of the deviations by the sample size minus 1. There is a lengthy theoretical and mathematical reason for why we use $(n - 1)$ instead of just $n$, you will find a brief explanation of this in the second For Your Information shown on page 91. By dividing the sums of squares by the sample (minus 1) we get an estimate of the average variability within the data.

So now we have all the information to calculate the sample variance.

$$s^2 = \frac{\Sigma(x - \bar{x})^2}{(n - 1)} = \frac{100,000}{(5 - 1)} = 25,000 \qquad \textbf{(3.6)}$$

**FIGURE 3.6**

**A Histogram of Salaries**

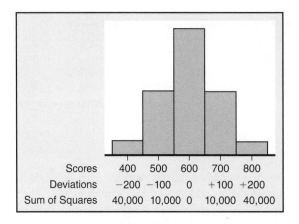

| Scores | 400 | 500 | 600 | 700 | 800 |
|---|---|---|---|---|---|
| Deviations | −200 | −100 | 0 | +100 | +200 |
| Sum of Squares | 40,000 | 10,000 | 0 | 10,000 | 40,000 |

So the variance ($s^2$) of our data (consisting of the five salaries) is 25,000. This indicates that the average of the squared deviations (sum of squares) of the observations from the mean is 25,000. Since this is in squared units of the observation, it can still be a bit difficult to interpret into everyday language. Because of this, researchers go one step further and estimate the standard deviation, which is much easier to interpret.

## The Standard Deviation

The **standard deviation** is the average amount, measured in standard units, in which the data scores vary (positively and negatively) from its mean.

The **standard deviation** is the average amount, measured in standard units, in which the data scores vary (positively and negatively) from the mean. It is probably the most commonly used measure of dispersion because it allows the researcher to report the deviation in the units of measurement used in the study. For example, if you measure weight in pounds, the standard deviation will be in pounds; if you measure height in centimetres, the standard deviation will be in centimetres. Higher standard deviation values indicate that the distribution is more dispersed (scores are further from the mean), low standard deviation values indicate the distribution is less dispersed (scores are closer to the mean). Distributions with a standard deviation of zero have no variability. As with the variance, the same distinction needs to be made between the sample standard deviation ($s$) and the population standard deviation ($\sigma$). We will focus here on the sample standard deviation.

Here's how it works. Recall that the variance is in squared units (deviations) of the observation. If we want to transform a number that is in squared units back to its original unit we simply take the square root of that number (e.g., $5^2 = \sqrt{25}$ and $5 = \sqrt{5^2}$). Therefore, the square root of the variance gives us the standard deviation ($s = \sqrt{s^2}$). More formally, the standard deviation is estimated using equation 3.7.

$$s = \sqrt{\frac{\Sigma(x - \bar{x})^2}{(n - 1)}} \qquad (3.7)$$

where: $s$ = sample standard deviation

$x$ = observation for each respondent

$\bar{x}$ = the mean value of $x$

$n$ = the sample size

## For Your Information

The equation for estimating the population standard deviation $\sigma$ is similar to the sample standard deviation. The difference is that the notation changes to indicate that we are referring to the population standard deviation ($\mu$) and population size ($N$), and the denominator becomes $N$ rather than $n - 1$:

$$\sigma = \sqrt{\frac{\Sigma(x - \mu)^2}{N}} \qquad \textbf{(3.8)}$$

## For Your Information

Why $n - 1$ in the sample variance and standard deviation? As shown in this chapter, the equations for calculating the sample variance [A] and standard deviation [B] are:

$$s^2 = \frac{\Sigma(x - \bar{x})^2}{(n - 1)} \qquad [A]$$

$$s = \sqrt{\frac{\Sigma(x - \bar{x})^2}{(n - 1)}} \qquad [B]$$

You may find that some textbooks and other resources, particularly in the social sciences, state that the formulas for calculating the sample variance and standard deviation are:

$$s^2 = \frac{\Sigma(x - \bar{x})^2}{n} \qquad [C]$$

$$s = \sqrt{\frac{\Sigma(x - \bar{x})^2}{n}} \qquad [D]$$

As we will discuss in later chapters, we often use the sample variance ($s^2$) to estimate the population variance ($\sigma^2$), and the sample standard deviation ($s$) to estimate the population standard deviation ($\sigma$). The mathematical proof provided in Dr. Book's article shows that when $n - 1$ is not used in the formula for either the sample variance or standard deviation (as in [C] and [D]), the sample variance tends to underestimate the population variance and the sample standard deviation tends to underestimate the population standard deviation. Thus, the use of $n - 1$ in the denominator.

Quite often, formulas [C] and [D] are used in order to keep it simpler for students who are new to statistics. However, the proper method for calculating the sample variance and standard deviation is as shown in [A] and [B], and this chapter. The mathematical proof behind using $n - 1$ is fairly technical. Readers who wish to explore the proof may want to read the paper by Stephen A. Book (1979), "Why $n - 1$ in the Formula for the Sample Standard Deviation?", *The Two-Year College Mathematics Journal*, Volume 10, Number 5, pages 330–333.

Looking again at our monthly income example in Table 3.8. We can now calculate the standard deviation as $s = \sqrt{s^2} = \sqrt{25,000} = \$158.11$. Now we know that the mean ($\bar{x}$) monthly income is $600 and the average amount that the scores deviate from the mean $158.11. So what does that indicate? That indicates that scores that are one standard deviation from the mean $= \$600 \pm \$158.11 = \$441.89$ and $\$758.11$.

This will mean more when we discuss the normal curve in chapter 4, but first it is important to see how the standard deviation relates to the distribution. Figure 3.7 shows the range of values that fall within one standard deviation of the mean—one standard deviation below the mean (441.89), and one standard deviation above the mean (758.11).

**FIGURE 3.7**

**A Histogram With Standard Deviations**

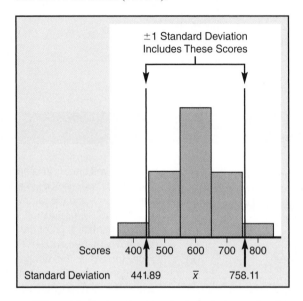

When calculating the standard deviation or variance manually, it is helpful to use a spreadsheet or table. Consider the following examples.

**Example 1:** Imagine you have data on the number of weekly video rentals for seven families. Table 3.9 provides the data and the calculations for the variance and the standard deviation.

**TABLE 3.9**

**Video Rentals for Seven Families**

| Family | Rentals/Week $x$ | Deviations $(x - \bar{x})$ | Squared Deviations $(x - \bar{x})^2$ |
|---|---|---|---|
| 1 | 1 | −1.857143 | 3.448980 |
| 2 | 2 | −0.857143 | 0.734694 |
| 3 | 2 | −0.857143 | 0.734694 |
| 4 | 3 | 0.142857 | 0.020408 |
| 5 | 3 | 0.142857 | 0.020408 |
| 6 | 4 | 1.142857 | 1.306122 |
| 7 | 5 | 2.142857 | 4.591837 |
| $n = 7$ | $\Sigma x = 20$ $\bar{x} = 2.857$ | $\Sigma(x - \bar{x}) = 0$ | $\Sigma(x - \bar{x})^2 = 10.85714$ Sum of Squares |

Using equation 3.7 we can calculate the standard deviation ($s$) as:

$$s = \sqrt{\frac{\Sigma(x - \bar{x})^2}{(n - 1)}} = \sqrt{\frac{10.85714}{7 - 1}} = \sqrt{1.809524} = 1.345185 \text{ or } 1.35 \quad \textbf{(3.9)}$$

## Take a Closer Look

**Step by Step Guide for Calculating a Standard Deviation**

**Step 1:** Find the sample size $n$ [the number of data values ($x$ values) you are using].

**Step 2:** Sum the numbers to get $\Sigma x$.

**Step 3:** Calculate the mean $\bar{x} = \dfrac{\Sigma x}{n}$.

**Step 4:** Calculate the deviations of each score from the mean using $x - \bar{x}$.

**Step 5:** Square the deviations of each score from the mean to get $(x - \bar{x})^2$.

**Step 6:** Sum the squared deviations to get $\Sigma(x - \bar{x})^2$.

**Step 7:** Divide the sum of squared deviations by $(n - 1)$ to get the sample variance

$$s^2 = \frac{\Sigma(x - \bar{x})^2}{n - 1}.$$

**Step 8:** Take the square root of the variance to get the sample standard deviation $s = \sqrt{s^2}$.

We can interpret this by saying that, on average ($\bar{x}$), these families rent 2.86 movies per week and the data varies by a standard deviation of 1.35 movies per week.

**Example 2:** Suppose we collected data from six respondents regarding how many cigarettes they smoked the previous day. Table 3.10 provides the data and the calculations for the variance and the standard deviation.

**TABLE 3.10**
**Number of Cigarettes Smoked Yesterday**

| Observation | Cigarettes Smoked $x$ | Deviations $(x - \bar{x})$ | Squared Deviations $(x - \bar{x})^2$ |
|---|---|---|---|
| 1 | 1 | −4 | 16 |
| 2 | 3 | −2 | 4 |
| 3 | 4 | −1 | 1 |
| 4 | 6 | 1 | 1 |
| 5 | 7 | 2 | 4 |
| 6 | 9 | 4 | 16 |
| $n = 6$ | $\Sigma x = 30$ $\bar{x} = 5$ | $\Sigma(x - \bar{x}) = 0$ | $\Sigma(x - \bar{x})^2 = 42$ Sum of Squares |

Using equation 3.7 we can calculate the standard deviation ($s$) as:

$$s = \sqrt{\frac{\Sigma(x - \bar{x})^2}{(n - 1)}} = \sqrt{\frac{42}{6 - 1}} = \sqrt{8.40} = 2.8982 \text{ or } 2.90 \quad \textbf{(3.10)}$$

## A Note on Measures of Dispersion

Measures of dispersion assign numerical values to the spread of the data, and therefore are really only applicable to interval and ratio data. As an example, suppose the responses are nominal categories such as "Dental Hygienist," "Veterinarian," or "Accountant." Given that there is no natural distance between the categories, measures of dispersion are not applicable. It is possible to take ordinal level data

**TABLE 3.11**
**Measuring Dispersions with Categories**

| Category | Midpoint | Frequency |
|----------|----------|-----------|
| 20 to 25 | 22 | 5 |
| 26 to 30 | 28 | 6 |

and artificially assign values to categories in order to assess dispersion. One common scenario is when the ordinal data has categories where a midpoint can be determined. For example, in Table 3.11 the variable age has categories where you can determine a midpoint and use the frequency to determine a mean age of 24.4: $[(5 \times 22) + (28 \times 6)] \div (5 + 6)$. However, at best this method can only provide a rough estimate, given that it artificially assigns the midpoint number to all respondents.

**EXERCISE 3.1**

In the month of November 2010, the University of British Columbia's women's basketball team, the Thunderbirds, played seven games, scoring the following points per game.

73    79    61    50    60    72    77

Answer the following questions:

1. What is the mean number of points the Thunderbirds scored in the month?
2. What is the standard deviation?
3. What are the 25th, 50th, and 75th percentiles?
4. What is the interquartile range?

Source: http://www.gothunderbirds.ca/custompages/Stats/Bballw/2010–11/teamcume.htm

# Describing the Shape of a Distribution

So far, we have discussed how to find and describe the centre (mean, median, and mode) and spread of a distribution (variance and standard deviation) but we have not yet discussed how to describe its overall shape. In this section, we will explore how to describe the shape of distributions from observed data using the terms skewness and kurtosis.

**LO6**

## Skewness

**Symmetric distribution** occurs if the left and right sides of the distribution are the same shape, only reversed.

When we talk about the shape of a distribution we are asking if it is symmetric or asymmetric and if it is tall or flat. A distribution is said to be a **symmetric** if the left and right sides of the distribution are the same shape, only reversed. Examine Figure 3.8 and imagine folding the histogram in half down the middle of the tallest (most frequent) column. The left side and the right side match because the distribution is symmetric.

**FIGURE 3.8**
**A Symmetric
Distribution**

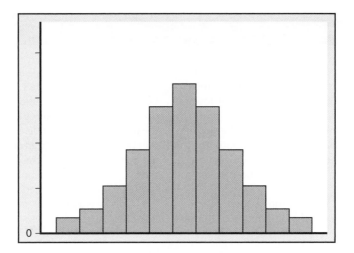

**Asymmetric
distribution** occurs
when the left and right
sides are not the same
shape in reverse.

**Skewness** is a
measure of the
amount to which a
distribution departs
from a symmetric
shape. Skewed
distributions are
asymmetric.

A distribution is said to be **asymmetric** (think lopsided) when the left and right sides are not the same shape in reverse. That is to say, the left and right sides are not mirror images of each other. The amount to which the shape of the distribution is asymmetric is referred to as **skewness**. There are two forms of skewness—positively skewed and negatively skewed. Figure 3.9 provides examples of skewed distribution shapes. The distribution on the left is said to be positively skewed since the bulk of the scores are low and few scores are high. The distribution on the right is said to be negatively skewed since the bulk of the scores are high and few scores are low. One way to remember whether the distribution is positively or negatively skewed is to look at the tail. If the tail is pointing to the high scores, then it is positively skewed. If the tail is pointing to the low scores then it is negatively skewed.

**FIGURE 3.9**  **Skewed Distributions**

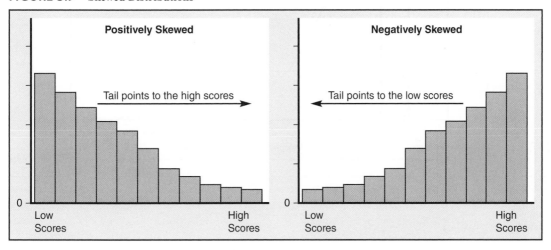

## For Your Information

The mean is very sensitive to skewness and extreme values (outliers). When a distribution is positively skewed the mean is pulled out towards the tail (higher values), and will therefore be higher than the median and mode. The opposite is true for negatively skewed distributions. The mean will be pulled toward the tail (lower values), and will therefore be less than the median and mode.

As an example, consider the frequency polygon below, which provides the distribution of the variable "number of people living in your household" from the Statistics Canada's 2004 Canadian Addiction Survey. This distribution is positively skewed since the bulk of the scores are at the lower end of the distribution. The mode is 2 (the most common number of people living in the household was 2), the median is 2 (50% of the observations had fewer than 2 people per household and 50% had more than 2 people per household), and the mean is 2.69 (on average there were 2.69 people per household).

**FIGURE 3.10** **Number of People Living in a Household**

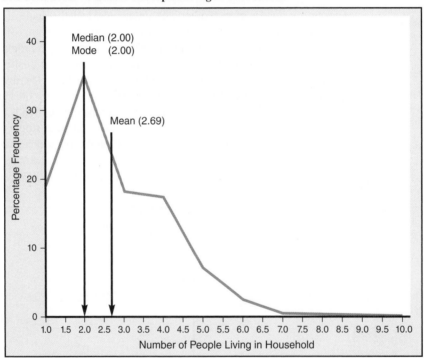

To give you an example of where you may see skewed distribution shapes, consider the following scenarios.

1. Several people are asked to consider their least favourite food and then rate on a scale of 1 (being low) to 10 (being high) whether they would like to eat it for dinner.

2. Several people are asked to consider their favourite ice cream and then rate on a scale of 1 (being low) to 10 (being high) whether they would like to eat it for dessert.

In the first scenario, it is likely that most people will not want their least favourite food for dinner, so a large percentage of the scores will be low. In this case, you will see the distribution of scores being positively skewed. In the second scenario, the majority are likely to say they would like to have their favourite ice cream for dessert, so most of the scores will be high. In this case, you will see the distribution of scores being negatively skewed.

## Kurtosis

While skewness is a measure of the amount to which the shape of the distribution departs from symmetry, **kurtosis** is a measure of the "peakedness" of a distribution. By peakedness, we mean how tall or flat the distribution is. Think of kurtosis as being similar to how you would describe two different hills, one that has a high peak versus one that is relatively flat. Examine the shape of the distribution on the left in Figure 3.11. When scores are clustered around the centre of a distribution, it tends to become tall with long left and right tails. We refer to this shape as **leptokurtic**. Now consider the shape of the distribution on the right of Figure 3.11. When scores are fairly evenly spread out across the possible range of values, the shape of the distribution becomes flat with short left and right tails. We refer to this shape as **platykurtic**. People have various ways to remember the difference between leptokurtic and platykurtic. One way to remember them is to equate them

**LO7**

**Kurtosis** is the measure of the "peakedness" of a distribution.

**Leptokurtic** refers to the shape of a distribution when scores are clustered around the centre point.

**Platykurtic** refers to the shape of a distribution when scores are fairly evenly spread out across the possible range of values.

**FIGURE 3.11**   **Leptokurtic and Platykurtic Distributions**

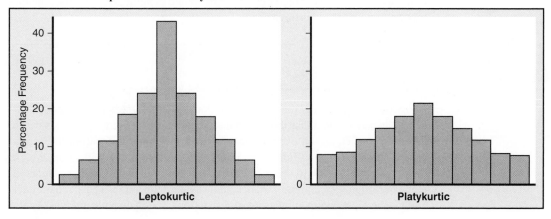

to a kangaroo and a platypus. Kangaroos are taller with a long tail and they leap. A leptokurtic distribution is tall with long tails. So think of "leap" like a kangaroo. A platypus on the other hand is pretty flat. A platykurtic distribution is also flat. So think of a platypus.

To give you an example of where you may see leptokurtic and platykurtic distribution shapes, consider the following scenarios.

1. Eleven runners time how long it takes to run five kilometres. The frequency table of the results is as follows:

| Time | Frequency |
|------|-----------|
| 18 minutes | 1 |
| 20 minutes | 2 |
| 25 minutes | 5 |
| 30 minutes | 2 |
| 32 minutes | 1 |
| Total | 11 |

2. Another eleven runners time how long it takes to run five kilometres. The frequency table of the results is as follows:

| Time | Frequency |
|------|-----------|
| 18 minutes | 2 |
| 20 minutes | 2 |
| 25 minutes | 3 |
| 30 minutes | 2 |
| 32 minutes | 2 |
| Total | 11 |

In the first scenario, you can see that the majority of the scores are at the centre (25 minutes) with smaller frequencies at the low and high end. In this case, the distribution will be leptokurtic in shape. In the second scenario, the frequencies of times are fairly evenly spread out across the range of values. In this case, the distribution will be platykurtic in shape.

# Conclusion

A key part in describing data includes reporting on the measures of central tendency, dispersion, and distribution shape. The level of measurement of a variable determines whether you use the mean, median, or mode in locating the central value. Variability tells us how spread out the data is from its mean value. We use measures of dispersion to describe the variability of our data. These measures include the range, percentiles, variance, and standard deviation. The standard deviation is the most common measure of dispersion (when you have interval or ratio data) because it allows the researcher to report the deviation in the units of measurement used in the study. Finally, we can describe the shape of our distribution using skewness and kurtosis. A skewed distribution indicates that the bulk of scores for that variable are situated at one end of the range of values. When the distribution is positively skewed, the mean will be numerically higher than the median and mode. When the distribution is negatively skewed, the mean will be numerically less than the median and mode. Kurtosis tells us how tall or flat the distribution is. When scores cluster around the centre value, the shape of the distribution tends to be taller with longer tails (leptokurtic). When scores are fairly evenly spread out across the range of values the shape of the distribution tends to be flatter with shorter tails (platykurtic).

Chapters 2 and 3 represent some of the fundamental concepts needed for understanding statistics. In the next chapter, we begin to discuss how we can make inferences about the population from our sample data. To do this, we need to begin with some elementary probability theory.

## Key Chapter Concepts and Terms

Central tendency, 76
Measures of central tendency, 76
Mode, 77
Median, 78
Mean, 79
Measures of dispersion, 84

Variability, 84
Percentiles, 85
Interquartile range, 87
Variance, 88
Deviation, 88
Sum of squares, 89
Standard deviation, 90

Symmetric distribution, 94
Asymmetric distribution, 95
Skewness, 95
Kurtosis, 97
Leptokurtic, 97
Platykurtic, 97

## Frequently Asked Questions

1. When calculating the mean, should the observations be arranged in ascending order as in the chapter? Or does it not matter?

   The numbers can be in any order for calculating the mean, or the standard deviation for that matter. We put them in ascending order to calculate medians and percentiles, and to make it easier to create a frequency table.

2. Is it possible to know ahead of time which measure of central tendency will be the best representation of the distribution of the sample? Or is it better to calculate all three and then decide based on the results?

   Since the variable's level of measurement determines which measure of central tendency you use, you should know the appropriate measure to use ahead of time. The tricky one is often with interval and ratio data when the mean and median may be appropriate. For example, suppose you were looking at house prices and want to know a typical value for a house. If there are a few $10 million homes being sold, then mean house price would be inflated and of little use. In this case, the median would be useful. Again, this is due to the data being denser on one side of the range than the other. We will cover this in more detail in chapter 4.

3. Why is the median calculated as the $(n + 1) \div 2$ position and not just the $n \div 2$ position? Why do you need to add 1?

If we have an odd number of values such as 1, 2, 3, 4, 5 then the middle point is the third number, which is in the $(5 + 1) \div 2$ position. If we only used $n \div 2$ to determine the position, then it would indicate the 2.5th position or $5 \div 2$. When you have an even number of values there usually is no exact middle value, so we need to take the mean of the middle two values. So for 1, 2, 3, 4, 5, 6 we have six values and the middle falls between the third and fourth value. In this case, if you used $n \div 2$ you would find only the first value (3) needed to calculate the median. You still need the number in the $(n + 1) \div 2$ position which is the second value (4). So the median value is $(3 + 4) \div 2$ or 3.5.

4. What does standard deviation help us to understand? Why do we use it?

Standard deviation measures the variability in the data. Suppose we have a scale from 1 (not acceptable) to 10 (highly acceptable) to measure the acceptability of using marijuana. A score of 7 with a very small standard deviation indicates that most of the sample provided a score close to 7. Conversely, a score of 7 with a large standard deviation indicates a lot of differing views, where some rated acceptability as very high and some as very low. A low standard deviation indicates little dissent from the mean, whereas a high standard deviation represents very diverse views.

**Research Example:**

The 2004 Canadian Addiction Survey, conducted by Statistics Canada, was meant to identify trend in drug and alcohol use. The survey, which included 13,700 Canadians, contained a series of questions regarding opinions and uses of drugs and alcohol, and demographics such as age, gender, province, education, gross family income, and employment status.

One particular question asked respondents to indicate their age when they first started drinking alcoholic beverages. The question asked for actual age and as a result produced ratio data. Specifically:

"Not counting small sips, how old were you when you started drinking alcoholic beverages? (Drinking does not include having a few sips of wine for religious purposes)."

Considering only a subset of the data—those who were 21 years old at the time the survey was completed—there were 181 respondents for this question. Table 3.12 provides a frequency table of their responses.

**Research Example Questions:**

**Question 1:** What is the median value?

**Question 2:** What was the mean age that 21-year-olds started to drink?

**Question 3:** What age occurs with the greatest frequency?

**Question 4:** What is the sample standard deviation?

**Question 5:** What percent of the sample started to drink by the age of 18?

**TABLE 3.12**   **Age of First Drink (For only those 21 years old at the time of the survey)**

| Age of First Drink | Frequency (f) | Relative Frequency (f/n) | Percentage Frequency (%f) | Cumulative Frequency (c.f) | Cumulative Percentage Frequency (c.%f) |
|---|---|---|---|---|---|
| 5 | 1 | 0.0055 | 0.55% | 1 | 0.55% |
| 8 | 2 | 0.0110 | 1.10% | 3 | 1.65% |
| 10 | 3 | 0.0166 | 1.66% | 6 | 3.31% |
| 11 | 2 | 0.0110 | 1.10% | 8 | 4.41% |
| 12 | 10 | 0.0553 | 5.53% | 18 | 9.94% |
| 13 | 13 | 0.0718 | 7.18% | 31 | 17.13% |
| 14 | 18 | 0.0994 | 9.94% | 49 | 27.07% |
| 15 | 27 | 0.1492 | 14.92% | 76 | 41.99% |
| 16 | 33 | 0.1823 | 18.23% | 109 | 60.22% |
| 17 | 22 | 0.1215 | 12.15% | 131 | 72.38% |
| 18 | 34 | 0.1878 | 18.78% | 165 | 91.16% |
| 19 | 11 | 0.0608 | 6.08% | 176 | 97.24% |
| 20 | 4 | 0.0221 | 2.21% | 180 | 99.45% |
| 21 | 1 | 0.0055 | 0.55% | 181 | 100.00% |
| Total | 181 | 1.0000 | 100.00% | | |

## Research Example Answers:

**Question 1:**  What is the median value?

With 181 observations the median occurs at the $(181 + 1) \div 2$ position. That is, we are looking for observation 91. We can obtain this from the cumulative frequency column. Since there is a total of 76 individuals up to 15 and a total of 109 up to 16, we know the 91st position must be 16. Therefore, the median age is 16. We could also find the median using the cumulative percentage frequency column by looking for the cumulative value of 50 percent. With 41.99 percent of the data including the age up to 15 and 60.22 percent up to the age 16, we know the 50 percent value must be 16.

**Question 2:**  What was the mean age that 21-year-olds started to drink?

The average can be calculated by summing all the numbers and dividing by 181. As we have frequencies or counts, we can say that there is one 5, two 8s, three 10s, etc. Summing them we get:

$$1 \times 5 + 2 \times 8 + 3 \times 10 + 2 \times 11 \cdots 1 \times 21 = 2,843$$

The sample mean is then $2,843 \div 181 = 15.7$. So the average age that 21-year-olds started drinking was 15.7.

**Question 3:**  What age occurs with the greatest frequency?

The highest frequency occurs at age 18 with 34 people out of 181. So the mode is 18. The mode is useful for this type of data as we can report that 18 is the most common age, and it is 18.78 percent of the sample.

**Question 4:** What is the sample standard deviation?

The sample standard deviation is:

$$s = \sqrt{\frac{\Sigma(x - \bar{x})^2}{(n - 1)}} = \sqrt{\frac{1,113.481}{181 - 1}} = \sqrt{6.1860} = 2.4872 \text{ or } 2.49$$

Therefore, one standard deviation includes the ages between $15.7 \pm 2.49 = 13.21$ to 18.19.

**Question 5:** What percent of the sample started to drink by the age of 18?

Looking in the age column for the age 18 and then moving horizontally across to the cumulative percentage frequency column, we can see that 91.16 percent of individuals aged 21 starting drinking alcohol by the age of 18.

---

**ANSWERS TO EXERCISE 3.1**

In the month of November 2010, the University of British Columbia's women's basketball team, the Thunderbirds, played seven games, scoring the following points per game.

73 79 61 50 60 72 77

Source: http://www.gothunderbirds.ca/custompages/Stats/Bballw/2010–11/teamcume.htm

| Question | Answer |
|---|---|
| 1. What is the mean number of points the Thunderbirds scored in the month? | 67.429 |
| 2. What is the standard deviation? | 10.628 |
| 3. What are the 25th, 50th, and 75th percentiles? | The 25th percentile is 60, the median is 72 and the 75th percentile is 77. |
| 4. What is the interquartile range? | $77 - 60 = 17$ |

---

**Problems**

1. The data shown represents the total compensation for the 20 top-paid CEOs for a recent year.

| 20 Top-Paid CEOs Compensation (in Millions) | | | |
|---|---|---|---|
| 17.5 | 18.0 | 29.6 | 14.8 |
| 17.3 | 24.3 | 31.9 | 24.8 |
| 23.7 | 16.5 | 19.7 | 29.4 |
| 37.6 | 19.7 | 25.6 | 31.9 |
| 19.3 | 20.0 | 25.7 | 29.5 |

a. Find the mean

b. Find the median

c. Find the mode

d. Compare the averages, then state which one you think is the best measure.

2. For each of the following wage groups, find:
   a. the mean for each group.
   b. the variance and standard deviation for each group.
   c. Based on the results, which data set is more variable?

| wages | |
|---|---|
| **group 1** | **group 2** |
| 12.00 | 13.28 |
| 14.74 | 16.03 |
| 16.41 | 17.71 |
| 20.19 | 21.51 |
| 18.62 | 19.93 |
| 16.41 | 17.71 |
| 16.03 | 17.32 |
| 13.74 | 15.02 |
| 18.41 | 19.73 |
| 16.74 | 18.05 |

3. The following frequency distribution for entrance exam scores was gathered for 108 randomly selected college applicants:

| Class limits | Frequency |
|---|---|
| 90–98 | 6 |
| 99–107 | 22 |
| 108–116 | 43 |
| 117–125 | 28 |
| 126–134 | 9 |

   a. Construct a histogram.
   b. Comment on the shape of the distribution.
   c. Is the data to be leptokurtic or platykurtic? Comment relative to the "peakedness" of the distribution.

# A Review of Probability Theory

# 4

**Learning Objectives:**

By the end of this chapter you should be able to:

1. Explain the concept of probability.
2. Describe simple, mutually exclusive, and non-mutually exclusive probability problems using a Venn diagram.
3. Calculate basic probabilities of events from a random experiment.
4. Use the additive and multiplicative rules of probability.
5. Describe the difference between frequency distributions and probability distributions.

## Abraham de Moivre (1667–1754)

Abraham de Moivre was born in France in 1667 as Abraham Moivre. As a French Huguenot, he and his family were forced to emigrate from France to England after the Louis XIV revoked the protection of Protestants from religious persecution. While in England, Moivre changed his name to de Moivre.

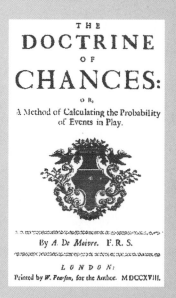

de Moivre was deeply interested in probability theory and is often credited for discovering the normal curve. His work—which he published in his 1773 book *The Doctrine of Chances: or, a Method of Calculating the Probability of Events in Play*—investigated such diverse topics as gambling outcomes and annuity payments based on an individual's lifespan. Although de Moivre's goal of becoming a university professor never came to be, fortunately for us he continued his desire to contribute to the field of statistics. His work in probability theory formed a significant part of what we do in applied statistics today.[1]

# Introduction

In the last chapter we looked at measures of central tendency, dispersion, and shape. This chapter builds on those topics to cover one of the most important concepts underlying statistical analysis: probability theory. Probability theory is an important part of the social sciences as it allows us to apply research findings to the broader population. Here are some examples of probability in different social science disciplines.

1. A criminologist uses probability to estimate the likelihood that an offender will repeat his or her offence.
2. A sociologist uses probability to determine how likely education is to reduce poverty within metropolitan areas.

3. An educational psychologist uses probability to estimate how likely bullying behaviour is to occur given specific character traits.

4. An economist uses probability to estimate the likely influence of interest rate hikes on debt defaulting.

5. A business person uses probability to estimate the potential for product defects.

6. A social worker uses probability to estimate the likelihood that a potential foster parent will meet the needs of children.

Traditionally, this topic involves a significant amount of mathematical formulas and notation. However, the approach here minimizes the number of formulas to only those necessary for your role as a social scientist. The figures accompanying the examples in this chapter are meant to help you visually see what the numbers say.

# What is Probability?

**LO1**

An **experiment** is a procedure or process that allows us to control specific conditions while observing a specific outcome.

An experiment has a **random outcome** if the outcome cannot be predicted with certainty.

A **random experiment** is any experiment that can be repeated, under the exact same conditions, and where the outcomes cannot be predicted with certainty.

In chapter 1 we stated that most of us informally use statistical language in our everyday conversation. A hockey coach may suggest that practicing more often will likely lead to more goal scoring. You might tell your friend that if she eats healthy food she probably won't get sick as often. Or you might say that you would be more likely to buy an Apple iPad if it were less expensive. All of these statements have probability hidden within them. So what is probability and why should social scientists care about it?

From a statistics perspective, probability as a mathematical theory was developed by the famous French mathematicians Fermat (1601–1665) and Pascal (1623–1662).[2] The word probability comes from the Latin word *probabilis* meaning "the appearance of truth or likelihood." Although too general for our purpose, you might consider probability to be "the extent to which something is likely to happen or not."

To adequately define probability, we first need to discuss two key terms: "experiment" and "random outcome." An **experiment** is a procedure or process that allows us to control specific conditions while observing a specific outcome. For example, a psychologist interested in testing memory performance may show participants a sequence of numbers and then ask them to recall those numbers. An experiment has a **random outcome** if the outcome cannot be predicted with certainty. We aim to conduct **random experiments** that can be repeated, under the exact same conditions, where the outcomes cannot be predicted with certainty.

Some common types of experiments with random outcomes (random experiments if you like) include tossing a coin, rolling dice, or choosing a card from a deck of 52 cards. Each experiment has a random outcome. In the case of tossing a coin

An **event** is a set of outcomes that we are interested in.

**Probability** is a measure of the proportion of times that the event would occur if the experiment were repeated many times, under the same conditions.

there are two possible outcomes, heads or tails. Another example is selecting Canadians at random and asking if they are in favour of harsher punishments for crimes committed with guns. The possible outcomes depend on the response options you provide but, for example, they could include "yes" versus "no," or "strongly disagree" versus "strongly agree," or even "refuse to answer." The responses will vary from one Canadian to the next and cannot be predicted with certainty.

When we conduct an experiment, we refer to the set of outcomes that we are interested in as an **event**. If we are interested in what proportion of coin tosses will be tails, we say that tails is the event of interest. **Probability** is a measure of the proportion of times that the event would occur if the experiment were repeated many times, under the same conditions.

# The Venn Diagram

**LO2**

Sample space refers to all of the possible outcomes of a random experiment.

The **complement of an event** refers to all of the possible outcomes within a sample space except for the event of interest.

One of the easiest ways to understand probability is by using Venn diagrams. A Venn diagram is a graphical way of looking at the relationship between different events. It was invented by British mathematician and philosopher John Venn (1834–1923), who first published this useful tool in 1880 in "The London, Edinburgh, and Dublin Philosophical Magazine and Journal of Science."[3]

A Venn diagram consists of a box called the **sample space** and at least one circle, referred to as the event(s) (see Figure 4.1). The term sample space simply refers to all the possible outcomes that can occur. Given that the event refers to the outcomes in which we are interested, it is a subset of the sample space. All other possible outcomes inside the sample space that are not the event we are interested in are called the **complement of the event**.

Suppose for a moment that you and a friend flip one coin to determine who is buying the coffee today. Ignoring the chance of the coin landing on its edge (the part between the two faces) there are only two possible outcomes (heads or tails) and we refer to these possible outcomes as the sample space. Now suppose you choose heads for the coin toss. The outcome that you are interested in, the coin

**FIGURE 4.1**
**Basic Venn Diagram**

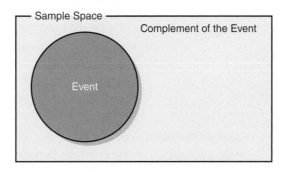

landing heads, is referred to as the event. The event of something other than your desired outcome occurring is referred to as the complement. So the coin landing heads is the event, and the coin landing tails is the complement.

Since an experiment can be repeated, probability is based on the proportion of times an event occurs when repeating the experiment over a long period of time. If you want to know the probability of certain outcomes in card games, such as bridge or poker, you can play cards for several years and observe what happens or you can use sophisticated counting procedures to obtain the probabilities. Another way to consider probability is to think of the lottery. Ask yourself how often you win a free ticket compared to winning a prize worth over $1,000. If you were to keep track of all the games you played, you would know the proportion of times you won versus lost. Even if you did not keep accurate records you would likely find that the probability of winning a free ticket is higher than the probability of winning over $1,000.

## Thinking About Probability

In the previous section, we introduced the Venn diagram as a way of looking at events. Now we will examine different types of probability problems using Venn diagrams. The different types of probability problems that we will cover include:

- simple probability problems, where you have one single event;
- mutually exclusive probability problems, where you have two events that can't overlap;
- non-mutually exclusive probability problems, where you have two events that can/do overlap;
- dependent events; and
- independent events.

**LO3**

*Simple Probability Problems*

We generally refer to a probability problem as simple probability when there is only one event being considered. The Venn diagram in Figure 4.2 shows an example where we consider only one event P(A). The probability of a single event occurring is equal to the number of ways that the event can happen divided by the total number of possible outcomes. We write this as:

$$P(A) = \frac{\text{Number of ways the event can happen}}{\text{Total number of possible outcomes}} \quad \text{(4.1)}$$

A simpler way of writing this is:

$$P(A) = \frac{s}{n} \quad \text{(4.2)}$$

where: P(A) is the probability of event A

$s$ = the number of ways the event can happen

$n$ = the total number of possible outcomes

**FIGURE 4.2**

**Venn Diagram,
Single Event**

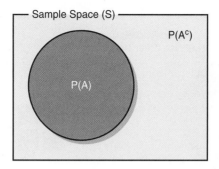

Within the Venn diagram we can now add some commonly used notation to refer to what we have just discussed. As you can see in Figure 4.2 we refer to the sample space as S, the event as A, and the complement of the event as $A^c$. We can also add in the notation for the probability, which is commonly shown as P( ), and is pronounced "probability of ( )". So the probability of A occurring is P(A) and the probability of the complement of A occurring is $P(A^c)$. In some textbooks you may see the complement represented as $\overline{A}$ or A′ (pronounced "A prime"). We will use $A^c$ in this textbook.

By now, you have likely figured out one of the crucial pieces to understanding probability: the sample space (S) is equal to the outcomes in event A plus all outcomes not in A. So we have:

$$P(S) = P(A) + P(A^c) \qquad \textbf{(4.3)}$$

Probabilities range from 0 to 1, where 0 means there is a 0 percent probability of the event happening and 1 means there is a 100 percent probability of the event happening. Since probabilities range from 0 to 1, then P(A) plus $P(A^c)$ must equal 1. If you think about it, this makes sense. If you have a 50 percent chance of the coin landing on heads (P(A) = 0.50) and a 50 percent chance of the coin landing on tails ($P(A^c)$ = 0.50), then you have a 100 percent chance (a probability of 1) of flipping either a head or a tail.

As the sample space represents all possible outcomes of an event, then P(S) must equal 1. So we can say:

$$1 = P(A) + P(A^c) \qquad \textbf{(4.4)}$$

which is the same as saying $P(A) = 1 - P(A^c)$
which is the same as saying $P(A^c) = 1 - P(A)$

Suppose we have a six-sided die and we want to know the probability of rolling a two. Figure 4.3 provides the Venn diagram for this problem and Figure 4.4 provides a diagrammatic view of the formula and the formula itself. The event we are interested in is "rolling a two" and there is only way to get that outcome. However, given that there are six sides to the die there are six possible outcomes. So there is a 0.166 (16.6 percent) probability of rolling a two. Although it is

**FIGURE 4.3**
**Venn Diagram, Roll Anything But Two**

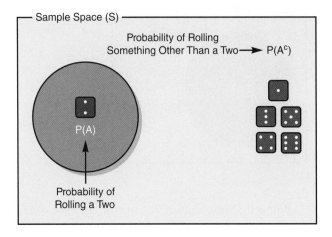

**FIGURE 4.4**
**Rolling Anything But Two**

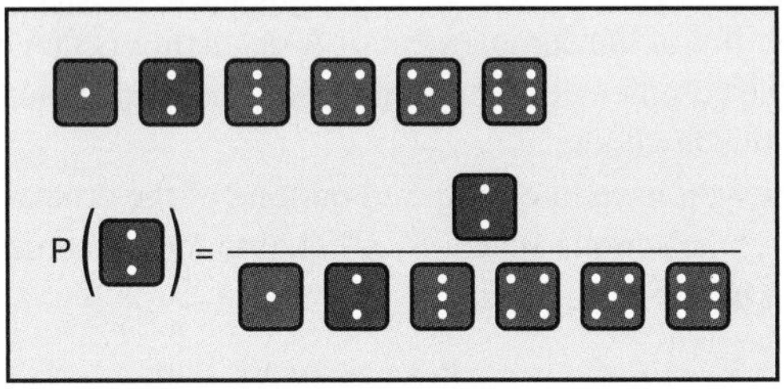

$$P(A) = \frac{s}{n} \tag{4.5}$$

$$P(\text{rolling a two}) = \frac{\text{One possible way of getting a two}}{\text{Six possible outcomes}}$$

$$P(A) = \frac{1}{6} = 0.166$$

possible to roll a two, two or three times in a row, what probability theory says is that on average and over a large number of rolls, 16.6 percent of the time you could expect to roll a two.

Let's look at another example. Suppose you have a draw for a door prize at a charity event. There are 148 male attendees and 172 female attendees. If you randomly select one attendee to win the door prize, what is the probability that a male will win the prize? Figure 4.5 provides the Venn diagram for this problem. The sample space consists of all 320 attendees. The event [P(A)] is the probability of selecting a male [P(Male)] and the complement [P(A^c)] is the probability of selecting a female [P(Female)].

**FIGURE 4.5**
**Venn Diagram,**
**Charity Event**

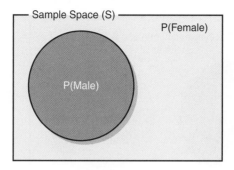

There are 148 ways that we could select a male out of the entire sample space of 320 attendees, so we write our formula as follows:

$$P(\text{male}) = \frac{\text{Number of ways the event can happen}}{\text{Total number of possible outcomes}} \quad \textbf{(4.6)}$$

$$= \frac{148}{320} = 0.4625$$

There is a 0.4625 probability (46.25 percent) that a male attendee will win the draw. Conversely, since we know that probabilities sum to equal 1, we can say that there is a $1 - 0.4625 = 0.5375$ probability (53.75 percent) that a female attendee will win the draw.

Now that you know how to solve a simple probability problem, let's consider other examples that build on our previous formula. Rather than focusing on the mathematical extensions to this formula, we'll focus more on the interpretation of the results.

**LO2**

*Mutually Exclusive Probability Problems*

In probability, we say that events are mutually exclusive when the outcomes of the events cannot occur at the same time. You can have either outcome A or outcome B but not both. This is similar to the simple probability problem where we flipped a coin, and the outcome is either heads or tails, but not both. However, now we are talking about more than one event of interest in the sample space.

Imagine that you have a chance to win \$100 if you roll a single die and get either a one or a six. Figure 4.6 provides a Venn diagram with two mutually exclusive events represented by the two circles labelled A and B. Event A is the probability that you will roll a one and event B is the probability that you will roll a six. We also have the complement, which represents all other outcomes that are not A or B, which is the probability that you role a two, three, four, or five. You hope that when you roll the die that it will be either a one *or* six, but you know that it is impossible for it to be both. This is so obvious that it seems silly to mention, but in understanding mutually exclusive events it is important to note that only one of the two events can happen, not *both*.

**FIGURE 4.6**
**Venn Diagram, Two Events**

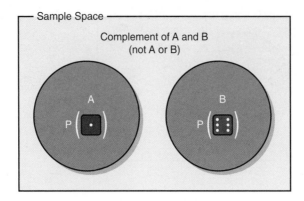

**LO4**

Estimating the probability of rolling a one, P(A), can be done with formula 4.4 (1 ÷ 6 = 0.166). Similarly, estimating the probability of rolling a six, P(B), can also be done with formula 4.4 (1 ÷ 6 = 0.166). However, with two events that are mutually exclusive, what we usually want to know is the probability that event A *or* B will happen. To estimate this, we need to extend our previous formula slightly using what is referred to as the addition rule for mutually exclusive events.

$$P(A \text{ or } B) = P(A) + P(B) = \frac{1}{6} + \frac{1}{6} = \frac{1}{3} \text{ or } 0.332 \text{ or } 33.2\% \quad \textbf{(4.7)}$$

As you can see, the probability of rolling a one or a six is 0.332, meaning 33.2 percent of the time we can expect to roll a one or a six and win the $100. Conversely, over time there is a 66.8 percent probability (1 − 0.332 = 0.668) that we will not win the $100.

Now let's look at an example with some real data. Table 4.1 provides the results of the number of seats won in the Fortieth Federal General Election in 2008 by the Conservative and Liberal parties by gender.[4] We are focussing on these two parties in order to keep the example manageable. A Venn diagram of this data is presented in Figure 4.7. There are 308 seats in the Canadian House of Commons, and these two parties hold 220 of them. For simplicity, we are only considering these two political parties with a total count of 220.

**TABLE 4.1**

Source: Elections Canada (from 40th General Election 2008 by the Conservative and Liberal Parties by Gender)

| | Conservative Party Seats | Liberal Party Seats | Total |
|---|---|---|---|
| Female | 23 (A) | 19 (C) | 42 |
| Male | 120 (B) | 58 (D) | 178 |
| Total | 143 | 77 | 220 |

**FIGURE 4.7**

**Venn Diagram, Political Party MPs**

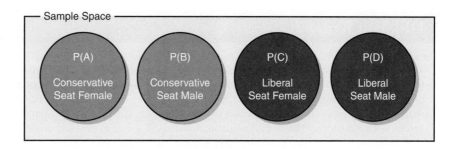

Figure 4.7 shows four mutually exclusive events. They are mutually exclusive because you can't be in both parties and you can't be both genders. If we randomly selected one seat from the entire sample space of 220 seats, we could calculate certain probabilities, such as:

1. The probability of selecting a seat held by a female from the Conservative party is P(female from the Conservative Party) = 23 ÷ 220 = 0.1045 or 10.45 percent.

2. The probability of selecting a seat held by a male from the Conservative party is P(male from the Conservative Party) = 120 ÷ 220 = 0.5454 or 54.54 percent.

3. The probability of selecting a seat held by a female from the Liberal party is P(female from the Liberal Party) = 19 ÷ 220 or 0.0864 or 8.64 percent.

4. The probability of selecting a seat held by a female is P(female from the Conservative Party or female from the Liberal Party) = (23 ÷ 220) + (19 ÷ 220) = 0.1909 or 19.09 percent.

Now that we have looked mutually exclusive probabilities, let's examine non-mutually exclusive events.

**LO2**

*Non-Mutually Exclusive Probability Problems*

Consider the data from Table 4.1 but in a slightly different form. If we look at the probability of choosing a seat held by a female or the probability of choosing a seat held by a Liberal, then the two events could have common outcomes. In fact, there are 19 seats that are held by people who are both female and Liberal. If we want to find the probability that a seat is held by a female or a Liberal, then we first add up the number of seats held by females and the number of seats held by Liberals and then subtract the seats we counted twice. This is referred to as the addition rule for non-mutually exclusive events:

P(Female or Liberal) = P(Female) + P(Liberal) − P(Female and Liberal)

$$P(\text{Female or Liberal}) = \left( \frac{23}{220} + \frac{19}{220} \right) + \left( \frac{19}{220} + \frac{58}{220} \right) - \left( \frac{19}{220} \right) = \frac{100}{220}$$

$$= 0.4545 \text{ or } 45.45\%$$

## Did You Know?

There is a famous statistics problem called "The Monty Hall Problem" that for a while caused a lot of controversy amongst statisticians and mathematicians. The problem, first proposed by Steve Selvin, is based on the 1960s/1970s game show "Let's Make A Deal" hosted by Monty Hall. A popular version of the problem shows a contestant with a chance to win a new car. Monty Hall shows the contestant three doors, from which the contestant must choose one. Behind two of the doors are goats and behind one door is the car. Once the contestant chooses a door, Monty always opens one of the remaining doors that has a goat behind it. The contestant is now free to stick with his or her original choice or to switch doors. What to do?

At this point people often think that with two doors remaining there is a 50 percent chance that they have chosen the correct door. The answer is that they are twice as likely to win if they switch doors. Here's how it works: Suppose you choose door number 2. When you chose this door, there was a one-in-three chance you were correct (the car is behind door number 2) and a two-in-three chance you were incorrect. Remember that regardless of the door you choose, Monty always opens a door that has a goat behind it. Suppose Monty now opens door number 1 and reveals the goat. The probabilities have not changed, there is still a one-in-three chance the car is behind the door you selected and a two-in-three chance the car is behind door 1 or door 3; now you know it isn't behind door number 1. Therefore, switching to door number 3 is like switching to door number 1 and 3 combined. So there is now a two-in-three chance the car is behind door number 3. On average, if you switch doors, you will win the car two out of every three times.

Here's how you can try this. Have someone hide a coin under one of three cups. Choose one cup and ask the person to turn over one of the two remaining cups that is not hiding the coin. Then switch your choice to the remaining cup. Repeat this 12 times (switching each time) and on average you will select the cup with the coin 8 of the 12 times.

**Sources:** S. Selvin, "Letters to the Editor," *The American Statistician,* 29 no. 1 (February 1975), pp. 67–71.

J.S. Rosenthal, *Struck by Lightning. The Curious World of Probabilities.* (Toronto: Harper Perennial, 2005), pp. 212–215.

---

**LO4**

For non-mutually exclusive events, the general addition rule for two events A and B can be written as follows:

$$P(A \text{ or } B) = P(A) + P(B) - P(A \text{ and } B)$$

The 2006 Statistics Canada report "Stress and Depression in the Employed Population"[5] found that among those reporting high levels of work and personal stress, approximately 32 percent of respondents felt they had low levels of co-worker support in their job and approximately 16 percent felt they had low levels of supervisor support in their job. Let's assume for a moment that these findings and estimates are representative of the entire population of Canadian workers of the same age as the original study. If we were to conduct a similar survey, what would be the probability that we would find respondents reporting low levels of co-worker support *or* low levels of supervisor support *or* both? Notice that unlike the previous example, we are now considering the possibility that two events (low co-worker support and low-supervisor support) could occur at the same time. This

**FIGURE 4.8**

**Venn Diagram, Non-Mutually Exclusive**

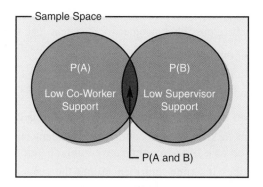

is what we refer to as a non-mutually exclusive probability problem. Figure 4.8 shows the Venn diagram for this problem.

As was the case in our previous example, when we estimate probabilities for non-mutually exclusive events like this one, P(A) or P(B) or P(A and B), we have to take the overlap into consideration. If 5 percent of workers have both low supervisor support and low co-worker support then, on average among those respondents reporting a high level of work and personal stress, there would be a 43 percent probability [(0.16 + 0.32 − 0.05) = 0.43] that these individuals would report experiencing either low co-worker support, low supervisor support, or both low co-worker and low supervisor support. This is calculated as follows:

$$P(A \text{ or } B) = P(A) + P(B) - P(A \text{ and } B)$$

P(low co-worker support or low supervisor support) = (0.16) + (0.32) − (0.05)
$$= 0.43 \text{ or } 43\%$$

**Note:** In this example we have percentages as opposed to fractions, but the formula works the same way.

*Dependent Events*

Sometimes probabilities depend on previous events. To calculate the probability for dependent events, we use the multiplicative rule.

For dependent events, the general multiplicative rule can be written as follows. For events A and B:

$$P(A \text{ and } B) = P(A) \, P(B \text{ given } A)$$

Consider a course in which students are allowed to write the exam a second time if they failed the first time. In one particular course 150 out of 200 passed the exam. Of the remaining 50 students who failed and took the exam again, 40 passed the second attempt and 10 did not. If we took a random student in the class, we can ask questions such as:

a) What is the sample space of possible outcomes?

b) What is the probability of failing the exam on the first try?

c) What is the probability of failing both exams?

**Answers**

a) There are three possible outcomes for a student. The student can:

    i) not fail the first time,

    ii) fail the first time and pass the second, or

    iii) fail both times.

b) P(failing on first attempt) = P(A) = 50 ÷ 200 = 0.25.

c) If we want to know the probability of a student failing both times we just multiply (because of the multiplicative rule). Therefore,

P(failing the first time and then failing the second) = P(failing the first time) P(failing the second time given that you failed the first time) = P(A) P(B given A) = 0.25 × 0.20 = 0.05. Therefore, 5 percent of the students failed both exams.

---

**EXERCISE 4.1**

This exercise is meant to help you learn to work with probability calculations. The answers are at the end of the chapter.

One hundred people were asked about the number of jobs and the number of residences they had over the last two years. Using the following table, calculate the probability for each outcome.

| Outcome | Count | Probability |
|---|---|---|
| One job and one residence | 20 | |
| One job and more than one residence | 10 | |
| More than one job but only one residence | 10 | |
| More than one job and more than one residence | 60 | |
| Total | 100 | |

Assuming that we randomly choose one person from the previous table, answer the following questions.

**Question**

1. What is the probability of having one residence?
2. What is the probability of having more than one job?
3. What is the probability of having more than one job or more than one residence?
4. What is the probability that an individual who had only one job will also have had only one residence in the two years?

## Take a Closer Look

**A Baseball Example (Sabremetrics)**
A baseball player has the probability of batting a hit of 0.200. That is, he gets a hit 20 percent of the time for his official at bats. What is the probability that he misses the ball in four consecutive at bats?

If he gets a hit with a 0.20 probability then he misses with the probability of 0.80. If we assume that his at bats are independent events, the probability that he misses four times is:

$$0.8 \times 0.8 \times 0.8 \times 0.8 = 0.41$$

There is a 41 percent chance that he will have no hits in four at bats. That is a pretty high probability

of no hits in a game. In reality, there are very few 0.200 players in professional baseball. If we have a probability of 0.400 then the probability of a miss is $1 - 0.4 = 0.6$. The probability of four consecutive misses is:

$$0.6 \times 0.6 \times 0.6 \times 0.6 = 0.13$$

In this case there is a low probability of the player not getting a hit. In fact, for a player with a 0.400 probability of getting a hit, we can expect one hit in most of the games played.

*Independent Events*

If we have two events, A and B, that are independent, then we say that the probability of A occurring does not depend on B. For example, the genders of two babies are not dependent on each other. Consider a mother having two children and let's say that A is the event that the first child is a girl and B the event that the second child is a girl. We assume that a child's gender is random and the gender of previous children has no effect on the gender of future children. In this case, we can assume that the probability of a girl is P(A) = P(B) = 0.5.

For independent events, such as the probability of having two girls, we use the multiplicative rule. Therefore, to determine the probability of having two girls, we multiply . . .

$$P(\text{Girl and Girl}) = P(\text{Girl}) \times P(\text{Girl}) = 0.50 \times 0.50 = 0.25.$$

. . . and find that there is a 25 percent chance of having two girls.

**LO4**

When event A has no effect on the probability of event B, we write the multiplicative rule for independent events as:

$$P(A \text{ and } B) = P(A)\,P(B)$$

# Frequency Distributions versus Probability Distributions

**LO5**

**Distribution** is the arrangement of any values based on the frequencies with which they occur.

In chapter 2 you learned how to graph the frequency of an event of interest. When we do this, we say we are graphing the frequency distribution of a variable that we have observed. A **distribution** is the arrangement of any values based on the frequencies with which they occur.

For example, a 2004 Statistics Canada report determined that of 11,860,932 Canadian males over the age of 18, over 2.7 million (22.9 percent) were considered to be obese (measured as having a body mass index (BMI) of 30.00 or

**TABLE 4.2**

| Age | Number | Percent | Cumulative Percent |
|---|---|---|---|
| 18—34 | 640,558 | 23.53% | 23.53% |
| 35—44 | 514,221 | 18.89% | 42.42% |
| 45—64 | 1,188,123 | 43.65% | 86.07% |
| 65 and over | 378,891 | 13.92% | 99.99% |
| Total | 2,721,793 | 100.00% | |

**Frequency distribution** is a graph showing the distribution of empirical data gathered.

**Empirical data** is data gathered from objects or participants.

**Probability distribution** is a theoretical frequency distribution with an infinite number of trials.

higher).[6] Table 4.2 provides a frequency table of this data and Figure 4.9 provides a frequency distribution of the values. We can see from this sample of males that obesity appears to occur more frequently in those within the 45–64 age category.

Understanding the difference between a frequency distribution and a probability distribution is important. **Frequency distributions** are based on **empirical data** that we gather using tools such as surveys, interviews, databases, and so on. For example, a sociologist might gather empirical data on cultural norms, a political scientist on voting behaviour, an economist on stock fluctuation, an educational psychologist on gender difference in academic performance, and so on. All social science disciplines gather some form of empirical data from the real world in one way or another and when graphing the frequency of their data, they are creating frequency distributions.

**Probability distributions** are theoretical distributions based on the mathematical formulas of probability theory. This sounds like a complicated mouthful but for our purposes it does not need to be. We have already covered a brief introduction to probability theory in the previous section. Based on formulas used to calculate probabilities, we can estimate what is theoretically most likely or least likely to occur.

**FIGURE 4.9**
**Frequency of High BMI**

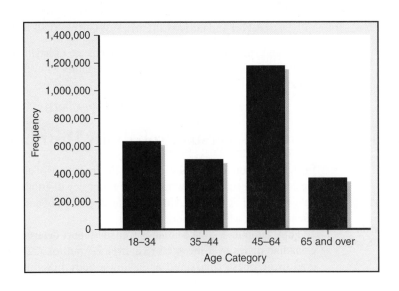

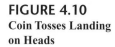

**FIGURE 4.10**
**Coin Tosses Landing on Heads**

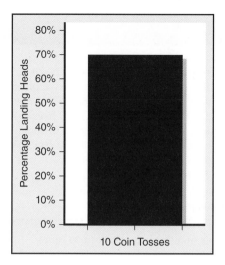

The difference between a frequency distribution and a probability distribution is this: A frequency distribution only includes the values that you gathered in the empirical data (e.g., a survey of stereotyping behaviour in a sample of 100 workers), whereas a probability distribution includes all theoretically possible values that could happen. You can think of it as what your frequency distribution would look like if you could take an infinite sample instead of a finite sample such as the 100 workers.

To ease into the idea of probability distributions and to tie everything together that we have learned in this chapter so far, let's work through the example of coin tossing. Suppose we flip a coin 10 times and find we get seven heads and three tails. Since this is empirical data (we gathered it), we can graph the frequency distribution of our results using a graph, such as the histogram in Figure 4.10. Based on this frequency distribution, we can say that we observed the coin landing on heads 70 percent of the time.

Now, this may seem a bit odd because we know from our formula for estimating simple probability problems that 50 percent of the time the coin should land on heads. However, we just found after flipping the coin 10 times that 70 percent of the time it landed on heads. So how do we reconcile this with what we learned in the probability section? This is an important question. When we talk about the probability that something will happen, we are saying that something is likely or not likely to occur based on what happens over a number of different times. We refer to these "number of different times" as trials or more specifically Bernoulli trials, named after Jacob Bernoulli. For example, suppose you ran a 10 km race 10 times in six months and in 8 of the 10 times, you did so in under 50 minutes. The next time you run that race, all things being equal, you can say that based on previous experience it is likely that you will run the race in under 50 minutes.

## For Your Information

In Figure 4.11, we simulated what the percentage of heads might be if we were to flip the coin 1,000 times. The numbers of coin tosses (trials) are on the x-axis, while the mean percentage of time the coin landed on heads is on the y-axis. The dashed line highlights where the 50 percent point is on the y-axis and the solid line represents the cumulative average after each trial. After 50 trials, the coin landed on heads approximately 55 percent of the time. After approximately 600 trials, the cumulative average is pretty much 50 percent. Based on the 1,000 trials, the coin landed just as our formula predicted it would, 50 percent heads and 50 percent tails. We refer to this effect as the Law of Large Numbers.

**FIGURE 4.11** **1,000 Coin Toss Results**

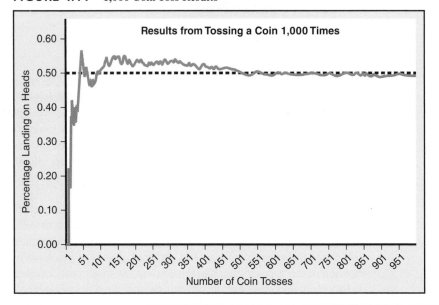

While we still haven't graphed probability distributions, we've just covered one of the main concepts you need to understand probability and, as you will soon see, the normal curve. That is that probability distributions are based on what is likely or not likely to occur over an infinite number of trials. Consider the coin toss results in Figure 4.10. If those are the potential results (frequency distribution) from flipping the coin 10 times—potential because it could be different results for the next 10—then what might a frequency distribution look like over an increasing number of different trials. Let's look at six different examples to find out. Each of the examples in Figures 4.12 and 4.13 has a set number of trials. Each trial represents the results of 10 coin tosses. The x-axis is the number (and percentage) of

**FIGURE 4.12**    **Coin Toss Trials**

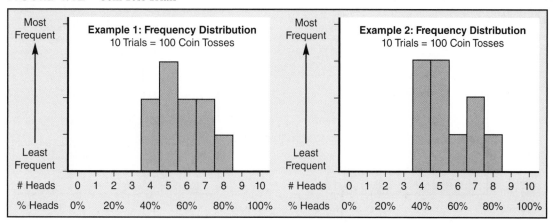

heads per trial, while the *y*-axis is the frequency labelled from least frequent to most frequent.

We'll use Figure 4.12 Example 1 as training for how these trials work. In this example, there were 10 trials of 10 coin tosses and the most frequent result was that 50 percent of the time, the coin landed on heads. In other words, across the 10 trials, the most frequent results were five heads out of 10 tosses per trial. This may seem to be an odd way of testing how frequently the coin will land on heads. Why not just toss the coin 100 times and count the number of heads? If we did that, we would not be able to examine the distribution of possible outcomes and their likelihood over time. We would simply have one column that would sit at approximately 50 percent, telling us that 50 percent of the time the coin will land on heads. But how likely is it that 30 percent of the time or 70 percent of the time the coin will land on heads? Running these trials provides us a means of looking at these possibilities using a frequency distribution with empirical data. Furthermore, you will see that our empirical data is similar to what a probability distribution would predict.

Figure 4.12 Example 2 is much like the previous example in that it had 100 trials, but the outcome was, not surprisingly, slightly different. In this example, the most frequent results were four heads and six tails (four out of 10) and five heads and five tails (five out of 10). Example 2 is here for two reasons. The first is to show you that given the same number of trials and tosses per trial the results can differ. The second is to show you how the distributions of these frequencies take shape as the number of trials increase. Looking at Figure 4.13 Examples 3, 4, 5, and 6, you can see that the shape of the distribution changes slightly and becomes more bell-shaped as we increase the number trials. We can see that on average, the coin lands on heads 50 percent of the time and the pattern of all heads or all tails evens out.

Over time, and many trials, our frequency distribution starts to look like a probability distribution. This makes sense because a probability distribution is simply a frequency distribution with an infinite number of trials.

**FIGURE 4.13    Coin Toss Trials**

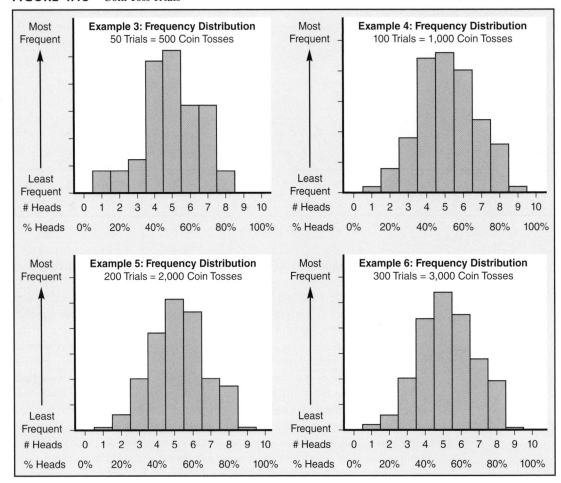

## Conclusion

Probability theory provides us with the ability to estimate the chances of events occurring. In this chapter we considered probability problems involving simple probability, mutually exclusive and non-mutually exclusive probability, and dependent and independent events. Perhaps the most important part of this chapter is the discussion of how probability theory helps us to create probability distributions. Probability distributions are based on what is likely or not likely to occur over an infinite number of trials. Over an infinite number of trials the distribution of probabilities begins to look like a bell-shaped curve. In the next chapter we will discuss a common probability distribution called the normal distribution, more frequently termed the normal curve. Keep in mind the bell shaped distribution in Figure 4.13 Example 6 and how increasing the number of trials creates its shape.

| Key Chapter Concepts and Terms | | |
| --- | --- | --- |
| Experiment, 106 | Probability, 107 | Frequency |
| Random outcome, 106 | Sample space, 107 | distribution, 119 |
| Random | Complement of an | Empirical data, 119 |
| experiment, 106 | event, 107 | Probability |
| Event, 107 | Distribution, 118 | distribution, 119 |

**Frequently Asked Questions**

1. What is the difference between mutually exclusive and independent events?

   Consider families with two children. We shall assume that the probability of having a boy in the family is 0.5 and similarly the probability of a girl is 0.5. Let A be the event that there are two girls and B be the event that there are two boys. The events A and B cannot occur together in a family with two children. So they are mutually exclusive events. P(A and B) = 0.

   On the other hand if we let A be the event that the first child is a boy and B be the event the second child is a boy, then P(A) = 0.5 and P(B) = 0.5. They are independent events as P(A and B) = P(A) P(B) = 0.5 × 0.5 = 0.25. The sex of the first child has no effect on the sex of the second child. So they are independent events.

2. What is the complement of an event?

   If I have two children and A is the event of two boys, then P(A) = 0.25. The complement of A consists of all those outcomes that are not two boys. In other words, it is the event of at least one girl. Also, if A occurs with probability 0.25, then it does not occur with probability 1 − 0.25 = 0.75. In general, $P(A^c) = 1 - P(A)$.

3. What is a probability distribution?

   If we could repeat an experiment a large number of times the probability distribution would be the proportion of times outcome occurs. It is a theoretical frequency distribution. If I roll a six-sided die, each number (one to six) occurs one out of six times. The interpretation of this distribution of the outcomes is that if I rolled the die a million times, each of the numbers (one to six) occurs with a relative frequency of approximately one out of six.

4. Are the outcomes referred to by a probability distribution always numbers?

   Yes. A probability distribution is always referred to as the probability of obtaining a number such as a one or a six. For example, a theoretical frequency distribution for the outcomes of rolling two dice (ranging from 2 to 12) would show that we could expect to roll a seven 16.6 percent ($6 \div 36 = 0.166$) of the time.

5. How do I calculate the probability of complicated events such as A or B?

Sometimes it is easier to just count all of the outcomes in the event and divide by the total number of possible outcomes. However, if we can calculate P(A), P(B), and P(A and B) then we can use the formula P(A or B) = P(A) + P(B) − P(A and B). The formula and method you use depends on the question you are trying to answer and the information that you have.

## Research Example:

In 2001, Drs. Montmarquette, Mahseredjian, and Houle, of the University of Montreal, published their study "The Determinants of University Dropouts" in the journal *Economics of Education Review*. The purpose of their research was to investigate how 14 different variables influence student decisions to continue or drop out of university within their first year. Their sample consisted of 3,418 undergraduate students from the University of Montreal. Their results included the following:

1. Students in university programs that had an entrance quota were more likely than others to continue their studies.
2. Students whose hometowns were further away from Montreal had a higher probability of dropping out of their program.
3. Younger students had a higher probability of remaining in their program than older students.
4. Students with larger class sizes were more likely to drop out of university than those with smaller class sizes.[7]

## Research Example Questions:

**Question 1:** The researchers provided the tree diagram in Figure 4.14, outlining the decisions of the 3,418 students. Use the diagram to calculate:

a) the probability that a student will still be in his or her program after the first semester

b) the probability that a student will still be in the program after the second semester

**FIGURE 4.14**
**Tree Diagram**

Source: C. Montmarquette, S. Mahseredjian, and R. Houle (2001). "The determinants of university dropouts: A bivariate probability model with sample selection." *Economics of Education Review,* 20, 475–484.

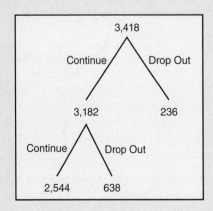

**Question 2:** Consider the students who continued into the second semester. Calculate the probability that a student who has entered the second semester will continue their university studies.

**Research Example Answers:**

**Question 1:** The researchers provided the tree diagram in Figure 4.14 outlining the decisions of the 3,418 students. Use the diagram to calculate:

a) The probability that a student will still be in his or her program after the first semester

$$P(A) = \frac{s}{n} \qquad\qquad (4.8)$$

Using the formula above to calculate the probability, $s$ is the total number of ways we can select a student who is still in the program after the first semester, and $n$ is the total number of possible outcomes. Given that $s = 3,182$ and $n = 3,418$, there is a 93.1 percent probability ($3,182 \div 3,418 = 0.931$) that a student who begins a program will still be enrolled in the program after the first semester.

Remember that: $1 = P(A) + P(A^c)$

Therefore:      $1 = 0.931 + 0.069$

The probability that a student is still in the program is 0.931 and the probability a student has dropped out of the program ($A^c$) is 0.069.

**FIGURE 4.15**

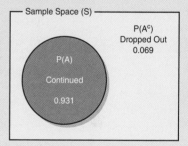

b) The probability that a student will still be in the program after the second semester

$$P(A) = \frac{s}{n} \qquad\qquad (4.9)$$

Similar to the previous question, we need to use the formula above to calculate the probability. Here $s$ is the total number of ways we can select a student who is still in the program after the second semester, and $n$ is the total number of possible outcomes. Given that $s = 2,544$ and $n = 3,418$, there is a 74.4 percent probability ($2,544 \div 3,418 = 0.744.$) that a student who begins a program will still be enrolled in the program after the second semester. The complement ($A^c$) is now $1 - 0.744 = 0.256$. So we can also say there is a 0.256 probability (25.6 percent) that a student will drop out of university by the end of the second semester.

**Question 2:** Consider the students who continued into the second semester. Calculate the probability that a student who has entered the second semester will continue their university studies.

We restrict our attention now to those students who continued into the second semester. Of the 3,182 students in university, 2,544 continue. So we apply the basic rule:

$$P(A) = \frac{s}{n}$$

$$= \frac{2,544}{3,182} = 0.80$$

Therefore, there is an 80 percent probability that a student who continued into the second semester will continue at university.

**ANSWERS TO EXERCISE 4.1**

One hundred people were asked about the number of jobs and the number of residences they had over the last two years; all had at least one job. To calculate the probability of each outcome in the table below, we divide the number of people in each particular event by the total number of people ($n = 100$).

| Outcome | Count | Probability |
|---|---|---|
| One job and one residence | 20 | $20 \div 100 = 0.20$ |
| One job and more than one residence | 10 | 0.10 |
| More than one job but only one residence | 10 | 0.10 |
| More than one job and more than one residence | 60 | 0.60 |
| Total | 100 | 1.00 |

Assuming that we randomly choose one person from the previous table, answer the following questions.

| Question | Answer |
|---|---|
| 1. What is the probability of having one residence? | $0.20 + 0.10 = 0.30$ |
| 2. What is the probability of having more than one job? | $0.60 + 0.10 = 0.70$ |
| 3. What is the probability of having more than one job or more than one residence? | $0.70 + 0.70 - 0.60 = 0.80$ |
| 4. What is the probability that an individual who had only one job will also have had only one residence in the two years? | $20 \div 30 = 0.67$ |

The probabilities in the previous table are calculated as follows:

1. Add the probabilities together: 0.20 + 0.10 = 0.30 (30%)
2. Add the probabilities together: 0.60 + 0.10 = 0.70 (70%)
3. There are two ways to calculate the probability of have more than one job or more than one residence:
   - Add the probabilities of the outcomes comprising the event of more than one job or more than one residence: 0.10 + 0.10 + 0.60 = 0.80 (80%)
   - Calculate the probability as P(more than one job) + P(more than one residence) − P(more than one job and more than one residence) = (0.10 + 0.60) + (0.10 + 0.60) − 0.60 = 0.80 (80%)
4. We know that there are 30 people who had one residence. Of the 30, 20 had only one job and 10 had more than one job. The probability of having only one job and one residence in the two year period is: 20 ÷ 30 = 0.67 (67%)

## Problems

1. When a card is selected from a deck, find the probability of getting a:
   a. heart
   b. face card or a spade
   c. two of spades
   d. a queen

2. At a clothing store, the managers found that 16 women bought white pants, four bought red pants, three bought blue pants, and seven bought yellow pants. If a customer is selected at random, find the probability that she bought:
   a. blue pants
   b. yellow or red pants
   c. white or yellow or blue pants
   d. pants that were not red

3. A vaccine for chickenpox has a 0.9 probability of being effective. The probability of getting chickenpox if a person is not vaccinated is 0.50. In Toronto, 25 percent of the children get vaccinated. If a child is selected at random, find the probability that he or she will contract the disease.

# Appendix

# Counting and the Lottery

Calculating the probability of winning a lottery prize requires counting all of the possible outcomes. However, since counting all of them would be tedious, we can use more sophisticated methods to make our life easier. In fact, most scientific calculators have a "Choose" button that will do the calculations for you.

Suppose you had three numbers 1, 2, and 3, and were asked to randomly choose two of them. If the order of the numbers mattered then the possible combinations of two would be:

$$(1,2), (2,1), (1,3), (3,1), (2,3), \text{ and } (3,2)$$

However, if the order of the numbers did not matter (for example, you considered (1,2) and (2,1) as being the same choice), then there are only three distinct sets of outcomes that you could have:

$$(1,2), (1,3), \text{ and } (2,3)$$

We can write this type of combination using the choice notation ($C_2^3$), which is read as "choose a combination of 2 out of the 3 possible." The formula for choosing $r$ numbers (or objects) from a total of $n$ possible numbers (or objects) is:

$$\frac{n!}{r!(n-r)!}$$

The exclamation mark (!) refers to the factorial operation. In our previous example, we would have:

$$C_2^3 = \frac{n!}{r!(n-r)!} = \frac{3!}{2!(3-2)!} = \frac{3!}{3!(1)!} = \frac{3 \times 2 \times 1}{(2 \times 1) \times (1 \times 1)} = \frac{3}{1} = 3$$

Considering Lotto 6/49, if we wanted to count how many ways to pick six numbers out of 49 (1 to 49), we would get:

$$C_6^{49} = \frac{n!}{r!(n-r)!} = \frac{49!}{6!(49-6)!} = \frac{49 \times 48 \times 47 \times 46 \times 45 \times 44}{6 \times 5 \times 4 \times 3 \times 2 \times 1}$$

$$= 13{,}983{,}816$$

Note: The 43! in the denominator cancels out everything from 43 down (43 × 42 × ... × 2 × 1) in the numerator, which makes our calculation easier.

Therefore, if you buy one ticket, you have one chance in approximately 14 million to win.

# Appendix B

# Binomial Experiments

Have you ever had someone come up to you with their hands behind their back and say "pick the left hand or right hand"? Well, imagine that your friend is holding a coupon for a free coffee in one hand and nothing in the other. Faced with two options—pick the left hand or the right—you ponder which to choose. Believe it or not, the proportion of the time that the coupon will be in the left hand (or the right hand) follows a binomial distribution.

Let's look at an example of a binomial experiment where we will assume that there is a 50 percent probability that the coupon is in the right hand. As part of the experiment, you observe your friend offering the coupon to two people (John and Jane) in the same manner as above. There are four possible combined choices that John and Jane could make. For simplicity, we'll denote choosing the left hand as L and the right hand as R. The possible outcomes are:

$$(L,L), (L,R), (R,L), \text{ and } (R,R)$$

The first response in the pair corresponds to John, and the second response corresponds to Jane. Since each of these four outcomes is equally likely, the probability of each outcome is $1 \div 4 = 0.25$. If we just looked at the number of times the right hand was chosen, we could summarize these as follows:

| Outcomes | Number of R | Probability |
|----------|-------------|-------------|
| (L,L) | 0 | 0.25 |
| (L,R) | 1 | 0.25 |
| (R,L) | 1 | 0.25 |
| (R,R) | 2 | 0.25 |

Since we are not really interested in the pairs of outcomes, we can combine the number of times that the right hand could have been chosen. So P(right hand is not chosen) = 0.25, P(the right hand was chosen once) = 0.25 + 0.25 = 0.50, and P(the right hand was chosen twice) = 0.25.

| # of R | Probability of R |
|--------|------------------|
| 0 | 0.25 |
| 1 | 0.50 |
| 2 | 0.25 |
| Total | 1.00 |

So, there is a 25 percent probability that neither John nor Jane would select the right hand, a 50 percent chance that either John or Jane would select the right hand, and a 25 percent chance that both would select the right hand.

This seems simple enough, but what if the probability of your friend putting the coupon in his right has was something other than 50 percent? For example, what if it was 40 percent? If we say that $p$ represents the probability of the coupon being in the right hand, then $1 - p$ must be the probability of the coupon being in the left hand. Similar to our last calculation, the probability of John and Jane both picking the right hand is $p \times p$, or $p^2$. Therefore, our previous table of outcomes becomes:

| Outcomes | Number of R | Probability |
|----------|-------------|-------------|
| (L,L) | 0 | $(1 - p)^2$ |
| (L,R) | 1 | $p(1 - p)$ |
| (R,L) | 1 | $p(1 - p)$ |
| (R,R) | 2 | $p^2$ |

Again, since we are not really interested in the pairs of outcomes, we can combine the number of times that the right hand could have been chosen.

| # of R | Probability of R |
|--------|------------------|
| 0 | $(1 - p)^2$ |
| 1 | $2p(1 - p)$ |
| 2 | $p^2$ |
| Total | 1.00 |

Therefore, if $p = 0.40$, there is a 36 percent probability that neither John nor Jane would select the right hand, a 48 percent chance that either John or Jane would select the right hand, and a 16 percent chance that both would select the right hand.

In general, if we sample $n$ people and count the number of people who chose one of two options (say, $x$ versus $y$) and the probability of choosing $x$ is $p$, then the probability of choosing $x$, is given by the formula:

$$p(x) = C_x^n \times p^x \times (1 - p)^{n - x}$$

When considering what constitutes a binomial experiment, there are three assumptions that must be met:

1. The probability of an $x$ response is $p$ for each individual.
2. Each individual is independent of one another.
3. There are $n$ subjects.

# The Normal Curve

5

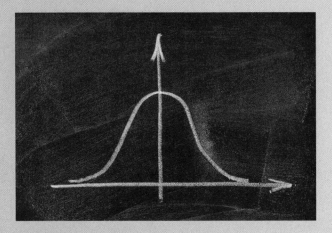

**Learning Objectives:**

By the end of this chapter you should be able to:

1. Identify why a probability distribution is a theoretical distribution.
2. Explain the concept of the normal curve and its importance.
3. Describe the areas under the normal curve.
4. Transform raw scores to standardized scores ($z$-scores) and percentiles.
5. Find the area(s) under the normal curve using Appendix A: Area Under the Normal Curve.
6. Draw inferences based on $z$-scores.
7. Transform $z$-scores to raw scores.
8. Transform percentiles to $z$-scores to raw scores.

### Johann Carl Friedrich Gauss (1777–1885)

Gauss was a mathematician who spent his life researching a wide range of areas. He received a stipend from the Duke of Brunswick to pursue these interests. He worked in algebra, geometry, numerical approximations, astronomy, physics, and special functions. Until 1817, Gauss spent his time on astronomy as a director of an observatory in Gottingen. While measuring the planets' orbits, he noticed that his calculations often had slight measurement errors. He therefore needed a way to fit theoretical models to data with errors. Gauss is credited with the theorem, now called the Gauss-Markov theorem, that shows an optimum way of drawing a line through a scatter plot of data points by using a least-squares method. In justifying this method he used the normal curve, which is often called the Gaussian distribution.

Gauss is credited with many important discoveries on a wide range of subjects, which probably explains why his portrait appeared on money and postage stamps.[1]

## Introduction

In the last chapter we discussed probability theory. Probability theory helps us to understand events with random outcomes that cannot be predicted with certainty. We concluded that chapter with a discussion of how to graph a probability distribution. The primary goal of this chapter is to show you how probability theory fits in with one of statistics' most important probability distributions, the normal curve.

## The Normal Curve

A **normal curve** is a theoretical probability distribution that has a symmetrical bell shape.

One of the most important probability distributions in statistics is the **normal curve**. The normal curve is actually a family of different distributions, but for our purposes we only need to focus on why the normal curve is so important to social scientists. You may hear others refer to this distribution as the bell curve, the normal distribution, or the Gaussian distribution, but we'll use the name normal curve here to keep things consistent. Figure 5.1 provides an example of the normal curve.

Does this shape look familiar? Think back to our coin toss trials where we found that as we increased the number of trials, the distribution of the results started to form a bell shape. Now look at Figure 5.2, where a normal curve overlaps the final coin toss results. As you can see, the frequency distribution (the columns), generally fits the pattern of the normal curve.

This is the basic mechanics behind the normal curve except that instead of going to the trouble of conducting a lot of research and gathering a lot of data, we can use

**LO1**

**FIGURE 5.1**
**The Normal Curve**

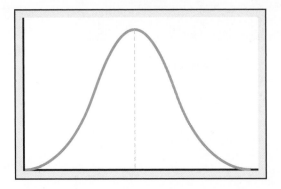

a mathematical formula (referred to as a mathematical function) to create it. We re-fer to the normal curve as a theoretical distribution because it is not based on empir-ical data (refer to the frequency distribution definition) but rather on probability theory (refer to the probability distribution definition), as it is meant to predict what may occur in the population rather than in a sample taken from the population.

This leads us to an important note before we move on. In chapter 1 we said that a population is the total number of individuals, objects, or items that you are interested in and that a sample is a subset of the population. An example of a population is the examination of work-related stress in all Canadians between the ages of 35 and 45. Since we can't survey all of the possible respondents in that population, we take a sample of 300 people and after gathering data, we use statistical analysis to draw reasonable conclusions about the population. We have two key groups here: the

**FIGURE 5.2**
**A Normal Curve Overlapped on a Histogram**

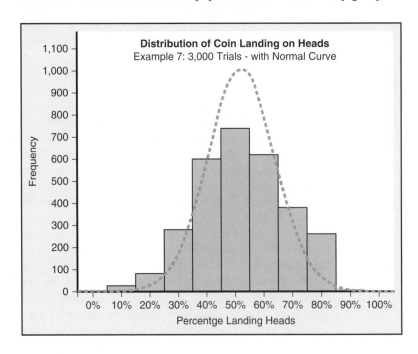

## For Your Information

Although we may not be aware of it, we think about the normal curve in our everyday lives. Many of us have likely used the Internet for one reason or another and thought that it was unusually slow at a particular time. We intuitively have an understanding (right or wrong) of the average speed we can expect from an Internet connection and know when it is performing above or below average. In this sense, we are considering a distribution of the speed of the Internet connection.

The normal curve is remarkable in its applicability to everyday life in both the social and natural sciences. Here are some interesting examples of the normal distribution in nature:

1. The spreading of diseases in cattle, such as bovine tuberculosis, appears to follow a normal distribution.*

2. Prostate-specific antigen values of healthy males between the ages of 50 and 60 follow a normal distribution.**

3. The gestation time for non-problematic pregnancies is approximately normally distributed.**

4. The length of the legs and bodies of fire-bellied toads follow a normal distribution.***

5. Many other natural phenomena have traits that follow a normal distribution, such as weight of tomatoes, height of humans, foot size, tree height and width, etc.**, ***

**Source:**
* Karo et al., "Mycobaterium bovis shedding patterns from experimentally infected calves and the effect of concurrent infection with bovine viral diarrhea virus," *Journal of the Royal Society: Interface,* 4, no. 14, (2007), pp. 545–551.

** Gerstman, *Basic Biostatistics: Statistics for Public Health Practice,* 2008. Jones and Bartlett Publishers, Inc.

*** Barton et al, *Evolution.* (Cold Spring Harbor, New York: Cold Spring, 2007.)

**Population mean** uses the symbol $\mu$, which is pronounced "mu."

**Population standard deviation** uses the symbol $\sigma$, which is pronounced "sigma."

**Population variance** uses the symbol $\sigma^2$, which is pronounced "sigma squared."

population and the sample. In chapter 3 you learned that the $\bar{x}$ (pronounced 'x bar') was the symbol for the mean, $s$ for standard deviation, and $s^2$ for variance. These describe the mean, standard deviation, and variance for a set of empirical (real) data gathered from a sample of the population. When we talk about the normal curve, we are referring to what may theoretically happen in the population rather than just a sample of the population. Therefore, when referring to the population we use the symbol $\mu$ (mu) for the **mean**, $\sigma$ for the **standard deviation**, and $\sigma^2$ for the **variance**.

As it turns out, a great number of variables in which social scientists are interested (such as test scores, recidivism rates, height, intelligence quotient (IQ) scores, mortgage default rates, etc.) fit the normal curve. Of course not all variables fit the normal curve perfectly. For example, income rarely fits as it tends to be positively skewed due to the disproportionate number of individuals at the lower to middle area of the income range.

While some variables don't fit perfectly, they are close enough that we can use the normal curve to make statistical inferences (i.e., statements) about real empirical data. We will take a look at the classic example of IQ scores, but first we need to fill in a bit more detail about the areas under the normal curve. This requires you to integrate your understanding of measures of central tendency (mean, median, and mode) and dispersion (standard deviation and variance), so if you need to, go back to chapter 3 to review these areas before moving on.

**FIGURE 5.3**
**Normal Curve with a**
**Mean and Standard**
**Deviations**

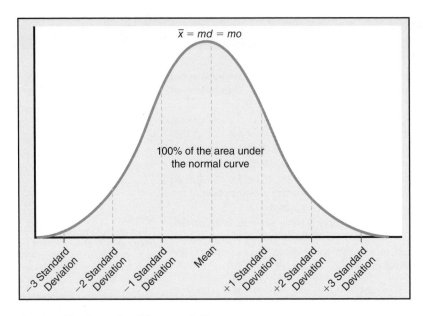

**FIGURE 5.3**
**Normal Curve with a Mean and Standard Deviations**

**LO2** **LO3**

## Areas Under the Normal Curve

The area under a normal curve represents 100 percent of the cases or possible outcomes. So just like the frequency distribution in Figure 5.1 we see that the highest frequency is around the mean value. Just like a frequency distribution, the normal curve also has mean ($\bar{x}$), median (*md*), and mode (*mo*). Fifty percent of the area under the normal curve falls to the right of the mean (positive) and 50 percent falls to the left of the mean (negative). The normal curve has a symmetrical shape where the mean, median, and mode (one mode or uni-modal) are all equal and represent the single maximum point of the curve. The normal curve can also be separated by standard deviations. Figure 5.3 provides an example of a normal curve with the mean and standard deviations included.

**Note:** Often, the notation *md* is used to represent the median, and *mo* to represent the mode.

We represent the population mean with the symbol $\mu$, the population standard deviation with the symbol $\sigma$, and the population variance with the symbol $\sigma^2$. Given that we have 100 percent of the cases of a variable under the normal curve, we use standard deviations to determine what percentage of cases will fall above or below the mean. We can also tell what percentages fall between specific standard deviations. In fact, as we will see later on, we can be precise about the probability that a case will occur at a given point under the normal curve. This curve is the basis upon which we conduct many of the statistical tests that we will learn about later. For now though, let's examine the normal curve in a bit more detail.

Figure 5.4 shows the normal curve with the population mean ($\mu$) and plus/minus three standard deviations ($\sigma$). We can see that 47.72 percent of the cases fall within two standard deviations from the mean and 49.87 percent of the cases fall within three standard deviations from the mean.

**FIGURE 5.4**
**Normal Curve and Areas Under the Curve**

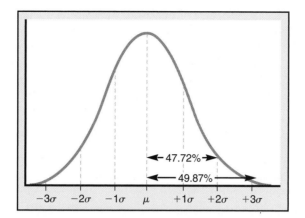

Figure 5.5 provides even more detail. Here we can see the following:

a) 68.26 percent of the area under the normal curve falls between $-1\sigma$ and $+1\sigma$ (34.13 percent on either side of the mean).

b) 95.44 percent of the area falls between $-2\sigma$ and $+2\sigma$ (47.72 percent on either side of the mean)

c) 99.74 percent of the area falls within $-3\sigma$ and $+3\sigma$ (49.87 percent on either side of the mean)

d) 99.99 percent of the area falls within $-4\sigma$ and $+4\sigma$ (49.99 percent on either side of the mean)

Just as a technical note, you will notice that Figure 5.5 includes $\pm 4\sigma$, whereas Figure 5.4 included only $\pm 3\sigma$. The curve theoretically goes for a plus and minus infinite number of standard deviations along the *x*-axis. You may also notice that

**FIGURE 5.5**
**Normal Curve and Areas Under the Curve**

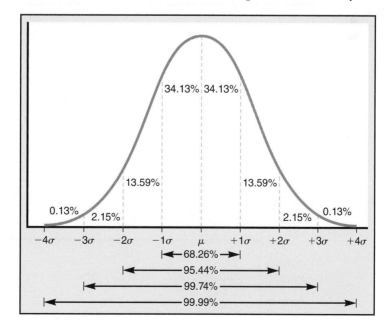

the percentages of area on either side of the mean in Figure 5.5 add to 50 percent. At four standard deviations from the mean, the area covered under the normal curve is actually 0.49997 and the additional 0.00003 is past four standard deviations. Given this is such a small amount, the convention is to round up the 0.49997 to 0.50 at four standard deviations from the mean. You will usually see a normal curve with either $\pm 3$ or $\pm 4$ standard deviations.

| EXERCISE 5.1 | Referring to Figure 5.5, try this exercise. Answers are at the end of the chapter. |
| --- | --- |

**Questions**

What percentage of area is between $+1\sigma$ and $+2\sigma$?

What percentage of area is between $-3\sigma$ and $-2\sigma$?

What percentage of area is $\leq +1\sigma$?

What percentage of area is $\geq -2\sigma$ and $\leq +1\sigma$?

Since we know the proportions of area under the normal curve, we can also calculate the percentiles. The percentiles are simply the cumulative percentages (see Figure 5.6). So $-2\sigma$ is the 2.28th percentile, $+1\sigma$ is the 84.13th percentile, and so on. The following example covers these concepts in more detail.

**Example: IQ Scores** Here is real example that provides a useful way of understanding the normal curve. An IQ score is considered by many to be a measure of an individual's mental intelligence. The distribution of IQ scores follows a normal curve

**FIGURE 5.6**
**Normal Curve with Percentiles**

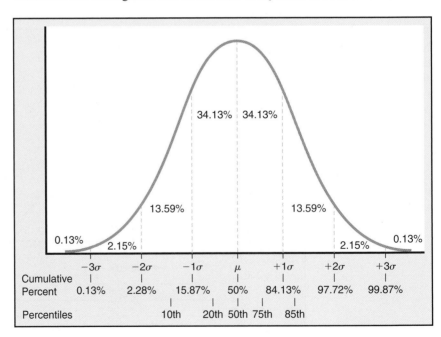

**FIGURE 5.7**
Normal Curve
with Cumulative
Percentages

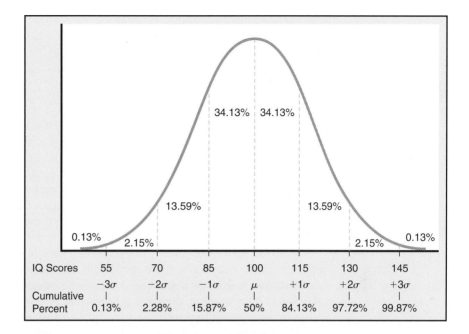

quite closely, and is considered to have a population mean ($\mu$) of 100 with a population standard deviation ($\sigma$) of 15 points. Figure 5.7 displays the distribution of IQ scores along with the standard deviations and cumulative percentages (percentiles).

Looking at Figure 5.7, how might we interpret this information? Suppose we randomly selected 100 individuals from the population and did not have access to their IQ scores. Based on the normal curve we could make the following inferences:

a) We would likely find that approximately 68 individuals (68.2 percent) have an IQ score ranging from 85 to 115.

b) It is likely that only two individuals (2.28 percent) have an IQ score of 70 or less ($-2$ standard deviations from the mean) and similarly it is likely that only two individuals (2.28 percent) have an IQ of 130 or more (2 standard deviations from the mean).

c) An individual with an IQ score of 130 is in the 97th percentile (97.72 percent), meaning that his or her score is higher than 97.72 percent of the group.

There are a number of other inferences we could make, but these will do for now. Now imagine that you have an IQ of 122 and want to know how you compare against the population. Your score is between 115 and 130. We know that it is likely that only 13.59 percent of the population fall within that range, so you are part small group of individuals. We could even say that being in at least the 84th percentile (your score is higher than 84.13 percent of the group) your IQ score is not only higher than average, but is fairly rare because only 15.87 percent (percentage under the normal curve with scores $\geq$ 115) of the population tend to have an IQ score above 115.

By now you're probably wondering how we determine the exact percentages of area under the normal curve when the standard deviation is not a whole number like 1 or 2 standard deviations. For example, what do we do if we want to know exactly how many standard deviations an IQ score of 122 is? To answer that, we need to discuss standardized scores.

**LO4**

A **raw score** is the natural unit of measurement for a variable.

## Standardized Scores

So far we have focused on the raw scores of variables. A **raw score** is the observed score of a variable, measured by its natural unit of measurement. For example, when we want to measure height, we use inches, centimetres, feet, etc. These units of measure are all measuring height, but in different units. So when we say John is six feet tall and Jane is 1.7526 metres tall, we are measuring the variable height as a raw score. One problem with raw scores is that when variables are measured in different units, it becomes a bit difficult to compare them. For example, if you want to compare the height of John and Jane you first have to convert either six feet into metres (1.8288 metres) or 1.7526 metres into feet (5 feet 9 inches).

We can use the normal curve to determine the extent to which a particular case differs from the mean score. More specifically, how many standard deviations a particular case is from the mean. Using raw scores, we might say that an IQ score of 115 is 15 IQ points from the mean. A score of 85 is also 15 IQ points the mean. When we use standardized scores (also called *z*-scores) we convert the raw score unit of measurement into the number of standard deviations that score is from the mean. So, a **standardized score** is a raw score that has been converted into the number of standard deviations that the score is from its mean. We use the terms standardized score and *z*-score interchangeably; this may be a bit confusing but they mean exactly the same thing. As you will see, we call it a *z*-score because the formula creates a *z*-value, but we call it a standardized score because we are creating a score that is measured in standard deviations. The value in doing this is that we can now compare any variable or case because it has been transformed into the same unit of measurement.

A **standardized score** (*z*-score) is a raw score that has been converted into the number of standard deviations that score is from its mean.

To transform a raw score to a *z*-score (a standardized score) we use the following formula:

$$z = \frac{x - \mu}{\sigma} \tag{5.2}$$

where: $z$ is the standardized score (also referred to as the *z*-score)

$x$ is any score along the *x*-axis that you want to convert

$\mu$ is the mean value of all of the scores

$\sigma$ is the standard deviation

As an example, suppose you want to calculate the *z*-score for $+2$ standard deviations. With IQ scores the population mean ($\mu$) is 100 and the population standard deviation ($\sigma$) is 15.

**First:** Subtract $100(\mu)$ from 130 (value at $+2\sigma$) to get $+30$.

**Second:** Divide $+30$ by the $\sigma$ of 15 to get a *z*-score of 2.

**FIGURE 5.8**   *z*-Scores and the Normal Curve

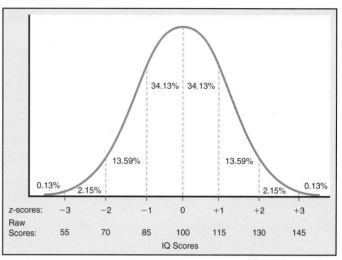

$$z = \frac{x - \mu}{\sigma}$$

a.  $IQ = 55$: $z = \dfrac{55 - 100}{15} = -3$

b.  $IQ = 70$: $z = \dfrac{70 - 100}{15} = -2$

c.  $IQ = 85$: $z = \dfrac{85 - 100}{15} = -1$

d.  $IQ = 100$: $z = \dfrac{100 - 100}{15} = 0$

e.  $IQ = 115$: $z = \dfrac{115 - 100}{15} = +1$

f.  $IQ = 130$: $z = \dfrac{130 - 100}{15} = +2$

g.  $IQ = 145$: $z = \dfrac{145 - 100}{15} = +3$

So a raw score of 130 is equal to a *z*-score of 2. Therefore, a score of 130 is $+2$ standard deviations from the mean ($\mu$).

Figure 5.8 illustrates the transformation of the raw IQ scores in Figure 5.7 to their *z*-scores. Look at the calculations on the left and the *z*-scores on the normal curve on the right. Do you notice how the mean value is now zero? Standardizing the scores creates a common scale from the raw scores, whereby the mean will always equal zero (in other words, it is zero standard deviations away from the mean) and the remaining numbers will express the positive and negative deviations from (or distance from) the mean.

Now let's go back to our previous example where we imagined that you wanted to compare your IQ of 122 to the population. Before we covered *z*-scores, we could only say that your score was between $+1$ and $+2$ standard deviations away from the population mean. Now we can calculate precisely what your standardized score is:

$$z = \frac{x - \mu}{\sigma} = \frac{122 - 100}{15} = 1.47 \qquad \textbf{(5.3)}$$

So we can say that you are $+1.47$ standard deviations from the mean. Since we know your *z*-score for the raw IQ score of 122, we can tell what percentage of people score higher and lower than you. While there is a formula to do this, the easiest way is to look up the values in the table in Appendix A: Area Under the Normal Curve, at the end of the textbook. The table provides the proportion of the area under the normal curve for up to four standard deviations from the mean. Given that the normal curve is symmetric, only the positive *z-values* are shown.

## For Your Information

As you have just seen, the formula for calculating z-scores (standardized scores) is:

$$z = \frac{x - \mu}{\sigma} \qquad \text{[A]}$$

You may find that some textbooks and resources suggest that the population mean ($\mu$) should be replaced with the sample mean ($\bar{x}$) and the population standard deviation ($\sigma$) replaced with the sample standard deviation ($s$). In such cases, the formula for calculating the z-scores (standardized scores) is said to be:

$$z = \frac{x - \bar{x}}{s} \qquad \text{[B]}$$

Quite often, this formula [B] is used to make the material easier for students to understand. When it is used this way, the idea is that the sample mean ($\bar{x}$) and standard deviation ($s$) are meant to be estimates

of the population mean ($\mu$) and standard deviation ($\sigma$) when the population values are not given. However, the proper method for calculating z-scores is as shown here [A]. The reason is that when standardizing scores to create a standard normal distribution, we need to be referring to the population, not the sample. Therefore, the formula must include the population mean ($\mu$) and population standard deviation ($\sigma$).

Formula [B] can be used if you want to create z-scores for your sample data. For example, suppose you converted the mid-term grades for your Canadian Geography class to standardized scores (z-scores). Since you have a sample mean ($\bar{x}$) and standard deviation ($s$), rather than the population mean ($\mu$) and standard deviation ($\sigma$), you use the sample statistics ($\bar{x}$) and ($s$) as estimates of the population parameters ($\mu$ and $\sigma$).

## Did You Know?

Did you know that what is good for men and women can be bad for people? This contradiction is called the Simpson's paradox. Although the issue had been noted as far back as 1903 by famous statisticians, such as Yule, the term itself was coined by Colin Blyth in 1972 based on the 1951 work of Edward Simpson.

Simpson's paradox is important for researchers. It states that if you ignore important factors, such as gender or age, then you can arrive at a completely opposite conclusion. Researchers are often unsure about what factors are important to include and measure in a study, so they need to be careful on reporting their results. Bickel (1975) gives an interesting example of sex discrimination in graduate admissions where, overall, women had lower admission rates than men. However, when the department the women were applying to was factored in, there was no difference in admission rates. The difference arose because women were applying to the more competitive programs, whereas men tended to favour the less competitive programs.

Here is as an illustration of the Simpson's paradox:

Suppose we have two different exercise programs, Program A and Program B, which we are evaluating for their effectiveness in weight loss.

For males, we find that of those in Program A, 20 out 25 (80 percent) lost weight, whereas of those in program B, six out of eight (75 percent) lost weight. So it appears that Program A is better than Program B. For females, we find that of those in Program A, 30 out of 60 (50 percent) lost weight, whereas of those in program B, two out of five (40 percent) lost weight. So once again it appears that Program A is better than Program B.

If we ignored gender and combine the results, we would find that of those in Program A, 50 out of 85 (59 percent ) lost weight, whereas of those in program B, eight out of 13 (62 percent) lost weight. Now, it appears that Program B is better than Program A.

So, what's happening? If you look at the data, a greater proportion of men lost weight compared to women. However, 24 percent of the men were in Program B compared to 14 percent of the women.

So when you ignore gender, we find that Program B is better than Program A simply because more men were assigned to B and overall more men than women lost weight.

The key concept to remember is that ignoring important factors can lead to erroneous conclusions.

**Sources:** G.H. Yule, G. H., "Notes on the theory of association of attributes in Statistics", *Biometrika,* 1903, no. 2 pp. 121–134.

E.H. Simpson, "The interpretation of interaction in contingency tables", *Journal of the Royal Statistical Society* (Series B, 1951), no. 13, pp. 238–241.

C.R. Blyth, "On Simpson's Paradox and the Sure Thing Principle", *Journal of the American Statistical Association,* (1972), no. 67, pp. 364–366.

P.J. Bickel, E.A. Hammel, and J.W. O'Connell, "Sex Bias in Graduate Admissions: Data From Berkeley," *Science,* 187, 4175, pp. 398–404.

**LO5**

## How to Read Appendix A: Area Under the Normal Curve

The table in Appendix A is a standard table found in almost every statistics textbook. This table provides you with the proportion of the area under the normal curve based on the $z$-scores.

We saw in Figure 5.5 that 50 percent of the of the area under the normal curve lies to the left of the mean and 50 percent lies to the right of the mean. We also saw that 0.3413 (34.13 percent) of the area lies between the mean and $+1$ standard deviations, and that 0.3413 (34.13 percent) of the area lies between the mean and $-1$ standard deviations. If you know the $z$-value of a raw score, you can use the table to look up the proportions of the area under the normal curve.

It can take a while to get used to working with the table, so first we will examine how to read the table and then look at the different ways you can use it. Figure 5.9 shows a sample of the table. To read the table, follow these steps:

1. Look down column I until you find the $z$-value you are looking for.
2. Move to the right to column II to find the area between the mean value and the $z$-value.
3. Move right once more to column III to find the area from the $z$-value to the end of the curve.

**FIGURE 5.9**

**Sample of Appendix A: Area Under The Normal Curve**

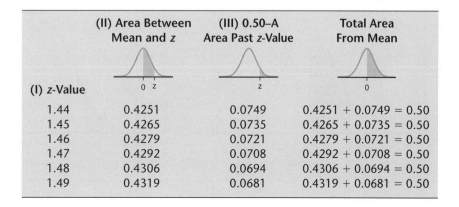

| (I) *z*-Value | (II) Area Between Mean and *z* | (III) 0.50–A Area Past *z*-Value | Total Area From Mean |
|---|---|---|---|
| 1.44 | 0.4251 | 0.0749 | 0.4251 + 0.0749 = 0.50 |
| 1.45 | 0.4265 | 0.0735 | 0.4265 + 0.0735 = 0.50 |
| 1.46 | 0.4279 | 0.0721 | 0.4279 + 0.0721 = 0.50 |
| 1.47 | 0.4292 | 0.0708 | 0.4292 + 0.0708 = 0.50 |
| 1.48 | 0.4306 | 0.0694 | 0.4306 + 0.0694 = 0.50 |
| 1.49 | 0.4319 | 0.0681 | 0.4319 + 0.0681 = 0.50 |

**LO6**

**Example: Reading the Table** We previously found that an IQ score of 122 (where $\mu = 100$ and $\sigma = 15$) has a standardized score ($z$-score) of $+1.47$. Looking at the sample above and the $z$-value 1.47 ($+1.47$ standard deviations from the mean) we can see that 42.92 percent (0.4292 in column II) of the area of the normal curve lies between the mean and the $z$-score of 1.47. Looking at column III we can see that 7.08 percent of the area of the curve lies beyond the $z$-score of 1.47. Suppose your $z$-value is $-1.47$ (IQ score of 78). Use the table exactly the way you would with positive $z$-values—just look up $|-1.47|$ (absolute value of $-1.47 = 1.47$).

In Figure 5.9 you will notice another column titled Total Area From the Mean. This is not included in Appendix A and is here just to illustrate the point that adding the values in column II and III equals 0.50. This is because 50 percent of the area falls to the right of the mean and 50 percent falls to the left of the mean.

To illustrate what Appendix A tells you, look at Figure 5.10. The $z$-value of 1.47 is marked on the $x$-axis and the shaded portions under the normal curve

**FIGURE 5.10** **Areas Under the Normal Curve**

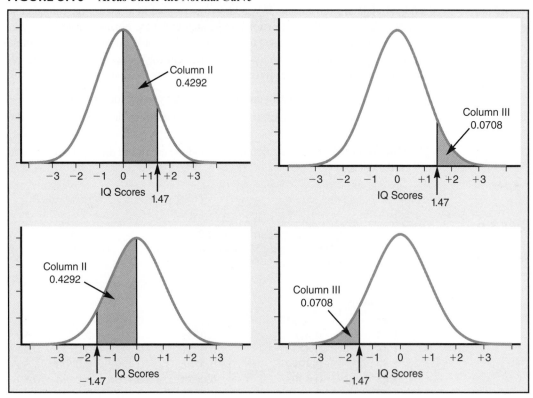

correspond to the columns in Appendix A. For comparison purposes, the z-score of $-1.47$ is also included. What can we infer from this information?

For a z-score of $+1.47$:

- A person with an IQ score of 122 is 1.47 standard deviations above the mean.
- 42.92 percent of the IQ scores fall between 100 and 122.
- 7.08 percent of the IQ scores are greater than 122.
- A person with an IQ score of 122 is in approximately the 93rd percentile ($0.50 + 0.4292 = 0.9292$ rounded).

For a z-score of $-1.47$:

- A person with an IQ score of 78 is 1.47 standard deviations below the mean.
- 42.92 percent of the IQ scores fall between 78 and 100.
- 7.08 percent of the IQ scores are less than 78.
- A person with an IQ score of 78 is in approximately the 43rd percentile (0.4292 rounded).

## Take a Closer Look

### Guide to Standardizing Scores at the Mean ($\mu$) and ± Three Standard Deviations ($\sigma$)

**Step 1:** Find the mean and the standard deviation.

For IQ raw scores, $\mu = 100$ and $\sigma = 15$.

**Step 2:** Chart the values at $-3, -2, -1, +1, +2, +3$ standard deviations.

2.1  Create a chart with two columns and seven rows. Put the raw score mean in the middle row of the first column and the standard deviations going up and down in the column.

**TABLE 5.1**

| Raw Scores | |
|---|---|
| +3 standard deviations | |
| +2 standard deviations | |
| +1 standard deviations | |
| Mean | 100 |
| −1 standard deviations | |
| −2 standard deviations | |
| −3 standard deviations | |

2.2  Calculate the raw scores at each standard deviation by adding or subtracting the standard deviation from the mean as appropriate.

## TABLE 5.2

| Raw Scores | |
|---|---|
| +3 standard deviations | 100 + 15 + 15 + 15 = 145 |
| +2 standard deviations | 100 + 15 +15 = 130 |
| +1 standard deviations | 100 + 15 = 115 |
| Mean | 100 |
| −1 standard deviations | 100 − 15 = 85 |
| −2 standard deviations | 100 − 15 − 15 = 70 |
| −3 standard deviations | 100 − 15 − 15 − 15 = 55 |

2.3 Calculate the standardized scores (*z*-score) for each value in the table.

## TABLE 5.3

| Raw Scores | | z-scores |
|---|---|---|
| +3 standard deviations | 100 + 15 + 15 + 15 = 145 | (145 − 100) ÷ 15 = 3 |
| +2 standard deviations | 100 + 15 +15 = 130 | (130 − 100) ÷ 15 = 2 |
| +1 standard deviations | 100 +15 = 115 | (115 − 100) ÷ 15 = 1 |
| Mean | 100 | (100 − 100) ÷ 15 = 0 |
| −1 standard deviations | 100 − 15 = 85 | (85 − 100) ÷ 15 = −1 |
| −2 standard deviations | 100 − 15 − 15 = 70 | (70 − 100) ÷ 15 = −2 |
| −3 standard deviations | 100 − 15 − 15 − 15 = 55 | (55 − 100) ÷ 15 = −3 |

# Take a Closer Look

### Guide to Calculating Ranges of Area Under the Normal Curve: With Two *z*-values.

We previously covered how to estimate the area under the normal curve when you have one *z*-value (e.g., area from the mean to *z* or area past *z*). But you will often want to estimate a range of area under the normal curve. This guide shows you how to estimate the ranges using the *z*-score formula and Appendix A.

### (1) Estimating a range that crosses the mean

Suppose you want to know the percentage of individuals with IQ scores between 90 and 105. IQ scores have a $\mu$ of 100 and a $\sigma$ of 15. To solve this, you need to:

1. Convert both raw scores to *z*-scores so that you can look up their values in Appendix A.

$$z = \frac{x - \mu}{\sigma} = \frac{90 - 100}{15} = \frac{-10}{15} = -0.67 \quad (5.4)$$

$$z = \frac{x - \mu}{\sigma} = \frac{105 - 100}{15} = \frac{5}{15} = 0.33 \quad (5.5)$$

2. Look up both *z*-values in Appendix A.

For $z = -0.67$, look in column II to find that the area between mean and $z = -0.67$ is 0.2486.

For $z = 0.33$, look in column II to find that the area between mean and $z = 0.33$ is 0.1293.

3. Add to two values together.

Since 0.2486 is the area from −0.67 to 0 and 0.1293 is the area from 0 to 0.33, the sum of the two represent the area between −0.67 and 0.33. Therefore, the area is 0.2486 + 0.1293 = 0.3779.

Figure 5.11 shows that the shaded area equals 0.3779. Approximately 33.79 percent of individuals have an IQ score between 90 and 105.

**FIGURE 5.11**   Areas Under the
Normal Curve

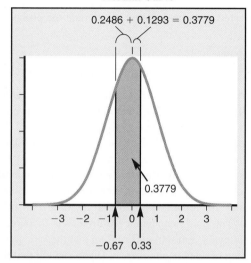

**FIGURE 5.12**   Areas Under the Normal Curve

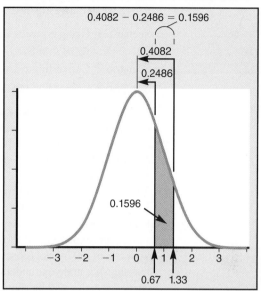

**(2) Estimating a range within one half of the normal curve**

Suppose you want to know the percentage of individuals with IQ scores between 110 and 120. IQ scores have a $\mu$ of 100 and a $\sigma$ of 15. To solve this, you need to:

1. Convert both raw scores to z-scores so that you can look up their values in Appendix A.

$$z = \frac{x - \mu}{\sigma} = \frac{110 - 100}{15} = \frac{10}{15} = 0.67 \text{ (5.6)}$$

$$z = \frac{x - \mu}{\sigma} = \frac{120 - 100}{15} = \frac{20}{15} = 1.33 \text{ (5.7)}$$

2. Look up both z-values in Appendix A.

   For $z = 0.67$, look in column II to find that the area between mean and $z = 0.67$ is 0.2486.

   For $z = 1.33$, look in column II to find that the area between mean and $z = 1.33$ is 0.4082.

3. Subtract the smaller from the larger.

   Since 0.2486 is the area from 0 to 0.67 and 0.4082 is the area from 0 to 1.33, subtracting the smaller area from the larger area gives you the area between 0.67 and 1.33. Therefore, the area is $0.4082 - 0.2486 = 0.1596$.

   Figure 5.12 shows that the shaded area equals 0.1596. Approximately 15.96 percent of individuals have an IQ score between 110 and 120.

# Putting it All Together: Probability and the Normal Curve

So far we have discussed probability, the normal curve, standardized scores (z-scores), and the area under the normal curve. In this section, we extend the use of the normal curve and z-scores to examine probabilities a bit more. The intent here is to tie everything you have learned in this chapter together by looking at three different scenarios and drawing inferences from the normal curve. The scenarios we will investigate are:

Scenario 1: Using *z*-scores (converted from raw scores) to estimate the probability of events.

Scenario 2: Converting *z*-scores to raw scores.

Scenario 3: Converting raw scores to percentiles, and percentiles to raw scores.

For each of these three scenarios, we will use life expectancy at birth values provided by Statistics Canada. [Statistics Canada defines life expectancy at birth as "the number of years a person would be expected to live, on the basis of the mortality statistics for a given observation period."[2] The mean and standard deviation were calculated using the data provided for each of the 10 provinces, from 2005 to 2007. It does not include the Yukon, Northwest Territories, or Nunavut. Figure 5.13 shows the distribution of life expectancies for females (grey) and males (blue). The $\mu$ life expectancy for females is 82.6 years with a $\sigma$ of 0.84 years (approximately 10 months). The $\mu$ life expectancy for males is 77.6 years with a $\sigma$ of 0.97 years (approximately 11.5 months). Based on just these descriptive statistics and your understanding of dispersion (chapter 3) you can tell that the curve for males will be shorter and wider (more dispersed) because it has a larger standard deviation than females. Likewise, since the standard deviation for

**FIGURE 5.13** **Distribution of Male and Female Life Expectancy**

| Male Raw Score | Male z-Score | Female Raw Score | Female z-Score |
|---|---|---|---|
| 80.51 | +3 | 85.12 | +3 |
| 79.54 | +2 | 84.28 | +2 |
| 78.57 | +1 | 83.44 | +1 |
| 77.60 | 0 | 82.60 | 0 |
| 76.63 | −1 | 81.76 | −1 |
| 75.66 | −2 | 80.92 | −2 |
| 74.69 | −3 | 80.08 | −3 |

Adapted from Statistics Canada publication *Life Tables, Canada, Provinces and Territories, 2000 to 2002*, Catalogue 84-537-XIE2006001, http://www.statcan.gc.ca/pub/84-537-x/2006001/4227757-eng.pdf. Date of extraction: May 18, 2011.

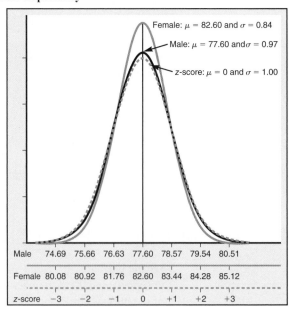

females is less than that for males, the curve for the females should be taller and narrower because there is less dispersion.

In this figure, both curves are shown together so you can visually see the difference of their shape when using raw life expectancy scores rather than standardized $z$-scores. Notice that one standard deviation below the mean for males is 76.63 years, whereas one standard deviation below the mean for females is 81.76 years. As mentioned earlier, when we standardize the scores, it creates a standard shape, which is represented by the grey dotted line. The blue line (males) looks more similar to the dotted grey line ($z$-scores) than the grey line (females) because the standard deviation for males is close to one ($\sigma$ males $= 0.97$).

Based on the previous section, we can immediately infer several things. Given that 68.26 percent of the population falls between $-1\sigma$ and $+1\sigma$, approximately 68 out of every 100 males have a life expectancy between 76.63 and 78.57 years, and approximately 68 out of every 100 females have a life expectancy between 81.76 and 83.44 years. Now let's look at the three scenarios and see how the normal curve can help us make inferences about the population.

## Scenario 1: Using *z*-Scores to Estimate Probability of Events

Given the $z$-score and Appendix A, we can easily estimate the probability of certain life expectancies. Let's look at two examples.

**Scenario 1 Example 1:** What is the probability of a randomly selected female from one of the 10 provinces having a life expectancy of up to 81 years? Consider the solution to this in steps:

**Step 1:** Convert the raw score to a standardized score.

Since this example is giving us a raw value, we first have to transform the value to a $z$-score.

$$z = \frac{x - \mu}{\sigma} = \frac{81 - 82.6}{0.84} = \frac{-1.6}{0.84} = -1.90 \qquad \textbf{(5.8)}$$

**Step 2:** Look up the area past the $z$-value (column III) in Appendix A.

Since this is asking us to find the percentage of females living to the age of 81, we need to find the area under the normal curve left of the $z$-value of $-1.90$. Look up the $z$-value of 1.90 in column I and move over to column III (Area Past the $z$-value) to find the value 0.0287.

**Step 3:** Interpret the meaning of the value of the area under the curve.

The value 0.0287 means that 2.87 percent ($0.0287 \times 100$) of the area of the normal curve lies to the left of the $z$-value $-1.90$. This means that we can expect to find that a randomly selected female from one of the 10 provinces has a 3 in 100 probability (2.87 percent rounded) of living until the age of 81. But think about what you have learned so far about probability. All of the possible life expectancy values are within the sample space (S). The sample space (S) is the sum of the probability of event A (living until age 81) plus the probability of all other outcomes $P(A^c)$ (living past age 81). So if the probability of living until age 81 is approximately 3 in 100 (2.87 rounded) then there is a 97 in 100 probability of living past 81 years of age. To be more precise, we add 0.4713 (Area Between Mean and $z$, column II) and 0.50 (which is the value of the area to the right of the mean) together to get 0.9713.

**Scenario 1 Example 2:** If we were to randomly select 100 males from the 10 provinces of Canada, how many would have a life expectancy between the ages of 78 and 80?

**Step 1:** Convert the raw score to a standardized score.

Again we have to transform the raw score into a $z$-score, but this time we have two raw scores, 78 and 80.

$$z = \frac{x - \mu}{\sigma} = \frac{78 - 77.60}{0.97} = \frac{0.40}{0.97} = 0.41 \qquad \textbf{(5.9)}$$

$$z = \frac{x - \mu}{\sigma} = \frac{80 - 77.60}{0.97} = \frac{2.40}{0.97} = 2.47 \qquad \textbf{(5.10)}$$

**Step 2:** Calculate the area between the two $z$-scores.

This situation is the same as in the Guide to Calculating Ranges of Area Under the Normal Curve. Since we are asked to find the percentage of males with a life expectancy between a range of ages (78 to 80), we first look up the areas between the mean and $z$-score for 78 ($z = 0.41$) and 80 ($z = 2.47$), and then subtract the smaller area from the larger.

Look up the $z$-value of 0.41 in column I and move over to column II (Area Between Mean and $z$) to find the value 0.1591. Look up the $z$-value of 2.47 in column I and move over to column II to find the value 0.4932. Subtract 0.1591 from 0.4932, and you get 0.3341.

**Step 3:** Interpret the meaning of the value of the area under the curve.

The value 0.3341 means that 33.41 percent (0.3341 × 100) of the area of the normal curve lies between a $z$-value of 0.41 (78 years old) and 2.47 (80 years old). So, we can expect to find that approximately 33 out of a random sample of 100 males have a life expectancy between 78 and 80 years of age.

**LO7**

## Scenario 2: Converting *z*-Scores to Raw Scores

Sometimes we need to convert $z$-scores into raw scores. If we want to find the raw score associated with a given $z$-score, then we need to solve for $x$ (raw score) by algebraically manipulating the $z$-score formula as follows:

If $$z = \frac{x - \mu}{\sigma} \qquad \textbf{(5.11)}$$

Then multiplying both sides by the standard deviation ($\sigma$) gives you

$$z\sigma = x - \mu \qquad (5.12)$$

Then, to isolate $x$ add the mean ($\mu$) to both sides to get

$$z\sigma + \mu = x \qquad (5.13)$$

**Scenario 2 Example 1:** What is the life expectancy age of males at $+1.25$ standard deviations and females at $-1.25$ standard deviations? Remember to keep the minus sign in front of negative $z$-scores or else you won't get a raw score less than the mean.
**Step 1:** Convert the $z$-scores into raw scores.
Since we are given the $z$-scores ($+1.25$ for males and $-1.25$ for females) and need to find the raw scores, we use the $z$-score formula to solve for $x$.

**Males:**

$$z\sigma + \mu = x \qquad (5.14)$$
$$(1.25 \times 0.97) + 77.60 = 78.81$$

**Females:**

$$z\sigma + \mu = x \qquad (5.15)$$
$$(-1.25 \times 0.84) + 82.60 = 81.55$$

Note: If you didn't include the negative sign in front of 1.25 in the equation for females, the result is 83.65, which is incorrect.

**Step 2:** Interpret the results.
The life expectancy age of males at $+1.25$ standard deviations is 78.81 years of age. The life expectancy age of females at $-1.25$ standard deviations is 81.55 years of age.

**Scenario 2 Example 2:** What is the range of life expectancy ages for males from 0.50 standard deviations to 1.50 standard deviations?
**Step 1:** Convert the $z$-scores into raw scores.
Again we have to transform the $z$-scores into raw scores, only this time we have two $z$-scores, 0.50 and 1.50. Similar to Example 1, we use the $z$-score formula to solve for both $x$-values.

**Males at 0.50 standard deviations:**

$$z\sigma + \mu = x \qquad (5.16)$$
$$(0.50 \times 0.97) + 77.60 = 78.09$$

**Males at 1.50 standard deviations:**

$$z\sigma + \mu = x \qquad (5.17)$$
$$(1.50 \times 0.97) + 77.60 = 79.06$$

**Step 2:** Interpret the results.
The life expectancy of males with a range of 0.50 standard deviations to 1.50 standard deviations is 78.09 years of age to 79.06 years of age.

LO8

## Scenario 3: Converting Raw Scores to Percentiles and Percentiles to Raw Scores

Sometimes we want to know what percentile a particular raw score falls into. For example, you may have a grade point average that falls in the 90th percentile. Recall that in chapter 3 we discovered how to calculate a percentile based on a given score and how to determine a score at a given percentile. Manually calculating percentiles is not difficult when you have a small number of observations. However, when you are dealing with a larger number of observations, manually calculating percentiles can become time-consuming. Another method of estimating percentiles is to use $z$-scores and Appendix A.

**Scenario 3 Example 1:** If a randomly selected female lived to 84.5 years of age, in what percentile would she be?
**Step 1:** Convert the raw score to a $z$-score.

$$z = \frac{x - \mu}{\sigma} = \frac{84.5 - 82.6}{0.84} = \frac{1.90}{0.84} = 2.26 \qquad \textbf{(5.18)}$$

**Step 2:** Look up the area between the mean and the $z$-score (column II) in Appendix A. 0.4881
Next, calculate the area under the normal curve from the left side ($z = 0.00$) up to the $z$-score of 2.26. According to Appendix A column II, the area between the mean and $z = 2.26$ is 0.4881. Given that the area left of the mean equals 0.50, adding 0.4881 and 0.50 gives you the total area to the left of $z = 2.26$. So 0.4881 + 0.50 = 0.9881.
**Step 3:** Interpret the meaning of the value of the area under the curve.
The value 0.9881 means that a female who lives to 84.5 years of age is in the 99th percentile (0.9881 rounded to 0.99 times 100).

**Scenario 3 Example 2:** What is the minimum age for the top 10 percent of male life expectancy?
This example requires us to (1) convert the percent to a percentile, (2) convert the percentile to the value for the area under the normal curve, (3) convert the area to a $z$-score, (4) convert the $z$-score to a raw score (age), and (5) interpret the results.
**Step 1:** Convert the percent to a percentile.
A male at the minimum value of the top 10 percent is at the 90th percentile ($1.0 - 0.10 = 0.90$).
**Step 2:** Convert the percentile to the area under the normal curve.
The 90th percentile is 0.90 (90 percent) of the area under the normal curve. Since Appendix A only provides area values for half of the normal curve, we need to subtract 0.50. The area under the normal curve to between the mean and 0.90 is 0.40 ($0.90 - 0.50 = .40$).

**Step 3:** Convert the area to a *z*-score.

Looking at Appendix A column II (Area Between Mean and *z*) we find that the closest value to the area of 0.40 is 0.3997. Looking in column I, we see that the *z*-value at 0.3997 is 1.28.

So far we have found that the minimum age for the top 10 percent is equal to a *z*-score of 1.28. We now have to convert the *z*-score to a raw score.

**Step 4:** Convert the *z*-score to a raw score (age).

We did this type of problem in the previous scenario by using the *z*-score formula and solving for *x*. So a *z*-score of 1.28 equals a raw score of 78.84 years of age.

$$z\sigma + \mu = x \qquad \textbf{(5.19)}$$
$$(1.28 \times 0.97) + 77.60 = 78.84$$

**Step 5:** Interpret the results.

If a male is at least 78.84 years old, he will be in the top 10 percent of male life expectancy.

## For Your Information

As another example of how social and natural phenomena seem to follow a normal distribution, the histogram below represents the percentage of homicide victims between the ages of 18 and 24 across 49 states in the U.S. for 2005.

### FIGURE 5.14

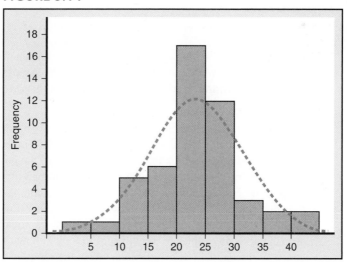

**Source:** Puzzanchera, C. and Kang, W. (2010). "Easy Access to the FBI's Supplementary Homicide Reports: 1980–2008." Online. Available: http://www.ojjdp.gov/ojstatbb/ezashr/. Data source: Federal Bureau of Investigation. Supplementary Homicide Reports 1980–2008 [machine-readable data files].

# Conclusion

The primary goal of this chapter was to provide you with an understanding of the normal curve and how probability theory is related to this theoretical distribution. Probability theory helps us to understand events with random outcomes that cannot be predicted with certainty. That is, it helps us to understand when we could expect to see a specific outcome. We saw at the end of chapter 4 that when we graph probabilities, a specific shape starts to form.

In this chapter, we saw that the probability distribution actually follows a normal curve. Given that the normal curve is a theoretical distribution of probabilities, we can use it to estimate probability in a wide range of phenomena (such as IQ, life expectancy, success of support programs, and product defects) in which we are interested. To use the normal curve we need to understand how to convert raw scores to *z*-scores, and vice versa. Using Appendix A: Area Under the Normal Curve, we can make inferences about what may occur in the population.

As we will see in the next chapter, we can also connect probability and the normal curve to how we take samples from a population. Furthermore, we will start to see how these last two chapters (4 and 5) coupled with the next chapter form the basis of different types of statistical tests.

## Key Chapter Concepts and Terms

Normal curve,  133
Population mean ($\mu$),  135
Population standard
  deviation ($\sigma$),  135

Population variance
  ($\sigma^2$),  135
Raw score,  140

Standardized ($z$)
  score,  140

## Frequently Asked Questions

1. If probability distributions are theoretical does that mean that they are meant to be applied to the whole population and not just the sample? Are they theoretical because they are based on the assumption that the sample is representative of the overall population?

   Probability distributions such as the normal curve (normal distribution) are called theoretical because we use a mathematical formula to determine what the distribution would look like if we could take all the possible combinations of samples into account. The idea behind the probability distribution is that it represents all possible samples that we can use to compare certain values and determine how likely or probable they are in the population. In this chapter, the focus was to introduce the idea of probability distributions and specifically the normal curve. In chapter 6, we will start to look at how to estimate the distribution of the population based on data from the sample. This involves changing the *z* formula to include potential error in the mean value.

2. If $\mu$ and $\sigma$ refer to the theoretical mean and standard deviation of the population (which we can't measure), do they simply represent an average of the means and standard deviations calculated on several samples?

This is topic will be dealt with specifically in chapter 6, but here's an example that answers the question. We rarely know what the values are for the mean and standard deviation in the population, but we can mathematically estimate what those values will be. This is where we get into the concept of sampling (chapter 6). Suppose you have 25 students in a classroom, which represents your population. Now imagine that you want to estimate the mean age of the students but could only base your calculation on samples of five students at a time. You may find that based on the first sample of five students the mean age is 20.1 years. Based on the second sample you may find the average age is 22 years. You have two different mean ages because you haven't sampled everyone in the classroom. However, if you keep sampling in groups of five you can eventually cover all the possible combinations of the sample (in this case there are 118,755 different combinations) and take the mean of all the mean ages from each sample to arrive at the population mean. What is actually happening is that as you increase your sample size, the error in your estimated mean decreases because you are getting closer to the size of the population.

3. If we only measure to four standard deviations from the mean, does that mean that any values that exceed ±4 standard deviations are considered irrelevant?

   Actually, we don't stop at ±4 standard deviations, we are only graphing ±3 or ±4 standard deviations.
   - 49.997 percent of cases fall between the mean and +4 standard deviations;
   - 49.997 percent of the cases fall between the mean and −4 standard deviations;
   - 0.003 percent of the cases fall beyond the +4 standard deviations; and
   - 0.003 percent fall beyond −4 standard deviations.

   The *x*-axis goes to infinity in both directions. However, given that the probability of a case being past ±4 standard deviations is small (0.003 in both directions), we usually state the probability of the case being beyond ±4 standard deviations is ≤ 0.003. In other words, that is usually accurate enough.

4. As a *z*-score becomes greater, what does this signify?

   The *z*-score increases the further away it gets from the mean. So a *z*-score of 1 is closer to the mean than a *z*-score of 2. Since *z*-scores are standard deviations we can determine how many standard deviations a score is from the mean and how likely that score is to occur. A high *z*-score means it is less likely to occur than a low *z*-score.

5. Would a shorter and wider curve still be considered a normal curve? Just with a greater standard deviation?

   Many times the data collected on phenomena do not fit the desired distribution (in this case the normal curve). However, they are either close enough that we can still use the normal curve, or we can treat the data using statistical methods (which are beyond the scope of this textbook) so that the analysis methods we use take the lack of fit into account.

6. How do you rearrange the $z$-formula to solve for $x$?

Rearranging formulas follows the basic rules of algebra. Take a look at the Math Review section on Connect for examples. To solve for $x$ in the $z$-score equation $z = (x - \mu) \div \sigma$, you first need to multiply both sides by $\sigma$, $z \times \sigma = (x - \mu) \div \sigma \times \sigma$. Since the $\sigma$s on the right side cancel each other out, $z \times \sigma = (x - \mu) \div \not\sigma \times \not\sigma$, you end up with $z\sigma = x - \mu$. Now add $\mu$ to both sides, $z\sigma + \mu = x - \mu + \mu$. Since $-\mu + \mu$ out cancel each other you end up with $z\sigma + \mu = x$. We usually write this as $x = \mu + z\sigma$ or, in words, $x$ equals the mean plus the $z$-value times the standard deviation.

## Research Example:

In 2008, Dr. Stephen W. Brown, of Queen's University in Kingston Ontario, published his study "Street Youth, Unemployment, and Crime" in the *Canadian Journal of Criminology and Criminal Justice*. The purpose of his research was to "examine the role that unemployment plays in the criminal behaviour of 400 homeless street youths." Along with other findings, Dr. Brown reported that:

a) Unemployment is associated with involvement in property crimes and drug dealing.

b) The association between unemployment and crime seems to be intensified when individuals are unhappy with their personal economic situation.

c) Those who actively sought employment but were unsuccessful in procuring it, tended to have higher levels of anger towards their unemployment which led to involvement in violent crimes and drug dealing.

Source: S.W. Brown, "Street youth, unemployment, and crime: Is it that simple? Using general strain theory to untangle the relationship." *Canadian Journal of Criminology and Criminal Justice*, 50, no. 4 (2008) pp. 399–434.

## Research Example Questions:

**Question 1:** Dr. Brown reported that the mean age of the 400 respondents was 19.90, with a standard deviation of 2.61 years.

a. Assuming that this is the population of homeless youth, standardize the scores ($z$-scores) for the mean and $\pm 3$ standard deviations.

b. What percentage of homeless youth can we expect to be age 24 and older ($\geq 24$ years old). Round the $z$-score to two decimals. Draw the normal curve, indicate where the $z$-score for age 24 is located, and shade in the proportion of the area representing those students $\geq 24$ years old.

**Question 2:** Dr. Brown asked respondents to report how often, over the past 12 months, they had committed a property crime or violent crime. For property crimes, the average was 5.46 with a standard deviation of 2.26. For violent crimes, the average was 1.56 with a standard deviation of 1.40.

a. Assuming that this is the population of homeless youth, in what percentile is a homeless street youth who committed eight property crimes?

b. Regarding violent crimes, if an individual has a $z$-score of 2.0, how many violent crimes will he or she have committed in the last 12 months?

**Research
Example
Answers:**

**Question 1:** Dr. Brown reported that the mean age of the 400 respondents was 19.90 with a standard deviation of 2.61 years.

a. Assuming that this is the population of homeless youth, standardize the scores (z-scores) for the mean and ±3 standard deviations.

| z-Scores for 1(a) | |
| --- | --- |
| Raw Scores | z-Scores |
| 27.73 | +3 |
| 25.12 | +2 |
| 22.51 | +1 |
| 19.90 | 0 |
| 17.29 | −1 |
| 14.68 | −2 |
| 12.07 | −3 |

b. What percentage of homeless youth can we expect to be age 24 and older (≥24 years old). Round the z-score to two decimals. Draw the normal curve, indicate where the z-score for age 24 is located and shade in the proportion of the area representing those students ≥24 years old.

$$z = \frac{x - \mu}{\sigma} = \frac{24 - 19.90}{2.61} = \frac{4.10}{2.61} = 1.57$$

We can expect to find that 5.82 percent of homeless youth is 24 years of age or older.

**FIGURE 5.15**
**Normal curve for question 1b.**

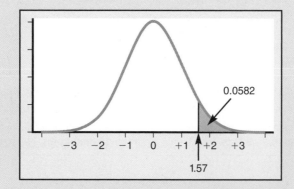

**Question 2:** Dr. Brown asked respondents to report how often, over the past 12 months, they had committed a property crime or violent crime. For property crimes, the average was 5.46 with a standard deviation of 2.26. For violent crimes, the average was 1.56 with a standard deviation of 1.40.

a. Assuming that this is the population of homeless youth, in what percentile is a homeless street youth who committed eight property crimes?

$$z = \frac{x - \mu}{\sigma} = \frac{8 - 5.46}{2.26} = \frac{2.54}{2.26} = 1.12$$

Since this is asking us to find the percentile that this individual is in, we need to calculate the area under the normal curve from the left side ($z = 0.00$) up to the z-score of 1.12. According to Appendix A column II, the area between the mean and $z = 1.12$ is 0.3686. If the area left of the mean equals 0.50, adding 0.3686 and 0.50 gives you the total area left of $z = 1.12$. So 0.3686 + 0.50 = 0.8686. The value of 0.8686 means that an individual who committed eight property crimes is be in the 87th percentile (0.8686 rounded to 0.87 times 100).

b. Regarding violent crimes, if an individual has a z-score of 2.0, how many violent crimes will he or she have committed in the last 12 months?

Since we know the z-value, the mean, and the standard deviation, we need to solve for $x$.

$$2.0 = \frac{x - 1.56}{1.4} \quad \therefore \quad 2.0 \times 1.4 = x - 1.56 \quad \therefore \quad (2.0 \times 1.4) + 1.56 = x$$
$$x = 4.36$$

With a z-value of two, $x$ must equal 4.36. Therefore, the individual will have committed 4.36 violent crimes in the last 12 months.

| ANSWERS FOR EXERCISE 5.1 | Referring to Figure 5.5, try this exercise. | |
|---|---|---|
| | **Questions** | **Answers** |
| | What percentage of area is between $+1\sigma$ and $+2\sigma$? | 13.59% |
| | What percentage of area is between $-3\sigma$ and $-2\sigma$? | 2.15% |
| | What percentage of area is $\leq +1\sigma$? | 84.13% (50% from left of the mean plus 34.13%) |
| | What percentage of area is $\geq -2\sigma$ and $\leq +1\sigma$? | 81.85% (47.72% from $-2\sigma$ to the mean plus 34.13%) |

**Problems**

1. For each of the following, find the appropriate area under the normal curve.
   a) Between $z = 0$ and $z = 1.76$
   b) Beyond $z = 2.01$
   c) Between $z = -1.09$ and $z = 1.11$
   d) Less than $-3.05$

2. According to the 1990 Canadian census, the average daily census totals for 116 government offices in Toronto equals 10,872. Suppose that the standard deviation of the daily census totals for these government offices is 1,505 patients. Assuming that daily census totals are normally distributed:
   a) What is the probability that the daily census totals will be less than or equal to 8,500?
   b) Using your result in a, what is the probability that the daily census totals will be greater than or equal to 8,500?
   c) What is the probability that the daily census totals will be somewhere between 6,000 and 12,000?

3. Scores on the junior high academic achievement tests are normally distributed with mean 400 and standard deviation 100.
   a) If the top 3 percent of students receive a $1,000 prize, then what is the minimum score needed to have a chance of receiving the prize?
   b) If a particular school accepts the top 30 percent of students, what minimum score do you need to be accepted?
   c) If the bottom 1.5 percent of the students must go to summer school, then what is the minimum score you need to avoid this fate?

# Getting From the Sample to the Population: Sample Distribution versus Sampling Distributions

## Learning Objectives:

By the end of this chapter you should be able to:

1. Define statistical inference.
2. Explain the difference between a sample statistic and a population parameter.
3. Explain the difference between a random and non-random sample.
4. State and explain four different random sampling methods.
5. Explain sampling error.
6. Explain the term "sampling distribution of means."
7. Briefly explain why the three statements of central limit theorem are true.
8. Explain what is meant by the mean of the sampling distribution means and standard error of the mean.
9. Describe why we can use the sampling distribution to make inferences about a population based on a random sample from that population.

## Thomas Bayes (1702–1761)

Born in Kent, England, and educated at Edinburgh University in Scotland, Reverend Thomas Bayes was a Presbyterian minister and mathematician who developed a mathematical approach to probability. Bayes published a number of papers on the field of mathematics, including a paper defending Sir Isaac Newton and his ideas on calculus. He is perhaps most famous for his theorem, called Bayes Rule, that establishes the relationship between probabilities. His rule allows us to estimate important probabilities such as the likelihood that a medical test for a disease will yield a positive result when it is actually negative.

Bayes was elected to the Royal Society in 1742 and passed away in 1761. Following his death, his friend Richard Price located an unpublished manuscript of Bayes' work. Price sent it, on Bayes' behalf, to the Royal Society who published it in 1763 in their journal *Transactions* under the title "Essay towards solving a problem in the doctrine of chance."[1]

# Introduction

**LO1**

**Statistical inference** is the process for making statements about the broader population based on the use of sample data from that population.

A **sample statistic** is a numeric value in the sample.

A **population parameter** is a numeric value in the population.

**LO2**

Social scientists research phenomena that occur in the population. Given that we are usually not able to conduct research on the entire population of interest, we take representative samples and use the findings from our sample to describe what is going on in the broader population. In chapter 5, we talked about the normal curve as a tool for understanding what theoretically may happen in the population. In this chapter, we will build on our understanding of the normal curve and examine how we apply the sample results to the larger population of interest.

The process for making statements about the broader population, based on the use of sample data from that population, is called **statistical inference**. To accomplish the objectives in this chapter we will start by discussing various techniques for drawing a sample from the population. Then we will discuss, in a little more detail, where statistical inference fits in the research process. From there we will talk about the role of sampling distributions in statistical inference and cover some of the basics of central limit theorem. Finally, we will pull all of the topics together to provide the foundation needed to understand how we actually go from sample results to making statements about the population. In chapter 7, we will learn how to estimate the population values.

Before we start, we need to discuss two new terms, **sample statistic** and **population parameter**. In previous chapters we made the distinction between the symbols and terms we use for the sample mean ($\bar{x}$) versus the population mean

($\mu$), sample variance ($s^2$) versus the population variance ($\sigma^2$), and sample standard deviation ($s$) versus population standard deviation ($\sigma$). When we want to refer to the value in the sample and the value in the population, we use the terms "statistic" and "parameter." The numeric value in the sample is called a "sample statistic" or just "statistic," whereas that value in the population is called a "population parameter" or just "parameter." So, to link statistical inference with these two new terms we say that we use the sample statistic to estimate the value of the population parameter.

## Take a Closer Look

**Hypothetical Example of Statistical Inference**
Suppose we we want to understand the effects of reducing the length of school recess time on grade 5 student academic performance. After collecting data from a random sample of 200 grade 5 students, we find that academic performance decreases when recess time drops below 15 minutes. While this statement describes what happened in our sample, we also want to describe what we should expect to see in the population of grade 5 students. Using statistical inference, we can make statements about the phenomena of interest in the population by using the results from our sample.

## Drawing a Sample From the Population

To **generalize** the sample results to the population means to apply information from the sample to the population. We say that our findings are generalizable if the conclusions from the sample can be applied to the population of interest.

**LO3**

In chapter 1 we discussed the difference between a sample and the population. Given that it is often impractical to study an entire population of individuals, social scientists conduct research on samples of the population. For example, suppose a sociologist wants to know how many hours a month teenagers who live in Alberta spend on social networking Web sites. Given that the population of Alberta teenagers using social networking sites is quite large, the researcher selects a sample of individuals from the population to participate in the research. Usually the researcher is not just interested in the sample of individuals but would like to be able to **generalize** the results to the entire population of Alberta teenagers using social networking sites (Figure 6.1). We will talk more about how we generalize the results in the next section, but first we will briefly cover a few of the most common methods of sampling.

There are two broad distinctions in the methods of creating a sample: **probability sampling** and **non-probability sampling**. Probability sampling is a method of creating a sample by using some form of random method for selecting the participants from the population. Non-probability sampling is a method of creating a sample that does not use a random method of sampling. In order to generalize the results from the sample to the population, the sample must be

**FIGURE 6.1**
**The Population and
the Sample**

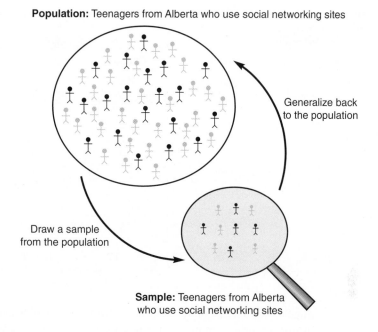

**Population:** Teenagers from Alberta who use social networking sites

Generalize back
to the population

Draw a sample
from the population

**Sample:** Teenagers from Alberta
who use social networking sites

**Probability sampling** is a method of creating a sample by using some form of random method for selecting the participants from the population.

**Non-probability sampling** is a method of creating a sample that does not use a random method of sampling.

representative of the population. That means that the sample must have the same characteristics or attributes as those in the population. For example, if we are interested in the population of Alberta teenagers using social networking sites, then we need our sample to exhibit the characteristics and attributes of that group of individuals. For a sample to be representative of the population, the sample must be drawn using a probability sampling approach. Given this, our focus here is only on probability sampling.

In probability sampling participants are selected at random, meaning everyone has an equal opportunity of being in the sample. As such, this method provides the best opportunity for making the sample results generalizable to the population. Sampling methods are usually covered quite extensively in research methods textbooks, so for our purposes we will focus on the four most commonly used probability sampling methods: simple random sampling, systematic random sampling, stratified random sampling, and cluster random sampling.

To make these examples easier to understand, suppose the entire population of Alberta teenagers using social networking sites consists of 50 individuals. This is widely out of sync with reality, but it makes it easier to show how the numbers work. Now further suppose that we are able to sample 10 individuals from the population of 50 (as is the case in Figure 6.1). Although we don't know the average number of hours the population spends on the sites, we do know that 40 percent of users are male, 60 percent are female, 40 percent live in Calgary, 40 percent live in Edmonton, and 20 percent live in Lethbridge. To draw any kind of random

**TABLE 6.1** 50 Alberta Teenagers Who Use Social Networking Sites, by Gender and City

| Males *n* = 20 | | | Females *n* = 30 | | |
|---|---|---|---|---|---|
| Calgary | Edmonton | Lethbridge | Calgary | Edmonton | Lethbridge |
| 1 | 2 | 11 | 12 | 3 | 7 |
| 5 | 4 | 23 | 16 | 6 | 14 |
| 8 | 10 | 46 | 20 | 13 | 28 |
| 9 | 18 | | 22 | 21 | 32 |
| 15 | 25 | | 27 | 24 | 35 |
| 17 | 29 | | 30 | 26 | 36 |
| 19 | 33 | | 31 | 34 | 42 |
| 48 | 40 | | 38 | 37 | |
| | 44 | | 39 | 43 | |
| | | | 41 | 49 | |
| | | | 45 | 50 | |
| | | | 47 | | |
| *n* = 8 | *n* = 9 | *n* = 3 | *n* = 12 | *n* = 11 | *n* = 7 |

sample, we first randomly assign a number from 1 to 50 to each person in the population, ensuring that no number repeats itself. Table 6.1 provides the number assigned to each of the 50 individuals, by gender and city. Normally, researchers are unlikely to have a list of the population of interest, so they may use other means such as telephone books, membership lists, and so on. Once we assign a number randomly to each individual we can employ one of the sampling methods to create our sample.

## Simple Random Sampling

Simple random sampling involves selecting potential respondents based on a random method. We refer to it as "simple" because we are not concerned about the structure of the population such as gender and location. That is, we are not worried about ensuring equal representation of different groups (e.g., gender). We are only interested in making sure that every potential respondent has an equal chance of being in the sample. In that respect, it is similar to pulling names from a hat to see who wins a prize.

In reality, researchers don't usually draw names from a hat, but the idea is the same. A typical process is as follows:

1. Generate a list of potential respondents.
2. Assign each respondent a unique number.
3. Randomly select a number either through a random number generator or a list of random numbers, such as the one in Appendix E online.
4. Match the number to the corresponding number assigned to a respondent.
5. Include that individual in the sample.
6. Continue the process until you reach your desired sample size.

**TABLE 6.2**   **Selected Samples by Sampling Method**

| Sample | Simple Random Sample Individual # | Systematic Random Sample Individual # | Stratified Random Sample Individual # | Gender | Cluster Random Sample Individual # | City |
|---|---|---|---|---|---|---|
| 1 | 10 | 3 | 10 | | 16 | |
| 2 | 45 | 8 | 23 | 40% | 8 | 40% |
| 3 | 13 | 13 | 1 | Males | 18 | Calgary |
| 4 | 21 | 18 | 25 | | 39 | |
| 5 | 4 | 23 | 14 | | 24 | |
| 6 | 30 | 28 | 20 | | 18 | 40% |
| 7 | 9 | 33 | 24 | 60% | 26 | Edmonton |
| 8 | 36 | 38 | 47 | Females | 37 | |
| 9 | 32 | 43 | 21 | | 14 | 20% |
| 10 | 26 | 48 | 36 | | 35 | Lethbridge |

Using our Alberta teenage population example, we would randomly select a number between 1 and 50 and then repeat that procedure for a total of 10 times. The outcome of this sampling method is shown under the Simple Random Sample column in Table 6.2.

## Systematic Random Sampling

Systematic random sampling is similar to simple random sampling in that it does not take into account details such as gender and location. Also like simple random sampling, the intent is to ensure that each potential respondent has an equal chance of being selected for the sample. The difference with this sampling technique is in how the sample is selected. In systematic random sampling, we randomly determine who the first individual will be on the list and then select every $n$th person thereafter until we reach our desired sample size. There are a few different ways of calculating who the first individual is and what the $n$th interval is, but they all more or less follow this process:

1. Generate a list of potential respondents.
2. Number each respondent from 1 to N.
3. Determine the $n$th interval by dividing the number of potential respondents (N) by your desired sample size ($n$). (N/$n$)
4. Determine who the first person is in the sample by randomly selecting a number between 1 and the $n$th interval.
5. Select every $n$th person thereafter until you reach your desired sample size.

Using our example, we first arrange our list in numerical order and then determine the $n$th interval (in this case, $50 \div 10 = 5$). We then randomly select a number between 1 and 5 (5 being the $n$th interval) to determine the first individual (in this

## For Your Information

In order to ensure that the sample is representative of the population, researchers often employ a mix of different random sampling methods. For example, we can combine stratified random sampling and cluster random sampling to create a more complex sampling method.

Suppose we want to determine the extent to which citizens are concerned about personal privacy when giving their personal information to a company over the Internet. We may decide our sample needs to include the potential for difference in age, geographical location, and gender. In this case we may create a clustered stratified random sample as follows:

1. Generate a list of those that qualify to be in the sample (the population).
2. Separate the list by province, and then by urban versus rural locations.
3. Separate the list even further by the age categories "under 50" and "50 and over."
4. Determine the percentage of males versus females within the age categories in the urban versus rural locations by province to determine what percentage of the sample should be male and female.
5. Conduct a simple random sampling from the list until we reach the desired proportionate sample size.

case it was individual #3) and then select every 5th person on the list until we have a sample size of 10. The Systematic Random Sample column in Table 6.2 displays our results.

### Stratified and Cluster Random Sampling

Stratified random sampling and cluster random sampling take into account different parts of the structure of the population such as gender and location.

In stratified random sampling you first create homogenous subgroups ("strata") based on a characteristic or trait of the population, and then perform a simple random sample from each subgroup. The groups in stratified sampling are usually based on personal rather than geographic characteristics, so in our example we break the population into gender groups and then perform a simple random sample within each. If we want proportionate representation, then we make sure that 40 percent of the sample comes from the male group and 60 percent from the female group. The Stratified Random Sample column in Table 6.2 displays the results.

In cluster random sampling you start by creating homogenous subgroups ("clusters") based on geographic characteristics and then perform a simple random sample from each cluster. In our example, we separate the sample into geographic clusters (Calgary, Edmonton, and Lethbridge) and then perform a simple random sample within each. Again, if we want proportionate representation, then we make sure that 40 percent of the sample comes from Calgary, 40 percent from Edmonton, and 20 percent from Lethbridge. The Cluster Random Sample column in Table 6.2 displays our results.

# Where Does Statistical Inference Fit?

Assuming that the sample of individuals is randomly drawn from the population, we can use statistical inference to generalize the results of the sample to the population. This is a bit of a mouthful and is an important statement to understand, so refer to Figure 6.2 and we'll break it down into sections. The numbers in the figure match the numbers in the following description.

1. We are interested in studying a phenomenon that is occurring in the population.
2. Since we cannot sample the entire population, we draw a sample of individuals that is representative of the population. Then, in order to make the sample representative, we use a random sampling method.
3. We gather data from the sample and conduct our analysis. For example, we may estimate the sample mean ($\bar{x}$), which we call the sample statistic.
4. The sample statistic ($\bar{x}$) is the value that we will use to estimate the population parameter ($\mu$). In plain language, we use the sample mean to estimate the population mean.

That is what is meant by statistical inference. Statistical inference is not the same as the term inferential statistics, which we will cover in later chapters. Rather, it is a process that allows us to make statements about the population based on a sample from that population.

## Sampling Error

As you can imagine, when we only take a sample of the population our sample statistic is not likely going to be the same as the population parameter. Sometimes the $\bar{x}$ will be less than $\mu$ and sometimes it will be more than $\mu$. So how do we deal with this problem if we want to use our sample mean ($\bar{x}$) as an estimator of the population mean ($\mu$)? To answer this we need to discuss sampling distributions and central limit theorem. However, in order to help you navigate your way through these

**FIGURE 6.2**
**From Population to Sample to Population**

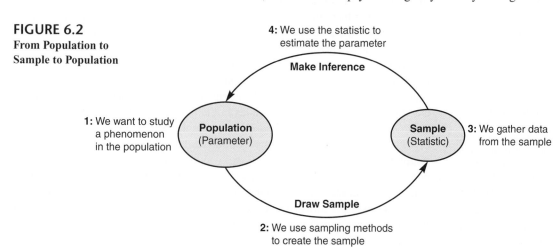

## Did You Know?

The courts require valid and acceptable statistical methods in determining probabilities when matching DNA samples with suspects. However, they often do not require probabilities of false positive results. What is the difference? Juries may be told that the DNA taken off the victim matches the suspect's DNA with a probability of such a match being one in a million or one in 500,000. Juries can then use this evidence to assess the suspect's guilt.

However, what is not reported is the probability that the match is wrong, which statisticians call the "false positive" result. In fact, subsequent testing has led to convictions being overturned. So what proportion of these positive matches in DNA are actually false? If one in three of these matches is false, then one third of the suspects identified may be wrongfully convicted.

Calculating these probabilities is difficult but not impossible. Thompson (2003) gives a discussion on many issues arising in DNA testing. Some of the issues he raises include: labs mixing up samples; a victim's DNA being mixed with the samples, making the DNA similar to the suspect's DNA; variations in labs and so on. As a result, Thompson suggests that courts should pay as much attention to false positives as they do for the probability of a match.

**Sources:** W.C. Thompson, "Are juries competent to evaluate statistical evidence?" *Law and Contemporary Problems* (1989), 9.

W.C. Thompson, "How the probability of a false positive affects the value of DNA evidence." *Journal of Forensic Science,* 48 (2003), pp. 1–4.

topics, we'll first spend some time talking generally about these concepts and how they relate to error.

Suppose we know that in a population of 10,000 individuals, people spend a mean ($\mu$) of six hours per month on Facebook with a standard deviation ($\sigma$) of 1.25 hours per month. We can see in Figure 6.3 that the distribution follows a normal distribution.

Now suppose we randomly select 50 people from the population and find they spend a mean ($\bar{x}$) of 6.7 hours. We can see right away that the sample mean is slightly greater than the population mean. If we select another 50 people we might find that this time the sample mean is 5.2, slightly less than the population mean.

As you can see in Figure 6.4, the seven sample means are within the population distribution, and sometimes a sample mean is less than the population mean while at other times it is greater than the population mean. This intuitively makes sense because each sample comes from the population; therefore, the mean of the sample is within the range of possible values in the population. The difference between the true population mean ($\mu$) and a single sample mean ($\bar{x}$) is called a **sampling error**. For example, our first sample of 50 yielded a mean of 6.7, which means the sampling error for that mean is 0.7 (6.7 – 6.0). Usually we don't know what the population mean is, so we cannot estimate the sampling error. In that case, given that we have an unknown sampling error amount, the best we can say is that the sample mean is an estimate of the population. More specifically, we call it a **point estimate** because we are not stating the range of sampling error involved in the estimate. So the sample mean ($\bar{x}$) is a point estimate of the population mean.

**Sampling error** is the difference between a sample mean ($\bar{x}$) and the population mean ($\mu$). This occurs as a result of only sampling a portion of the population.

A **point estimate** is a statistic that is used to estimate a parameter.

**FIGURE 6.3**
**Histogram of**
**Population Hours**
**Spent on Facebook**

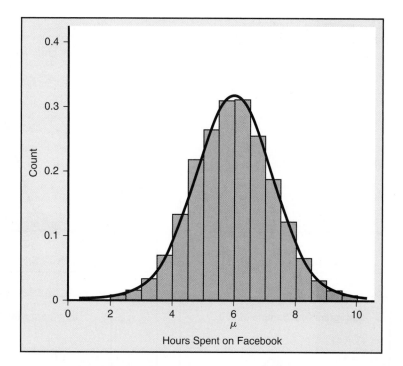

We can decrease the sampling error amount by increasing our sample size. As we increase the sample size, we take in more information about the population—since we are including more people from the population—which decreases the amount of discrepancy between the sample mean and the population mean. Consider the histograms in Figure 6.5: as we increase our sample size, two things happen. First, our sample distribution becomes more normally distributed and second, the sample mean ($\bar{x}$) gets closer to the true population mean ($\mu$).

Now that we understand sampling errors, we are ready to cover how we can use a sample mean ($\bar{x}$) as an estimator for the population mean. To do this, we need to move on to sampling distributions and central limit theorem.

**FIGURE 6.4**
**Population**
**Distribution and**
**Sample Means**

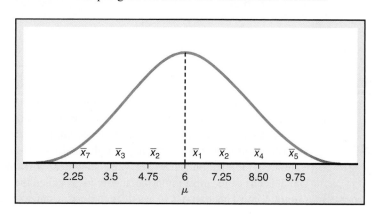

**FIGURE 6.5** **Increasing Sample Size**

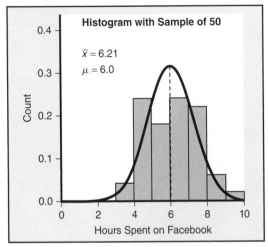

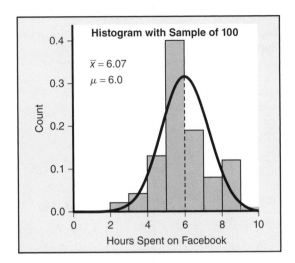

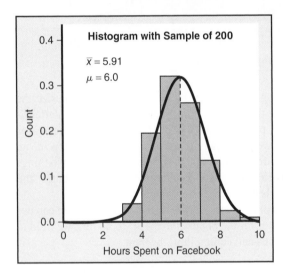

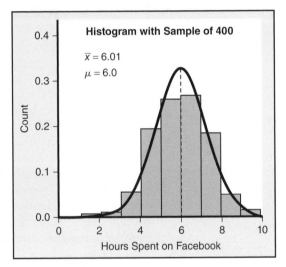

# The Sampling Distribution of Means

To recap what we've covered so far: We know that we can use a random sampling method to draw a sample from the population. We also know that due to sampling error, the sample mean ($\bar{x}$) will likely not equal the population mean ($\mu$), but that as we increase our sample size the amount of sampling error decreases. However, we still haven't covered the mechanism, that allows us to use a sample statistic to estimate a population parameter (i.e., statistical inference). This mechanism, which is one of the most important theorems, is called the Central Limit Theorem. Central Limit Theorem (CLT) has three important statements that allow us to make

**FIGURE 6.6**
**Central Limit Theorem**

| If you have a sample size *n* that is greater than or equal to ($\geq$) 30 then: |
| --- |
| Statement #1:   The mean of the sampling distribution of means (mean of the sampling means $\mu_{\bar{x}}$) will equal the population mean ($\mu$). |
| Statement #2:   The standard deviation of the sampling distribution of means (standard deviation of sampling means $\mu_{\bar{x}}$) will be equal to the population standard deviation ($\sigma$) divided by the square root of the sample size ($\sqrt{n}$). |
| Statement #3:   Even if the population distribution is not normally distributed, the sampling distribution of means will become more normally distributed as the sample size increases. |

inferences about the population parameter from our sample statistic. Figure 6.6 summarizes the three statements.

One important caveat to this theorem is that it applies to situations where the sample (*n*) is greater than or equal to 30.

## Central Limit Theorem Statement #1

*The mean of the sampling distribution means (mean of the sampling means $\mu_{\bar{x}}$) equals the population mean ($\mu$).*

A statistic is an
**unbiased estimator**
if its value equals the
value of the parameter
being estimated.

As we saw earlier, our sample statistics (as a point estimate) may not necessarily be equal to the population parameter given our sample size and sampling error. However, based on CLT we can say that our sample mean is an **unbiased estimator** (more specifically, an unbiased point estimate) of the population mean because of what we call the **sampling distribution**. A sampling distribution is a theoretical distribution of all the potential values of a sample statistic that you would find if you could draw all of the possible combinations of random samples. That part can be challenging to grasp, so let's look at it from another angle.

A **sampling distribution** is a theoretical distribution of all the potential values of a sample statistic that you would find if you could draw all possible combinations of random samples.

### *Example of a Sampling Distribution*

We said that CLT applies only when the sample is greater than or equal to 30. With sample sizes less than 30 it tends to not work. However, for the purpose of providing a simple example of a sampling distribution, we will use a small population and a small sample size. Following this, we will show you how this works with a more appropriate sample size.

Suppose you are in a room with five people and you want to find the average age and standard deviation. They are:

- Judy, age 20
- Mark, age 18
- Sam, age 21
- Lora, age 22
- John, age 24

The easiest way is to ask all five people (the population) what their age is and then calculate the mean age ($\mu = 21$) and standard deviation ($\sigma = 2.24$), which would be the population parameters. However, suppose you are constrained in that you are only allowed to ask the age of two people at time. If you randomly select every possible permutation of two people at a time from a population of five people, you would have 25 possible combinations of $n = 2$. Refer to the next For Your Information to see how we got the number 25 and what the samples would be.

A **sampling distribution of means**, also referred to as the distribution of sampling means, is a theoretical distribution of all potential values of a sample mean that you would find if you could draw all possible combinations of random samples.

Now, if we calculate the sample mean ($\bar{x}$) for each of the 25 samples, we get the results in Table 6.3, which is called the **sampling distribution of means** or the distribution of sampling means. While this sounds complex, it is just the distribution of the means from all of the samples we took. For now, we can ignore how the sampling means ($\mu_{\bar{x}}$) shown in Table 6.3 is calculated; we'll come back to that. What is important to understand at this point is that this is called a sampling distribution of means because we took all of the possible combinations of samples, and then calculated and recorded the mean for each sample.

**TABLE 6.3**
**The Sampling Distribution of Means**

| Sample Number ... | ...includes | ...has a sample $\bar{x}$ age of |
|---|---|---|
| 1 | {Judy, Judy} | 20.0 |
| 2 | {Judy, Mark} | 19.0 |
| 3 | {Judy, Sam} | 20.5 |
| 4 | {Judy, Lora} | 21.0 |
| 5 | {Judy, John} | 22.0 |
| 6 | {Mark, Judy} | 19.0 |
| 7 | {Mark, Mark} | 18.0 |
| 8 | {Mark, Sam} | 19.5 |
| 9 | {Mark, Lora} | 20.0 |
| 10 | {Mark, John} | 21.0 |
| 11 | {Sam, Judy} | 20.5 |
| 12 | {Sam, Mark} | 19.5 |
| 13 | {Sam, Sam} | 21.0 |
| 14 | {Sam, Lora} | 21.5 |
| 15 | {Sam, John} | 22.5 |
| 16 | {Lora, Judy} | 21.0 |
| 17 | {Lora, Mark} | 20.0 |
| 18 | {Lora, Sam} | 21.5 |
| 19 | {Lora, Lora} | 22.0 |
| 20 | {Lora, John} | 23.0 |
| 21 | {John, Judy} | 22.0 |
| 22 | {John, Mark} | 21.0 |
| 23 | {John, Sam} | 22.5 |
| 24 | {John, Lora} | 23.0 |
| 25 | {John, John} | 24.0 |
| The mean of the sampling means ($\mu_{\bar{x}}$) is: | | 21.0 |

## For Your Information

There are five people: Judy, Mark, Sam, Lora, and John. How many permutations* of two people can you get from the population of five people?

This is what is referred to as a permutation with repetition and is calculated using the following formula, where $n$ is the population of five and $r$ is the sample of two:

$$n^r = 5^2 = 5 \times 5 = 25$$

These possible combinations include:

\* Some textbooks may refer to this as a combination but technically it is a permutation because the order is important. Meaning that we want to treat Judy and Mark as a different sample from Mark and Judy even though the mean will be the same. For a more detailed look at combinations and permutations refer to the Math Review Module on Connect.

| | | | | |
|---|---|---|---|---|
| {Judy, Judy} | {Judy, Mark} | {Judy, Sam} | {Judy, Lora} | {Judy, John} |
| {Mark, Judy} | {Mark, Mark} | {Mark, Sam} | {Mark, Lora} | {Mark, John} |
| {Sam, Judy} | {Sam, Mark} | {Sam, Sam} | {Sam, Lora} | {Sam, John} |
| {Lora, Judy} | {Lora, Mark} | {Lora, Sam} | {Lora, Lora} | {Lora, John} |
| {John, Judy} | {John, Mark} | {John, Sam} | {John, Lora} | {John, John} |

We just saw a small example of a sampling distribution. Let's go back to our Facebook example to see how this works with a more appropriate sample size. To recap, we said there is a population of 10,000 individuals who spend a mean ($\mu$) of six hours per month on Facebook with a standard deviation ($\sigma$) of 1.25 hours per month.

Now suppose we could take every possible permutation of samples of 50 from the population of 10,000 and record the mean ($\bar{x}$) of each. That is a lot of samples ($1 \times 10^{200}$, or 1 with 200 zeros) so we can't possibly list them all here. However, we would have a sampling distribution of means just like the one in Table 6.3 (only much longer) with the means of each sample of 50 in the right hand column.

Now let's take it one step further to get to the point of CLT's first statement. If we were to calculate the mean of all of the means that were listed in the sampling distribution, we would have what we call the **mean of the sampling distribution means**. We use the notation $\mu_{\bar{x}}$ (pronounced "mu" with the subscript $x$-bar) to refer to the mean of the sampling distribution means, which is calculated as:

The **mean of the sampling distribution means** is the average of all of the means in the sampling distribution. It is the mean value of the sampling distribution means.

$$\mu_{\bar{x}} = \frac{\Sigma \bar{x}}{n} \qquad\qquad (6.1)$$

The formula for the mean of the sampling distribution of means is similar to the formula for the arithmetic mean (chapter 3). However, instead of summing individual values of $x$, we are summing individual values of "values of sampling means ($\bar{x}$)."

How can we prove that the statement is correct? If we had a computer that was powerful enough to run the simulation required to run all of our samples, we would see that it works. However, since we can't do that, we can look at our small example in Table 6.3 to prove that the mathematics works for this statement of CLT. In that scenario we said the population mean ($\mu$) age was 21. Using the formula to calculate the mean of the sampling distribution of means (Table 6.3), we see that $\mu_{\bar{x}}$ equals 21.0, which also equals the population mean of 21.0 for Judy, Mark, Sam, Lora, and John.

$$\mu_{\bar{x}} = \frac{\Sigma \bar{x}}{n} = \frac{21 + 19 + \cdots + 23 + 24}{25} = \frac{525}{25} = 21.0 \quad \textbf{(6.2)}$$

We have just seen how a sampling distribution works and found the first statement of CLT to be true. We found that the mean of the sampling distribution means ($\mu_{\bar{x}}$) does in fact does equal the population mean ($\mu$). This indicates that the distribution of the sampling means will be normal distributed with a mean value ($\mu_{\bar{x}}$) that is equal to the population mean ($\mu$). As evidence of this statement, the histogram on the left side of Figure 6.7 shows 50,000 samples of $n = 100$ from our Facebook population with the normal curve overlaid. The plot on the right shows the distribution of the sampling means ($\bar{x}$) where the mean ($\mu_{\bar{x}}$) equals $\mu$.

**FIGURE 6.7** **Sampling Distribution of Means**

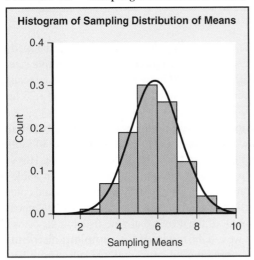
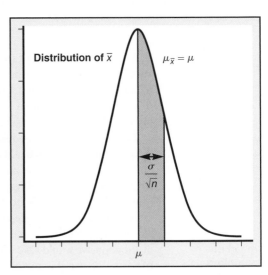

A key piece to the first CLT statement is that it relies on our ability to use the sample mean ($\bar{x}$) as an unbiased estimate of the population mean ($\mu$). That is, the sample mean ($\bar{x}$) can be considered an unbiased estimator of the population mean ($\mu$) if the mean of the sampling distribution of means ($\mu_{\bar{x}}$) equals the true population mean ($\mu$).

There are two reasons that this is true. First, although the sample mean ($\bar{x}$) may be slightly less or slightly more than the population mean ($\mu$) it differs randomly. Meaning there is an equal chance the sample mean will be less than or greater than the population mean. Second, over the course of a large of number of samples (such as 500 samples of $n = 50$), the sample mean ($\bar{x}$) will on average be equal to the population mean ($\mu$). In a nutshell, if we have a sample size greater than 30, this first statement tells us that we can use the sample mean as an unbiased estimator (an unbiased point estimate) of the population mean.

## Take a Closer Look

We stated that given computational limitations, we could not run a simulation large enough to include all of the possible $1 \times 100^{200}$ samples in our Facebook example to prove the first statement of CLT. However, we are able to run smaller versions. Simulating 1,000,000 random samples of size $n = 50$, which is the same as gathering the data from a sample of 50 people one million times, the mean of the 1,000,000 means was 6.02. Very close to the population mean ($\mu$) of six hours on Facebook, and there are still $1 \times 100^{194}$ samples yet to draw.

## Central Limit Theorem Statement #2

*The standard deviation of the sampling distribution of means ($\sigma_{\bar{x}}$) will be equal to the population standard deviation ($\sigma$) divided by the square root of the sample size ($\sqrt{n}$).*

Notice that in Figure 6.7 one standard deviation is shown as $\sigma/\sqrt{n}$. Think back to chapter 3 where we discussed measures of central tendency, dispersion, and shape. In that chapter we found that we can estimate the mean and standard deviation of a variable. In the first CLT statement we found that we can estimate the mean of a distribution of sampling means. The same is true with standard deviation of the distribution of sampling means. However, when referring to the standard deviation of the sampling means we call it the **standard error of the mean**. The plot on the right side of Figure 6.7 shows that the distribution of the sampling means not only follows a normal curve with a mean equal to $\mu$, but it also has a standard deviation (more appropriately called the standard error of the mean) that is equal to the population standard deviation divided by the square root of the sample size.

> The **standard error of the mean** ($\sigma_{\bar{x}}$) is the standard deviation of the sampling means.

Why do we care about the standard error of the mean? Remember that the standard deviation(s) tells us how far individual values vary from the mean ($\bar{x}$). The same is true with the standard error of the mean. Only this time it tells us how far individual sample means ($\bar{x}$) vary from the population mean ($\mu$).

The equation for estimating the standard error of the mean is:

$$\sigma_{\bar{x}} = \frac{\sigma}{\sqrt{n}} \qquad \textbf{(6.3)}$$

The symbol for the mean of the sampling distribution of means is $\mu_{\bar{x}}$ and the symbol for the standard deviation of the sampling distribution of means is $\sigma_{\bar{x}}$.

This means that if we take the standard deviation of the population ($\sigma$) and divide it by the square root of our sample size ($\sqrt{n}$) the result is the standard error of the mean.

Using our Facebook example, the standard deviation of the population ($\sigma$) is 1.25. Therefore, the standard error of the mean is 0.177.

$$\sigma_{\bar{x}} = \frac{\sigma}{\sqrt{n}} = \frac{1.25}{\sqrt{50}} = \frac{1.25}{7.07} = 0.177 \qquad \textbf{(6.4)}$$

So how do we know that the second CLT statement is correct if we don't know the real value of $\sigma_{\bar{x}}$? One way we can test this is to manipulate the equation to find the value for the population standard deviation ($\sigma$), which was 1.25, and insert our estimated value of the standard error (0.177).

$$\sigma_{\bar{x}} = \frac{\sigma}{\sqrt{n}}$$

Therefore:

$$\sigma = \sigma_{\bar{x}} \times \sqrt{n} \qquad \textbf{(6.5)}$$
$$= 0.177 \times \sqrt{50} = 0.177 \times 7.07 = 1.25$$

So simply by manipulating equation 6.3 we can see that CLT statement number 2 is correct.

Because the standard error of the mean is a function of sample size, as we increase our sample size two things happen. First, the standard error will decrease. Second, the distribution of the sampling means will become narrower. Consider Figure 6.8. On the left we see that as we increase the sample, the standard error decreases dramatically. On the right we can see how the standard error affects the distribution of the sampling means.

Like the first CLT statement, the second statement has important implications to our ability to make statistical inferences. Recall that a sample mean is an unbiased point estimate of the population mean even though sometimes the value may

**FIGURE 6.8   Standard Error and Sampling Distributions**

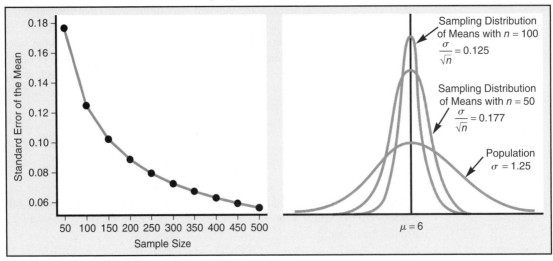

be slightly less or more than the true population mean. The standard error of the mean allows us to account for the difference between the sample mean and the population mean. We will see more on how this works in the next chapters where we will be covering confidence intervals. With confidence intervals we can use the sample mean as an estimate of the population and the standard error as a method for determining a range of where the true population mean lies.

## Central Limit Theorem Statement #3

*Even if the population distribution is not normally distributed, the sampling distribution of means will become more normally distributed as the sample size increases.*

We previously said that not all social phenomena follow a normal distribution. There are a number variables, such as social economic status and household income, that are not normally distributed in the population. Income in the population tends to be positively skewed, where most people earn average incomes and few people earn much higher than average incomes.

The third CLT statement is important in that it tells us that even if the population distribution is not normally distributed, the sampling distribution of means will be normally distributed. Furthermore, as we increase the sample size, the sampling distribution becomes even more normally distributed. This is good news because our ability to use the first two statements relies on having a distribution of sampling means that are normally distributed.

To illustrate this point, we have simulated a distribution of incomes that range from $1,000 a year to over $164,000 per year; see Figure 6.9. If the third CLT

**FIGURE 6.9**
**Histogram of Income**

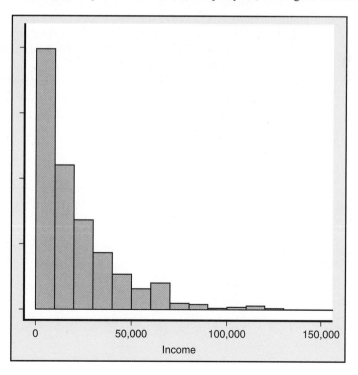

**FIGURE 6.10** **Two Different Histograms of Sampling Means of Income**

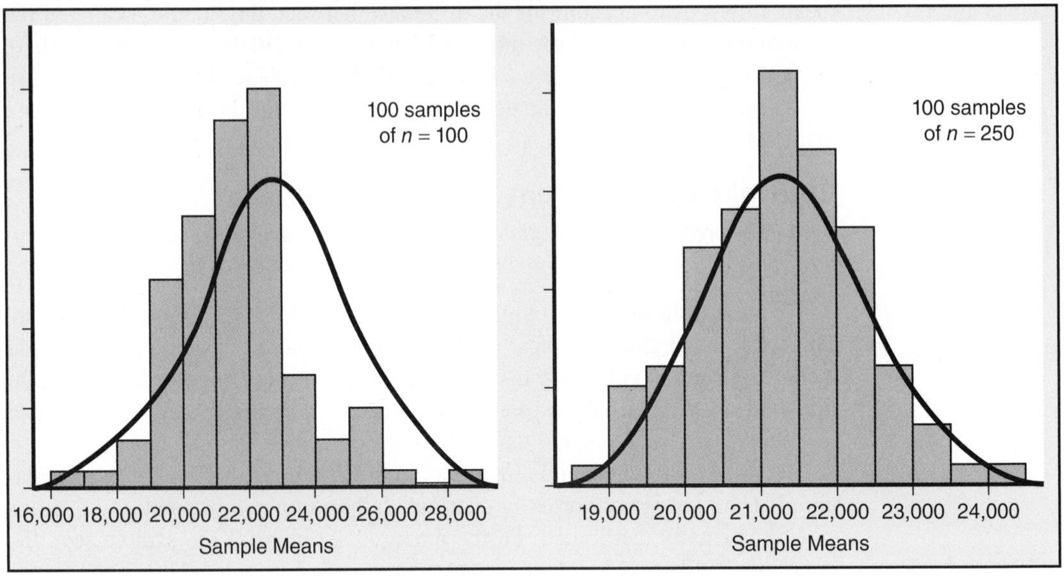

statement is correct, we should find that (a) the distribution of sampling means will be normally distributed, and (b) that distribution will become increasingly more normally distributed as the sample size increases.

Figure 6.10 provides the histograms of two sampling distributions of means from the population of income in Figure 6.9. The histogram on the left represents 100 samples of 100 people. As you can see, the data appear to be approaching a normal distribution. The histogram on the right represents 100 samples of 250 people, where you can definitely see that the data is fairly normally distributed. So by graphing our distribution of sampling means, we have found that in fact the third CLT statement is also correct.

**EXERCISE 6.1**    Consider the ages of three students. Answers are at the end of the chapter.

| Student | Age |
|---------|-----|
| A | 20 |
| B | 22 |
| C | 27 |
| Mean | 23 |

1. Suppose we want to sample two students from these three. List the nine possible permutations of the students, along with their ages.
2. Compute the mean of the two students' ages for all nine pairs of numbers.
3. Compute the mean of the nine averages.
4. The average of the three ages is 23. Is the average of the nine means still 23?

| Pairs | Ages | Mean |
|---|---|---|
| (A,A) | (20,20) | 20 |
| (A,B) | (20,22) | 21 |
| (A,C) | | |
| (B,A) | | |
| (B,B) | | |
| (B,C) | | |
| (C,A) | | |
| (C,B) | | |
| (C,C) | | |
| Average of means | | |

# The Sampling Distribution of Means, the Normal Curve, and Statistical Inference

So what does all of this mean to us in our quest to determine how we use our sample statistic to make inferences about the population? The answer is that we make statistical inferences about the population by way of the sampling distribution. Furthermore, we know we have the authority to do this because of the CLT. How do we know that? Consider this:

1. Statement one of the CLT states that we can use the sample mean as an unbiased point estimator of the population mean if the mean of the sampling distribution of means is equal to the population mean.
2. Statement two tells us that we can estimate the variability around the sample mean using the standard error of the mean.
3. Statement three tells us that even though a variable may not be normally distributed in the population the sampling means will be. Therefore, we are justified in using statements one and two in such situations.

The topic of sampling distributions is sometimes a difficult one to get your mind around. So let's look at one final example that ties this all together. Suppose we have 1,000 undergraduate students in our university and we want to determine the average age of the student body. As is usually the case with researchers, we have no idea what the value is of the population mean ($\mu$) or population standard deviation ($\sigma$). So we take a random sample of 125 students and find that the sample mean age ($\bar{x}$) is 21.03 with a sample standard deviation ($s$) of 0.97 years. Now what? We can't create a sampling distribution for this example because it would be far too much work. In fact, it would probably just be easier to take ask all 1,000 students their age.

Thankfully, we don't have to create the sampling distribution ourselves because it is a theoretical distribution based on probability theory. Remember, as the sample size increases the sampling distribution will be normally distributed. A normal curve, which we covered in chapter 5, is based on probability theory. So we can use our knowledge about the normal curve to estimate what is happening in the population. If you're not sure why this true, think back to our research example of the homeless street youth in chapter 5. Using standardized scores ($z$-scores) and areas under the normal curve, we could estimate what we should expect to find in the population. For example, in question 1 of that research example, we were able to state that "we can expect to find that 5.82 percent of homeless youth is 24 years of age or older."

We use statistical methods to test our hypotheses, and central limit theorem is the basis for the majority of the statistical methods. Before we can move on to the analysis methods, we first need to determine how to set up a hypothesis for statistical analysis. That is the subject of the next chapter.

## Conclusion

Statistical inference is a process that enables us to makes statements about a population based on our sample data, provided that it is a representative sample. To create a representative sample we use a random sampling method in order to ensure that key population characteristics and attributes are picked up in the sample. A sampling distribution is a theoretical distribution, based on probability, which includes all of the possible sample outcomes that we would find if we could gather data using every possible combination of samples. Central limit theorem tells us that we can estimate the mean (central tendency) of the population parameter, the variability of the scores around the population mean (dispersion), and its distribution (shape).

## Key Chapter Concepts

Statistical inference, 161
Sample statistic, 161
Population parameter, 161
Generalize, 162
Probability sampling, 163

Non-probability sampling, 163
Sampling error, 168
Point estimate, 168
Unbiased estimator, 171
Sampling distribution, 171

Sampling distribution of means, 172
Mean of the sampling distribution of means, 173
Standard error of the mean, 175

# Frequently Asked Questions

1. What is the difference between a parameter and a statistic?

   A statistic is calculated from a sample. A parameter can be theoretically calculated from the population. In practice we really cannot measure parameters except in rare cases. We use sample statistics to estimate population parameters.

2. When can we directly measure parameters?

   When Statistics Canada conducts a census and everyone responds, we can calculate parameter values. The point being, to directly measure the population parameter we have to collect data from everyone in the population of interest.

3. Why is the central limit theorem important?

   If you take a reasonably sized sample, then you know that the sample mean will follow a normal distribution centered around the mean of the population. We use this fact for the rest of the book.

4. What happens to the standard error when we increase the sample size?

   As the sample size increases, the standard error of a statistic—such as the standard error of the sample mean—usually decreases. It decreases by the square root of the sample size. The more people you sample, the more accurate the statistic.

5. Why do we have different sampling methods?

   Essentially, the point behind random sampling is to make the sample as representative of the population as possible. Different sampling methods have different ways of getting a representative sample.

# Research Example:

In 2009, Dr. Fiona Kay of Queen's University and Dr. Jean Wallace of the University of Calgary published their paper "Mentors as Social Capital: Gender, Mentors, and Career Rewards on Law Practice" in the journal *Sociological Inquiry.* One of the aims of this research was to examine the effects of mentors on the personal careers of those being mentored. Furthermore, they were interested in determining if these effects differed between females and males. To accomplish this, the researchers needed to survey younger lawyers who had mentors to assist them in developing their legal career. To gather the data, the researchers randomly sampled approximately 2,348 Ontario lawyers from a Law Society of Upper Canada membership list. The researchers sent out 50 percent of the surveys to females and 50 percent to males. Among other findings reported in the research, Kay and Wallace found that:

- Male lawyers with mentors experienced greater salary increases than their female counterparts.

- Female lawyers with mentors experienced greater work satisfaction than their male counterparts.

- There was no difference in the abilities of male and female lawyers to obtain high quality mentors.

**Source:** F.M. Kay and J.E. Wallace, "Mentors as Social Capital: Gender, Mentors, and Career Rewards on Law Practice" *Sociological Inquiry*, 79 no. 4 (2009), pp. 418–452.

**Research Example Questions:**

**Question 1:** What type of random sampling method was used in this research?

**Question 2:** What other sampling method(s) might the researchers have used?

**Question 3:** Based on their sample results regarding the variable "salary increases," about what population would they be interested in making inferences?

**Research Example Answers:**

**Question 1:** What type of random sampling method was used in this research?

Since the researchers divided the sample by gender, this is a stratified random sample.

**Question 2:** What other sampling method(s) might the researchers have used?

The researchers might also have used cluster random sampling in order to account for the locations of lawyers. It is likely that there is a greater proportion of Ontario lawyers in metropolitan areas versus rural areas. Another idea is to include the type of law practice in the stratified random sample. Males and females may be distributed differently across different types of legal practice (e.g., criminal versus corporate) which may influence the results.

**Question 3:** Based on their sample results regarding the variable "salary increases," about what population would they be interested in making inferences?

The researchers would be interested in using their sample results to make inferences about the population of Ontario lawyers. Inferences about the population should only include Ontario as that is where the sample was drawn. There may be other factors that limit to whom these results may apply that are not identified here. For example, if the sample only included law firms in metropolitan locations, then the results may apply only to Ontario lawyers in metropolitan locations.

---

**ANSWERS TO EXERCISE 6.1**

Consider the ages of three students.

| Student | Age |
|---------|-----|
| A | 20 |
| B | 22 |
| C | 27 |
| Mean | 23 |

1. Suppose we wanted to sample two students from the list. List the nine possible permutations of the students along with their ages.
2. Compute the average of the two students' ages for all nine pairs of numbers.
3. Compute the mean or the average of the nine averages.

| Pairs | Ages | Mean |
|-------|------|------|
| (A,A) | (20,20) | 20.0 |
| (A,B) | (20,22) | 21.0 |
| (A,C) | (20,27) | 23.5 |
| (B,A) | (22,20) | 21.0 |
| (B,B) | (22,22) | 22.0 |
| (B,C) | (22,27) | 24.5 |
| (C,A) | (27,10) | 23.5 |
| (C,B) | (27,22) | 24.5 |
| (C,C) | (27,27) | 27.0 |
| Average of means | | 207.0 ÷ 9 = 23.0 |

4. The average of the three ages is 23. Is the average of the nine means 23?

Yes. The average of the means of all pairs of observations drawn from the population is 23.

## Problems

1. Suppose the population of those in a running club consists of 4 people (Erin, John, Mike, and Denise). The number of kilometers per day that each person runs is: two (Erin), four (John), six (Mike), and eight (Denise). The population mean ($\mu$) is 5 kilometers, and the population standard deviation ($\sigma$) is 2.236. The following table represents all the possible samples of $n = 2$ that you could take from this population, and includes a column for you to calculate each sample mean.

| Sample Number ... | ...Includes | ...has a sample mean ($\bar{x}$) |
|-------------------|-------------|----------------------------------|
| 1 | 22 | |
| 2 | 24 | |
| 3 | 26 | |
| 4 | 28 | |
| 5 | 42 | |
| 6 | 44 | |
| 7 | 46 | |
| 8 | 48 | |
| 9 | 62 | |
| 10 | 64 | |
| 11 | 66 | |
| 12 | 68 | |
| 13 | 82 | |
| 14 | 84 | |
| 15 | 86 | |
| 16 | 88 | |

a) Calculate the mean of the sampling distribution means ($\mu_{\bar{x}}$).

b) Calculate the standard error of the mean ($\sigma_{\bar{x}}$).

c) Show that the population standard deviation is equal to the standard error of the mean multiplied by the square root of the sample size ($n = 2$).

2. Aptitude scores for the general population are normally distributed with a mean of 100 and standard deviation of 15. Suppose that many samples are taken and each time the aptitude test is recorded.

a) What is the standard deviation for all samples of size 16?

b) What about a sample of size 25?

c) What if, from b, the population was not normally distributed with the size of the population equal to 40, yet the mean was still 100 and standard deviation 15?

3. Assume that kindergarten students' heights have a standard deviation of two inches. For each of the following, indicate the standard error of the sampling distribution of the sample mean.

a) Sample mean height for random samples of $n = 16$ students.

b) Sample mean height for random samples of $n = 25$ students.

c) Sample mean height for random samples of $n = 36$ students.

d) Sample mean height for random samples of $n = 49$ students.

# The Foundations of Inferential Statistics: The Scientific Method and Hypotheses Testing

**Learning Objectives:**

By the end of this chapter you should be able to:

1. Explain the importance of the scientific method.
2. Describe the difference between a null and alternative hypothesis.
3. Write hypotheses including both the null and alternative.
4. Explain the difference between one-tailed and two-tailed hypotheses.
5. Describe the importance of significance levels and critical values.
6. Explain what it means to reject and fail to reject the null hypothesis.
7. Describe the five steps of hypothesis testing.
8. Explain Type I and Type II errors.

## Ronald Aylmer Fisher (1890–1962)

Ronald Fisher is credited for coining the term "null hypothesis." Born in Hampstead, England, the son of a London auctioneer, he was one of seven children. Tragically Robert's brother, Alan, died in 1881 at the age of three. His mother, Katie, held a superstitious belief that Alan should have had the letter "y" in his name. Hence, every child after Alan (e.g., Sibyl, Phyllis, and Alwyn) had the letter "y" in his or name.

Fisher studied mathematics and astronomy at the University of Cambridge. He worked briefly on a farm in Canada, before returning to England where he took a position as a statistician for an investment firm. He volunteered to serve during World War I, but was rejected due to poor eyesight. He then taught mathematics in public school for a few years until 1919 when he took a position as a statistician at an agricultural research station.

In 1933, Fisher became a Professor at University College London where he wrote about the null hypothesis. In his book *The Design of Experiments* (1935, p. 18) he wrote "In relation to any experiment we may speak of this hypothesis as the 'null hypothesis,' and it should be noted that the null hypothesis is never proved or established, but is possibly disproved, in the course of experimentation. Every experiment may be said to exist only in order to give the facts a chance of disproving the null hypothesis." And the null hypothesis, as they say, was born. Fisher later became a Professor at the University of Cambridge and retired in 1957. He died in Australia in 1962.[1]

# Introduction

**Population parameter estimation** is the analytical method for calculating the expected population parameter based on a sample statistic.

**Statistical hypothesis testing** is the use of statistical methods to test a hypothesis.

In chapter 6 we said that statistical inference is a process for making statements about the broader population based on the use of sample data from that population. We also discussed the difference between a sample statistic (a numeric value in the sample), and a population parameter (a numeric value in the population). Starting with this chapter, we are going investigate how we make statistical inferences. Two of the fundamental concepts in statistical inference are **population parameter estimation** and **statistical hypothesis testing**. This chapter will deal specifically with the process behind hypothesis testing. In chapter 8 we will introduce population parameter estimation using confidence intervals. However, before we do that, we need to discuss why these two concepts are important and how they relate to the scientific method.

# The Scientific Method

**LO1**

Social scientists are interested in using data to test theories about society. For example, in 2007 Professor Robin Wright, of McGill University, and colleagues published a paper titled "Effects of School-Based Interventions on Secondary School Students with High and Low Risks for Antisocial Behaviour."[2] These

**FIGURE 7.1**
**The Scientific Method**

Reference: W. Wallace, The Logic of Science in Sociology (Chicago: Aldine-Atherton, 1971).

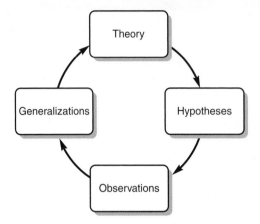

researchers were testing a theory, called the social development model, which hypothesizes that students who feel a strong personal connection to their school and its social and behavioural rules are more likely to engage in pro-social behaviour rather than anti-social behaviour. To accomplish their goal of testing the theory, the researchers followed the research process outlined in Figure 1.2 in chapter 1. This included creating hypotheses, gathering data, and using statistical methods to test their hypotheses and ultimately the theory.

In chapter 1 we discussed how statistics fits within the research process, but we did not discuss the underlying reason for following the research process. That reason is the **scientific method**, a process by which we investigate phenomena whether they be natural or social in nature. Figure 7.1 graphically displays the scientific method in what is commonly referred to as the Wheel of Science.[3] When we want to investigate a particular phenomenon or issue, we need a logical process to guide our investigation. The scientific method provides us with a way to obtain knowledge and present our findings in such a manner that others can replicate and confirm or disconfirm our results.

There are a number of ways of displaying the scientific method, but generally they follow the same idea as Figure 7.1. This includes the following:

The **scientific method** is a process by which we investigate phenomena whether natural or social in nature.

1. **Theory:** We start with a theory of why the phenomena is occurring (or acting in such a way). In our previous example, the researchers were using the social development model as the theory.

2. **Hypotheses:** Theory helps us create predictions about what we expect will happen within our sample. These predictions are made by way of hypotheses. Drawing again from Wright's research, it was hypothesized that students who felt a strong personal connection to their school and its social and behavioural rules would be more likely to engage in pro-social behaviour.

3. **Observations:** In order to test a theory, we need to observe what is happening in a sample of the population. This might involve collecting data using a survey instrument, an experiment, or other type of data collection method. In Wright's research, they used a survey questionnaire consisting of 98 questions.

4. **Generalizations:** Once we have the data, we can test our hypotheses using statistical analysis. Wright and colleagues tested their hypotheses using a form of analysis called Analysis of Variance, or ANOVA for short. We will learn more about this type of analysis later in the book. If we conduct our research with a random sample, we can then make generalizations about the population of interest. This is where population parameter estimation often comes in.

To recap, the scientific method provides us with steps to systematically test theories and advance knowledge. The research process is essentially the scientific method, except that it includes more details as to how to integrate it into your research. By following the scientific method, researchers (such as Wright et al., 2007) can test theories about the social world and extend our understanding. Other researchers can then use that information to test other hypotheses or to confirm the findings of previous researchers. We can also making inferences about what is happening in the population by using population parameter estimation. However, it is important to remember that, as discussed in chapter 6, in order to make an inference about a population parameter from a sample statistic our sample must have been randomly drawn from the population of interest. Given that not all research uses a random sample, making inferences about the population parameter is not always possible.

# Understanding Hypotheses and Significance Levels

**LO2**

## The Null and Alternative Hypotheses

In the previous section, we discussed the notion of hypothesis testing and population parameter estimation. In this section, we will specifically deal with how to set up a hypothesis for statistical testing. Testing hypotheses involves using a process called the Null Hypothesis Significance Test (NHST), often referred to as significance testing. To understand this concept, let's consider the following example before we look at the definition.

Suppose we want to test whether university students majoring in a social science discipline differ in IQ score from the population of university students. Now suppose we hypothesize that the social science majors will on average have a higher IQ score than the population of university students. Finally, suppose we know from prior literature that the population mean ($\mu$) IQ score for university students is 100 with a standard deviation ($\sigma$) of 15. Now we randomly select 150 individuals from a population of social science majors, collect their IQ scores, calculate the mean ($\bar{x}$), and find that on average their IQ score of ($\bar{x} = 102$) was higher than the population mean ($\mu$) of 100. We might be tempted to conclude that our hypothesis is correct. Now imagine that we replicate the study on a different random sample of 150 social science majors, only this time we find the opposite result. The mean ($\bar{x} = 98$) IQ scores for the social science students is lower than the population mean of university students ($\mu = 100$). This time we might conclude that our hypothesis is incorrect. What happens now?

**FIGURE 7.2**
**Population Means and Sample Means**

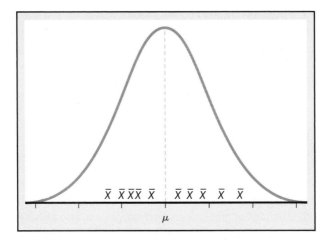

Results are considered to be **statistically significant** when it is unlikely that they occurred by chance.

A **null hypothesis** states that the result was due to chance (from sampling error) and as such is not a true difference.

An **alternative hypothesis** states that the result was not due to chance and represents a real difference or effect or relationship.

In this example, our results differed even though we took a random sampling of the population. However, we have to remember that since we only considered a subset of the population and not the entire population, the mean of our sample ($\bar{x}$) will not necessarily be the same as the mean of the population ($\mu$). Consider Figure 7.2. Here you can see that we have 10 different sample means that fall above or below the population mean. This is exactly what we saw in our discussion on sampling distributions, only this time we aren't calculating every possible sample. In statistics, we conclude that there could be two reasons why there is a difference between a sample mean ($\bar{x}$) and the population mean ($\mu$). The first is that, given that we only took a sample of the population, the result we obtained is just due to chance. One sample mean could be higher and another sample mean could be lower. The second is that the result we obtained is not due to chance, but represents a true difference. When a result represents a true difference, we say that it is **statistically significant**.

This brings us back to our hypothesis about social science majors and IQ scores. We know that our results could be due either to chance or to the existence of a true difference (statistically significant). Since there are two possible explanations for the result we found, we actually have two hypotheses rather than one. The first is that the difference is due to chance and the second is that the difference is real. If the first is true, then by default the second is false, and vice versa. We refer to these hypotheses as the null and the alternative. We should point out that a real difference does not mean that the difference is substantive or of practical importance. A diet that claims to help you lose weight might provide a weight loss that is proven statistically significant. But if the average weight loss was one pound, no one would find the diet useful. Statistical significance only tells us whether a difference exists, it does not tell us anything about the importance of the difference.

A **null hypothesis** states that the result was due to chance (from sampling error) and as such is not a true difference. An **alternative hypothesis** states that the result that was not due to chance and represents a real difference. The alternative hypothesis, often referred to as the research hypothesis, is usually the hypothesis that the researcher believes is true. Since the null hypothesis represents the case where the result doesn't reflect a true difference, we simplify it by saying that the null hypothesis is that there is no difference. Similarly, since the alternative hypothesis represents the case where the result reflects a statistically significant difference, we often simplify it by saying that the alternative hypothesis is that there is a difference.

To recap, while the null hypothesis always states that there is no difference (or no effect or no relationship), the alternative hypothesis always states that there is a difference (or effect, or relationship). Using our previous example, we can state the null and alternative hypotheses as follows:

Null Hypothesis: There is no difference in IQ scores between social science majors and other university students.

Alternative Hypothesis: Social science majors have a higher IQ score than other university students.

**Note:** The notation for a null hypothesis is usually $H_0$, whereas the notation for the alternative hypothesis is $H_A$. Quite often you have more than one hypothesis, in which case the A in $H_A$ is replaced with a number, such as $H_1$.

When we think about the null hypothesis in the context of the population mean of IQ scores (let's refer to that for the time being as $\mu_0$) versus the mean ($\bar{x}$) from our sample, what we are saying is that if that our sample came from the same population from which our population mean ($\mu_0$) is calculated, then there shouldn't be a difference. That is because the sample mean is one of a vast amount of possible samples in the sampling distribution that can be used to estimate the population distribution. In the same context, the alternative hypothesis states that if the mean of our sample ($\bar{x}$) is statistically different from the population mean ($\mu_0$), then it must be calculated from a different population with a different population mean (which we'll refer to as $\mu_A$). Therefore, what we are testing is whether $\mu_A$ is greater (in the sense of statistically significant) than $\mu_0$. Thus we can write the null and alternative hypotheses as:

$$H_0: \mu_A = \mu_0$$
$$H_A: \mu_A > \mu_0$$

The scientific method requires that a testable hypothesis can be falsified. This means that if the hypothesis truly is false then it can be shown to be false. In that regard, we never confirm that a hypothesis is true since we may later find evidence that shows it was false. This seems like a bit of a roundabout way of testing hypotheses, but remember that when we test hypotheses, we are actually testing the null hypothesis to see if it is false. If it is false, then we say we reject the null hypothesis and accept the alternative as a plausible explanation. If we cannot find evidence to show that the null hypothesis is false, then we say we fail to reject the null hypothesis and reject the alternative as a plausible alternative. We say "fail to reject" as opposed to "accept" because we can never truly confirm a hypothesis, given that we may later find evidence to the contrary. In short, when statistically testing a hypothesis, we test the null hypothesis to see if it is false. If there is evidence to suggest it is false then we reject it and accept (albeit temporarily) the alternative. If we can't find evidence to suggest that the null hypothesis is false, then we fail to reject it and, in return, we reject the alternative.

As was the case in our social science student IQ example, hypotheses can be stated in such a way as to specify the direction of the difference, relationship, or effect. When a hypothesis states a specific direction (such as higher or lower, increased or decreased, positively or negatively) we say it is a **one-tailed hypothesis**. The following are examples of one-tailed hypotheses.

$H_A$: Females experience <u>greater</u> levels of discrimination in the workplace than males.

$H_A$: 30mg of drug XYZ will <u>reduce</u> the risk of cancer.

$H_A$: Anti-social behaviour is <u>positively</u> related to bullying behaviour.

When we have a one-tailed alternative hypothesis, we need to set up the null hypothesis such that it considers all of the other possibilities not included in the alternative hypothesis. You'll notice that in our social science student IQ example we stated the null hypothesis as ". . . no difference in IQ scores." Given that the alternative hypothesis is directional, in that it states "Social science majors have a higher IQ score . . .," the null hypothesis should be "the IQ scores of social science majors is equal to or less than other university students. We kept the previous example simple in order to get the point across, but now it is time to restate the hypotheses.

Null Hypothesis: The IQ scores of social science majors is equal to or less than other university students.

Alternative Hypothesis: Social science majors have a higher IQ score than other university students.

Or,

$$H_0: \mu_A \leq \mu_0$$
$$H_A: \mu_A > \mu_0$$

When hypotheses do not have a specified direction of the difference, relationship, or effect, we refer to them as **two-tailed hypotheses**. The following are examples of two-tailed hypotheses.

$H_A$: Females experience <u>different</u> levels of discrimination in the workplace than males.

$H_A$: 30mg of Drug XYZ will <u>have an effect</u> on the risk of cancer.

$H_A$: Anti-social behaviour is <u>related</u> to bullying behaviour.

As you can see with a two-tailed hypothesis, the null hypothesis becomes $\mu_A = \mu_0$, whereas the alternative hypothesis is $\mu_A \neq \mu_0$. We will explore the importance of differentiating between the one- and two-tailed hypotheses later in the chapter. However, now that we understand how to set up a hypothesis for statistical testing, we need to cover when we reject or fail to reject the null hypothesis. This involves using significance levels and critical values.

## Significance Levels and Critical Values

A **significance level** ($\alpha$, pronounced "alpha") is the value used to determine whether to reject or fail to reject the null hypothesis. It is the portion of area

---

**LO4**

A **one-tailed hypothesis** states a predicted direction (directional).

---

**LO5**

The **significance level** ($\alpha$) value is used to determine whether to reject or fail to reject the null hypothesis

A **two-tailed hypothesis** does not state a predicted direction (non-directional).

under the sampling distribution curve that represents the probability of observing a score either above or below that point. In the social sciences it is common to set this value at either 0.05 or 0.01. Take a look at the sampling distribution on the left in Figure 7.3. Here you can see that the alpha value ($\alpha$) has been set at 0.05 in the left tail of the distribution. This indicates that 5 percent of the scores fall to the left of our alpha value and 95 percent fall to the right. Conversely, the sampling distribution on the right shows an alpha of 0.05 in the right tail of the distribution. In this case, 5 percent of the scores fall to the right of the alpha value and 95 percent fall to the left. Likewise, setting our alpha value at 0.01 in the left tail means that 1 percent of the scores will fall to the left of our alpha value and 99 percent will fall to the right. If our alpha value of 0.01 is in the right tail, 1 percent of the scores will fall to the right of this value, and 99 percent will fall to the left. The way in which the **critical value** under the distribution curve is calculated (based on your desired alpha value) differs by the type of statistical analysis and whether the hypothesis is one-tailed or two-tailed. For our purposes in this chapter, we will consider situations—similar to our current example— in which the data is either interval or ratio and where we can use the standard normal distribution.

> A **critical value** is the corresponding value to the significance level that determines the boundary for rejecting or failing to reject the null hypothesis.

Consider our discussions in chapter 5 pertaining to the areas under the normal curve. Since the sampling distribution is equal to the standard normal distribution and the alpha value represents a portion of the area under the sampling distribution curve, we can look up our desired alpha value of 0.05 in column III in Appendix A: Area Under the Normal Curve, and find its corresponding critical value, which is the $z$-score in this case. The $z$-score that corresponds to our desired alpha value is our critical value. More specifically, we call this the critical value of $z$ because we are dealing with $z$-scores. Based on Appendix A, we can see that the critical value of $z$ is $\pm 1.645$. It is $\pm$(plus or minus) because it is giving us the value for the right and left tails. Now, looking at the distribution on the left of Figure 7.3, the critical value corresponding to the alpha value of 0.05 is $-1.645$ (it is negative because it is on the left), meaning that we can expect 5 percent of the scores to be less than $-1.645$. Conversely, for the distribution on the right, the critical value is $+1.645$ (it is positive because it is in the right tail), meaning that we can expect 5 percent of the scores to be greater than $+1.645$.

**Note:** You will often see the critical value written with the notation $z_{(\alpha)}$ when dealing with $z$-scores. With other tests, the $z$ is replaced with the letter of the test. For example $t_{(\alpha)}$ for $t$-tests.

**LO6**

The shaded area in Figure 7.3 not only represents the values greater than or less than our alpha value. It also represents the region in which we *reject the null hypothesis*. The area that is not shaded represents the region where we *fail to reject the null hypothesis*. As you can see, both of these distributions are highlighting just one tail of the distribution (left or right). When we test a one-tailed hypothesis the entire 5 percent ($\alpha$) rejection region is placed in one tail. This is because our alternative hypothesis is stating directionality in either the positive/greater than ($+/>$) or negative/less than ($-/<$) direction.

**FIGURE 7.3** $\alpha = 0.05$ One-Tailed (left tail)      $\alpha = 0.05$ One-Tailed (right tail)

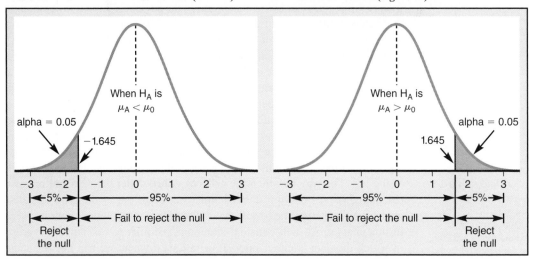

Contrast Figure 7.3 with the shaded area in Figure 7.4. Notice that our 5 percent alpha value is split equally across both tails. Since a two-tailed hypothesis does not specify directionality, we need to split the 5 percent across the two tails. Therefore, when we look up the $z$-value that corresponds with a two-tailed alpha value of 0.05, we first need to divide the alpha value by two ($0.05 \div 2 = 0.025$). We then look for the value 0.025 in column III of Appendix A. The corresponding $z$-score for a two-tailed alpha value of 0.05 is $\pm 1.96$.

**FIGURE 7.4**

$\alpha = 0.05$ Two-Tailed

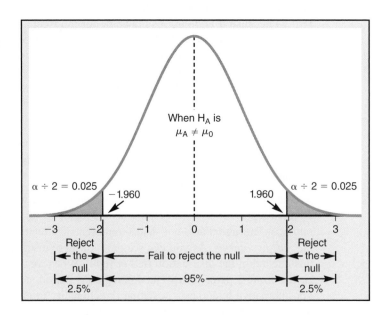

# For Your Information

As you can see in Figure 7.5, decreasing the $\alpha$ value from 0.05 to 0.01 increases the critical value $(Z_{(\alpha)})$, which makes it harder to reject the null hypothesis. Having higher confidence levels (i.e., 99 percent versus 95 percent) results in lower signifance levels ($\alpha$), which in turn creates more stringent tests since the "reject the null" region, based on the critical value, is further from the mean. You can also see that in two-tailed distribution the critical values $(Z_{(\alpha)})$ are based on $\alpha \div 2$, creating lower critical values $(Z_{(\alpha)})$ than their respective one-tailed distributions. As such, tests based on the two-tailed critical values are considered to be more stringent than those based on the one-tailed values because the "reject the null" region, based on the critical value, is further from the mean. Therefore, in the social sciences it is common to see tests based on the two-tailed critical values regardless of whether the hypothesis is a one-tailed or two-tailed hypothesis.

**FIGURE 7.5** **One-Tailed Alpha ($\alpha$) and Critical Values ($Z_{(\alpha)}$) versus Two-Tailed Alpha ($\alpha$) and Critical Values ($Z_{(\alpha)}$)**

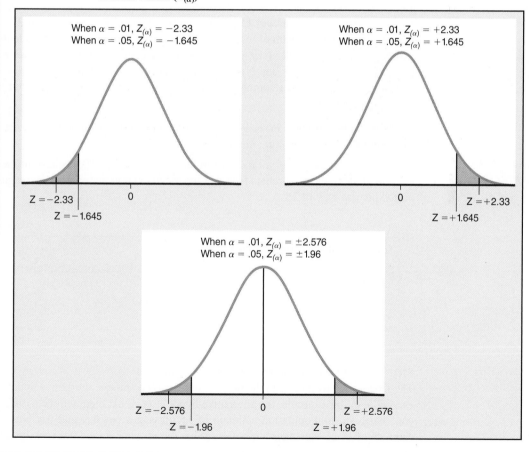

# The Five Steps of Hypothesis Testing

Now that we understand hypotheses, significance levels, and the basic concepts of rejecting versus failing to reject the null hypothesis, we need to discuss how to statistically test a hypothesis. As previously mentioned, the critical values for alpha ($\alpha$) depend on the type of analysis you use and whether the hypothesis is one-tailed or two-tailed. In this section, we will cover the steps for testing hypotheses using a simple one-sample $z$-test as an example. While the statistical test will change over the course of the remaining chapters, the steps involved for testing a hypothesis will remain the same. Furthermore, the process is the same whether you have one-tailed or two-tailed hypothesis tests. For this section we will use the following example.

Privacy issues have become a significant concern with social networking Internet sites. Of particular concern is the type of content that teenagers post about themselves and others that could potentially put them at physical and/or psychological risk. Suppose that the mean ($\mu$) number of posted messages (that included potentially risky content) for all 2,000 teens (the population) that attend high school in a specific region was 15 per day, with a standard deviation ($\sigma$) of 2.75. Further suppose that a team of researchers is currently studying whether students with higher average grades (say, greater than 85 percent) differ in the number of risky messages posted per day. Not knowing whether students with higher grades will post a higher or lower number of risky messages than the population, the researchers hypothesize:

$H_A$: The number of risky messages posted by teens with higher grade averages will differ from the population mean.

After collecting data from a random sample of 100 students (who have higher average grades), the researchers find that the mean ($\bar{x}$) number of risky messages posted per day was 14.25.

| Summary of Research Scenario Data | |
| --- | --- |
| Population of All 2,000 Teens in a High School in a Specific Region | Sample of 100 Teens with Higher Average Grades (Same Region) |
| $\mu = 15$ per day | $\bar{x} = 14.25$ |
| $\sigma = 2.75$ | $n = 100$ |

### Step 1: Define the Null and Alternative Hypotheses

The first step is to state both the null hypothesis ($H_0$) and the alternative hypothesis ($H_A$). In this example, the alternative hypothesis is that there will be a difference between the population estimate of 15 messages per day and the sample estimate of 14.25 messages a day. Given that the researchers did not specify that the number of messages, posted by those with higher average grades, would be more or less than the population (no specified direction), we know that this hypothesis is a two-tailed hypothesis. So we have:

$$H_0: \mu_A = \mu_0$$
$$H_A: \mu_A = \mu_0$$

## Step 2: Define the Sampling Distribution and Critical Values

Although the sample that the researchers took ($n = 100$) was a random sample, we know from our previous discussion that since there are many ways we could potentially draw a sample of 100 respondents from the population, the sample mean ($\bar{x} = 14.25$) will inevitably have some error when we consider it as representative of the population mean ($\mu = 15$). In chapter 6, we found that we could create a sampling distribution that represents the distribution of the means ($\bar{x}$) from every possible sample. Furthermore, the Central Limit Theorem (CLT) tells us that the mean of the sampling distribution ($\mu_{\bar{x}}$) will equal the population mean ($\mu$) and the standard error of the mean ($\sigma_{\bar{x}}$) of the sampling distribution will equal the population standard deviation ($\sigma$) divided by the square root of the sample size.

In hypothesis testing, the sampling distribution represents the distribution of the null hypothesis where the mean ($\mu_{\bar{x}}$) equals the value of the null hypothesis if it were true, and the standard error of the distribution ($\sigma_{\bar{x}}$) represents how far potential values deviate from the mean.

Let's consider this logic in a bit more detail.

1. The null hypothesis is that $\mu_A = \mu_0$. Written another way we can say that $\mu_A - \mu_0 = 0$.
2. If the null hypothesis is true, then we can say that the sample mean ($\bar{x} = 14.25$) came from the population where the mean ($\mu$) was 15 and not from a different population.
3. Therefore, if we create a sampling distribution that represents the null hypothesis ($\mu_0$), the mean ($\mu_{\bar{x}}$) of this distribution will have a $z$-score (standardized) value of 0 (representing the raw score of $\mu_{\bar{x}} = 15$) where the null hypothesis is true.
4. Furthermore, we can add standard deviations to the null hypothesis distribution by using the standard error of the mean ($\sigma_{\bar{x}}$). Based on our understanding of the CLT, the standard deviations will be $\sigma_{\bar{x}} = \sigma \div \sqrt{n}$. (Refer to chapter 6.)

So what we have is a distribution with a mean of 0 representing the null hypothesis and standard errors that represent how far potential values deviate from the mean. Using our population values and the formula for calculating the standard error of the mean (shown above), we can visually create the sampling distribution for the null hypothesis (Figure 7.6).

Now that we have the sampling distribution for the null hypothesis, the next step is to set the decision criteria by which we will either reject the null or fail to

**FIGURE 7.6**

The standard error is:

$$\sigma_{\bar{x}} = \frac{\sigma}{\sqrt{n}} = \frac{2.75}{\sqrt{100}}$$

$$= 0.275$$

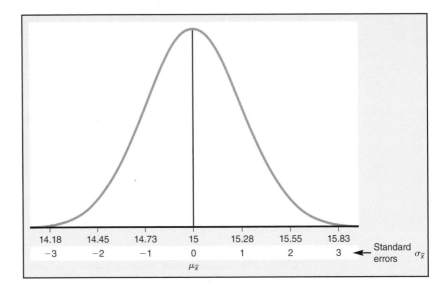

reject the null. Given that we are dealing with a two-tailed hypothesis, we need the two-tailed critical values. Assuming that we are interested in a 95 percent confidence level, which equates to an alpha ($\alpha$) of 0.05, our critical values will be $\pm 1.96$. Figure 7.7 shows the shaded regions where we would reject the null with an alpha of 0.05.

Let's step back for a moment and consider what we have at this point and how we will use it. We have a sampling distribution that represents the null hypothesis. Similar to our exercises in chapter 5, we can use $z$-scores to determine the probability of any given value (say, $\bar{x}$ value of 14.25) occurring under this distribution representing the null hypothesis. Meaning that, if the $z$-score for our sample mean ($\bar{x} = 14.25$) falls in the shaded areas, then we will *reject the null hypothesis* that $\mu_A = \mu_0$ and conclude that, given the probability of this score occurring when the null hypothesis were true is less than 5 percent (our alpha value), our sample mean ($\bar{x} = 14.25$) is therefore not likely from the population $\mu_0$ where $\mu = 15$, but is from another population ($\mu_{(A)}$). Alternatively, if the $z$-score for our sample mean ($\bar{x} = 14.25$) falls between $-1.96$ and $+1.96$, then we will *fail to reject the null hypothesis* that $\mu_A = \mu_0$ and conclude that it is quite likely that our sample mean ($\bar{x} = 14.25$) came from the population $\mu_0$ where $\mu = 15$. Looking at the $x$-axis in Figure 7.7, we can tell that the $\bar{x}$ of 14.25 is going to fall somewhere in the left tail between $-2$ and $-3$ standard errors from the mean.

A **test statistic** is a summary value (statistic), based on our sample data, that indicates how far our sample estimate (such as $\bar{x}$) differs from zero under the null hypothesis distribution.

**Step 3: Calculate the Test Statistic Using the Sample Data**

Now that we have the sampling distribution for the null hypothesis and our critical values, we need to calculate the **test statistic**. Given that we are using interval/ratio level data and the normal distribution, our test statistic is a $z$-score.

**FIGURE 7.7**

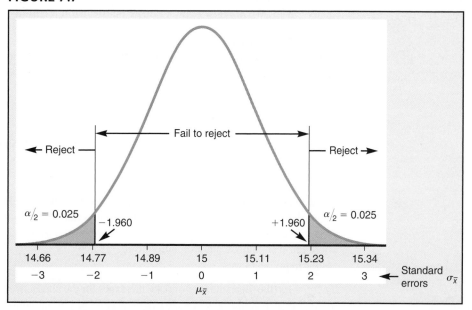

In chapter 5 we introduced the $z$-score formula:

$$z = \frac{x - \mu}{\sigma} \qquad (7.1)$$

We use this formula when we are interested in calculating the $z$-score for a normal distribution when we know the values for $\mu$ and $\sigma$. However, when dealing with sampling distributions, we need to modify the formula as shown in 7.2.

$$z = \frac{\bar{x} - \mu_0}{\sigma_{\bar{x}}} = \frac{\bar{x} - \mu_0}{(\sigma \div \sqrt{n})} \qquad (7.2)$$

Our justification for doing this is that since we are dealing with testing a sample mean against a population mean, the notation changes from that which represents an individual value ($x$) to that which represents a sample mean value ($\bar{x}$). Similarily, the value $\sigma_{\bar{x}}$ replaces $\sigma$. Recall from chapter 6 that standard error of the sampling distribution ($\sigma_{\bar{x}}$) is equal to the standard deviation of the population ($\sigma$) divided by the square root of the sample size ($\sqrt{n}$). Thus, our denominator is $\sigma \div \sqrt{n}$ and our result is:

$$z = \frac{\bar{x} - \mu_0}{(\sigma \div \sqrt{n})} = \frac{14.25 - 15}{\left(\dfrac{2.75}{\sqrt{100}}\right)} = \frac{-0.75}{0.275} = -2.73 \qquad (7.3)$$

Based on our sample mean of 14.25 our test statistic (z-score in this case) equals $-2.73$. We are now ready to make our decision regarding our hypothesis.

### Step 4: Make the Decision Regarding the Hypothesis

Now we are at the point where we can decide to either reject or fail to reject the null hypothesis. As we noted in Step 2, based on our two-tailed alpha value of 0.05, the critical value that our test statistic must pass in order to reject the null hypothesis was $\pm 1.96$. Meaning our test statistics must be either greater than $+1.96$ or less than $-1.96$.

**Note:** Remember although our alpha ($\alpha$) value is 0.05, it is split in half because we are conducting a two-tailed test. If we used a one-tailed test, then the critical value would be $-1.645$ instead of $\pm 1.96$.

Our test statistic is $-2.73$, which means that our sample $\bar{x}$ of 14.25 is $-2.73$ standard errors from the $\mu_{\bar{x}}$ of 15. Since this is less than the critical value of $-1.96$ we can reject the null hypothesis. Figure 7.8 provides a graphic representation of where our test statistic sits in relation to $\mu_{\bar{x}}$.

Our hypothesis was:

$H_0$: $\mu_A = \mu_0$ (the mean number of risky messages for the alternative population is 15).

$H_A$: $\mu_A \neq \mu_0$ (the mean number of risky messages for the alternative population is not 15).

### FIGURE 7.8

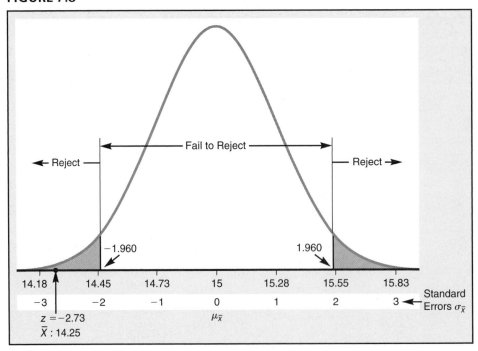

Our decision to *reject the null hypothesis* means that we can accept the alternative hypothesis as true, at least until future evidence proves otherwise.

We rejected the null hypothesis because our test statistic passed the critical value. We can also look at the probability associated with our test statistic. Consider Figure 7.9. With a two-tailed significance level ($\alpha$) of 0.05 the probability of finding a score less than $z = -1.96$ is 2.5 percent. We know this because we can look up the $z$-score of $|1.96|$ in Appendix A and find the proportion of area past the $z$-value is 0.025. We refer to the probability value as the *p*-value. We can also find the *p*-value for our test statistic value ($-2.73$) by looking up the $z$-score of $-2.73$. Using Appendix A, we find that the proportion of area past the $z$-value is 0.003. Therefore, we can say that our test statistic of has a *p*-value of 0.003. Lower *p*-values for our test statistics indicate stronger evidence against the null hypothesis. Therefore, we can say that the probability of obtaining a test statistic as as low as $-2.73$ or lower is 0.3 percent when the null hypothesis is actually true. A simpler statement is that there is only a three in 1,000 chance that we would find this particular value (result) if the null hypothesis were really true. That's pretty strong evidence against the null hypothesis.

### Step 5: Interpret the Results

Our researchers had the following hypothesis about posting risky personal messages.

$H_A$: The number of risky messages posted by teens with higher average grades will differ from the population mean.

**FIGURE 7.9**

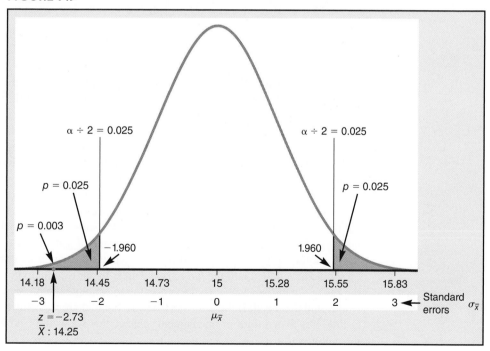

## Take a Closer Look

### *p*-Values and Alpha Values

Alpha values are the significance levels that we assign in order to determine the critical value that a test statistic must pass in order to reject the null hypothesis. We can also determine the *p*-value that is associated with a given alpha value. In the two-tailed situation, an alpha value of 0.05 has a *p*-value of 0.025 on both the right and left tails. In the one-tailed situation, the same alpha value has a *p*-value of 0.05, because we are only considering one tail of the distribution.

It is common to refer to a test statistic as being statistically significant at the $p < 0.05$ (or $p < 0.01$) level. Although different disciplines have different reporting conventions, to distinguish between one- and two-tailed situations, we often state this as:

Our test statistic was significant at $p < 0.05$ level (two-tailed).

*Or*

Our test statistic was significant at the $p < 0.05$ level (one-tailed).

Two things are worth noting here. First, in statistics we use the term "significant" to refer to something being statistically significant; that is, it is unlikely to have occurred by chance. Second, even though an alpha value of 0.05 has a two-tailed *p*-value of 0.025 we often report it as a $p < 0.05$ and include "(two-tailed)" so that readers can determine the significance level we set.

When considering the test statistic *p*-values, here is a way to remember whether to reject or fail to reject the null: When the test statistic *p*-value is less than alpha ($p < \alpha$) you reject the null. When the test statistic *p*-value is greater than alpha ($p > \alpha$) you fail to reject the null. It is quite difficult to calculate the exact *p*-value of a test statistic without the help of a computer. So we will leave our discussion of *p*-values at this.

Since our test statistic ($z = -2.73$) was statistically significant at the $p < 0.05$ level (two-tailed) we rejected the null hypothesis and accepted the alternative. When we state that we accept the alternative, we are saying that there is enough evidence to suggest that this sample mean is significantly different from the population mean of 15. Therefore, the number of risky messages posted by students with higher average grades did differ (fewer in this case) significantly from the population mean.

It is important to remember that when we reject the null hypothesis at the $p < 0.05$ level we are stating the probability that we would observe the result we did if the null hypothesis were true. This is not the same as the probability of the null hypothesis being true. Sometimes the language of statistics is confusing, so here's another way to think of it. If the null hypothesis were true, our test statistic should have fallen into the *fail to reject* area. In our example, the result fell in the *reject the null* area. We used the *p*-value to estimate the probability that we would find that result if the null was true and found there was only a 0.3 percent (a little less than a third of one percent) chance that we would find that result if the null was true.

# Did You Know?

Since 1991, the organization Improbable Research has sponsored the now-famous Ig Nobel Prize which is meant to celebrate research that "first makes people laugh, then makes them think." In a nutshell, these prizes are meant to commemorate those researchers who have conducted research that might be considered a bit unusual. According to the organization, "the prizes are intended to celebrate the unusual, honor the imaginative and spur people's interest in science, medicine, and technology."

Five interesting hypotheses that have earned researchers an Ig Noble Prize are:

1. Parkin and colleagues tested the hypothesis that wearing socks over your shoes decreases your risk of slipping on icy paths. Results suggest that it works.[1]

2. Bertenshaw and Rowlinson tested whether cows that are named by the farmer yield more milk than those without names. Evidence suggests they do.[2]

3. Stephens and colleagues tested the hypothesis that swearing can increase one's pain tolerance. Results suggest that in some situations it might.[3]

4. Bolliger and colleagues investigated whether empty or full beer bottles were sturdier and if that influenced the potential for head injury during a physical conflict. Results show that while empty bottles are sturdier, both can cause serious head injury.[4]

5. Stack and Gundlach tested the hypothesis that country music increases the risk of suicide. Results suggest that it can increase suicide rates in those already at risk of suicide.[5]

**Sources:** M. Abrahams, The Ig Nobel Prizes: *The Annals of Improbable Research,* (Dutton, published by Penguin Group (USA) Inc., 2003)

http://improbable.com/

[1] L. Parkin, S. M. Williams, P. Priest, "Preventing winter falls: a randomised controlled trial of a novel intervention," *Journal of the New Zealand Medical Association* Volume 122 (2009), pp. 31–38.

[2] C. Bertenshaw and P. Rowlinson, "Exploring Stock Managers' Perceptions of the Human-Animal Relationship on Dairy Farms and an Association with Milk Production," *Anthrozoos: A Multidisciplinary Journal of The Interactions of People & Animals,* Volume 22, no. 1 (2009), pp. 59–69

[3] R. Stephens, J. Atkins, A. Kingston, "Swearing as a response to pain." *Neuroreport,* 20 no. 12 (2009), pp. 1056–1060.

[4] S. A. Bolliger et al., "Are full or empty beer bottles sturdier and does their fracture-threshold suffice to break the human skull?" *Journal of Forensic and Legal Medicine,* 16 no. 3 (2009), pp. 138–142

[5] S. Stack and J. Gundlach, "The Effect of Country Music on Suicide." *Social Forces,* 71, no. 1 (1992), pp. 211–218.

## Example of a One-Tailed Hypothesis Test

*Scenario:*

Generally, the mean ($\mu$) IQ score in the population is considered to be 100 with a standard deviation ($\sigma$) of 15. Suppose you hypothesize that individuals who play the piano have higher IQ scores than the population. Your study of a random sample of 125 people indicates that the mean score ($\bar{x}$) for this sample is 102.

**Step 1: Define the null and alternative hypotheses**
$H_0$: $\mu_A \leq \mu_0$ (the mean IQ of people who play the piano is 100)
$H_A$: $\mu_A > \mu_0$ (the mean IQ of people who play the piano is greater than 100)

**Step 2: Define the sampling distribution and critical values**
The mean of the sampling distribution ($\mu_{\bar{x}}$) is 100 and the standard error of the mean ($\sigma_{\bar{x}}$) is 1.34. Therefore $-2\sigma_{\bar{x}} = 97.32$, $-1\sigma_{\bar{x}} = 98.66$, $+1\sigma_{\bar{x}} = 101.34$, $+2\sigma_{\bar{x}} = 102.68$.

$$\sigma_{\bar{x}} = \frac{\sigma}{\sqrt{n}} = \frac{15}{\sqrt{125}} = 1.3416$$

With an alpha ($\alpha$) value of 0.05 and the hypothesis being one-tailed (right tail), the critical value ($z_\alpha$) is +1.645.

**Step 3: Calculate the test statistic using the sample data**
The test statistic is $z = 1.49$.

$$z = \frac{\bar{x} - \mu}{\sigma / \sqrt{n}} = \frac{102 - 100}{1.3416} = 1.49$$

**Step 4: Make the decision regarding the hypothesis**
The test statistic of $z = 1.49$ is less than the critical value ($z_\alpha$) of +1.645; therefore, you fail to reject the null hypothesis. Another way to make the decision is to use *p*-values. The *p*-value for the test statistic of $z = 1.49$ is $p = 0.07$. Since the *p*-value is greater than the alpha value ($\alpha$) ($0.07 > 0.05$), you fail to reject the null hypothesis.

**Step 5: Interpret the results**
The mean IQ ($\bar{x} = 102$) of the sample does not differ significantly from the mean IQ ($\mu = 100$) of the population. Therefore, based on this sample, people who play the piano do not have higher IQs than the population.

---

### Take a Closer Look

**The Five Steps of Hypothesis Testing**

**Step 1:** Define the null and alternative hypotheses.

**Step 2:** Define the sampling distribution and critical values.

**Step 3:** Calculate the test statistic using the sample data.

**Step 4:** Make the decision regarding the hypothesis.

**Step 5:** Interpret the results.

---

# Type I and Type II Errors

**LO8**

What happens if our conclusion is wrong? Figure 7.10 shows that there are two ways we can come to the incorrect conclusion. We could have rejected the null hypothesis when it was actually true, or we could have failed to reject the null hypothesis when it was really false.

Let's consider a real research scenario to clarify the difference between the two. In 2009, Catherine Sabiston and colleagues published the paper "School Smoking Policy Characteristics and Individual Perceptions of the School Tobacco Context: Are They Linked to Students' Smoking Status" in the *Journal of Youth Adolescence*. Among a number of interesting findings, they discovered that high school students (in Canada) who have a low sense of connection to their school (dislike the school, don't feel part of the school, don't feel that they are treated fairly, etc.) are more likely to smoke.

**FIGURE 7.10**

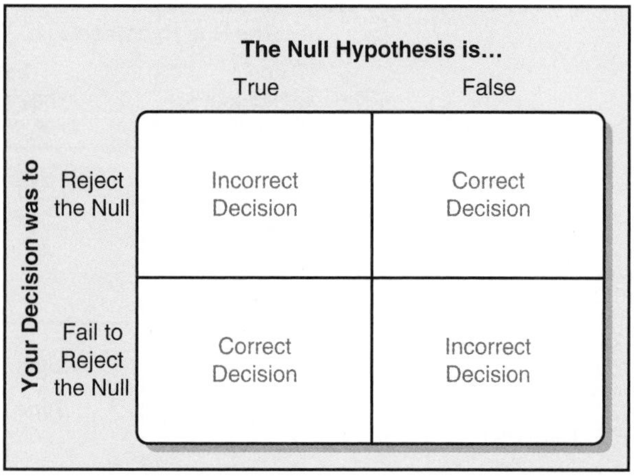

| | The Null Hypothesis is... | |
|---|---|---|
| | True | False |
| **Reject the Null** | Incorrect Decision | Correct Decision |
| **Fail to Reject the Null** | Correct Decision | Incorrect Decision |

*Your Decision was to*

Now suppose we conducted a study to replicate this particular finding. Our one-tailed hypothesis is:

$H_0$: High school students who do not feel connected to their school are not more likely to smoke or are less likely to smoke than those who feel connected to their school.

$H_A$: High school students who do not feel connected to their school are more likely to smoke than those who feel connected to their school.

If we take Figure 7.10 and add our research scenario and the possible errors we can make, we come up with Figure 7.11. When we reject a null that is actually true, we commit what is called a Type I error. The probability that we will commit a Type I error is the alpha value ($\alpha$) that we set as our significance level. So if we say that we are setting our significance level at $\alpha = 0.05$, we are also saying that we are willing to accept a 5 percent chance that we will commit a Type I error. Put another way, if we repeat this study 100 times, we are likely to make an incorrect decision about the null hypothesis (reject it when it was true) five times out of 100. The other 95 times we are likely to make the correct decision about the null (fail to reject it when it was true). So now you can see the importance of the significance level alpha ($\alpha$) and why changing the level from $\alpha = 0.05$ to $\alpha = 0.01$ makes the test more stringent. An alpha of 0.01 versus 0.05 means your probability of committing a Type I error is only 1 percent instead of 5 percent.

So to recap, a Type I error is the probability that you will reject the null hypothesis when it is actually true. In the context of our research example, it is the equivalent of saying that students who do not feel connected to their school are more likely to smoke, when in fact the likelihood that they will smoke is no different than those students who feel connected to their school. We control the probability of committing Type I error when we set our significance level ($\alpha$) in step 2 of our

**FIGURE 7.11**

|  | | The Null Hypothesis is... | |
|---|---|---|---|
|  | | **True**<br>"They are not more<br>likely to smoke" | **False**<br>"They are more<br>likely to smoke" |
| **Reject the Null**<br>You say...<br>"They are<br>more likely to<br>smoke" | | Incorrect Decision<br>**Type I Error**<br>$\alpha$ | Correct<br>Decision |
| **Fail to Reject<br>the Null**<br>You say...<br>"They are not<br>more likely to<br>smoke" | | Correct<br>Decision | Incorrect Decision<br>**Type II Error**<br>$\beta$ |

*(Your Decision was to)*

hypothesis testing. You may wonder, why don't we just set our alpha at the lowest possible value in order to decrease the probability of Type I error as much as possible? The answer has to do with our second type of error, Type II error, which we refer to with the symbol beta ($\beta$).

Refer back to Figure 7.11. Suppose that after testing our hypothesis we decide to fail to reject the null hypothesis, when it is actually false. In this case we are saying that students who do not feel connected to their school are not more likely to smoke, when in fact they are more likely to smoke. You can see that this is the opposite to a Type I error. We commit a Type II error when we fail to reject a false null hypothesis. Type I and Type II are related in that as you decrease the risk of a Type I error you increase the risk of a Type II error and vice versa. Figure 7.12 graphically shows how this works. Imagine the line representing the critical value ($z_{(\alpha)}$) on the null hypothesis distribution moving to the right and left. As it moves to the left, the alpha area increases, indicating an increased Type I error rate, and the beta decreases, indicating a decreased Type II error rate. Similarly, as the critical value line moves to the right, the alpha gets smaller, indicating a decreased Type I error rate, and the beta gets larger, indicating an increased Type II error rate.

While there is a lot more that we can cover about Type I and II errors, we will leave our discussion of this issue at this point. The main thing to take from this is that the significance level ($\alpha$) not only determines the critical value at which we reject or fail to reject the null hypothesis, but it also represents the probability that we will commit a Type I error. Although it is common in social science to set alpha values at 0.05 or 0.01 (and even 0.001), we need to remember that doing so is a bit of a balancing act between requiring more evidence to reject the null and potentially making the wrong decision about your hypotheses.

**FIGURE 7.12**

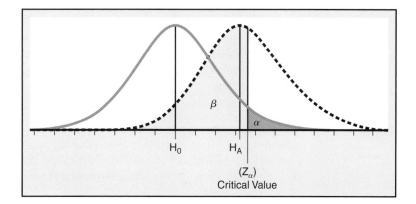

## Conclusion

In this chapter we covered one of the core concepts in inferential statistics, the hypothesis test. The scientific method provides us with a process for testing theories by way of hypotheses. Testing a hypothesis requires that you set up the hypothesis in such a way that it can be tested statistically. This means defining the null and alternative hypotheses. From there, we can follow the five steps of hypothesis testing and determine whether to reject or fail to reject the null hypothesis. By doing so, we are accepting or rejecting the alternative hypothesis. When setting our significance value $(\alpha)$ we must always be conscious of how that influences our probability of committing a Type I error.

In the next chapter, we will cover another core concept of inferential statistics, population parameter estimation. This topic will introduce you to confidence intervals and how we can test hypotheses using them.

**Key Chapter Concepts and Terms**

Population parameter
  estimation, 187
Statistical hypothesis
  testing, 187
Scientific method, 188
Statistically
  significant, 190

Null hypothesis, 190
Alternative
  hypothesis, 190
One-tailed
  hypothesis, 192
Two-tailed
  hypothesis, 192

Significance
  level $(\alpha)$, 192
Critical value, 193
Test statistic, 198

**Frequently Asked Questions**

1. Do researchers always use 5 percent for the significance level?

   Researchers typically use 5 percent for the significance level. Often the results are corroborated by other similar studies. However, you may want to have a much smaller significance level if your results may have dire consequences if you are wrong.

2. Why do different surveys and research papers give different results sometimes?

   It is possible that with all the research being conducted in the world, some significant results occur by chance. When that happens there are often other researchers that will report that they could not draw the same conclusions from their data. However, it is important that scientific results should be replicable by other researchers.

3. Why is the normal distribution used so much?

   We can prove mathematically that sums of independent numbers or averages of numbers tend to follow a normal or bell-shaped distribution. Sample means and proportions are averages and so they tend to have a normal distribution. This makes the normal distribution useful in hypothesis testing.

4. What is the Type II error used for?

   We know that if we reject the null hypothesis with a 5 percent significance level that we have a one in 20 chance of being wrong. The Type II error is the probability of not rejecting the null hypothesis when we actually should be rejecting it. Researchers often use the Type II error to determine how many people to sample in order to be able to obtain a significant result, if one does exist, given values of the parameter of interest.

**Research Example:**

In 2010, Dr. Christel Kesler (University of Oxford) and Dr. Irene Bloemraad (University of California, Berkeley) published their study "Does Immigration Erode Social Capital? The Conditional Effects of Immigration-Generated Diversity on Trust, Membership, and Participation across 19 Countries, 1981–2000" in the *Canadian Journal of Political Science*.

Their research focused on "immigration-driven diversity" and the possible effects it may have on "social policy and democratic participation." Specifically, the researchers were interested in "whether diversity undermines the willingness of citizens to trust one another, to participate in collective endeavours and to be politically engaged" (p. 319–320). The following represents an altered version of the alternative hypotheses in Kesler and Bloemraad's paper. Each alternative hypothesis is numbered.

Hypotheses:

$H_1$: Some countries experience higher social benefits from increased immigration than other countries.

$H_2$: A country's multiculturalism policy influences the level of trust citizens have in one another.

$H_3$: A country's multiculturalism policy influences citizen engagement in the country's political process.

**Source:** C. Kesler, I. Bloemraad, "Does Immigration Erode Social Capital? The Conditional Effects of Immigration-Generated Diversity on Trust, Membership, and Participation across 19 Countries, 1981–2000" *Canadian Journal of Political Science,* 43 no. 2 (2010), pp. 319–347.]

**Research Example Questions:**

**Question 1:**  Are these hypotheses one-tailed or two-tailed? Explain your answer and include a discussion of the critical value in relation to the test of the hypothesis.

**Question 2:**  Write the null and alternative hypotheses for each of the three hypotheses using the mathematical notation and explain the notation for each.

**Question 3:**  Explain how a Type I error may be committed with the first hypothesis.

**Research Example Answers:**

**Question 1:**  Are these hypotheses one-tailed or two-tailed? Explain your answer and include a discussion of the critical value in relation to the test of the hypothesis.

$H_1$: Some countries experience higher social benefits from increased immigration than other countries.

The first hypothesis is one-tailed because it states directionality. The word "higher" in the hypothesis indicates directionality. Since it states "higher" the critical value will be in the right tail of the distribution.

$H_2$: A country's multiculturalism policy influences the level of trust citizens have in one another.

The second hypothesis is two-tailed because it does not state directionality. The word "influence" in the hypothesis can mean that it is either positive or negative. Therefore, there will be a critical value for both the left and right tails of the distribution.

$H_3$: A country's multiculturalism policy influences citizen engagement in the country's political process.

The third hypothesis is also two-tailed because it does not state directionality. The word "influence" in the hypothesis can mean that it is either positive or negative. Therefore, there will be a critical value for both the left and right tails of the distribution.

**Question 2:**  Write the null and alternative hypotheses for each of the three hypotheses using the mathematical notation and explain the notation for each.

$H_1$: Some countries experience higher social benefits from increased immigration than other countries.

$$H_0: \mu_A \leq \mu_0$$
$$H_A: \mu_A > \mu_0$$

The $\mu_0$ represents the null distribution where there is no difference in social benefits experienced. The $\mu_A$ represents the alternative distribution where there are higher social benefits experienced.

$H_2$: A country's multiculturalism policy influences the level of trust citizens have in one another.

$$H_0: \mu_A = \mu_0$$
$$H_A: \mu_A \neq \mu_0$$

The $\mu_0$ represents the null distribution where there is no difference in the level of trust citizens have in one another. The $\mu_A$ represents the alternative distribution there is a difference in the level of trust citizens have in one another.

$H_3$: A country's multiculturalism policy influences citizen engagement in the country's political process.

$$H_0: \mu_A = \mu_0$$
$$H_A: \mu_A \neq \mu_0$$

The $\mu_0$ represents the null distribution where there is no difference in the citizen engagement in the political process. The $\mu_A$ represents the alternative distribution there is a difference in the citizen engagement in the political process.

**Question 3:**  Explain how a Type I error may be committed with the first hypothesis.

$H_1$: Some countries experience higher social benefits from increased immigration than other countries.

A Type I error occurs when the researcher rejects the null hypothesis when in fact it is true. The alpha value ($\alpha$) represents the significance level of the test and the probability of committing Type I error if the null hypothesis is true. Therefore, if the researchers concluded that some countries experience higher social benefits than others (thus rejecting the null hypothesis) when in reality they do not, then a Type I error has been committed.

## Problems

1. For each of the following, indicate the null and alternative hypotheses.
   a) A researcher claims that the average cost of jeans for men is less than $75.
   b) A sceptic would like to know if the average income for Canadians working for governmental agencies differs from $50,000.
   c) A trucking company comptroller would like to know if average corporate income is statistically more than $2.5 million.

2. The weight of drained fruit found in 21 randomly selected cans of peaches packed by the Sunny Fruit Company were (in ounces):

| | | | | | | |
|---|---|---|---|---|---|---|
| 11.0 | 11.6 | 10.9 | 12.0 | 11.5 | 12.0 | 11.2 |
| 10.5 | 12.2 | 11.8 | 12.1 | 11.6 | 11.7 | 11.6 |
| 11.2 | 12.0 | 11.4 | 10.8 | 11.8 | 10.9 | 11.4 |

The standard deviation of canned fruit weight is 1.25.

a) Compute the sample mean and sample standard deviation.

b) Using the five steps, is there sufficient evidence to believe that the mean weight per can is significantly different from 11 ounces (assume $\alpha = 0.05$)?

3. The concierge at the Grand Hotel in Atlantic City would like to know if the average age of porters is greater than 24. A sample of 36 porters at the hotel finds that the average age is 24.7, with standard deviation of two years. Is there sufficient evidence to support the claim at a level of significance of 5 percent?

 McGraw-Hill Connect provides you with a powerful tool for improving academic performance and truly mastering course material. You can diagnose your knowledge with pre- and post-tests, identify the areas where you need help, search the entire learning package, including the eBook, for content specific to the topic you're studying, and add these resources to your personalized study plan. Visit  to register.

# Parameter Estimation Using Confidence Intervals

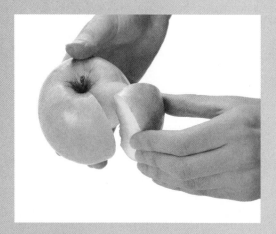

 Visit **connect** for additional study tools.

## Learning Objectives:

By the end of this chapter you should be able to:

1. Describe the concept and use of confidence intervals.
2. Calculate the confidence interval of a mean when the population standard deviation is known.
3. Calculate the confidence interval of a mean when the population standard deviation is unknown.
4. Calculate the confidence interval of a proportion.
5. Describe the Student's *t*-distribution.
6. Explain when and why the *t*-distribution is used.
7. Interpret confidence intervals.

8

## Jerzy Neyman (1894–1981)

Jerzy Neyman was born in Russia with Polish ancestry. He studied physics but soon switched to mathematics because of his clumsiness in the lab. When problems arose after the First World War, Neyman was jailed as an enemy alien. He was freed in 1921 and went to Poland. Although Neyman liked mathematics he could only find work as an agricultural statistician. He later moved to Warsaw as a lecturer in mathematics and statistics. Neyman spent time in London and Paris but eventually landed at the University of Berkeley in 1938 where he later established the Department of Statistics.

Neyman formalized the concepts of testing hypotheses using Type I and II errors and the power of statistical tests. Neyman also made major advances in sampling, confidence intervals, and experimental design. He later received the Medal of Science from President Johnson in 1969.[1]

# Introduction

**LO1**

A **confidence interval** is a range of values that we expect will contain the true population parameter.

In chapter 7 we introduced two fundamental concepts in statistical inference: population parameter estimation and statistical hypothesis testing. At the beginning of that chapter we stated that, except for defining the term, we would defer the discussion of parameter estimation to this chapter. Chapter 7 was concerned with how to set up a hypothesis for statistical testing. In this chapter we continue the discussion of parameter estimation—more specifically, parameter estimation using **confidence intervals**—focusing specifically on confidence intervals for the population mean ($\mu$) and population proportion ($p$). This chapter represents your leap into inferential statistics. Chapters 9 through 13 will draw on your knowledge of setting up hypotheses by focussing on various statistical methods for testing them.

**Note:** A proportion can also be referred to as a percentage. For example, saying the proportion of children who play soccer is the same as saying the percentage of children who play soccer.

**Note:** A proportion that is estimated based on data from a random sample is referred to as a sample proportion and written as $\hat{p}$ (pronounced "$p$-hat"). Some textbooks write this as $p$ prime ($p'$) or $P_s$ but the meaning is the same. A population proportion is written as $p$.

To start our discussion on parameter estimation, consider the following example. On April 1, 2010, political pollsters EKOS Politics issued the press release "Canadians Decisively Pro-Choice on Abortion." In the report, EKOS stated that 52 percent of Canadians, over the age of 18, considered themselves to be pro-choice. EKOS further qualified this statement by stating that their sample consisted of 2,162 randomly selected Canadians who were 18 years of age or older and that the results are accurate within $\pm 2.1$ percentage points, 19 times out of 20. How can a statement be made regarding the opinion of all Canadians over the age of 18, without actually polling the entire population over the age of 18? Consider the qualifying statement. When EKOS states that the results are accurate within $\pm 2.1$ percentage points, 19 times out of 20, they are saying that based on their sample, they are 95 percent confident (19 times out of 20) that the true proportion of Canadians 18 years of age and older that consider themselves to be pro-choice falls somewhere between 49.9 percent and 54.1 percent ($\pm 2.1$ percentage points). Stated another way, and based on statistical inference, they are saying that if they continuously take random samples from the same population (Canadians over the age of 18), 95 percent of the time the true population parameter will fall within their confidence interval of 49.9 percent to 54.1 percent.[2]

In chapter 6 we introduced the term "statistical inference" as the process for making statements about the broader population based on the use of sample data from that population. To make statements about the opinion of the broader population, pollsters take a random sample of the population and make inferences about the population parameter (in this case, the proportion of the Canadian population who identify themselves as pro-choice) using the sample statistic (proportion of the sample of Canadians who identify themselves as pro-choice) as the point estimate. The point estimate is the statistic used to estimate the population parameter. In this case, we can only estimate a range (interval) of where we could expect the true population parameter to fall within a certain **level of confidence**. In this chapter, we discuss why this is the case, but for now it is sufficient to understand that this is a typical example of a confidence interval—more specifically, a confidence interval using a sample proportion ($\hat{p}$).

> A **level of confidence**, also referred to as the confidence level, is the estimated probability that the true value of the population parameter falls within the stated confidence interval.

Confidence intervals should be based on a sample that has been obtained with a random sampling method. This is because the sample must be representative of the population. For our purposes in this chapter, we won't worry about the type of random sampling method needed for each example; however, remember that you should use the random sampling approach that provides the greatest likelihood of obtaining a representative sample of the population. We begin this chapter by discussing what confidence intervals are, and then progress to how we calculate confidence intervals for the population mean ($\mu$) using sample means ($\bar{x}$), and confidence intervals for the population proportion ($p$) using sample proportions ($\hat{p}$). However, before you proceed you may wish to review Table 8.1, which provides a list of the different notation (symbols) used in this chapter.

**TABLE 8.1**
**Statistical Notation Associated with Confidence Intervals**

| | |
|---|---|
| Symbols for Parameter and Statistic | $\mu$ = population mean (parameter) |
| | $p$ = population proportion (parameter) |
| | ($\bar{x}$) = sample mean (statistic) |
| | $\hat{p}$ = sample proportion (statistic, and pronounced "p-hat") |
| Symbols for Standard Error | $\sigma_{\bar{x}}$ = standard error of the mean |
| | $\sigma_{\hat{p}}$ = standard error of the proportion |
| Symbols for Estimated Standard Error | $s_{\bar{x}}$ = estimated standard error of the mean |
| | $s_{\hat{p}}$ = estimated standard error of the proportion |

# Understanding Confidence Intervals

Before we discuss how to calculate confidence intervals (CI), we must look at what makes up a confidence interval. The advantage of covering this material now is that once you grasp the concept, the calculations for the means and proportions are much easier to cover and understand. We have already discussed most of what is needed to create confidence intervals, we just need to put the pieces together. A confidence interval is a range of values with a lower and an upper limit, based on the sample statistic that we expect—with a certain level of confidence—will contain the population parameter. Think of confidence intervals as similar to giving friends a range of time that you think you will arrive at their house. You may be aiming to arrive at 7:15 p.m., but you say you'll be there between 7:00 p.m. and 7:30 p.m.

Since our sample statistic is the point estimate of the population parameter, a confidence interval can really be thought of as our sample statistic plus or minus some amount. Figure 8.1 shows how we arrive at the formula for calculating confidence intervals. The plus or minus some amount means that we have a lower limit that consists of our sample statistic minus that amount, and an upper limit that consists of our sample statistic plus that amount.

As Figure 8.1 indicates, we need to know three things in order to estimate our confidence interval:

1. What is our sample statistic? For our purposes we will discuss sample means ($\bar{x}$) and sample proportions ($\hat{p}$).
2. What level of confidence do we want and what is its associated $z$-score (or $t$-score)?
3. What is the standard error (SE) of our sample statistic?

## Sample Statistic

We already know what a sample mean ($\bar{x}$) and sample proportion ($\hat{p}$) are so we don't need to cover that here. However, the general formula for confidence intervals differs slightly for each. While the formula for each is shown below we won't

**FIGURE 8.1**
**What Makes Up a Confidence Interval**

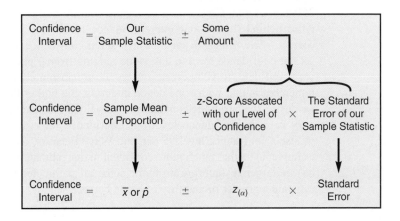

fill in the details until a little further on in our discussion. At that point, we will also be more specific about how we deal with the standard error, which for now we will refer to as SE. As you will later see, SE will be replaced with the proper notation ($\sigma_{\bar{x}}$, $s_{\bar{x}}$, $\sigma_{\hat{p}}$, or $s_{\hat{p}}$).

| **Confidence Interval for the Mean** | **Confidence Interval for the Proportion** |
|---|---|

$$CI = \bar{x} \pm z_{(\alpha)}(SE) \quad \textbf{(8.1)}$$

$$CI = \hat{p} \pm z_{(\alpha)}(SE) \quad \textbf{(8.2)}$$

where: $CI$ = confidence interval

$\bar{x}$ = sample mean

$z_{(\alpha)}$ = z-score associated with the level of confidence

$SE$ = standard error of the mean

where: $CI$ = confidence interval

$\hat{p}$ = sample proportion

$z_{(\alpha)}$ = z-score associated with the level of confidence

$SE$ = standard error of the proportion

**Note:** Some textbooks refer to $z_{(\alpha)}$ as $z_{(CL)}$; however, they both refer to the same thing—the z-score associated with a given confidence level. For example, an alpha ($\alpha$) of 0.05 is the same as a confidence level (CL) of 95 percent. Therefore, $z_{(.05)}$ and $z_{(95\%)}$ are the same in that they both equate to a z-score of $\pm 1.96$.

## Level of Confidence

The accuracy of a confidence interval is set by our desired level of confidence. The level of confidence is the estimated probability that the true value of the population parameter falls within the stated confidence interval. To grasp the idea of a level of confidence (or confidence level), imagine someone asks you to guess his age. He may look like he is in his twenties but if you had to guess a specific age, say 23, you may not be confident about that estimate. In fact, you might even say to yourself that you're only 50 percent sure (confident) that you are correct. Now imagine you're given the opportunity to estimate his age within a range (interval) of ages. If you said you thought he was somewhere from 22 to 24 years of age you might be 90 percent confident about your guess. Better yet, you may even think to yourself that to be more confident in your estimate (say 95 percent confident) you should increase the age range (interval) to 21 to 25 years of age, since doing so means you are more likely to be correct. The point behind this is that our confidence level—the probability that we are correct—determines, in part, the size of our confidence interval (range). We can set our confidence level to any value ranging from 1 percent, where we are not very confident, to 100 percent, where we are absolutely certain. A key thing to remember is that with confidence intervals, the higher the level of confidence we desire, the larger the confidence interval will be, and vice versa. So if we use a 99 percent confidence level our confidence interval will be larger than if we use a confidence level 95 percent. Why? Because, as with our age guessing example, to be that much more confident in our estimate the range of the interval has be larger to incorporate more potential parameter values. This gives our estimate a greater probability of being correct.

**FIGURE 8.2**
**95 Percent and 99 Percent Confidence Levels and Associated *z*-scores**

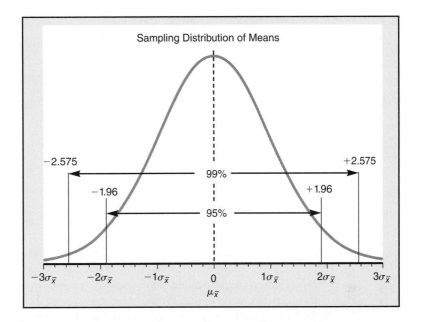

This concept should sound familiar to you now. Recall our discussions about the normal curve in chapter 5, sampling distribution in chapter 6, and critical values in chapter 7. There we found that 95 percent of the values under the normal curve fall within the critical values (*z*-scores) of ±1.96 and 99 percent fall within ±2.576. For confidence intervals, we always use the two-tailed *z*-values because intervals have both a lower and an upper limit. That is why 95 percent corresponds to a *z*-score of 1.96 and not 1.645 and so on (see figure 8.2). In chapter 7 we also covered the idea of significance levels ($\alpha$) and found that a significance level of 0.05 (which equals a critical value *z*-score of ±1.96) means that 95 percent of the values under the normal curve will fall between the lower and upper critical values. Recall that alpha ($\alpha$) represents not only the significance level, but also the percentage of error (Type I error to be specific) that we are willing to accept. Putting these concepts together gives us our level of confidence, which we write as follows:

$$\text{Level of Confidence} = 100 \times (1 - \alpha) \qquad \textbf{(8.3)}$$

If we are willing to accept a 5 percent chance that we are wrong (meaning that 5 percent of the time the true population parameter will fall outside of our confidence interval) that means our confidence level is 95 percent, which is $100 \times (1 - 0.05) = 95$ percent. When we write the notion for a *z*-score at a given alpha ($\alpha$), we write it as $z_{(\alpha)}$, which is pronounced "*z*-sub-alpha." It is not uncommon to see other textbooks refer to the confidence level instead of alpha, writing the notation as $z_{(CL)}$, which is pronounced "*z*-sub-CL." Both refer to the same thing, which is the *z*-score associated with our desired level of confidence. Table 8.2 provides a quick reference for alpha ($\alpha$), confidence levels, and *z*-scores.

**TABLE 8.2**
**Levels of Confidence and *z*-scores**

| Alpha ($\alpha$) | Level of Confidence $100 \times (1 - \alpha)$ | z-score $z_{(\alpha)}$ |
|---|---|---|
| 0.05 | 95% | ±1.96 |
| 0.01 | 99% | ±2.576 |
| 0.001 | 99.9% | ±3.29 |

## Standard Error

In chapters 6 and 7, we discussed the standard error of the mean. However, just as a refresher, the standard error of the mean ($\sigma_{\bar{x}}$) represents how far individual sample means ($\bar{x}$) vary from the population mean ($\mu$). Similarly, the standard error of the proportion ($\sigma_{\hat{p}}$), represents how far the individual sample proportion ($\hat{p}$) varies from the population proportion ($p$).

Our previous calculations of the standard error of the mean have only included the situation where we knew the value of the population standard deviation ($\sigma$). Most of the time, we actually don't know the value of $\sigma$ and require an alternative formula. The same is true for the standard error of the proportion. Most of the time we do not know the true value of the population proportion, which is needed to calculate the standard error of the proportion. In both cases, we use what is referred to as an estimated standard error. That is, we estimate the standard error based on information from our sample. We will keep our discussion of standard error, as it pertains to confidence intervals, to just this at this point. As we get in to the actual calculation of the interval we will expand on this subject.

# Calculating Confidence Intervals for the Mean and Proportion

Now that we have some of the preliminary discussion out of the way, aside from more detail about the standard error, we can focus on the mechanics of calculating confidence intervals. In this section we will cover the following scenarios:

1. Confidence intervals for the mean when we *know* the value of the population standard deviation ($\sigma$).
2. Confidence intervals for the mean when we *do not know* the value of the population standard deviation ($\sigma$).
3. Confidence intervals for the proportion when we *do not know* the proportion in the population ($p$).

**LO2**

### Confidence Intervals for the Mean When the Population Standard Deviation Is Known

Suppose we randomly select 125 students who have written the Law School Admissions Test (LSAT) and calculate the mean ($\bar{x}$) test score to be 150.44 with a standard deviation ($s$) of 9.83. Furthermore, based on reports from the Law School Admissions Council, we know that the standard deviation in the population ($\sigma$) is 9. If we want to estimate the confidence interval we can use the following formula to calculate confidence intervals for the population mean.

$$CI = \bar{x} \pm z_{(\alpha)}(SE) \qquad (8.4)$$

To work through this calculation, we'll break this down into five steps.[3]

**Step 1:** Calculate the sample mean.
We know from the Central Limit Theorem (CLT; chapter 6) that a sample mean is considered an unbiased estimator of the population mean. Therefore, we can use our sample statistic in the confidence interval formula. We have already calculated that sample mean, so adding this to our equation gives us:

$$CI = 150.44 \pm z_{(\alpha)}(SE) \qquad (8.5)$$

**Step 2:** Determine the level of confidence and associated $z$-score.
In the social sciences, the norm for confidence levels tends to be either 95 percent or 99 percent. For this example, we will calculate the confidence interval for both 95 percent and 99 percent so that we can compare them. To find the $z$-scores associated with these confidence intervals we use the process we followed in chapter 6. A confidence level of 95 percent equals an alpha ($\alpha$) value of 0.05 and a 99 percent confidence interval equals an alpha ($\alpha$) value of 0.01. Using Appendix A: Area Under the Normal Curve we look up values for the area past $z$, remembering to first divide alpha ($\alpha$) by two, and then moving to the left to find the corresponding $z$-value. For quick reference in this chapter, refer to Table 8.2. The $z$-value for $\alpha = 0.05$ is $\pm 1.96$ and the $z$-value for $\alpha = 0.01$ is $\pm 2.576$. Adding this to our equation gives us:

**For a 95 percent Confidence Level**

$$CI = 150.44 \pm z_{(\alpha = .05)}(SE) \qquad (8.6)$$
$$= 150.44 \pm 1.96\,(SE)$$

**For a 99 percent Confidence Level**

$$CI = 150.44 \pm z_{(\alpha = .01)}(SE) \qquad (8.7)$$
$$= 150.44 \pm 2.576\,(SE)$$

**Step 3:** Calculate the standard error.
We know from CLT that the standard error of the mean, which you will recall is the standard deviation of the sampling means, is a calculated as:

$$\text{Standard error of the mean} = \sigma_{\bar{x}} = \frac{\sigma}{\sqrt{n}}$$

Therefore, our formula for the confidence interval of the mean is expanded to:

$$CI = \bar{x} \pm z_{(\alpha)}(\sigma_{\bar{x}}) \qquad (8.8)$$

Which is the same as:

$$CI = \bar{x} \pm z_{(\alpha)}\left(\frac{\sigma}{\sqrt{n}}\right) \qquad (8.9)$$

Note, the standard error (SE) from 8.1 is replaced with the actual formula for the standard error of the mean, $\sigma/\sqrt{n}$.

Now if we add this to our equation we get:

**For a 95 percent Confidence Level**        **For a 99 percent Confidence Level**

$$CI = 150.44 \pm z_{(\alpha=.05)}\left(\frac{\sigma}{\sqrt{n}}\right) \quad \textbf{(8.10)}$$   $$CI = 150.44 \pm z_{(\alpha=.01)}\left(\frac{\sigma}{\sqrt{n}}\right) \quad \textbf{(8.11)}$$

$$= 150.44 \pm 1.96\left(\frac{9}{\sqrt{125}}\right)$$   $$= 150.44 \pm 2.576\left(\frac{9}{\sqrt{125}}\right)$$

$$= 150.44 \pm 1.96(0.805)$$   $$= 150.44 \pm 2.576(0.805)$$

**Step 4:** Complete the calculation of the confidence interval.

Let's stop here for a moment and consider what we have at this point. Recall in Figure 8.1 that we said the confidence interval consists of our sample statistics plus or minus some amount. The some amount is made up the $z$-score associated with our desired level of confidence plus or minus the standard error of the mean from the sampling distribution of means. So if 1 standard error equals $\pm 0.805$, then what does 1.96 standard error equal (for a 95 percent confidence) and what does 2.576 standard error equal (for a 99 percent confidence level)? As you can see in Figure 8.3, $\pm 1.96$ standard error (95 percent confidence) is equal to $\pm 1.578$ ($1.96 \times \pm 0.805$), and $\pm 2.576$ standard error (99 percent confidence) is equal to $\pm 2.074$ ($2.576 \times \pm 0.805$).

**FIGURE 8.3**
**Sampling Distribution with $\pm 1.578$ and $\pm 2.576$ Standard Error**

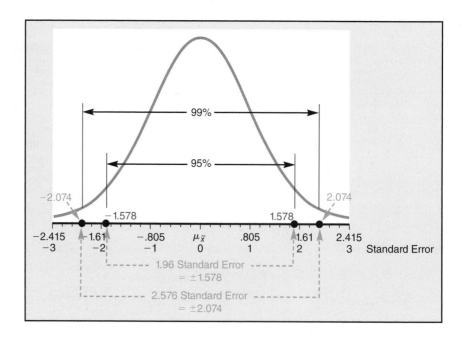

Let's continue with our formula, which can now be completed. You will notice that we are now replacing SE with the proper notation for the standard error, which is $\sigma_{\bar{x}} = \sigma/\sqrt{n}$.

**For a 95 percent Confidence Level**

$$CI = 150.44 \pm z_{(\alpha = .05)}\left(\frac{\sigma}{\sqrt{n}}\right) \quad \textbf{(8.12)}$$

$$= 150.44 \pm 1.96\left(\frac{9}{\sqrt{125}}\right)$$

$$= 150.44 \pm 1.96(0.805)$$

$$= 150.44 \pm 1.578$$

equals:

$150.44 - 1.578 = 148.86$ (lower limit)

and

$150.44 + 1.578 = 152.02$ (upper limit)

**For a 99 percent Confidence Level**

$$CI = 150.44 \pm z_{(\alpha = .01)}\left(\frac{\sigma}{\sqrt{n}}\right) \quad \textbf{(8.13)}$$

$$= 150.44 \pm 2.576\left(\frac{9}{\sqrt{125}}\right)$$

$$= 150.44 \pm 2.576(0.805)$$

$$= 150.44 \pm 2.074$$

equals:

$150.44 - 2.074 = 148.37$ (lower limit)

and

$150.44 + 2.074 = 152.51$ (upper limit)

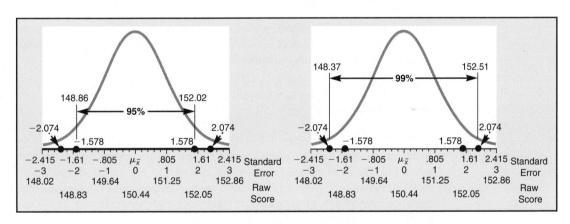

Now we can see, from both the formula and the respective plot of the results, that for a 95 percent confidence interval the lower limit is an LSAT score of 148.86 and the upper limit is an LSAT score of 152.02. Similarly, for a 99 percent confidence interval the lower limit is 148.37 and the upper limit is 152.51. We are now ready for the final step, the interpretation.

**LO7**

**Step 5:** Interpret the confidence interval.

What we have just done is use our sample statistics ($\bar{x}$) to estimate the population parameter ($\mu$). When interpreting a confidence interval, we write the result as follows:

For a 95 percent confidence interval: $148.86 \le \mu \le 152.02$

For a 99 percent confidence interval: $148.37 \le \mu \le 152.51$

This means that based on our sample statistic (150.44) we can expect that 95 percent of the time the population mean ($\mu$) will be greater than or equal to 148.86 (148.86 $\leq \mu$) and less than or equal to 152.02 ($\mu \leq$ 152.02). This means that if we take 100 random samples, 95 times out of 100 the true population mean will fall between 148.86 and 152.02. Five times out of 100 (or 5 percent, our alpha ($\alpha$) level) we will be wrong and the true value of the population will fall outside of our confidence interval. Similarly, 99 percent of the time the population mean will fall between 148.37 and 152.51, while 1 percent of the time it will fall outside of our confidence interval.

The following is an example of how to explain confidence intervals.

**Sample:** Based on our sample statistic, we are (<u>insert level of confidence</u>) per-cent confident that the population mean for (<u>insert variable of interest</u>) is between (<u>insert lower limit</u>) and (<u>insert upper limit</u>).

Based on our results, and using the wording above for our interpretation, we may conclude the following.

**For 95 percent CI:** Based on our sample statistic, we are 95 percent confident that the population mean for LSAT scores is between 148.86 and 152.02.

**For 99 percent CI:** Based on our sample statistic, we are 99 percent confident that the population mean for LSAT scores is between 148.37 and 152.51.

In fact, based on a 2010 report by the Law School Admission Council the popula-tion mean ($\mu$) score for the Canada LSAT test is approximately 151 with a standard deviation ($\sigma$) of 9. So, our confidence intervals are correct.

**Source:** "LSAT Performance with Regional, Gender, and Racial/Ethnic Breakdowns: 2001–2002 through 2009–2010 Testing Years," Dalessandro, Sitwell, Lawlor, and Reese, October 2010.

### A Follow-up Note on Confidence Intervals

At this point, you may be asking yourself when the true population parameter would fall outside of our confidence interval. Consider Figure 8.4. Imagine if we took 100 random samples of 125 students (as per our previous example) and then calculated the 95 percent confidence interval for each mean (from $\bar{x}_1$ to $\bar{x}_2$) and plotted them under the sampling distribution. We can expect that 95 percent of the time, the confidence interval (represented with horizontal bars in Figure 8.4) will cross the population mean, meaning that the population mean will fall within the confidence interval. Five percent of the time the confidence interval won't cross the population mean. This is because it is possible that our sample mean ($\bar{x}$) might come from the far left or right tails representing the 5 percent (or 2.5 percent in the left tail and 2.5 percent in the right tail).

**LO3**

## Confidence Intervals for the Mean When the Population Standard Deviation Is Unknown

In the previous scenario, we wanted to estimate the confidence interval of the population mean and we knew the value of the population standard deviation ($\sigma$).

**FIGURE 8.4**  **Example of 100 Random Samples and Confidence Intervals**

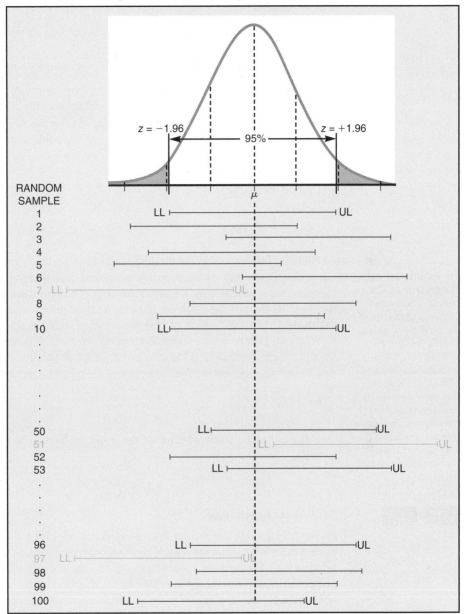

**Note:** Only 3 out of 5 confidence intervals that would not include the value of the population parameter are shown here.

Unfortunately, we usually don't know the value of the population standard deviation, so we need to take a slightly different approach. This approach includes:

1. Using an estimated standard error of the mean ($s_{\bar{x}}$) instead of the standard error of the mean ($\sigma_{\bar{x}}$).
2. Using Student's *t*-distribution instead of the normal distribution.

Before we get into the estimated standard error of the mean and the Student's *t*-distribution, we are going to change our general formula for confidence intervals slightly by replacing the *z*-score with a *t*-score. At this point, don't worry about why this is the case, we will cover that shortly. At this point, just recognize that we need to make this small change.

Therefore, we are changing this:

$$CI = \bar{x} \pm z_{(\alpha)}(SE)$$

to this:

$$CI = \bar{x} \pm t_{(\alpha)}(SE)$$

### Estimated standard error of the mean ($s_{\bar{x}}$)

The **estimated standard error of the mean** is the estimate of the standard error of the mean based on the sample standard deviation (*s*). This differs from the standard error of the mean where the true population standard deviation is used ($\sigma$) in the formula. The sample standard deviation (*s*) is used as an estimate of the population standard deviation ($\sigma$).

Given that we don't know the population standard deviation ($\sigma$), we can't directly calculate the standard error of the mean ($\sigma_{\bar{x}}$). Therefore, we need to estimate the standard error of the mean based on the sample information. We call this the **estimated standard error of the mean**, represented as $s_{\bar{x}}$.

When we calculate the estimated standard error of the mean ($s_{\bar{x}}$), we use the sample standard deviation (*s*) as an estimate of the population standard deviation ($\sigma$). Therefore, whereas the standard error of the mean is calculated as…

$$\sigma_{\bar{x}} = \frac{\sigma}{\sqrt{n}} \qquad \textbf{(8.14)}$$

…the estimated standard error of the mean replaces $\sigma$ with *s* to obtain the formula:

$$s_{\bar{x}} = \frac{s}{\sqrt{n}} \qquad \textbf{(8.15)}$$

### Student's t-distribution

As you read through this section, keep in mind that what we are doing is simply replacing the *z*-value (from the normal distribution) with a *t*-value (from the Student's *t*-distribution). Furthermore, remember that the normal curve is referred to as the normal distribution. When we replace raw scores with *z*-values (standardized scores) we refer to the normal distribution as the standard normal distribution. Sometimes you will also hear this referred to as the *z* distribution but the meaning is the same.

When we don't know the population standard deviation, we can use the sample standard deviation as an estimate of the population standard deviation. As we saw in our alcohol-related questions (Ontario high schools; chapter 2), we replaced $\sigma$ with *s*. The problem with using this approach is that the sample standard deviation (*s*) varies around the population standard deviation ($\sigma$), particularly when using

**FIGURE 8.5**
**Comparison of a**
**Normal Distribution**
**and *t*-Distribution**
**With 2 *df***

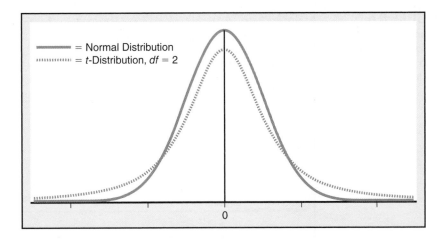

smaller samples. However, the amount of variability decreases as we increase our sample size. The reason for this is complex and not necessary to cover in detail for our purposes. Suffice it to say that as a result of replacing $\sigma$ with $s$ in our equation for the standard error, we get more variability in the sampling distribution. However, as we increase the sample size, the sampling distribution becomes less variable. Given the issue of variability, the sampling distribution no longer follows a normal distribution and, as a result, we must use the *t*-distribution to account for this.

The *t*-distribution is similar to the standard normal distribution in that it is bell shaped and symmetric with a mean of 0 and a standard deviation of 1. What differs is the spread (variability) of the distribution. The smaller the sample size, the more variable (think wider and shorter) the distribution. As we increase the sample size, the distribution becomes less variable (think narrower and taller) until it reaches the same shape of the normal distribution. Consider Figure 8.5. The solid-line curve represents the normal distribution and the dotted-line curve represents the *t*-distribution with 2 **degrees of freedom**. When we create a confidence interval for a single mean (and tests for single mean, as we will see in the next chapter), the degrees of freedom are calculated as $n - 1$. Therefore, based on a sample size of 3, the *t*-distribution in Figure 8.5 has 2 degrees of freedom (written *df*).

The *t*-distribution is a family of distributions with a separate distribution for each degree of freedom (*df*). Since the distribution variability is based on *df* (the sample size minus one), the *t*-distribution begins to take the shape of the normal distribution as the degrees of freedom increase. As you can see in Figure 8.6, at 30 *df*, the *t*-distribution looks similar to the normal distribution.

Whereas the standard normal distribution gives us a *z*-statistic (*z*-score), the *t*-distribution gives us the equivalent, called the *t*-statistic (or *t*-score). Just as we used a table to look up the *z*-score, we use a separate table called the *t*-Distribution Table (appendices B and C in the back of the textbook) to find the critical values of *t* for a given significance level, alpha ($\alpha$) and degrees of freedom (*df*). Looking up the critical values of *t* is easy (see Table 8.3). First, determine whether you want

**Degrees of freedom**
are the number of independent observations/ pieces of information used in estimating a parameter. For single sample confidence intervals, degrees of freedom is calculated as $n - 1$.

**FIGURE 8.6**

**Comparison of a Normal Distribution and 3 *t*-distributions with 2, 10, and 30 *df***

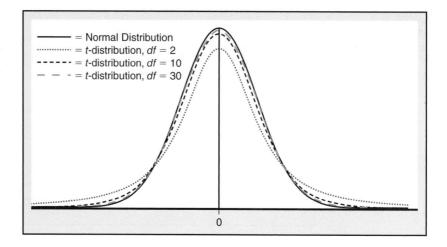

one- or two-tailed values. For our purposes we'll use the two-tailed values. Then, determine at what level of alpha ($\alpha$) you are interested. To be consistent with our previous examples we'll use $\alpha = 0.05$. Following that, determine how many degrees of freedom you have. If we have a sample size of 11, we will have 10 degrees of freedom ($n - 1$). Now we follow the column labelled *df* down until we come to

**TABLE 8.3**

**Excerpt From the Table of Critical Values of the *t*-Distribution**

| df | Two-Tailed Tests | | | | |
|---|---|---|---|---|---|
| | $\alpha = 0.1$ | $\alpha = 0.05$ | $\alpha = 0.025$ | $\alpha = 0.01$ | $\alpha = 0.001$ |
| 1 | 6.314 | 12.706 | 25.452 | 63.657 | 636.619 |
| 2 | 2.920 | 4.303 | 6.205 | 9.925 | 31.599 |
| 3 | 2.353 | 3.182 | 4.177 | 5.841 | 12.924 |
| 4 | 2.132 | 2.776 | 3.495 | 4.604 | 8.610 |
| 5 | 2.015 | 2.571 | 3.163 | 4.032 | 6.869 |
| 6 | 1.943 | 2.447 | 2.969 | 3.707 | 5.959 |
| 7 | 1.895 | 2.365 | 2.841 | 3.500 | 5.408 |
| 8 | 1.860 | 2.306 | 2.752 | 3.355 | 5.041 |
| 9 | 1.833 | 2.262 | 2.685 | 3.250 | 4.781 |
| 10 | 1.812 | 2.228 | 2.634 | 3.169 | 4.587 |
| 11 | 1.796 | 2.201 | 2.593 | 3.106 | 4.437 |
| 12 | 1.782 | 2.179 | 2.560 | 3.055 | 4.318 |
| 13 | 1.771 | 2.160 | 2.533 | 3.012 | 4.221 |
| 60 | 1.671 | 2.000 | 2.299 | 2.660 | 3.460 |
| 70 | 1.667 | 1.994 | 2.291 | 2.648 | 3.435 |
| 80 | 1.664 | 1.990 | 2.284 | 2.639 | 3.416 |
| 90 | 1.662 | 1.987 | 2.280 | 2.632 | 3.402 |
| 100 | 1.660 | 1.984 | 2.276 | 2.626 | 3.390 |
| 110 | 1.659 | 1.982 | 2.273 | 2.621 | 3.381 |
| 120 | 1.658 | 1.980 | 2.270 | 2.617 | 3.373 |
| $\infty$ | 1.645 | 1.960 | 2.240 | 2.576 | 3.300 |

**FIGURE 8.7**

Normal Distribution
and *t*-Distribution
with Critical Values
for a 95 percent
Confidence Level

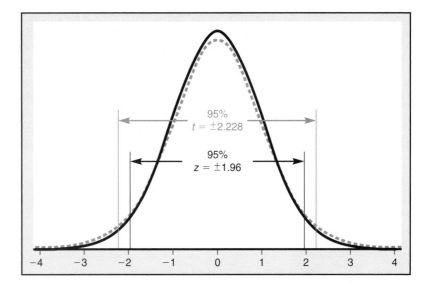

10 and then look across (right) until we get to the column for $\alpha = 0.05$. In this example, the *t*-value is 2.228. This represents the critical value for the significance level of $\alpha = 0.05$. To picture this, look at Figure 8.7. Now consider the implication of this. When we used the normal distribution, the critical value for a two-tailed alpha ($\alpha$) value of 0.05 was 1.96 (*z*-value). Now that we are using the *t*-distribution, the critical value for a two-tailed alpha ($\alpha$) value of 0.05 is 2.228 (*t* value). As shown in Figure 8.7, whereas 95 percent of the area under a normal curve falls between $\pm 1.96$ standard deviations (*z*-scores), 95 percent of the area under a *t*-distribution with 10 *df* falls between $\pm 2.228$.

If you keep going down the *df* column, you will see that as the *df* increases the critical values become similar to those from the normal distribution. As the *df* approaches infinity, the critical value for *t* is the same as the critical value for *z*. In fact, after 30 *df* there really isn't much difference between the calculation using *t* and *z*. As such, you'll often see individuals using *z*-scores for confidence intervals involving means once the sample size is greater than 30. We don't recommend this approach though, as the correct method is to use the *t*-distribution when you do not know the value of the population standard deviation ($\sigma$).

*A Recap*

Now that we have covered the estimated standard error of the mean and the *t*-distribution, let's take a minute to recap where we are. When we want to calculate the confidence interval for a population mean ($\mu$) and we do not know the value of the population standard deviation ($\sigma$), we need to do two things:

1. Use the estimated standard error of the mean $[s_{\bar{x}} = (s/\sqrt{n})]$ instead of the standard error of the mean $[\sigma_{\bar{x}} = (\sigma/\sqrt{n})]$.

2. Use the *t*-distribution instead of the normal distribution.

Knowing this, we can follow the five steps for calculating the confidence interval of a mean when we do not know the population standard deviation ($\sigma$). To give some context to what we are doing, we will use the following example. According to the 2000/01 "Courts Personnel and Expenditures Report" by the Canadian Centre for Justice Studies there were 2,262 personnel working in the court system within Quebec with a mean ($\mu$) annual salary of approximately \$61,900. Suppose we randomly selected 26 individuals from this population and found the sample mean ($\bar{x}$) was \$63,129 with a sample standard deviation ($s$) of \$5,503. Based on this sample information, we are now interested in calculating the confidence interval for the mean.[4]

**Step 1:** Calculate the sample mean.
We know based on the information in our example that the mean ($\bar{x}$) salary is \$63,129. Therefore, our formula starts as:

$$CI = 63,129 \pm t_{(\alpha)}(s_{\bar{x}}) \tag{8.16}$$

**Step 2:** Determine the level of confidence and associated $z$-score.
Similar to our previous examples, we use both a 95 percent and 99 percent confidence level just so that you can compare them. Usually you would only compute the confidence interval for one level of confidence. Again, a confidence level of 95 percent equates to an alpha ($\alpha$) value of 0.05 and a 99 percent confidence interval equates to an alpha ($\alpha$) value of 0.01.

Since we don't know the value of the population standard deviation ($\sigma$), we are going to use the $t$-distribution. To get the $t$-value, we first need to determine how many degrees of freedom ($df$) we have. Since $df = n - 1$ and our sample is $n = 26$ we have 25 $df$. Using the $t$-distribution table we find that an alpha ($\alpha$) level of 0.05 (two-tailed) equals a $t$-value of 2.060 and an alpha ($\alpha$) level of 0.01 (two-tailed) equals a $t$-value of 2.787. Therefore, we get:

**For a 95 percent Confidence Level**

$$CI = 63,129 \pm t_{(\alpha = .05)}(s_{\bar{x}}) \tag{8.17}$$
$$= 63,129 \pm 2.060(s_{\bar{x}})$$

**For a 99 percent Confidence Level**

$$CI = 63,129 \pm t_{(\alpha = .01)}(s_{\bar{x}}) \tag{8.18}$$
$$= 63,129 \pm 2.787(s_{\bar{x}})$$

**Step 3:** Calculate the standard error.
Because we don't know the standard deviation of the population, our standard error is the estimated standard error of the mean. Filling in the information for $s$ and $n$, the equation becomes:

**For a 95 percent Confidence Level**

$$CI = 63,129 \pm t_{(\alpha = .05)}(s_{\bar{x}}) \tag{8.19}$$
$$CI = 63,129 \pm 2.060\left(\frac{5,503}{\sqrt{26}}\right)$$
$$CI = 63,129 \pm 2.060(1,079.23)$$

**For a 99 percent Confidence Level**

$$CI = 63,129 \pm t_{(\alpha = .01)}(s_{\bar{x}}) \tag{8.20}$$
$$CI = 63,129 \pm 2.787\left(\frac{5,503}{\sqrt{26}}\right)$$
$$CI = 63,129 \pm 2.787(1,079.23)$$

**TABLE 8.4**
**Five Steps for Calculating Confidence Intervals for Means**

Step 1: Calculate the sample mean.
Step 2: Determine the level of confidence and associated *z*-score or *t*-score.
Step 3: Calculate the standard error.
Step 4: Complete the calculation of the confidence interval.
Step 5: Interpret the confidence interval.

**Step 4:** Complete the calculation of the confidence interval.
Continuing, we get:

**For a 95 percent Confidence Level**

$$CI = 63,129 \pm t_{(\alpha=.05)}(s_{\bar{x}}) \qquad \textbf{(8.21)}$$

$$CI = 63,129 \pm 2.060\left(\frac{5,503}{\sqrt{26}}\right)$$

$$CI = 63,129 \pm 2.060(1,079.23)$$

$$CI = 63,129 \pm 2,223.21$$

equals:

$63,129 - 2,223.21 = 60,905.79$ (lower limit)

and

$63,129 + 2,222.78 = 65,352.21$ (upper limit)

**For a 99 percent Confidence Level**

$$CI = 63,129 \pm t_{(\alpha=.01)}(s_{\bar{x}}) \qquad \textbf{(8.22)}$$

$$CI = 63,129 \pm 2.787\left(\frac{5,503}{\sqrt{26}}\right)$$

$$CI = 63,129 \pm 2.787(1,079.23)$$

$$CI = 63,129 \pm 3,007.81$$

equals:

$63,129 - 3,007.81 = 60,121.19$ (lower limit)

and

$63,129 + 3,007.23 = 66,136.81$ (upper limit)

**LO7**

**Step 5: Interpret the confidence interval.**
For a 95 percent confidence interval: $\$60,905.79 \leq \mu \leq \$65,352.21$
For a 99 percent confidence interval: $\$60,121.19 \leq \mu \leq \$66,136.81$
   Based on our results, and using the sample for wording, we may conclude the following.

**For 95 percent CI:** Based on our sample statistic, we are 95 percent confident that the population mean annual salary for personnel working in the court system within Quebec is between $60,905.79 and $65,352.21.

**For 95 percent CI:** Based on our sample statistic, we are 99 percent confident that the population mean annual salary for personnel working in the court system within Quebec is between $60,121.19 and $66,136.81.

**EXERCISE 8.1**

Based on their research involving 97 First Nations young people between the ages of 10 to 17 who were living in and out of home care, Filbert and Flynn (2010) found the sample mean ($\bar{x}$) developmental asset score of the participants was 28.28 with a sample standard deviation ($s$) of 7.26. Developmental assets included personal attributes such as being honest, supportive, trustworthy, etc. This variable is measured on a scale of 0 (low) to 40 (high).
   Calculate the 95 percent confidence interval for the mean. The answers for this exercise are at the end of the chapter.

## For Your Information

Recall from chapter 3 that the formula for calculating the sample standard deviation was...

$$s = \sqrt{\frac{\Sigma(x - \bar{x})^2}{(n - 1)}} \qquad \text{[A]}$$

...while the formula for the population standard deviation was:

$$\sigma = \sqrt{\frac{\Sigma(x - \bar{x})^2}{n}} \qquad \text{[B]}$$

Some textbooks and various statistical resources do not differentiate between the two in that they do not use $n - 1$ in the denominator for the sample standard deviation. Thus, calculating the sample standard deviation as:

$$s = \sqrt{\frac{\Sigma(x - \bar{x})^2}{n}} \qquad \text{[C]}$$

We discussed this discrepancy in chapter 3; however, it is important to point out the implication in calculating the estimated standard error of the mean when the formula for the sample standard deviation does not include $n - 1$, as in [C]. If the sample standard deviation is calculated using formula [C], then the estimated standard error of the mean would need to be calculated using $n - 1$ in the denominator, such as:

$$s_{\bar{x}} = \frac{s}{\sqrt{n - 1}} \qquad \text{[D]}$$

Again, the proper method for calculating the sample standard deviation is as we discussed in chapter 3 and shown in [A] above. When executed this way, the estimated standard error of the mean is calculated as shown in this chapter. That is:

$$s_{\bar{x}} = \frac{s}{\sqrt{n}} \qquad \text{[E]}$$

We hope that this will help you understand these differences when you see them in other textbooks and/or resources.

---

**LO4**

## Confidence Intervals for a Proportion Where the Population Proportion is Unknown

Confidence intervals for proportions are usually only calculated when the sample size is greater than 30 ($n > 30$). Furthermore, we always use the standard normal distribution ($z$-scores) for confidence intervals for proportions. The process for calculating a confidence interval for a proportion is similar to calculating the confidence interval of a mean.

As introduced earlier, the general formula for the confidence interval of a proportion is:

$$CI = \hat{p} \pm z_{(\alpha)}(SE) \qquad \text{(8.23)}$$

The confidence interval for the proportion is the sample proportion ($\hat{p}$) plus or minus the $z$-score associated with the chosen level of confidence multiplied by the standard error of the proportion. Therefore, we are trying to find an interval that, given a specified level of confidence, will contain the population proportion ($p$). Now that you have experience calculating confidence intervals, this will be fairly straightforward.

**TABLE 8.5**
**Five Steps for Calculating Confidence Intervals for Proportions**

Step 1: Calculate the proportion.
Step 2: Determine the level of confidence and associated *z*-score.
Step 3: Calculate the estimated standard error of the proportion.
Step 4: Complete the calculation of the confidence interval.
Step 5: Interpret the confidence interval.

To explore confidence intervals of proportions, consider the following scenario. The 2009 Ipsos-Reid report "What Canadians Wouldn't Give Up to Add Five Healthy Years to Their Lives," stated that of the 507 randomly-sampled Canadian women, 227 said they would not give up chocolate to add five years to their life.

**Source:** Canadian online Ipsos-Reid Express, December 8, 2009; http://www.ipsos-na.com/news-polls/pressrelease.aspx?id=4627.

As a guide, we can adjust our five steps for calculating a confidence interval to suit our needs for proportions.

**Step 1:** Calculate the proportion.
The proportion of women who would not give up chocolate to add five years to their lives is $227 \div 507 = 0.448$, which we will round to 0.45 to keep it simple. Therefore, $\hat{p} = 0.45$ and our formula starts as:

$$CI = \hat{p} \pm z_{(\alpha)}(SE) \qquad \textbf{(8.24)}$$
$$CI = 0.45 \pm z_{(\alpha)}(SE)$$

**Step 2:** Determine the level of confidence and associated *z*-score.
As we did with the confidence intervals for the mean, we will use both a 95 percent and 99 percent confidence level for comparison. A confidence level of 95 percent equals an alpha ($\alpha$) value of 0.05 and a 99 percent confidence interval equals an alpha ($\alpha$) value of 0.01. An alpha ($\alpha$) level of 0.05 equates to a *z*-value of 1.96 and an alpha ($\alpha$) level of 0.01 equates to a *z*-value of 2.576. Therefore, we get:

**For a 95 percent Confidence Level**

$$CI = 0.45 \pm z_{(\alpha = .05)}(SE) \quad \textbf{(8.25)}$$
$$CI = 0.45 \pm 1.96(SE)$$

**For a 99 percent Confidence Level**

$$CI = 0.45 \pm z_{(\alpha = .01)}(SE) \quad \textbf{(8.26)}$$
$$CI = 0.45 \pm 2.576(SE)$$

**Step 3:** Calculate the estimated standard error of the proportion ($S_{\hat{p}}$).
This is where calculating confidence intervals get a little more complex when dealing with proportions as opposed to means. As a result, we need to diverge from our discussion of calculating the estimated standard error and discuss why we are not looking at the standard error of the proportion ($\sigma_{\hat{p}}$). Recall that the population proportion is written as $p$. The standard error of the proportion ($\sigma_{\hat{p}}$) is calculated as:

$$\sigma_{\hat{p}} = \sqrt{\frac{p(1 - p)}{n}} \qquad \textbf{(8.27)}$$

The **estimated standard error of the proportion** $(s_{\hat{p}})$ is the estimate of the standard error of the proportion based on the sample proportion $(\hat{p})$. This differs from the standard error of the proportion $(\sigma_{\hat{p}})$ where the population proportion $(p)$ is used in the formula. The sample proportion $(\hat{p})$ is used as an estimate of the population proportion $(p)$.

Ignoring most of the formula for now, you'll notice that $p$ is required in order to calculate the standard error. This is problematic because we usually do not know the value of $p$. Furthermore, if we did know $p$ we wouldn't need to estimate the confidence interval. So we are dealing with a situation where we need to calculate the confidence interval but we cannot calculate the standard error $(\sigma_{\hat{p}})$. Thus, we need to skip straight to the **estimated standard error of the proportion**.

To calculate the estimated standard error of the proportion, we can use the sample proportion $(\hat{p})$ as an estimate of the population proportion $(p)$. So, substituting $\hat{p}$ for $p$, we arrive at the formula for the estimated standard error of the proportion:

$$s_{\hat{p}} = \sqrt{\frac{\hat{p}(1-\hat{p})}{n}} \qquad \textbf{(8.28)}$$

At this point, it is worth spending a little bit more time on what is happening in the numerator $\hat{p}(1-\hat{p})$. If $\hat{p}$ is the sample proportion and proportions are a value with a maximum of 1, then $(1-\hat{p})$ is the remaining proportion after $\hat{p}$ is considered. In our example, $\hat{p}$ is 0.45, which represents the proportion of women who would not give up chocolate; therefore, $(1 - \hat{p} = 1 - 0.45 = 0.55)$ is the proportion of women who would give up chocolate to add five years to their lives.

Now that we have dealt with the concept of the estimated standard error of the proportion, we can substitute the values in our example. Doing so gives us:

**For a 95 percent Confidence Level**

$$CI = 0.45 \pm z_{(\alpha=0.05)}(s_{\hat{p}}) \qquad \textbf{(8.29)}$$

$$CI = 0.45 \pm z_{(\alpha=.05)}\left(\sqrt{\frac{\hat{p}(1-\hat{p})}{n}}\right)$$

$$CI = 0.45 \pm 1.96\left(\sqrt{\frac{.45(1-.45)}{507}}\right)$$

$$CI = 0.45 \pm 1.96\left(\sqrt{\frac{.2475}{507}}\right)$$

$$CI = 0.45 \pm 1.96(0.022)$$

**For a 99 percent Confidence Level**

$$CI = 0.45 \pm z_{(\alpha=0.05)}(s_{\hat{p}}) \qquad \textbf{(8.30)}$$

$$CI = 0.45 \pm z_{(\alpha=.01)}\left(\sqrt{\frac{\hat{p}(1-\hat{p})}{n}}\right)$$

$$CI = 0.45 \pm 2.576\left(\sqrt{\frac{.45(1-.45)}{507}}\right)$$

$$CI = 0.45 \pm 2.576\left(\sqrt{\frac{.2475}{507}}\right)$$

$$CI = 0.45 \pm 2.576(0.022)$$

**Step 4:** Complete the calculation of the confidence interval. Continuing, we get:

**For a 95 percent Confidence Level**

$$CI = 0.45 \pm z_{(\alpha=0.01)}(s_{\hat{p}}) \qquad \textbf{(8.31)}$$

$$CI = 0.45 \pm z_{(\alpha=.05)}\left(\sqrt{\frac{\hat{p}(1-\hat{p})}{n}}\right)$$

**For a 99 percent Confidence Level**

$$CI = 0.45 \pm z_{(\alpha=0.01)}(s_{\hat{p}}) \qquad \textbf{(8.32)}$$

$$CI = 0.45 \pm z_{(\alpha=.01)}\left(\sqrt{\frac{\hat{p}(1-\hat{p})}{n}}\right)$$

$$CI = 0.45 \pm 1.96\left(\sqrt{\frac{.45(1 - .45)}{507}}\right) \qquad CI = 0.45 \pm 2.576\left(\sqrt{\frac{.45(1 - .45)}{507}}\right)$$

$$CI = 0.45 \pm 1.96\left(\sqrt{\frac{.2475}{507}}\right) \qquad CI = 0.45 \pm 2.576\left(\sqrt{\frac{.2475}{507}}\right)$$

$$CI = 0.45 \pm 1.96(0.022) \qquad CI = 0.45 \pm 2.576(0.022)$$

$$CI = 0.45 \pm 0.04 \qquad CI = 0.45 \pm 0.06$$

equals:                                       equals:

0.45 − 0.04 = 0.41 (lower limit)          0.45 − 0.06 = 0.39 (lower limit)

and                                             and

0.45 + 0.04 = 0.49 (upper limit)          0.45 + 0.06 = 0.51 (upper limit)

**LO7**

**Step 5:** Interpret the confidence interval.
For a 95 percent confidence interval: $0.41 \le p \le 0.49$
For a 99 percent confidence interval: $0.39 \le p \le 0.51$
Based on the calculations, we can now interpret the results.

**For 95 percent CI:** Based on our sample statistic, we are 95 percent confident that the proportion of Canadian women who would not give up chocolate to add five years to their lives is between 0.41 (or 41 percent) and 0.49 (or 49 percent).

**For 99 percent CI:** Based on our sample statistic, we are 99 percent confident that the proportion of Canadian women who would not give up chocolate to add five years to their lives is between 0.39 (39 percent) and 0.51 (51 percent).

**Note:** Remember that you can only make inferences about the population from which the random sample was taken. So if the random sample consists only of teens living in Regina, Saskatchewan, then the inference must be restricted to the population of teens living in Regina.

**Note:** A confidence interval for the mean is written as: <u>lower limit</u> $\le \mu \le$ <u>upper limit</u>. A confidence interval for the proportion is written as: <u>lower limit</u> $\le p \le$ <u>upper limit</u>.

---

**EXERCISE 8.2**

The Ipsos-Reid report "What Canadians Wouldn't Give Up to Add Five Healthy Years to Their Lives," stated that, based on a random sample of 525 Canadian men, 39 percent said they would not be willing to give up beer, wine, or alcohol to add five years to their life.

Calculate the 95 percent confidence interval for the population proportion. The answer for this exercise is at the end of the chapter.

**Source:** Canadian online Ipsos-Reid Express, December 8, 2009; http://www.ipsos-na.com/news-polls/pressrelease.aspx?id=4627.

## Take a Closer Look

Polsters often report confidence intervals with the margin of error.

For example, CBC News reported the results of a 2007 poll commissioned by the Canadian Medical Association regarding Canadians' opinions of the connection between the environment and their health. The report stated that, "27 percent of Canadians believe they have environment-related illnesses such as asthma and allergies." Furthermore, using a random sample of 1,001 Canadians, they stated that, "The sample provides a 3.2 percentage point margin of error for the overall national findings, 95 times out of 100."

The margin of error is the plus or minus ($\pm$) value we have been calculating (the critical value multiplied by the standard error). When you see a confidence interval reported like the example above ("... a 3.2 percentage point margin of error ..."), this usually indicates that the plus or minues ($\pm$) number is 3.2. So the lower and upper confidence intervals are 23.8 and 30.2 respectively. However, sometimes you will see the term "margin of error" reported with the $\pm$ symbol such as "... a $\pm$ 1.6 percentage point margin of error ..." This does not mean the results are reported incorrectly. It is just another way of reporting the same thing. This highlights the need to be careful in interpreting the results of the confidence interval. For example, the "3.2 percentage point margin of error" "accurate within $\pm 3.2$ percentage points" should be interpreted as. Another way to report these results would have been to state that '27 percent of Canadians believe they have environmental related illness and that results are accurate within $\pm 3.2$ percentage points, 95 times out of 100.'

**Source:** "Canadians link environment, health problems: CMA poll" (August 20, 2007), http://www.cbc.ca/news/canada/story/2007/08/19/cma-reportcard.html. Permission granted by CBC Radio-Canada and The Canadian Press.

## Did You Know?

### That 1 = 2 ?

Suppose we have two numbers, $a$ and $b$, that are equal.

Then we can say:

$$a = b \qquad [1]$$

That being the case, multiplying both sides by $b$ we get:

$$ab = b^2 \qquad [2]$$

If we subtract both sides by $b^2$ we get:

$$ab - b^2 = b^2 - b^2 \qquad [3]$$

Since $b^2$ is the same as $a^2$ we can swap the first $b^2$ on the right side for $a^2$ and get:

$$ab - b^2 = a^2 - b^2 \qquad [4]$$

Using simple algebra we can change each side to an equivalent form and get:

$$b(a - b) = (a + b)(a - b) \qquad [5]$$

If we then divide both sides by $(a - b)$ we get:

$$\frac{b(a - b)}{(a - b)} = \frac{(a + b)(a - b)}{(a - b)} \qquad [6]$$

Working that through we get:

$$\frac{b(a - b)}{(a - b)} = \frac{(a + b)(a - b)}{(a - b)} \qquad [7]$$

This leaves us with:

$$b = (a + b) \qquad [8]$$

Since $a$ is equal to $b$ we can replace $a$ with $b$ to get:

$$b = (b + b) \qquad [9]$$

Therefore, we have:

$$b = 2b \qquad [10]$$

Now if $b = 1$ then:

$$1 = 2(1) \qquad [11]$$

And:

$$1 = 2 \qquad [12]$$

This is commonly known as a mathematical fallacy where the logic of the math might appear to be reasonable but the result is definitely incorrect. Apart from the fact that we intuitively know we have done something wrong, what really happened here? Our error occurred in Step 6. If $a = b$, then $a - b$ must be zero. That means the numerator is divided by zero. Any number divided by zero is considered to be undefined. The proof of this is that if $2 \div 0 = a$, then $a \times 0$ would have to equal 2 and anything multiplied by 0 is 0.

**Source:** Weisstein, Eric W. "Fallacy." From MathWorld—A Wolfram Web Resource. http://mathworld.wolfram.com/Fallacy.html.

## Conclusion

This chapter represents your leap into inferential statistics. We use confidence intervals to make inferences about population parameters based on our sample statistic. The sample statistic is the point estimate that we use to estimate the population parameter. We interpret confidence intervals as a range of values that we believe, given a certain level of confidence, will contain the population parameter. It is important to remember that we are not stating what the population parameter is, but rather we are providing a range of values that we believe—within a certain level of confidence—will contain the true population value.

In this chapter we covered confidence intervals for means and proportions. It is important to remember that we use the normal distribution when we know the value of the population standard deviation ($\sigma$) and the $t$-distribution when we do not know the value of $\sigma$. For proportions, we always use the normal distribution. In the next chapter, we will expand on the use of the $t$-distribution and our knowledge about hypothesis testing and begin discussing methods for statistically analyzing hypotheses. We begin with testing hypothesis regarding a single mean.

**Key Chapter Concepts**

Confidence intervals, 213
Level of confidence, 214
Estimated standard error of the mean, 223
Estimated standard error of the proportion, 232
Degrees of freedom, 225

# Frequently Asked Questions

1. I have seen other textbooks or resources where the confidence interval of the mean is separated into small sample (usually $n < 30$) and large sample (usually $n \geq 30$) when the population standard deviation is unknown. Why do these resources show it this way?

   You may find other resources split confidence intervals of the mean by sample size even when the population standard deviation is unknown. The reason some authors choose this method is that when you have larger sample sizes, the standard normal distribution is similar to the $t$-distribution. As a result, some use the $z$-scores from the standard normal distribution instead of $t$-scores when they have a larger sample size. In smaller samples, $t$ and $z$ are quite different, so they may decide to switch to the $t$-distribution only when they are dealing with smaller samples. Technically, the difference in the confidence interval when using $z$ versus $t$ in larger samples is pretty small. However, the most accurate way of dealing with confidence intervals is as presented in this chapter.

   For example, say that you take a random sample of 30 individuals and find their mean score (on a scale of 1 to 15) is 10 with a standard deviation of 1.2. If you use a $z$-score of 1.96 (for $\alpha = 0.05$) you would get the confidence interval $9.57 \leq \mu \leq 10.43$. However, if you used the $t$-value (2.045), the confidence interval for the same alpha ($\alpha$) value (0.05) is $9.55 \leq \mu \leq 10.45$.

   Although this difference doesn't look like much (0.02 difference on both the lower and upper limits) remember that our goal is to be able to say that we are 95 percent confident that this interval contains the population parameter. When using the $z$-scores, the confidence interval does not consider the larger variability and therefore has a smaller range. As such, it may not be the case that the interval will contain the population mean 95 percent of the time, yet we are saying it will. Therefore, using the $t$-distribution when the standard deviation of the population is unknown provides the more accurate confidence interval.

2. I'm a little confused by what we mean when we say we are 95 percent confident. Are we 95 percent confident that we know the population mean?

   Consider the confidence interval $8 \leq \mu \leq 12$, which we might interpret by saying that we are 95 percent confident that the population mean will fall between 8 and 12. We are not saying that we know the value of the population. What we are saying is that whatever the value of the population mean is, we are 95 percent sure that it is between 8 and 12. By saying this we are also saying that there is a 5 percent chance we are wrong and that the value of the population mean falls outside that range.

3. What is the difference between the margin of error and a confidence interval?

   The confidence interval is the range of values that we expect will contain the true parameter. The margin of error is what is used to calculate the lower and upper values of the confidence interval. It is the critical value multiplied by the standard error.

4. How do we know what value we should use for our level of confidence?

Usually we follow the norms of our disciplines when it comes to levels of confidence. In the social sciences the norm is to use either 95 percent or 99 percent. In the natural sciences (such as astronomy, physics, and medicine) it is not uncommon to have higher levels of confidence such as 99.9 percent or 99.99 percent.

5. Why is the *t*-distribution called the Student's *t*-distribution? Was there a person named Student?

William Sealy Gosset was a statistician who worked for the beer brewer Guinness. Gosset was prohibited by his employer to publish papers under his real name, so he wrote under the pseudonym "Student." In 1908, Gosset published his paper formulating the *t*-distribution ("The Probable Error of a Mean") in the journal *Biometrika* under this pseudonym. Thus, the *t*-distribution became known as Student's *t*-distribution.

## Research Example:

Hovespeian et al. (2010) recruited 328 adolescent girls who were sheltered by child protective services (CPS) in the province of Quebec (between 2000 and 2002). The researchers were interested in understanding the relationship between prior sexual and physical abuse, and the ability of individuals to communicate with their partners about their sexuality and the use of contraception with partners. Of the 328 participants, 271 indicated that they had had sexual intercourse. Of the remaining 57, 16 stated that they had not had sexual intercourse and 41 did not answer the question. The mean age of those who had intercourse was 13.0 with a standard deviation of 1.7. Participants were also asked if they had been sexually abused in the past. Of the 264 who responded to the question, 192 stated Yes and 72 stated No. The researchers also measured a variable, "Perceived Ability to Communicate about Sexuality and Contraception." Of those who had indicated that they had a prior history of sexual abuse ($n = 192$), the mean score on this variable was 3.99 with a standard deviation of 0.8.[5]

## Research Example Questions:

**Question 1:** What is the population under study?

**Question 2:** What is the proportion of females under CPS care who have had sexual intercourse?

**Question 3:** What is the 95 percent confidence interval for the proportion of females under CPS care who have had sexual intercourse?

**Question 4:** What is the 95 percent confidence interval for the average age of first intercourse for females under CPS care?

**Question 5:** Of the 192 respondents who indicated that they had experienced sexual abuse, what is the 95 percent confidence interval for their average score (3.99) on the variable "Perceived Ability to Communicate about Sexuality and Contraception"?

**Research Example Answers:**

**Question 1:** What is the population under study?

The population is females under CPS care in Quebec.

**Question 2:** What is the proportion of females under CPS care who have had sexual intercourse?

Estimating the proportion of females under CPS care who have had sexual intercourse can be difficult, because 41 respondents did not answer the question. We could say that since 271 out of 328 said Yes, that the proportion is 0.83, or 83 percent. However, doing this implies that the 41 answered No, which is not the case. Therefore, we may wish to say that of those who responded to the question, 271 out of 287 said Yes, for a proportion of 0.94, or 94 percent.

**Question 3:** What is the 95 percent confidence interval for the proportion of females under CPS care who have had sexual intercourse?

Using 271 out of 287, or 0.94 as the proportion, the 95 percent confidence interval for the population proportion would be:

$$0.94 \pm 1.96\sqrt{\frac{0.94 \times 0.06}{287}} = 0.94 \pm 0.03, \text{ or } 0.91 \leq p \leq 0.97$$

**Question 4:** What is the 95 percent confidence interval for the average age of first intercourse for females under CPS care?

For a sample of 271 the average age of first intercourse was $\bar{x} = 13.0$ with a standard deviation of $s = 1.7$. The 95 percent confidence interval for the mean of the population is therefore:

$$13.0 \pm 1.96\left(\frac{1.7}{\sqrt{271}}\right)$$

which equals

$$13 \pm 0.20$$

or

$$12.80 \leq \mu \leq 13.20$$

So, we are 95 percent sure that the mean age of first sexual intercourse for females under CPS care (given that they have had sexual intercourse) is between 12.8 and 13.2.

**Question 5:** Of the 192 respondents who indicated that they had experienced sexual abuse, what is the 95 percent confidence interval for their average score (3.99) on the variable "Perceived Ability to Communicate about Sexuality and Contraception"?

With the mean ($\bar{x}$) of 3.99 and a standard deviation ($s$) of 0.8 and $n = 192$, the standard error of mean is:

$$\frac{s}{\sqrt{n}} = \frac{0.8}{\sqrt{192}} = 0.06$$

The 95 percent confidence interval for the mean is then:

$$3.99 \pm 1.96\left(\frac{0.8}{\sqrt{192}}\right)$$

which equals:

$$3.99 \pm 0.12$$

or

$$3.87 \leq \mu \leq 4.11$$

---

**ANSWERS TO EXERCISE 8.1**

Since we do not know the population standard deviation ($\sigma$), the formula for the 95 percent confidence interval is:

$$CI = \bar{x} \pm t_{(\alpha = .05)}\left(\frac{s}{\sqrt{n}}\right)$$

Most tables for the $t$-distribution don't provide all of the degrees of freedom ($df$) values. You'll notice that the $df$ numbers often jump from 90 to 100 and don't include 96 ($n - 1 = 96$). When this happens move down to the next lower $df$ value. In this case that is 90. If you are using a statistical software program to calculate the confidence interval, it will likely provide you with the exact $t$-value for the given $df$.
   Therefore,

$$CI = 28.28 \pm 1.987\left(\frac{7.26}{\sqrt{97}}\right)$$

$$CI = 28.28 \pm 1.46$$

equals:

28.28 − 1.46 = 26.82 (lower Limit)

and

28.28 + 1.46 = 29.74 (upper limit)

We interpret this result as: We are 95 percent confident that the mean developmental asset score of all First Nation youth in and out of home care is between 26.82 and 29.74.

**EXERCISE 8.2**

The formula for calculating the confidence interval of a proportion is:

$$CI = P_s \pm z_{(\alpha = .05)}\left(\sqrt{\frac{P_s(1 - P_s)}{n}}\right)$$

We are already given the proportion (39 percent), so we can fill in the formula with the appropriate values to get:

$$CI = 0.39 \pm 1.96\left(\sqrt{\frac{.39(1 - .39)}{525}}\right)$$

$$CI = 0.39 \pm 1.96(0.02)$$

$$CI = 0.39 \pm 0.04$$

equals:

0.39 − 0.04 = 0.35 (lower limit)

and

0.39 + 0.04 = 0.43 (upper limit)

We interpret this result as: We are 95 percent confident that the proportion of Canadian men who would not be willing to give up beer, wine, or alcohol to add five years to their life is between 35 percent and 43 percent.

## Problems

1. The weight (in ounces) of drained fruit found in 21 randomly selected cans of peaches packed by the Sunny Fruit Company were:

| | | | | | | |
|---|---|---|---|---|---|---|
| 11.0 | 11.6 | 10.9 | 12.0 | 11.5 | 12.0 | 11.2 |
| 10.5 | 12.2 | 11.8 | 12.1 | 11.6 | 11.7 | 11.6 |
| 11.2 | 12.0 | 11.4 | 10.8 | 11.8 | 10.9 | 11.4 |

The standard deviation of the canned fruit weight is 1.25.

a) Calculate the sample mean and sample standard deviation.

b) Assuming normality, construct a 95 percent confidence interval for the estimated mean weight of peaches per can.

c) How would your answer change if you were interested in 90 percent instead?

d) In this context, what does 95 percent mean?

2. While talking about the cars that fellow students drive, Tom claims that 15 percent of all college students that drive cars drive convertibles. Tom's friend, Jody, finds this hard to believe and decides to check the validity of Tom's claim using the data Justine already collected. Justine, in a recent survey of the student parking lot, found 17 convertibles out of 200 selected cars.

a) Define $p$ in this setting.

b) What is a 90 percent confidence interval for the proportion of students driving convertibles at the college?

c) What is the 99 percent confidence interval?

d) What do you notice about the intervals as the confidence level rises?

3. A group of 22 hockey players can hit, on average, 86 hockey pucks in a 5-minute interval with standard deviation 5. What is the 90 percent confidence interval for the average number of hockey pucks?

4. The length of time it takes to complete a Rubik's cube is known to be normally distributed. The times (in seconds) for 16 individuals is given below.

| | | | |
|----|----|----|----|
| 33 | 12 | 52 | 71 |
| 38 | 12 | 56 | 77 |
| 42 | 20 | 61 | 85 |
| 47 | 27 | 66 | 97 |

a) When should the *t*-distribution be used to find a confidence interval for the mean?

b) What is a 90 percent confidence interval for the mean time to complete the Rubik's cube?

c) What is the 99 percent confidence interval?

# Estimation and Hypothesis Testing I: Single Sample *T*-Test and *Z*-Test

*9*

**Learning Objectives**

By the end of this chapter you should be able to:

1. Describe the importance of a single sample test of a mean and proportion.
2. Describe when to use a *z*-test versus a *t*-test when testing a hypothesis about a single mean.
3. Prepare a hypothesis for testing using a single sample test.
4. Conduct a single sample *z*-test of a mean.
5. Conduct a single sample *t*-test of a mean.
6. Conduct a single sample *z*-test of a proportion.
7. Describe why you might favour a two-tailed test over a one-tailed test.
8. Report the *p*-values for a *z*-test and/or a *t*-test.

### William Sealy Gossett (1876–1937)

William Sealy Gossett graduated from Oxford having studied chemistry and mathematics. He then worked for the Guinness Brewery in Dublin, performing statistical analyses to improve barley production and the quality of the brewery's beer. While employed at Guinness, Gossett derived the *t*-test for testing means with small samples. Although his work was theoretical in nature, the brewery would not allow him to publish his work, fearing that the competition would learn of their trade secret. However, the company did allow him to publish the work under the pseudonym "student." Hence, the Student *t*-test was established.[1]

## Introduction

**LO1**

In chapter 7 we introduced two fundamental concepts in statistical inference: population parameter estimation and statistical hypothesis testing. In the last chapter we covered how we make inferences about the population by using confidence intervals. For the remaining chapters in this book we will focus on how to statistically test hypotheses. In this chapter, we look specifically at hypothesis testing with a single sample mean and hypothesis testing with a single sample proportion.

Actually, you already have some experience with this type of analysis. In chapter 7, we used a single sample test when discussing the Five Steps of Hypothesis Testing. However, we were not really concerned with the type of test we were using. Therefore, to clarify what is meant when we say "hypothesis testing with a single sample mean" and "hypothesis testing with a single sample proportion" let's consider an example for each.

### Single Sample Mean Example

An organizational sociologist is interested in determining if those with university undergraduate degrees earn higher hourly wages than the population. Based on the data from the 2008 Statistics Canada Labour Force Survey she knows that the mean ($\mu$) hourly wage of Canadian full-time employees between the age of 30 and 34 is approximately $21.69. The sociologist randomly selects a sample of 100 individuals with a university bachelor's degree and finds that their mean ($\bar{x}$) hourly wage is $26.38. Using a single sample test the sociologist compares the mean hourly wage from the single sample of 100 individuals ($26.38) to the population mean ($21.69) and finds that there is a significant difference between the two.

So what do we mean by hypothesis testing with a single sample mean? In the previous example, we have a sample mean ($\bar{x} = \$26.38$) that we wanted to compare to a known population mean ($\mu = \$21.69$). The sample is called a "single sample" because the sociologist only took one sample of 100 individuals out of the population as opposed to multiple samples. Given that she calculated the mean based on a single sample, it is called a single sample mean. Therefore, **hypothesis testing with a single sample mean** is the statistical evaluation of a hypothesis whereby we compare a single sample mean to a known mean which is often, but not always, the population mean.

**Hypothesis testing with a single sample mean** is the statistical evaluation of a hypothesis whereby we compare a single sample mean to a known mean which is often, but not always, the population mean.

## Single Sample Proportion Example

A political scientist is interested in determining if the proportion of female Members of Provincial Parliaments across Canada differs significantly from 50 percent. Based on data provided by the Library of Parliament he finds that across Canada, females hold 23.97 percent of the seats in Provincial legislatures. Using a single sample test he compares the proportion of female Members of Parliament (23.97 percent) to the goal of 50 percent representation, and finds that the difference between 50 percent and 23.97 percent is significant.

Similar to hypothesis testing with a single sample mean, **hypothesis testing with a single sample proportion** is the statistical evaluation of a hypothesis whereby we compare a single sample proportion to a known proportion which is often, but not always, the population proportion.

**Hypothesis testing with a single sample proportion** is statistical evaluation of a hypothesis whereby we compare a single sample proportion to a known proportion which is often, but not always, the population proportion.

In both cases, we stated that we are comparing a sample mean or proportion to a known mean or proportion. Often, the "known mean" or "known proportion" is the population mean or proportion. However, we can also use a desired mean or proportion as the comparison value. Below are some examples of hypothesis tests using a single sample mean or proportion that we compare to a population or a desired mean or proportion.

1. A researcher has starting salary data for a sample of 85 nurses in Manitoba who were not born in Canada. Using the known provincial average of starting salary for nurses, the researcher wants to determine if those born outside of Canada receive the same average starting salary as the population of nurses in Manitoba.

2. A social worker knows that last year the average number of community service hours imposed on young offenders for a first offense was 122.5 hours. He takes a sample of 35 young offenders sentenced this year to determine if the average number of community service hours imposed has changed from last year.

3. The Mayor has a goal for workplace diversity. She wants at least 25 percent of the city staff to come from visible minority groups. Using the current proportion of 21.5 percent, she wants to determine if the difference (between the current proportion and the known goal of 25 percent) is significantly different.

4. A high school English teacher believes that if students spend an average of four hours per week studying the class material they would do well in the course. He selects a sample of 20 students to determine if the current average number of hours studying for his course differs from the desired four hours.

5. A hockey coach calculated that this year his team won 25 percent of their games in overtime. He compared his team's proportion of games won in overtime this year against the known proportion in the league to determine how they compare.

The important thing to note in these examples is that the sample mean or proportion is compared to the either the population mean or proportion or a desired mean or proportion. By making this comparison, we can test hypotheses about the differences between the two. Knowing this, we are now ready to get in to the "how" of testing hypotheses with a single sample mean. We start by comparing the single sample $z$-test with the single sample $t$-test.

# Single Sample $z$-Test or Single Sample $t$-Test

**LO2**

In chapter 8 we learned the following regarding the normal distribution and the $t$-distribution:

1. When dealing with sample means ($\bar{x}$), we use the normal distribution ($z$-scores) if we know the value of the population standard deviation ($\sigma$).
2. When dealing with sample means ($\bar{x}$), we use the $t$-distribution ($t$-scores) if we do not know the value of the population standard deviation ($\sigma$).
3. When dealing with tests involving sample proportions ($\hat{p}$) we use the normal distribution ($z$-scores).

A **single sample z-test of a mean** involves the comparison of a single sample mean ($\bar{x}$) to a known (or desired) population mean ($\mu$) when the population standard deviation ($\sigma$) is known.

The same is true with single sample tests:

1. For a single sample test for a mean, we use the normal distribution ($z$-scores) if we know the population standard deviation ($\sigma$).
2. For a single sample test for a mean, we use the $t$-distribution ($t$-scores) if we do not know the population standard deviation ($\sigma$).
3. For a single sample test for a proportion, we use the normal distribution ($z$-scores).

A **single sample t-test of a mean** involves the comparison of a single sample mean ($\bar{x}$) to a known (or desired) population mean ($\mu$) when the population standard deviation ($\sigma$) is unknown.

We refer to single sample tests of hypotheses as either the **single sample z-test for a mean,** the **single sample t-test for a mean** or the **single sample z-test for a proportion.** More specifically:

1. We use a single sample $z$-test for a mean if we know the population standard deviation ($\sigma$).
2. We use a single sample $t$-test for a mean if we do not know the value of the population standard deviation ($\sigma$).

A **single sample z-test of a proportion** involves the comparison of a single sample proportion ($\hat{p}$) to a known (or desired) population proportion ($p$).

3. We use a single sample $z$-test for a proportion if we are interested in testing hypotheses about a single proportion.

**Note:** There are situations in which we would not use a single sample $z$-test. However, this is beyond the scope of this textbook and so it is not covered here. As such, we only discuss the single sample $z$-test of a proportion.

**TABLE 9.1**
*z*-**Test or** *t*-**Test**

| Test Contains a Mean ($\bar{x}$) | When $\sigma$ is known: | Single sample *z*-test for a mean |
|---|---|---|
| | When $\sigma$ is unknown: | Single sample *t*-test for a mean |
| Test Contains a Proportion ($\hat{p}$) | | Single sample *z*-test for a proportion |

**Note:** It is common for the single sample *z*-test or *t*-test to be called a one sample *z*-test or *t*-test. The meaning is the same.

The rest of this chapter is devoted to the discussion of the single sample *z*-test for a mean, the single sample *t*-test for a mean, and the single sample *z*-test for proportion. However, before moving on, let's quickly review some of the important information from chapter 7 regarding setting up a hypothesis for statistical testing.

# Setting Up a Hypothesis for Statistical Testing

**LO3**

We covered how to set up a hypothesis for statistical testing in chapter 7 and provided the five steps for hypothesis testing. Let's briefly review that material in the context of a single sample hypothesis test.

Suppose we hypothesize that students at our university who prefer to take their classes in the evening are not the same age as the population of all students at the university. Further suppose that we know the mean age of the population (of all students at our university) is 21.5 and, based on a sample of 125 students, the mean age of those who prefer to take their class at night is 22.5. Our hypothesis is non-directional (two-tailed) and so we write the notation for this as:

$$H_0: \mu = \mu_0$$
$$H_A: \mu \neq \mu_0$$

Within this hypothesis you'll notice two population mean symbols, $\mu$ and $\mu_0$. $\mu_0$ represents the population mean (21.5) of all students at our university. This is the population mean for the null hypothesis. Conversely, $\mu$ represents the population mean for the alternative hypothesis. We are stating that our sample mean ($\bar{x}$) of 22.5 came from this population ($\mu$) where its mean is not 21.5 but is some other value. If we "fail to reject" the null hypothesis, then we are saying that $\mu$ is the same as $\mu_0$ (meaning, $\mu = \mu_0$). If we "reject" the null hypothesis, then we are saying that $\mu$ is not the same as $\mu_0$ (meaning, $\mu \neq \mu_0$). The concept of null hypothesis testing takes a little while to get used to. Figure 9.1 provides a flowchart of our hypothesis and the possible "reject" or "fail to reject" decision.

**FIGURE 9.1**
**Flowchart of**
**Hypothesis Testing**

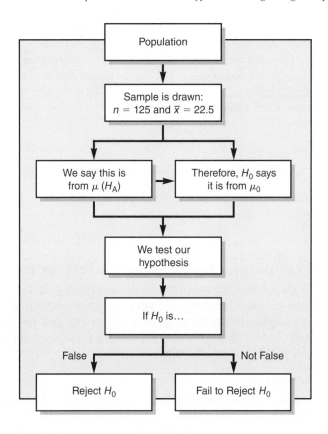

## The Single Sample z-Test for a Mean

**LO4**

When we want to compare a single sample mean to a known population mean and we know the value of the population standard deviation, we use a single sample z-test for a mean. To cover this test, we'll first look at the formula, then use a scenario to work through the hypothesis test.

### Formula for the Single Sample z-Test for a Mean

The formula for this test is:

$$z = \frac{\bar{x} - \mu_0}{(\sigma_x)} \tag{9.1}$$

where: $\bar{x}$ = the sample mean

$\mu_0$ = the population mean

$\sigma_{\bar{x}}$ = the standard error of the mean

You should notice right away that this formula is similar to the formula we covered in chapter 5 for calculating z-scores. That is because we are calculating a z-score for the difference between our given sample mean and the population mean. In hypothesis testing we refer to this z-score as a z-statistic. In the numerator $(\bar{x} - \mu_0)$ we are subtracting the known population mean from our sample mean. In the denominator, we have the standard error of the mean. This is the same standard error of the mean that we discussed in the previous chapter. The standard error of the mean is:

$$\sigma_{\bar{x}} = \frac{\sigma}{\sqrt{n}} \tag{9.2}$$

Therefore, the z-statistic formula is:

$$z = \frac{\bar{x} - \mu_0}{\left(\dfrac{\sigma}{\sqrt{n}}\right)} \tag{9.3}$$

## Example of a Single Sample z-Test for the Mean

To demonstrate the use of the single sample z-test for the mean, consider the following scenario and our five steps for hypothesis testing. We will use the two-sided test as this provides us with a more stringent test of the null hypothesis. Refer to the Take a Closer Look following the scenario for a more detailed explanation of why this is the case.

## Scenario:

Suppose the mean waiting time for non-emergency surgeries in your hospital is 87.5 days (12.5 weeks) with a standard deviation of 14 days (2 weeks). Over the last year the hospital's CEO has been implementing various programs to try to reduce waiting time. You are asked to test whether the wait times have changed from the previous average. Not knowing if the wait times have increased or decreased, you hypothesize that the wait times are not 87.5 days (a two-tailed hypothesis). You randomly select 100 cases and calculate the average wait time. Your data shows the following:

$\mu = 87.5$ days      $\bar{x} = 84$ days
$\sigma = 14$ days       $n = 100$

---

## Take a Closer Look

**The Five Steps of Hypothesis Testing**

**Step 1:** Define the null and alternative hypothesis.

**Step 2:** Define the sampling distribution and critical values.

**Step 3:** Calculate the test statistic using the sample data.

**Step 4:** Make the decision regarding the hypothesis.

**Step 5:** Interpret the results.

**Step 1:** Define the null and alternative hypotheses.

$$H_0: \mu = 87.5$$
$$H_A: \mu \neq 87.5$$

Notice that we have replaced $\mu_0$ with the actual value of 87.5. Since $\mu_0$ represents the situation where the population mean is 87.5, replacing $\mu_0$ with the actual value makes the hypothesis a little easier to read.

**Step 2:** Define the sampling distribution and critical values.

The mean of the sampling distribution ($\mu_{\bar{x}}$) is equal to the population of the mean ($\mu$) of 87.5 days. The standard error of the mean ($\sigma_{\bar{x}}$) is:

$$\sigma_{\bar{x}} = \frac{\sigma}{\sqrt{n}} = \frac{14}{\sqrt{100}} = 1.40 \qquad \textbf{(9.4)}$$

Therefore, 1 standard error equals 1.40 days. Given an alpha ($\alpha$) of 0.05 and a two-tailed hypothesis, our critical value for $z$ is $\pm 1.96$. While it is not necessary for us to estimate and draw the sampling distribution to test this hypothesis, for this example we provide it diagrammatically in Figure 9.2.

**Step 3:** Calculate the test statistic using the sample data.

Using the formula for a single sample $z$-test we get:

$$z = \frac{\bar{x} - \mu_0}{\left( \dfrac{\sigma}{\sqrt{n}} \right)} = \frac{84 - 87.5}{\left( \dfrac{14}{\sqrt{100}} \right)} = \frac{-3.5}{1.40} = -2.50 \qquad \textbf{(9.5)}$$

**FIGURE 9.2**
**Sampling Distribution and Critical Values at $\alpha = 0.05$**

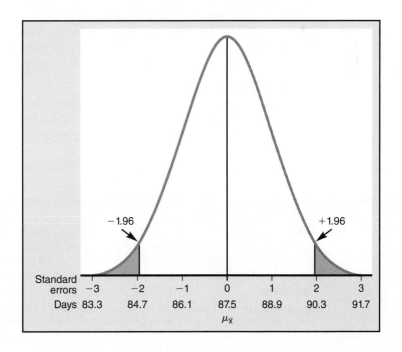

**FIGURE 9.3**
*z*-Statistic From
Hypothesis Test

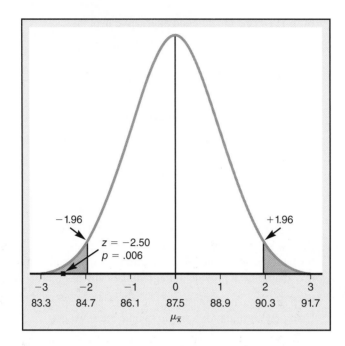

**LO8**

**Step 4:** Make the decision regarding the hypothesis.
Our *z*-statistic is −2.50, meaning that our sample mean of 84 days is 2.50 standard errors less than the population mean of 87.5 days. The two-tailed critical value for an alpha (α) value of 0.05 (meaning 5 percent chance of rejecting a false null) is ±1.96. Given that our *z*-statistic is past the critical value (i.e., −2.50 < −1.96) we reject the null hypothesis that $\mu = 87.5$ (see Figure 9.3).

**LO8**

**Step 5:** Interpret the results.
Based on our sample, we can say that there appears to be a statistically significant decrease in wait times. Our sample mean of 84 days is significantly lower than the population mean of 87.5 days at an alpha (α) level of 0.05.

**EXERCISE 9.1**

You work for your provincial probation officers association. Based on a sample of 50 probation officers in your province you find the mean number of cases handled per probation officer is 100. In addition, you know that the national mean (μ) is 95 cases per officer with a standard deviation (σ) of 15. You want to conduct a two-tailed hypothesis test, with an alpha (α) of 0.05, to determine if there is a significant difference between your sample mean and the population mean.

**Source:** This scenario is loosely based on a February 15th, 2000 presentation to the Ministry of Finance found on the website for the Ontario Probation Officers Association; http:\\www.poao.org.

# Take a Closer Look

### One-Sided or Two-Sided Hypothesis Test?

As we saw in Figure 7.5 of chapter 7, two-tailed tests are considered to be more stringent than one-tailed tests, because it is harder to "reject the null." Using our scenario of wait times for non-emergency surgeries, consider why this is the case. What would happen if our *z*-statistic (our test statistic) was $-1.85$ and not $-2.50$? With a two-tailed test and the critical value of $\pm 1.96$ we would "fail to reject the null" and state that the difference is not significant. However, with a one-tailed test, our critical value would be $-1.645$. This means we would "reject the null" stating that there is a significant difference. So, the null is harder to reject using a two-tailed test.

It should also be stated that in using a one-tailed test, you also run the risk of not testing for the opposite effect. For example, suppose you thought that implementing a program to help first year students adapt to university life would significantly increase their grades. Now imagine that—after an appropriate amount of time has passed since implementing the program—you take a random sample of first year students and compare the sample mean grades to the previous first year student population grades. To your surprise you find that first year student grades have decreased rather than increased. Since you used a one-sided test you are not be able to test if the decrease is significantly different from the previous population grades.

Switching tests after we create a hypothesis because we didn't anticipate the opposite effect or because we want to obtain a significant result is considered to be bad science. Therefore, it is often recommended to use the two-sided hypothesis test.

# The Single Sample *t*-Test for a Mean

When we want to compare a single sample mean to known population mean but we do not know the value of the population standard deviation, we use a single sample *t*-test for a mean. The process is similar to the single sample *z*-test, only this time we use the *t*-distribution (as we did when calculating confidence intervals) and the estimated standard error of the mean instead of the standard error of the mean. For this test, we'll first look at the formula, then use a scenario to work through the hypothesis test.

## Formula for the Single Sample *t*-Test for a Mean

The formula for this test is:

$$t = \frac{\bar{x} - \mu_0}{s_x} \tag{9.6}$$

where: $\bar{x}$ = the sample mean

$\mu_0$ = the population mean

$\sigma_{\bar{x}}$ = the estimated standard error of the mean

As we saw in chapter 8, we cannot calculate the standard error of the mean when we do not know the population standard deviation ($\sigma$). Therefore, we use the estimated standard error of the mean instead. As in chapter 8, the formula is:

$$s_{\bar{x}} = \frac{s}{\sqrt{n}} \qquad (9.7)$$

Therefore the *z*-statistic formula is:

$$z = \frac{\bar{x} - \mu_0}{\left(\dfrac{s}{\sqrt{n}}\right)} \qquad (9.8)$$

## Example of a Single Sample *t*-Test for the Mean

Consider the following scenario as we work through the single sample *t*-test using a two-tailed hypothesis.

## Scenario:

You recently read a report, published two years ago, that asked 21-year-old students what age they were when they had their first alcoholic drink. The report stated the mean ($\mu$) was 17 years of age. To test if the age of first drink has changed since the report was published you collect data from a random sample of 91 students who are 21 years old. To determine if there is a significant difference between your sample mean and the population mean, you conduct a two-tailed hypothesis test with an alpha ($\alpha$) value of 0.01. Based on your data you find that the mean ($\bar{x}$) age of the first drink is 16.3 with a standard deviation (*s*) of 2.60.

**Step 1:** Define the null and alternative hypotheses.

$$H_0: \mu = 17$$
$$H_A: \mu \neq 17$$

**Step 2:** Define the sampling distribution and critical values.
The mean of the sampling distribution ($\mu_{\bar{x}}$) is 17 years of age. The estimated standard error of the mean ($s_{\bar{x}}$) is:

$$s_{\bar{x}} = \frac{s}{\sqrt{n}} = \frac{2.60}{\sqrt{91}} = 0.273 \qquad (9.9)$$

Given an alpha ($\alpha$) value of 0.01 and a two-tailed hypothesis, our critical value for *t* with $n - 1$ degrees of freedom (*df*) is $\pm 2.632$. Our sampling distribution out to $\pm 3s_{\bar{x}}$ is show on the line below. Picture the line as the *x*-axis for the sampling distribution curve, similar to the one in Figure 9.2.

| $-3s_{\bar{x}}$ | $-2s_{\bar{x}}$ | $-1s_{\bar{x}}$ | $\mu_{\bar{x}}$ | $+1s_{\bar{x}}$ | $+2s_{\bar{x}}$ | $+3s_{\bar{x}}$ |
|---|---|---|---|---|---|---|
| 16.18 | 16.45 | 16.73 | 17.00 | 17.27 | 17.55 | 17.82 |

**Step 3:** Calculate the test statistic using the sample data.
Using the formula for a single sample *t*-test we get:

$$t = \frac{\bar{x} - \mu_0}{\left(\frac{s}{\sqrt{n}}\right)} = \frac{16.3 - 17}{\left(\frac{2.60}{\sqrt{91}}\right)} = \frac{-0.7}{.273} = -2.56 \qquad \textbf{(9.10)}$$

**LO8**

**Step 4:** Make the decision regarding the hypothesis.
Our *t*-statistic is $-2.56$. The two-tailed critical value for an alpha ($\alpha$) value of 0.01 is $\pm 2.632$. Since our test statistic does not pass the critical value ($-2.56 > -2.632$), we fail to reject the null hypothesis.

This scenario is a good case of using a one-tailed versus two-tailed test. Using a two-tailed test—which we previously said is more stringent as it makes it harder to reject the null and consequently harder to commit a Type I error—we failed to reject the null. Had we used a one-tailed test, the critical value would have been $-2.369$ and we would have rejected the null. If the null was true (in which case we correctly failed to reject it) we would have committed a Type I error by using the one-tailed approach.

**LO8**

**Step 5:** Interpret the results.
Based on the sample, you can say that there does not appear to be a statistically significant difference between the mean age of first drink reported two years ago ($\mu = 17$) and the sample mean ($\bar{x} = 16.3$) at an alpha ($\alpha$) level of 0.01.

---

**EXERCISE 9.2**

A 2006 Statistics Canada report stated that Montreal residents spend an average of $1,670 annually on utilities (water, fuel, and electricity) for their residence. You are interested in determining if this amount has significantly changed since then. You select a random sample of 40 residents living in Montreal and record their 2010 utilities expenditures. You find that $\bar{x} = \$1,850$ and $s = \$465$. Based on this information, test the hypothesis that there is a significant difference using a two-tailed hypothesis test and an alpha ($\alpha$) value of 0.025.

**Source:** "Measuring housing affordability" by Jacqueline Luffman, adapted from Statistics Canada publication *Perspectives on Labour and Income,* Catalogue 75-001-XIE2006111, Vol. 7, No. 11, page 18, http://www.statcan.gc.ca/bsolc/olc-cel/olc-cel?catno=75-001-XIE&lang=eng.

---

## Did You Know?

The prisoner's dilemma was a game proposed by computer scientists in the 1950s.

Consider two offenders who have committed a crime. They are placed in separate cells so that they can be interrogated separately. If they both do not confess, they will serve one year in jail. If they both confess, they will receive five years in jail. However, if one confesses and the other does not, the confessor goes free and the other gets 10 years in jail. What is the best strategy? We can put the decisions in the form of a chart.

|  | Offender B | |
| :--- | :---: | :---: |
|  | Do Not Confess | Confess |
| **Do Not Confess** | A Gets 1 Year<br>B Gets 1 Year | A Gets 10 Years<br>B Goes Free |
| **Confess** | A Goes Free<br>B Gets 10 Years | A Gets 5 Years<br>B Gets 5 Years |

*(Offender A labels the rows: Do Not Confess, Confess)*

If the two offenders trust each other, not confessing is the best choice. However, without information about the other offender the strategy that minimizes the loss—regardless of the other's decision—is to confess. The idea of minimizing the maximum loss is called a mini-max strategy.

We can frame a similar model used in labour relations and social interactions. Consider a game in which you can choose to be good or bad with the following payouts.

|  |  | Person B | |
| :--- | :--- | :---: | :---: |
|  |  | **Good** | **Bad** |
| **Person A** | **Good** | A wins $1,000<br>B wins $1,000 | A loses $2,000<br>B wins $2,000 |
|  | **Bad** | A wins $2,000<br>B loses $2,000 | A loses $1,000<br>B loses $1,000 |

What strategy will you choose? If you decide to be good and your opponent decides to be bad you will lose. But if you choose to be bad and your opponent chooses to be bad, then you both lose. The ideal situation is for both to be good. That requires trust. What if the game was played repeatedly? What strategy is best then? If you choose to be bad your opponent will have to choose to be bad and then you are both guaranteed to lose. You may choose to be good for a while and then stab your opponent in the back and win that round. But you will likely end up losing $1,000 every turn thereafter. You will have more money than your opponent but not as much as if you both choose to be good throughout. Try to think of situations in social interactions where you have to make these types of choices. The television show "Survivor" may be considered an extreme case of this type of decision making.

**Source:** http://en.wikipedia.org/wiki/Prisoner%27s_dilemma.

# The Single Sample *z*-Test for a Proportion

When we want to compare a single sample proportion ($\hat{p}$) to a known population proportion ($p$) we use a single sample *z*-test for a proportion. For this test, we'll first look at the formula, then use a scenario to work through the hypothesis test.

## Formula for the Single Sample *z*-Test for a Proportion

The formula for this test is:

$$z = \frac{\hat{p} - p_0}{\sigma_{\hat{p}}} \qquad (9.11)$$

where: $\hat{p}$ = the sample proportion

$p_0$ = the population proportion

$\sigma_{\hat{p}}$ = the estimated standard error of the proportion

To calculate the estimated standard error of the proportion, we use the following formula:

$$\sigma_{\hat{p}} = \sqrt{\frac{p_0(1 - p_0)}{n}} \qquad (9.12)$$

The *z*-statistic formula then becomes:

$$z = \frac{\hat{p} - p_0}{\left(\sqrt{\frac{p_0(1 - p_0)}{n}}\right)} \qquad (9.13)$$

Often there is confusion with what is happening in this formula, so it is worth spending the time to clarify. The first area of confusion usually is about why we are using the standard error of the proportion ($\sigma_{\hat{p}}$) and not the estimated standard error of the proportion ($s_{\hat{p}}$) as we did in chapter 8. In chapter 8, we dealt with confidence intervals where we did not know the value of the population proportion ($p$). There, we said that because we do not know the value of the population proportion ($p$), we must use the estimated standard error of the proportion ($s_{\hat{p}}$) instead of the standard error of the proportion ($\sigma_{\hat{p}}$). However, in a single sample *z*-test for a proportion, we know the value of the population proportion ($p$) since that is what we are comparing to our sample proportion ($\hat{p}$). That is why we use the standard error of the proportion ($\sigma_{\hat{p}}$) in the *z*-statistic formula. The second area of confusion is usually around why we are using $p_0$ to represent the population proportion in the formula and not $p$. The reason for this is due to the hypothesis. Consider the hypothesis:

$$H_0: p = p_0$$
$$H_A: p \neq p_0$$

Remember with the single sample *t*-test for means, we said that $\mu_0$ represents the known population mean, whereas $\mu$ represents the population mean that our sample mean ($\overline{x}$) came from. Well, the same is true with single sample *z*-test for proportions—we say that $p_0$ represents the known population proportion, whereas $p$ represents the population proportion from which our sample proportion ($s_{\hat{p}}$) came.

## Example of a Single Sample *z*-Test for the Proportion

Consider the following scenario as we work through the test using a two-tailed hypothesis.

## Scenario:

In the 2009 Canadian Tobacco Use Monitoring Survey, Health Canada reported that in 1999 83 percent of current smokers over the age of 15 smoked on a daily basis. Interested in the change in the smoking behaviour in Canada, you take a random sample of 200 Canadians who smoke and find that 77.5 percent of current smokers smoke on a daily basis. You would like to test the hypothesis that the proportion of those who smoke daily is now significantly different than it was in 1999. You are using a two-tailed hypothesis test with an alpha ($\alpha$) of 0.05.[2]

**Step 1:** Define the null and alternative hypotheses.

$$H_0: p = 0.83$$
$$H_A: p \neq 0.83$$

You will notice that we have replace $p_0$ with its actual value (0.83) in order to make the hypothesis easier to read. We are hypothesizing (the alternative hypothesis) that our sample proportion ($\hat{p}$) does not come from the population of smokers ($p_0$) where the proportion is 0.83 ($p_0 = 0.83$) but rather from an alternative population ($p$) where the proportion is not 0.83. If this is correct, then $p$ should not be the same as $p_0$ ($p \neq 0.83$). If it is not correct, then $p$ should be the same as $p_0$ ($p = 0.83$).

**Step 2:** Define the sampling distribution and critical values.

The proportion ($p_0$) is 0.83. The standard error ($\sigma_{\hat{p}}$) of the proportion is:

$$\sigma_{\hat{p}} = \sqrt{\frac{p_0(1 - p_0)}{n}} = \sqrt{\frac{0.83(1 - 0.83)}{200}} = \sqrt{\frac{.1411}{200}} = 0.027 \quad \textbf{(9.14)}$$

Given an alpha ($\alpha$) of 0.05 and a two-tailed hypothesis, our critical value of $z$ is $\pm 1.96$. Our sampling distribution out to $\pm 3\sigma_{\hat{p}}$ is shown on the line below. Picture this line as the $x$-axis for the sampling distribution curve, similar to Figure 9.2.

| $-3\sigma_{\hat{p}}$ | $-2\sigma_{\hat{p}}$ | $-1\sigma_{\hat{p}}$ | $p_0$ | $+1\sigma_{\hat{p}}$ | $+2\sigma_{\hat{p}}$ | $+3\sigma_{\hat{p}}$ |
|---|---|---|---|---|---|---|
| 0.749 | 0.776 | 0.803 | 0.830 | 0.857 | 0.884 | 0.911 |

**Step 3:** Calculate the test statistic using the sample data.

Using the formula for a single sample $z$-test we get:

$$z = \frac{\hat{p} - p_0}{\left(\sqrt{\frac{p_0(1 - p_0)}{n}}\right)} = \frac{.775 - .83}{\left(\sqrt{\frac{.83(1 - .83)}{200}}\right)} = \frac{-0.055}{.027} = -2.04 \quad \textbf{(9.15)}$$

**LO8**

**Step 4:** Make the decision regarding the hypothesis.

The $z$-statistic is $-2.04$. The two-tailed critical value for an alpha ($\alpha$) of 0.05 is $\pm 1.96$. Since our $z$-statistic passes our critical value ($-2.04 < -1.96$), we reject the null hypothesis.

**LO8**

**Step 5:** Interpret the results.

Based on the sample, you can say that there appears to be a statistically significant difference between the 1999 proportion of smokers who smoke on a daily basis and the sample proportion of current smokers who smoke on a daily basis at the alpha ($\alpha$) level of 0.05.

---

**EXERCISE 9.3**

Suppose that prior to introducing the distracted driving law in British Columbia, 16 percent of drivers texted while driving. One year later you are interested in determining if the law is reducing the proportion of drivers who text while driving. You randomly sample 300 drivers and find that the sample proportion of drivers who text while driving is 11 percent. Using a two-tailed hypothesis test with an alpha ($\alpha$) of 0.05, test the hypothesis that the sample proportion differs from the previous population proportion.

# Conclusion

In this chapter we learned how to test hypotheses with a single mean or proportion. Hypothesis testing with a single sample mean or proportion is the statistical evaluation of a hypothesis whereby we compare a single sample mean or proportion to a known mean or proportion. Often the known mean or proportion comes from the population; however, that is not always the case. We can use target values, such a reduction in the proportion of families who live in poverty, as our known value.

Our journey into hypothesis testing has just begun. In the next chapter we will build on the single sample test and look at how to test hypotheses about two means. For example, is there a difference between males and females in the average starting salary for a given job? This involves collecting data from two different samples and comparing the means. We will also investigate the case where we collect data from individuals over two time periods. For example, does a certain type of therapy decrease anxiety over two different time periods (e.g., prior to therapy exposure and after therapy exposure). As with this chapter, we will also cover the comparison of two proportions. Chapter 10 will require you to pull together what you have learned in chapters 8 and 9. Therefore, we recommend that before you proceed, you go back and review any information that you are not entirely comfortable with.

## Key Chapter Concepts and Terms

Hypothesis testing with a single sample mean,  246

Hypothesis testing with a single sample proportion,  246

Single sample $z$-test of a mean,  247

Single sample $t$-test of a mean,  247

Single sample $z$-test of a proportion,  247

## Frequently Asked Questions

1. How do we know when to use the single sample $z$-test of a mean instead of the single sample $t$-test for a mean?

   The key thing to look for when determining if the test is a $z$-test or a $t$-test is the population standard deviation ($\sigma$). If you have the value for $\sigma$, then use the $z$-test. If you don't have the value for $\sigma$, but you do have the sample standard deviation ($s$), then use the $t$-test. Try to remember this key phrase "if you don't have the value for $\sigma$, then you use the $t$-test."

2. If we use a one-tailed hypothesis test and we find that we should have used a two-tailed test, why can we not just switch the critical values?

   Good practice of the scientific method requires us to state our hypotheses $a$-prior, which means that we state them before we collect and analyze our data. Switching your hypotheses after you have collected and analyzed your data leaves you open to the criticism that you are simply mining your data for things to report. Furthermore, given the importance of the concept of falsifiability to the scientific method, it is important for us to ensure that we apply as stringent a test as possible when testing the null hypothesis.

3. Does the critical value affect the value of the test statistic? (i.e., $z$-test or $t$-test)

The critical value, based on your desired alpha ($\alpha$) level, does not affect the value of your test statistic. The critical value is the value to which you compare your test statistic in order to determine whether you fail to reject or reject the null hypothesis.

4. What is the difference between the standard error of the mean and the estimated standard error of the mean?

The standard error of the mean is what we calculate when we know the value of the population standard deviation ($\sigma$). It is $\sigma$ divided by the square root of the sample size. As discussed in chapter 6, this represents the standard deviation of the sampling distribution as per the Central Limit Theorem. When we don't know the value of $\sigma$ we cannot calculate the standard error of the mean. The best we can do is get an estimate of the standard error of the mean. In this case, we use the sample standard deviation ($s$) instead of $\sigma$. Since we are using $s$ as an estimate of $\sigma$ we call the result of the formula the estimated standard error of the mean.

5. Why do we always use a $z$-test for test of a proportion?

Proportions follow a binomial distribution. However, we can use the normal distribution ($z$) to approximate the binomial distribution as long as the sample proportion times the sample size is greater than 10 ($\hat{p} \times n > 10$) and the value from 1 minus the sample proportion times the sample size is greater than 10 $[(1 - \hat{p}) \times n > 10]$. If this assumption is met, then we can use the normal distribution, which means using the $z$-test. When this assumption is not met, we need to use the binomial distribution instead of the normal distribution. However, this is beyond the scope of this textbook and so it is not covered here. As such, we state that we use the $z$-test for hypothesis tests using a single proportion.

**Research Example:**

In 2008, Professor Michael Martinez presented his paper "Voters and Nonvoters in Canadian Federal Elections," at the Annual Meeting of the Canadian Political Science Association in Vancouver, British Columbia. Using data from the 1997 and 2006 Canadian Election Studies, Martinez examined voter/non-voter attitudes toward a host of social issues. A sample of the issues considered included:

"How much do you think should be done for Quebec: more, less, or about the same as now?"

"Society would be better off if more women stayed at home with their children."

"Do you think Canada should admit more immigrants, fewer immigrants, or about the same as now?"

"How much do you think should be done for racial minorities: more, less, or about the same as now?"

For this example, we'll focus specifically on the opinions of non-voters regarding the Canadian economy. In 2006, 308 non-voters were asked the following question:

"Over the past year, has Canada's economy gotten better, gotten worse, or stayed about the same?"

Of the 308 non-voters, 25.3 percent stated they felt the economy had gotten better.

In the next chapter, we continue with this example and examine differences between voters and non-voters; however, for now, consider the following questions regarding hypotheses and confidence intervals for one population proportion.

**Research Example Questions:**

**Question 1:** What is the population of interest for this data?

**Question 2:** Suppose that prior to collecting the data, we hypothesized that 40 percent of non-voters would state that the economy was getting better. Using the 2006 non-voter data mentioned above, test this hypothesis using a two-tailed test.

**Research Example Answers:**

**Question 1:** What is the population of interest for this data?

The sample is representative of non-voters in a Canadian federal election.

**Question 2:** Suppose that prior to collecting the data, we hypothesized that 40 percent of non-voters would state that the economy was getting better. Using the 2006 non-voter data mentioned above, test this hypothesis using a two-tailed test.

**Step 1:** Define the null and alternative hypotheses.

$$H_0: p = 0.40$$
$$H_A: p \neq 0.40$$

**Step 2:** Define the sampling distribution and critical values.
The proportion $(p_0)$ is 0.40. The standard error of the proportion $(\sigma_{\hat{p}})$ is:

$$\sigma_{\hat{p}} = \sqrt{\frac{p_0(1 - p_0)}{n}} = \sqrt{\frac{0.40(1 - 0.40)}{308}} = \sqrt{\frac{0.24}{308}} = 0.028$$

Given an alpha $(\alpha)$ of 0.05 and a two-tailed hypothesis, our critical value of $z$ is $\pm 1.96$.

| $-3\sigma_{\hat{p}}$ | $-2\sigma_{\hat{p}}$ | $-1\sigma_{\hat{p}}$ | $p_0$ | $+1\sigma_{\hat{p}}$ | $+2\sigma_{\hat{p}}$ | $+3\sigma_{\hat{p}}$ |
|---|---|---|---|---|---|---|
| 0.316 | 0.344 | 0.372 | 0.400 | 0.428 | 0.456 | 0.484 |

**Step 3:** Calculate the test statistic using the sample data.
Using the formula for a single sample $z$-test we get:

$$z = \frac{\hat{p} - p_0}{\left( \sqrt{\frac{p_0(1 - p_0)}{n}} \right)} = \frac{0.253 - 0.40}{\left( \sqrt{\frac{0.40(1 - 0.40)}{308}} \right)} = \frac{-0.147}{0.028} = -5.30$$

**Step 4:** Make the decision regarding the hypothesis.
The z-statistic is $-5.30$. The two-tailed critical value for an alpha ($\alpha$) of 0.05 is $\pm 1.96$. Given that our z-statistic passes the critical value ($-5.30 < -1.96$), we reject the null hypothesis.

**Step 5:** Interpret the results.
Based on our results, we conclude that the proportion of non-voters in the population who, in 2006, stated they felt the economy was better, differed significantly from the hypothesized value of 0.40. In fact, our sample estimate was 0.253.

---

**ANSWER TO EXERCISE 9.1**

**Step 1:** Define the null and alternative hypotheses.

$$H_0: \mu = 95$$
$$H_A: \mu \neq 95$$

**Step 2:** Define the sampling distribution and critical values.
The mean of the sampling distribution ($\mu_{\bar{x}}$) is 95 cases. The standard error of the mean ($\mu_{\bar{x}}$) is:

$$\sigma_{\bar{x}} = \frac{\sigma}{\sqrt{n}} = \frac{15}{\sqrt{50}} = 2.12$$

Given an alpha ($\alpha$) of 0.05 and a two-tailed hypothesis, our critical value for z is $\pm 1.96$. Our sampling distribution out to $\pm 3\sigma_{\bar{x}}$ is:

| $-3\sigma_{\bar{x}}$ | $-2\sigma_{\bar{x}}$ | $-1\sigma_{\bar{x}}$ | $\mu_{\bar{x}}$ | $+1\sigma_{\bar{x}}$ | $+2\sigma_{\bar{x}}$ | $+3\sigma_{\bar{x}}$ |
|---|---|---|---|---|---|---|
| 88.64 | 90.76 | 92.88 | 95.00 | 97.12 | 99.24 | 101.36 |

**Step 3:** Calculate the test statistic using the sample data.
Using the formula for a single sample z-test we get:

$$z = \frac{\bar{x} - \mu_0}{\left(\frac{\sigma}{\sqrt{n}}\right)} = \frac{100 - 95}{\left(\frac{15}{\sqrt{50}}\right)} = \frac{5}{2.12} = 2.36$$

**Step 4:** Make the decision regarding the hypothesis.
Our z-statistic is 2.36. The two-tailed critical value for an alpha ($\alpha$) of 0.05 is $\pm 1.96$. Given that our z-statistic passes our critical value ($2.36 > 1.96$), we can reject the null hypothesis.

**Step 5:** Interpret the results.
Based on the sample, you can say that there appears to be a statistically significant difference between your provincial mean number of cases handled per probation officer and the national mean number of case handle per probation officer. Your sample mean of 100 cases is significantly higher than the population mean of 95 cases at an alpha ($\alpha$) level of 0.05.

**ANSWER TO EXERCISE 9.2**

**Step 1:** Define the null and alternative hypotheses.

$$H_0: \mu = \$1{,}670$$
$$H_A: \mu \neq \$1{,}670$$

**Step 2:** Define the sampling distribution and critical values.
The mean of the sampling distribution ($\mu_{\bar{x}}$) is \$1,670. The estimate standard error of the mean ($s_{\bar{x}}$) is:

$$s_{\bar{x}} = \frac{s}{\sqrt{n}} = \frac{465}{\sqrt{40}} = 73.52$$

Given an alpha ($\alpha$) of 0.025 and a two-tailed hypothesis, our critical value for $t$ with $n - 1$ $df$ is $\pm 2.331$. Our sampling distribution out to $\pm 3\sigma_{\bar{x}}$ is:

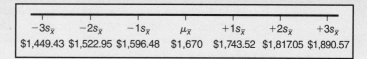

| $-3s_{\bar{x}}$ | $-2s_{\bar{x}}$ | $-1s_{\bar{x}}$ | $\mu_{\bar{x}}$ | $+1s_{\bar{x}}$ | $+2s_{\bar{x}}$ | $+3s_{\bar{x}}$ |
|---|---|---|---|---|---|---|
| \$1,449.43 | \$1,522.95 | \$1,596.48 | \$1,670 | \$1,743.52 | \$1,817.05 | \$1,890.57 |

**Step 3:** Calculate the test statistic using the sample data.
Using the formula for a single sample $z$-test we get:

$$t = \frac{\bar{x} - \mu_0}{\left(\dfrac{\sigma_s}{\sqrt{n}}\right)} = \frac{1850 - 1670}{\left(\dfrac{465}{\sqrt{40}}\right)} = \frac{180}{73.52} = 2.45$$

**Step 4:** Make the decision regarding the hypothesis.
Our $t$-statistic is 2.45. The two-tailed critical value for an alpha ($\alpha$) of 0.025 is $\pm 2.331$. Therefore, we reject the null hypothesis, since our test statistic falls past the critical value (2.45 > 2.331).

**Step 5:** Interpret the results.
Based on the sample, you can say that there is a statistically significant difference between the 2006 reported value and your sample mean, at an alpha ($\alpha$) level of 0.025.

**ANSWER TO EXERCISE 9.3**

**Step 1:** Define the null and alternative hypotheses.

$$H_0: p = 0.16$$
$$H_A: p \neq 0.16$$

**Step 2:** Define the sampling distribution and critical values.
The proportion ($p_0$) is 0.16. The estimated standard error of the proportion ($\sigma_{\hat{p}}$) is:

$$\sigma_{\hat{p}} = \sqrt{\frac{p_0(1 - p_0)}{n}} = \sqrt{\frac{0.16(1 - 0.16)}{300}} = \sqrt{\frac{0.1344}{300}} = 0.021$$

Given an alpha ($\alpha$) of 0.05 and a two-tailed hypothesis, our critical value of $z$ is $\pm 1.96$. Our sampling distribution out to $\pm 3\sigma_{\hat{p}}$ is:

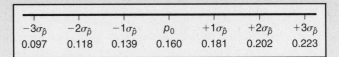

| $-3\sigma_{\hat{p}}$ | $-2\sigma_{\hat{p}}$ | $-1\sigma_{\hat{p}}$ | $p_0$ | $+1\sigma_{\hat{p}}$ | $+2\sigma_{\hat{p}}$ | $+3\sigma_{\hat{p}}$ |
|---|---|---|---|---|---|---|
| 0.097 | 0.118 | 0.139 | 0.160 | 0.181 | 0.202 | 0.223 |

**Step 3:** Calculate the test statistic using the sample data.
Using the formula for a single sample $z$-test we get:

$$z = \frac{\hat{p} - p_0}{\left(\sqrt{\dfrac{p_0(1 - p_0)}{n}}\right)} = \frac{0.11 - 0.16}{\left(\sqrt{\dfrac{0.16(1 - 0.16)}{300}}\right)} = \frac{-0.05}{0.021} = -2.38$$

**Step 4:** Make the decision regarding the hypothesis.
The $z$-statistic is $-2.38$. The two-tailed critical value for an alpha ($\alpha$) of 0.05 is $\pm 1.96$. Therefore, we reject the null hypothesis given that our test statistic passes our critical value ($-2.38 < -1.96$).

**Step 5:** Interpret the results.
Based on the sample, there appears to be a statistically significant decrease in the proportion of drivers who text while driving.

## Problems

1. Building on Problem 1 in Chapter 8, you'll recall that the weight (in ounces) of drained fruit found in 21 randomly selected cans of peaches packed by the Sunny Fruit Company were:

| | | | | | | |
|---|---|---|---|---|---|---|
| 11.0 | 11.6 | 10.9 | 12.0 | 11.5 | 12.0 | 11.2 |
| 10.5 | 12.2 | 11.8 | 12.1 | 11.6 | 11.7 | 11.6 |
| 11.2 | 12.0 | 11.4 | 10.8 | 11.8 | 10.9 | 11.4 |

The standard deviation of canned fruit weight is 1.25.

a) Calculate the sample mean and sample standard deviation.

b) Is there sufficient evidence to believe that the mean weight per can is significantly different from 11 ounces (assume $\alpha = 0.05$)?

c) What $p$-value would you report for your test statistic?

2. While talking about the cars that fellow students drive, Tom claims that 15 percent of all college students that drive cars drive convertibles. Tom's friend, Jody, finds this hard to believe and decides to check the validity of Tom's claim using the data Justine already collected. Justine, in a recent survey of the student parking lot, found 17 convertibles out of 200 selected cars.

a) Define $p$ in this setting.

b) At a level of significance of 1 percent, is there enough evidence to support Tom's claim? (assume a two-tailed test)

c) What $p$-value would you report for your test statistic?

3. The length of time it takes to complete a Rubik's cube is known to be normally distributed. The times (in seconds) for 16 individuals is given below:

| | | | |
|---|---|---|---|
| 33 | 12 | 52 | 71 |
| 38 | 12 | 56 | 77 |
| 42 | 20 | 61 | 85 |
| 47 | 27 | 66 | 97 |

a) Is there sufficient evidence to believe that average time to complete the cube is greater than 75 seconds (assume $\alpha = 0.05$)?

b) What $p$-value would you report for your statistic?

# Estimation and Hypothesis Testing II: Independent and Paired Sample $T$-Test

# 10

**Learning Objectives:**

By the end of this chapter you should be able to:

1. Describe the difference between an independent and a dependent sample.
2. Describe the difference between and uses of an independent sample $t$-test and a paired sample $t$-test.
3. List the assumptions for the independent sample $t$-test.
4. Test a hypothesis using two independent samples.
5. Construct confidence intervals for the difference in means for the independent sample $t$-test.
6. List the assumptions for the paired sample $t$-test.
7. Test a hypothesis using two dependent samples.
8. Construct confidence intervals for the difference in means for the paired sample $t$-test.

## Egon Sharpe Pearson (1885–1980)

Born in Hampstead, England, Egon Pearson, son of the famous statistician Karl Pearson, began studying mathematics at Cambridge University in 1914. He left after his first year in order to serve England during the First World War. While his health prohibited him from combat duties, he served his country through the Ministry of Supply. Egon completed his studies in 1920 and in 1921 was granted a faculty position at University College, London, in his father's department, the Department of Applied Statistics.

Even though his mathematics education prepared him to be a top scholar, one could only imagine the pressure Egon must have felt working in the same field, not to mention department, as his famous father. However, Egon rose brilliantly to the challenge. In 1925 he became friends with Jerzy Neyman. In the years leading up to Egon and Jerzy's friendship, Robert A. Fisher, who was fiercely attacking the work of Karl Pearson, began creating and publishing his theory of the null hypothesis test. Convinced that Fisher's theories lacked consideration for the alternative hypothesis, Egon and Jerzy began developing their idea of the alternative hypothesis, which Egon partially credits to conversations he had with William Sealy Gossett. In 1928, two papers on the Neyman-Pearson theory of hypothesis testing were published in the journal *Biometrika*. In their papers, Egon and Jerzy laid out the idea of deciding between the null and alternative hypotheses. Their combined work changed the very nature of how we test hypotheses today. Egon Pearson went on to be the editor of *Biometrika* and a Fellow of the Royal Society. He remained at University College, London, until his retirement in 1960.[1]

# Introduction

In chapter 9, we looked at hypothesis testing when we have a mean or a proportion for a single group and we want to compare the sample statistic from that group to a known mean or proportion. But what if you have two groups, such as LSAT scores for females versus males, or political involvement scores for unionized workers versus non-unionized workers? In these situations we need a test that allows us to compare the means of the two groups. In this chapter, we extend our understanding of hypothesis testing with means to incorporate the situation where we have two samples (or groups) instead of just one. However, before we begin we need to clarify what we mean by two samples (also referred to as groups). To do this, consider the following three scenarios.

**Scenario 1:** You want to determine whether grade 9 students involved in after-school extracurricular activities have different grade point averages than grade 9 students who are not involved in after-school extracurricular activities. In this example, you have two groups of people. You randomly select 10 students who are involved in the after-school activities and record their grade point averages. You then randomly select 10 students who are not involved in after-school activities and record their grade point averages. You now have two samples (or two groups).

**Scenario 2:** You want to know if a certain diet is effective at reducing LDL cholesterol levels (the bad kind of cholesterol). You randomly select 20 individuals and measure their LDL cholesterol level. You then have the 20 individuals participate in the diet for three months. At the end of the three months, you measure the LDL cholesterol levels of the same 20 individuals. You now have two samples (or groups).

**Scenario 3:** You want to know if parents' rating of their child's academic ability differs from the teacher's rating. You randomly select 25 parents and record their rating of their child's ability (e.g., 1 = poor, to 10 = genius). You contact the teacher of each child and record his or her rating of the child's academic ability. You now have two samples (or groups).

**Note:** You will often hear the term "two samples" referred to as "two groups," but the meaning is the same.

**LO1**

**Independent samples** are considered to be independent of one another if they consist of different individuals and the selection of the individuals in the first group does not influence the selection of the second group.

**Dependent samples** are considered to be dependent on one another if they consist of the same individuals and/or the selection of the individuals in the first group determines the selection of the second group.

You'll notice each of the three scenarios involved two samples, with a slight difference in how they were related or connected to each other. The samples in the first scenario are referred to as **independent samples**, whereas those in the second and third scenarios are referred to as **dependent samples**.

The first two scenarios are fairly straightforward to identify. In the first scenario, the sample of students in group 1 (involved in extracurricular activities) was completely different from the sample of students in group 2 (not involved in extracurricular activities) and so they are considered to be independent samples. In the second scenario, the sample of individuals who had their cholesterol level measured before participating in the diet (time 1) was the same as those measured at the end of their three month participation in the diet (time 2), which makes them dependent samples. The third scenario is a little trickier. A dependent sample doesn't necessarily have to include the same individuals in both groups. They are still considered dependent if the selection of the first group determines the selection of the second group. Since we want to know if the parents' rating of their child's academic ability differs from the teacher's rating of the child's academic ability, the samples are connected because they are rating the same child. Accordingly, selecting a specific parent determines the selection of a specific teacher (through the connection with the same child). In other words, they are dependent because they are providing a rating on the same child.

Now that we understand the difference between independent samples and dependent samples, we can move on to learning how to test a difference in means across two samples. There are two types of tests that we will cover: the independent sample *t*-test (for independent samples) and the paired sample *t*-test (for dependent samples).

# Take A Closer Look

Often students tell us that they find it hard to keep track of what statistical tests go with which situations. Starting with this chapter, we are including a Take a Closer Look feature in the introduction that briefly summarizes the analysis we have covered in previous chapters and the analysis we will cover in the current chapter.

| | Matching the Research Situation to the Type of Analysis | | |
| --- | --- | --- | --- |
| Situation | Example | Statistical Test | Refer to... |
| I need to estimate the population parameter based on my sample statistic. The variable is measured at the interval or ratio level. | You calculate the mean score of the Law School Admission Test (LSAT) for a random sample of students who did not study criminology during their undergraduate education, and you want to estimate what the mean LSAT score might be in the population of students who did not study criminology during their undergraduate education. | Confidence Intervals: Use confidence intervals when you need to make an inference about a population mean or proportion and you have a sample mean or proportion. | Chapter 8 |
| I calculated a mean based on data from one sample of respondents and want to compare it to a known mean such as the one I found in a published report. Both my variable and the one in the report are measured at the interval or ratio level. | You calculate the mean LSAT score of students in your university who just took the test. You want to test the alternative hypothesis that the mean score from your sample is higher than the mean LSAT score for all of Canada as published by the Law School Admission Council. | Single Sample Mean (or Proportion): Use a single sample test for a mean (or proportions when you have proportions) when you need to compare your sample mean to a known mean (or proportion) value. | Chapter 9 |
| I have two means from two independent samples and need to determine if they differ from one another. The variable is measured at the interval or ratio level. | Based on a random sample you have calculated the mean LSAT score for students from your university and the mean LSAT score for students from another university. You want to test the hypothesis that the mean score from your university is higher than the mean score of the other university. | Independent Sample *t*-Test: Use an independent sample *t*-test when you are comparing the means from two samples that are independent of each other. | Chapter 10 |
| I have two means from a paired sample and need to determine if they differ from one another. The variable is measured at the interval or ratio level. | Ten students took the LSAT exam last year and again this year. You want to test the hypothesis that the mean LSAT score from last year is lower than the mean LSAT score from this year. | Paired Sample *t*-Test: Use a paired sample *t*-test when you are comparing the means samples that are not independent of one another. | Chapter 10 |

**Note:** We would like to thank our former student Lynn Roodbol for suggesting we include this in the book.

# Test of Difference in Means Across Two Groups

As we saw in chapters 8 and 9, we use the *t*-distribution when we do not know the value of the population standard deviation ($\sigma$). Since we rarely know that value ($\sigma$) you generally see tests of difference in means across two groups using the *t*-distribution. Furthermore, we know that as our sample size increases, the *t*-distribution becomes less variable, and eventually taking the shape of the normal distribution. Given this, you will find that most statistical software packages also use the *t*-distribution and *t*-test for differences in means across two groups regardless of whether the groups consist of independent or dependent samples. As such, we will focus on the independent sample *t*-test for independent samples and the paired sample *t*-test for dependent samples.

# Independent Sample *t*-Test of Two Means

When we have two samples that are independent of one another (such as males and females) and we want to compare the sample mean of the first sample with that of the second, we use an independent sample *t*-test. Consider the following examples where an independent sample *t*-test for means would be used.

1. Does access to post-secondary education differ between Canadians born within Canada versus those born outside of Canada?
2. Does trust in governmental foreign policy differ between young people and seniors?
3. Does the number of songs illegally downloaded from the Internet differ between low income earners and high income earners?
4. Does the amount of money spent on environmental restoration differ between those companies that are subject to lower versus higher governmental regulation?
5. Does the number of community service hours that judges sentence young offenders differ between those from lower income families versus higher income families?

In all of these examples, we want to compare the sample mean from the first sample to the sample mean of the second sample. By making this comparison, we can test hypotheses about the differences between the two samples. Knowing this, we are now ready to cover the "how" of hypothesis testing with two sample means.

To start, we'll first discuss the key assumptions that must be met in order for the test to be valid. Then we will cover how to set up the null and alternative hypotheses. From there we will discuss the formula and finally, using an example, we will work through the hypothesis test.

## Assumptions for the Independent Sample *t*-Test

Starting with this chapter, you will find that a number of the statistical tests we employ require certain assumptions about the data to be met in order to use them. Think of assumptions for statistical tests as being similar to the assumption that you must have a driver's license in order to drive a car. If our data doesn't meet these assumptions then we need to conduct a different type of analysis (some of which we cover in chapter 13). Similarly, if you don't meet the requirements to legally drive a vehicle then you need to take a different mode of transportation.

To conduct an independent sample *t*-test we must meet the following assumptions:

1. The variables must be measured at either the interval or ratio level of measurement (otherwise we can't calculate the mean, variance, and standard deviation).
2. The two groups from which you collect the data must be independent of one another.
3. The data must be normally distributed so that we can use the *t*-distribution.
4. The variance in the population must be equal for both groups. Meaning that the variance ($\sigma^2$) for group 1 must be equal to the variance ($\sigma^2$) for group 2. By equal, we mean that they are not statistically different from one another. We often call this assumption the **assumption of homogeneity of variances**.

**Assumption of homogeneity of variances** is the assumption that the variances are equal across the groups under investigation. In the case of an independent sample *t*-test this means the variance of group 1 equals the variance of group 2.

**Violating an assumption** is the situation where our data has not met one of the assumptions of a test.

If our data does not meet an assumption we say that it is **violating the assumption**. This term simply means that we have not met the requirements of that assumption. For example, if our variances are not equal, we say that our data violates the assumption of homogeneity of variances.

If we violate the first assumption, then we need to use a different type of test. Chapter 13 covers some of the alternative tests for these situations. If our groups consist of dependent samples and not independent samples then we are in violation of the second assumption and would likely use the paired sample *t*-test, discussed later in this chapter. There are ways to correct the data when it violates the third assumption; however, that is out of the scope of this textbook and so for this chapter we will assume that this assumption has been met. Finally, if the fourth assumption is violated, meaning our variances are not equal, we can adjust our test to account for this violation. We will briefly discuss this adjustment later in the chapter.

## Setting up the Null and Alternative Hypotheses for an Independent Sample *t*-Test

Suppose you are the coach for The Greens soccer team, and you want to know if there is a difference between the mean number of shots your team takes on an opponent's net versus your rival team The Blues. The data you collect may look something like this:

| The Greens | | The Blues | | The Greens | The Blues |
|---|---|---|---|---|---|
| Game | # of Shots | Game | # of Shots | $\bar{x}_1 = 20.80$ | $\bar{x}_2 = 19.25$ |
| 1 | 20 | 1 | 21 | $s_1^2 = 77.70$ | $s_2^2 = 76.25$ |
| 2 | 17 | 2 | 17 | $s_1 = 8.81$ | $s_2 = 8.73$ |
| 3 | 23 | 3 | 30 | $n_1 = 5$ | $n_1 = 4$ |
| 4 | 10 | 4 | 9 | | |
| 5 | 34 | | | | |

So that we can tell which sample mean ($\bar{x}$), sample variance ($s^2$), sample standard deviations ($s$), and sample size ($n$) belongs to which group, we add the subscript 1 for group 1, and 2 for group 2, to the notation. So for group 1, The Greens, we have the mean $\bar{x}_1$, the variance $s_1^2$, the standard deviation $s_1$, and the sample size $n_1$. For group 2, The Blues, we have the mean $\bar{x}_2$, the variance $s_2^2$, the standard deviation $s_2$, and the sample size $n_2$.

The Greens and The Blues are independent samples, meaning that they are two samples from two different populations. We'll say that The Greens are from population $\mu_1$, whereas The Blues are from population $\mu_2$. When we test the hypothesis that there is a difference in the mean number of shots on net between The Greens and The Blues, what we are really asking is whether there is a difference in the population means $\mu_1$ and $\mu_2$. Therefore, our null and alternative hypotheses are:

$$H_0\text{: } \mu_1 = \mu_2$$
$$H_A\text{: } \mu_1 \neq \mu_2$$

The null hypothesis says that there is no difference between the two population means (they are equal), whereas the alternative hypothesis says that there is a difference (they are not equal). Often you will see these written in a slightly different format, such as:

$$H_0\text{: } \mu_1 - \mu_2 = 0$$
$$H_A\text{: } \mu_1 - \mu_2 \neq 0$$

These two approaches are saying the same thing. The alternative format simply states that the difference between the two populations for the null hypothesis is 0 and for the alternative hypothesis is not 0. Now that we understand how to set up the hypothesis for testing using an independent sample *t*-test, we can move on to the formula itself.

## Formula for the Independent Sample *t*-Test for Two Means

*The General Formula for the Independent Sample* t-*Test*

The general formula for the independent sample *t*-test is:

$$t = \frac{\bar{x}_1 - \bar{x}_2}{s_{\bar{x}_1 - \bar{x}_2}} \tag{10.1}$$

where: $\bar{x}_1$ = the sample mean for group 1

$\bar{x}_2$ = the sample mean for group 2

$s_{\bar{x}_1 - \bar{x}_2}$ = the estimated standard error of the difference in the means

You'll see a few similarities between this formula and the formula for the single sample *t*-test. Both subtract means in the numerator and both have an estimated standard error in the denominator. However, there are two key differences in this formula.

The first is that we are subtracting the sample mean of group 2 ($\bar{x}_2$) from the sample mean of group 1 ($\bar{x}_1$) in the numerator (versus subtracting $\mu_0$ from $\bar{x}$ in the single sample *t*-test).

The second difference requires a bit of backtracking. Recall that there is only one sample mean in the single sample *t*-test, so we only have one standard error of the mean ($s_{\bar{x}}$). In the independent sample *t*-test there are two sample means so we need a standard error of the difference between the mean of group 1 and the mean of group 2. We call this the estimated standard error of the difference in the means.

### The Estimated Standard Error of the Difference of the Means

We have found that the calculation of this estimated standard error generally needs a fair bit of discussion in order to fully grasp the idea, so we will devote this section to detailing this calculation. Remember that since we do not know the value of the population standard deviation ($\sigma$) or variance ($\sigma^2$) for either group, we need to estimate it using our sample statistics. In an independent sample *t*-test we work with variances rather than standard deviations for reasons that we'll discuss shortly. Therefore, we estimate the population variance ($\sigma^2$) for group 1 ($\sigma_1^2$) and group 2 ($\sigma_1^2$) using our sample variance for group 1 ($s_1^2$) and group 2 ($s_2^2$). There are two ways we can calculate the estimated standard error. The first way, and probably the most common method shown in introductory textbooks, is to use pooled sample variances. The second is to use separate variance estimates. We will focus on the first method for this chapter, but include the second method in the Take A Closer Look feature at the end of this section.

## Take a Closer Look

Technically, the formula for the independent sample *t*-test is:

$$t = \frac{(\bar{x}_1 - \bar{x}_2) - (\mu_1 - \mu_2)}{s_{\bar{x}_1 - \bar{x}_2}}$$

Since we are testing the null hypothesis where $\mu_1 = \mu_2$, and in the null hypothesis $\mu_1 - \mu_2 = 0$, we set the term ($\mu_1 - \mu_2$) to zero. Since $(\bar{x}_1 - \bar{x}_2) - 0$ is the same as writing $(\bar{x}_1 - \bar{x}_2)$ we often leave the term ($\mu_1 - \mu_2$), which equals 0, out of the equation.

The **pooled estimated standard error of the difference in the means** is the estimated standard error used when the assumption of homogeneity of variances has been met.

### The Estimated Standard Error Using Pooled Sample Variances

Introductory textbooks generally provide the calculation of the estimated standard error for the condition where the assumption of homogeneity of variance has been met ($\sigma_1^2 = \sigma_2^2$). We call this the **pooled estimated standard error of the difference of the means**; however, you will find that most people, textbooks, and resources just call it the estimated standard error of the difference of the means. We'll start by showing you the full formula for the pooled estimated standard error of the difference of the means and then disect the formula to show you what is happening. The formula is:

$$s_{\bar{x}_1 - \bar{x}_2} = \sqrt{\frac{(n_1 - 1)s_1^2 + (n_2 - 1)s_2^2}{(n_1 + n_2 - 2)} \times \left(\frac{1}{n_1} + \frac{1}{n_2}\right)} \quad \textbf{(10.2)}$$

Why do we call it the pooled estimated standard error of the difference of the means? To make a long story short, we call it the pooled estimated standard error because we are using just one pooled sample variance to estimate the population variance, and we are saying that both groups have this population variance. When the variances are equal (the assumption of homogeneity of variances), it is easier for us to calculate and work with just one **pooled sample variance**. The pooled variance is an unbiased estimator of the population variance that both groups have in common. While this may sound complicated, just remember that when we talk about a pooled estimate of the population variance what we are saying is that while the sample means may differ, the true variance of both populations will be equal.

The **pooled sample variance** is an unbiased estimator of the variance that both groups have in common.

### The Pooled Sample Variance

Now, let's break down the formula for the pooled estimated standard error of the difference of the means (10.2) by starting with the pooled sample variance. It usually helps if you keep in the back of your mind the fact that the variance ($s^2$) is the standard deviation ($s$) squared, and to convert from variance to standard deviation you take the square root of the variance ($s = \sqrt{s^2}$). The pooled sample variance ($s_p^2$) is calculated as:

$$s_p^2 = \frac{(n_1 - 1)s_1^2 + (n_2 - 1)s_2^2}{(n_1 + n_2 - 2)} \quad \textbf{(10.3)}$$

where: $s_p^2$ = the pooled sample variance (the subscript $p$ indicates that it is pooled)

$s_1^2$ = the sample variance for group 1

$s_2^2$ = the sample variance for group 2

$n_1$ = the sample size for group 1

$n_2$ = the sample size for group 2

What happens when we pool the variances together using this formula is that we are allowing for the situation where we may have different sample sizes in group 1 versus group 2. If the sample sizes are equal, then the pooled sample variance is just the average variance. Consider the following data to show why this is true.

|  | Group 1 | Group 2 |
|---|---|---|
| Sample Variances | $s_1^2 = 21.43$ | $s_2^2 = 19.38$ |
| Samples Sizes | $n_1 = 10$ | $n_2 = 10$ |

Since the sample sizes are equal, then the pooled sample variance is the average of 21.43 and 19.38 as shown below:

$$s_p^2 = \frac{21.43 + 19.38}{2} = 20.405 \qquad (10.4)$$

To confirm this we could use the pooled sample variance formula to get:

$$s_p^2 = \frac{(n_1 - 1)s_1^2 + (n_2 - 1)s_2^2}{(n_1 + n_2 - 2)} \qquad (10.5)$$

$$s_p^2 = \frac{(10 - 1)21.43 + (10 - 1)19.38}{(10 + 10 - 2)}$$

$$= \frac{192.87 + 174.42}{18} = \frac{367.29}{18} = 20.405$$

As expected, we get the same value.

Now, if we have different sample sizes, we need to take a weighted average of the variances such that the pooled sample variance takes into account the fact that one sample has more weight to it [because it has a larger sample size ($n$)] than the other [because it has a smaller sample size ($n$)]. Consider the data in our example above, but this time, make the sample size in group 2 smaller than group 1. Our data is then:

|  | Group 1 | Group 2 |
|---|---|---|
| Sample Variances | $s_1^2 = 21.43$ | $s_2^2 = 19.38$ |
| Samples Sizes | $n_1 = 10$ | $n_2 = 8$ |

$$s_p^2 = \frac{(n_1 - 1)s_1^2 + (n_2 - 1)s_2^2}{(n_1 + n_2 - 2)} \qquad (10.6)$$

$$s_p^2 = \frac{(10 - 1)21.43 + (8 - 1)19.38}{(10 + 8 - 2)}$$

$$= \frac{192.87 + 135.66}{16} = \frac{328.53}{16} = 20.533$$

Recall that with equal sample sizes the pooled sample variance ($s_p^2$) was 20.405. Now with unequal sample sizes the pooled sample variance is 20.533; we have a weighted average of the two sample variances. Therefore, the pooled sample variance allows us to take unequal samples sizes into account.

### Moving from Pooled Sample Variance to Pooled Estimated Standard Error of the Difference of Means

Remember, we are working on how we get the pooled estimated standard error of the difference of means ($s_{\bar{x}_1 - \bar{x}_2}$) in equation 10.2, and so far have the pooled sample variance portion ($s_p^2$) in equation 10.3. To calculate the estimated standard error (of the difference of the means), we need information about the variability of the sample data and information about the size of the sample. The numerator is the standard deviation (which is our variability information) and the denominator is the square root of the sample size (which is our sample size information). Thinking back to chapter 8, we found that the standard error of the mean ($s_{\bar{x}}$) is calculated as:

$$s_{\bar{x}} = \frac{s}{\sqrt{n}} = \sqrt{\frac{s^2 \leftarrow \text{Variability information}}{n \leftarrow \text{Sample size information}}} \qquad \textbf{(10.7)}$$

As you can see, we can calculate the estimated standard error of the mean ($s_{\bar{x}}$) using the variance ($s^2$) so long as we remember to take the square root of the variance. This is important to note because the same is true when we want to convert our pooled sample variance ($s_p^2$) to a pooled sample standard deviation ($s_p$). Therefore, to calculate the pooled standard deviation ($s_p$), we take the square root of the pooled sample variance ($s_p^2$) to get:

$$s_p = \sqrt{s_p^2} \qquad \textbf{(10.8)}$$

Remember, a standard error has two pieces of information: information about the variability, and information about the size of the sample. However, since we have two sample means ($\bar{x}_1$ and $\bar{x}_2$), we have a numerator and a denominator for the first mean ($\bar{x}_1$) and for the second mean ($\bar{x}_2$). Therefore, our pooled estimated standard error of the difference of the means ($s_{\bar{x}_1 - \bar{x}_2}$) becomes:

$$s_{\bar{x}_1 - \bar{x}_2} = \sqrt{\frac{s_p^2}{n_1} + \frac{s_p^2}{n_2}} \qquad \textbf{(10.9)}$$

This is the same as:

$$s_{\bar{x}_1 - \bar{x}_2} = \sqrt{s_p^2 \times \left(\frac{1}{n_1} + \frac{1}{n_2}\right)} \qquad \textbf{(10.10)}$$

If we expand $s_p^2$ (meaning replace $s_p^2$ with its actual formula) we return to the estimated standard error of the difference of the means from equation 10.2.

$$s_{\bar{x}_1 - \bar{x}_2} = \sqrt{\frac{(n_1 - 1)s_1^2 + (n_2 - 1)s_2^2}{(n_1 + n_2 - 2)} \times \left(\frac{1}{n_1} + \frac{1}{n_2}\right)} \qquad \textbf{(10.11)}$$

So what was the point of going through all of that? There are two reasons. The first is that different textbooks will show you the formula in different ways. Algebraically manipulating the formula here provides you with other ways you may see it in others resources. The second is to show you that although the formula looks a little daunting, it is really made up of the same components that you have already grasped. It just contains a variance part and a sample size part. In other words, think of it as:

$$s_{\bar{x}_1 - \bar{x}_2} = \sqrt{Variance\ Part \times Sample\ Size\ Part} \qquad \textbf{(10.12)}$$

*The Expanded Formula for the Independent Sample* t-*Test*

Now we can conclude our discussion of the formula for the independent sample *t*-test. Since we know that the general formula for the independent sample *t*-test is…

$$t = \frac{\bar{x}_1 - \bar{x}_2}{s_{\bar{x}_1 - \bar{x}_2}}$$   **(10.13)**

… and we know how to calculate the estimated standard error of the difference of the means, our expanded formula for the independent sample *t*-test becomes:

$$t = \frac{\bar{x}_1 - \bar{x}_2}{\sqrt{\frac{(n_1 - 1)s_1^2 + (n_2 - 1)s_2^2}{(n_1 + n_2 - 2)} \times \left(\frac{1}{n_1} + \frac{1}{n_2}\right)}}$$   **(10.14)**

Now that we have covered the assumptions, the set-up of the null and alternative hypotheses, and the formula for the independent sample *t*-test, we are ready to conduct the hypothesis test of difference in two sample means.

**LO4**

## Independent Sample *t*-Test Example

We'll use the following scenario and our five steps for hypothesis testing to conduct a hypothesis test using an independent sample *t*-test. As we did in the previous chapters, we will focus on the two-tailed hypothesis test.

## Scenario:

In 2007, Stinson, Patry, and Smith published the paper "The CSI Effect: Reflections from Police and Forensic Investigators" in the *Canadian Journal of Police and Security Services*. The researchers were interested in understanding how television crime shows affect the way forensic investigators and police officers do their jobs and interact with the community. The researchers collected data from 127 forensic professionals and 36 police officers in Canada.

One of the questions the researchers asked was, "To what extent have changes in science and technology changed the way you do your job?" The question was measured with a 7-point scale ranging from 1 (low) to 7 (high). The follow summary data includes the means and variances reported in the paper. However, the sample sizes have been changed for the purpose of this example.[2]

|  | Forensic Professionals | Police Officers |
|---|---|---|
| Sample Means | $\bar{x}_1 = 5.67$ | $\bar{x}_2 = 4.36$ |
| Sample Variances | $s_1^2 = 1.37$ | $s_2^2 = 3.72$ |
| Samples Sizes | $n_1 = 30$ | $n_2 = 27$ |

\* Note: This is fictitious data created based on the paper.

Let's test the alternative hypothesis that there is a significant difference between forensic professionals and police officers in how they feel technology has changed how they do their job. For this test we will use the alpha value ($\alpha$) of 0.05.

**Step 1:** Define the null and alternative hypotheses.

$$H_0: \mu_1 = \mu_2$$
$$H_A: \mu_1 \neq \mu_2$$

**Step 2:** Define the sampling distribution and critical values.

In chapter 9, we learned that the mean of the sampling distribution ($\mu_{\bar{x}}$) is set to the value of the null hypothesis. In two sample tests, the null hypothesis is that there is no difference between $\mu_1$ and $\mu_2$, so the sampling distribution mean ($\mu_{\bar{x}}$) is 0 because $\mu_1 - \mu_1 = 0$. This represents a key part of understanding hypothesis testing with two samples. The sampling distribution represents the distribution where the null hypothesis is true. Therefore, it is the distribution of no difference.

The standard error for this distribution is the pooled estimated standard error (of the difference of the means) that we discussed previously. Using pooled variances, our estimated standard error is:

$$s_{\bar{x}_1 - \bar{x}_2} = \sqrt{\frac{(n_1 - 1)s_1^2 + (n_2 - 1)s_2^2}{(n_1 + n_2 - 2)} \times \left(\frac{1}{n_1} + \frac{1}{n_2}\right)} \qquad (10.15)$$

$$s_{\bar{x}_1 - \bar{x}_2} = \sqrt{\frac{(30 - 1)1.37 + (27 - 1)3.72}{(30 + 27 - 2)} \times \left(\frac{1}{30} + \frac{1}{27}\right)}$$

$$s_{\bar{x}_1 - \bar{x}_2} = \sqrt{\frac{39.73 + 96.72}{55}} \times 0.07 = \sqrt{0.174} = 0.418 \approx 0.42$$

While it is not necessary to draw the sampling distribution, it is helpful in understanding what is happening within the hypothesis test and where the numbers are coming from. For this example, we provide the sampling distribution in Figure 10.1.

**FIGURE 10.1**
**Sampling Distribution for $H_0: \mu_1 = \mu_2$**

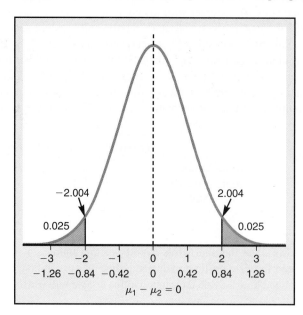

Since we are using the *t*-distribution, we need to know the number of degrees of freedom (*df*) in order to draw the distribution and determine the critical values. For an independent sample *t*-test, the *df* are calculated as:

$$df = n_1 + n_2 - 2 \qquad \textbf{(10.16)}$$

This is the same as our *df* in the single sample mean tests in chapter 9, where *df* was $n - 1$. However, since we have two variables in an independent sample *t*-test versus one variable in a single sample test, we have $df = n - 1 + n - 1$. Therefore, our *df* for this example are:

$$df = n_1 + n_2 - 2 = 30 + 27 - 2 = 55 \qquad \textbf{(10.17)}$$

Looking up our critical value of *t* in the *t*-distribution table, we find that with 55 *df* and a two-tailed alpha value ($\alpha$) of 0.05, our critical value of $t_{(\alpha = 0.05)}$ is $\pm 2.004$.

**Step 3:** Calculate the test statistic using the sample data.
Using the formula for the independent sample *t*-test we get:

$$t = \frac{\bar{x}_1 - \bar{x}_2}{s_{\bar{x}_1 - \bar{x}_2}} = \frac{5.67 - 4.36}{0.42} = \frac{1.31}{0.42} = 3.12 \qquad \textbf{(10.18)}$$

We can see in Figure 10.2 that the *t*-statistic of 3.12 is well within the shaded area of the right tale of the distribution.

**FIGURE 10.2**
**Sampling Distribution and the *t*-test Statistic**

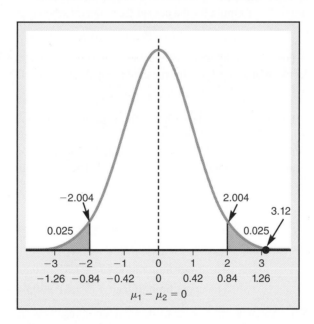

**Step 4:** Make the decision regarding the hypothesis.
Our *t*-statistic is 3.12 and the two-tailed critical value for an alpha value ($\alpha$) of 0.05 is $\pm 2.004$. Given that our *t*-statistic is past the critical value (3.12 > 2.004) we reject the null hypothesis.

## Take a Closer Look

Had we used a one-tailed hypothesis test for our forensic professionals and police officers scenario we would have had to *a-priori* determined that forensic professionals would score higher than police officers; then our critical value ($\alpha = 0.05$) would have been 1.673. Therefore, the difference would have still been significant. Keep in mind that we would have had to know *a-priori* which direction (positive indicating right tail or negative indicating left tail) the difference would be.

**Step 5:** Interpret the results.

Based on our sample, there appears to be a statistically significant difference in how forensic professional and police officers view the impact that science and technology has had their job functions. The perceived impact is higher in forensic professionals ($\bar{x} = 5.67$) than in police officers ($\bar{x} = 4.36$).

## Confidence Interval of the Difference in Two Population Means

Recall in chapter 8 that we found that we can estimate population parameters by using confidence intervals with the sample mean or sample proportion. We can also use confidence intervals to estimate the difference in the means in the population. The formula for the confidence interval when using the *t*-distribution is:

$$CI = Point\ Estimate \pm t_{(\alpha)}(s_{\bar{x}}) \qquad \textbf{(10.19)}$$

For a test of difference in two means, the point estimate is the difference between the mean of group 1 and the mean of group 2. Therefore, the formula becomes:

$$CI = (\bar{x}_1 - \bar{x}_2) \pm t_{(\alpha)}(s_{\bar{x}}) \qquad \textbf{(10.20)}$$

Using our example with the forensic professionals and police officers, the point estimate is 1.31 ($5.67 - 4.36$). With an alpha value ($\alpha$) of 0.05 the critical value of *t* was $\pm 2.004$ and our estimated standard error of the difference of the means (using pooled variances) was 0.42. Therefore, our confidence interval for the difference in the means is:

$$CI = 1.31 \pm 2.004(0.42) \qquad \textbf{(10.21)}$$
$$CI = 1.31 \pm 0.84$$

Therefore,

$$\text{The lower limit of the } CI = 1.31 - 0.84 = 0.47$$
$$\text{The upper limit of the } CI = 1.31 + 0.84 = 2.15$$

**Note:** You will often see confidence interval results written as [0.47, 2.15]

Therefore, we can say that we are 95 percent confident that the difference in the means for the population is between 0.47 and 2.15. This may be written more formally as:

$$0.47 \leq (\mu_1 - \mu_2) \leq 2.15$$

The main reason for estimating the confidence intervals of the difference in means is that you want to be able to see what the population parameter might be. Remember that our sample from each of the two populations represents one of many possible samples. Therefore, it is possible that in one sample we will find a difference, but in another sample we may not. This leads us to an important use of confidence intervals of the difference in means. Suppose we found a confidence interval to be:

$$-1.47 \leq (\mu_1 - \mu_2) \leq 1.15$$

You can see right away that the confidence interval includes negative to positive numbers, which means that we could have a zero value. A zero value means there is no difference. So if we are 95 percent confident that the difference in the means for the population is between $-1.47$ and $1.15$, then we are saying that 95 percent of the time it is feasible that there is no difference in the mean. That is an important thing for us to report.

We should always include the confidence intervals for the difference in the mean in our decision and interpretation steps. Let's revisit steps 4 and 5 from our previous results for the forensic professionals and the police officers and incorporate the confidence intervals.

**Step 4:** Make the decision regarding the hypothesis.
Our $t$-statistic is 3.12 and the two-tailed critical value for an alpha value ($\alpha$) of 0.05 is $\pm 2.004$. Given that our $t$-statistic is past the critical value ($3.12 > 2.004$) we reject the null hypothesis. The difference between the mean score for forensic professionals and police officers was 1.31 ($5.67 - 4.36$). Furthermore, our 95 percent confidence intervals are $1.31 \pm 2.004(0.42)$ which is $[0.47, 2.15]$.

**Step 5:** Interpret the results.
Based on the sample, there appears to be a significant difference in how forensic professionals and police officers view the impact that science and technology has had on their job functions. The perceived impact is higher in forensic professionals ($\bar{x} = 5.67$) than in police officers ($\bar{x} = 4.36$). The 95 percent confidence interval for the difference is $[0.47, 2.15]$, which means we are 95 percent confident that the difference in the means for the population is between 0.47 and 2.15. Given that the interval does not contain a zero value, 95 out of 100 times we can expect to find a difference in the means.

---

**EXERCISE 10.1**

Suppose you are interested in determining if male teens with high self-esteem perform better academically in grade 11 than male teens with low self-esteem. Prior to collecting any data you hypothesize the following:

$H_A$: Males with high self-esteem will perform better academically than males with low self-esteem.

You collect data from 450 teenage males in high schools across your province. Using the Rosenberg Self-Esteem Scale, you separate the males into the two categories, high self-esteem ($n = 220$) versus low self-esteem ($n = 230$).

Using their grade 11 grade point average you construct the following table of summary data:

| Grade Point Average | High Self-Esteem (n = 220) | Low Self-Esteem (n = 230) |
|---|---|---|
| Mean | $\bar{x}_2 = 3.05$ | $\bar{x}_1 = 2.85$ |
| Standard deviation | $s_2 = .68$ | $s_1 = .75$ |

Conduct an independent sample *t*-test to test your hypothesis. Use a two-tailed hypothesis test with an alpha value ($\alpha$) of 0.01.

## Take a Closer Look

### What if the variances are not equal?

In the independent sample *t*-test for difference of the means, we said that there are two ways to calculate the estimated standard error of the difference of the means. The first uses pooled sample variances, the second uses separate variance estimates. Most introductory textbooks provide the first method only. Unfortunately, it is difficult to cover each of the introductory topics in specific detail, so we usually just assume the variances across the two groups are equal and use the pooled variance method. So how do you know if the variances are equal and what do you do if they aren't?

The answer to the first part of that question is beyond the scope of an introductory textbook, but it is worth noting that researchers usually use one of three different tests to determine whether the variances are equal across the groups. These are the Levene's test, the Bartlett's test, and the Brown-Forsythe test. The most common test is the Levene's test, formally known as the Levene's Test for Equality of Variances. The Levene's test tests the null hypothesis that the variances are equal ( $H_0$: $s_1^2 = s_2^2$). If you fail to reject the null hypothesis then you can assume that the variances are equal and you can use the pooled variances for the estimate of the standard error. If you reject the null hypothesis, this means the variances are not equal and you must use the second method, which involves calculating separate variance estimates. Tests of equality of variance are not something you really want to be doing manually. Fortunately, most statistical software packages, such as SPSS, SAS, STATA, etc., provide you with at least one of the tests in their output.

More discussion about the independent sample *t*-test using separate variance estimates can be found in the supplemental material on Connect. **connect**

## Did You Know?

In the United States, there were 450 deaths attributed to falling from a bed in 2004. In Canada, there were 62 deaths attributed to falling from a bed in 2004. Does that mean that our southern neighbours are more likely to die from falling out of a bed than us?

Actually, that is not the case. In 2004, Canadians were 1.46 times more likely to have died as a result of falling from a bed than Americans when considering total number of deaths. Consider the following data:

| | 2004 Cause of Death | | 2004 Total |
| --- | --- | --- | --- |
| | Fall from Bed[3] | Other | Deaths[4&5] |
| Canada | 62 | 226,522 | 226,584 |
| United States | 450 | 2,397,165 | 2,397,615 |
| Total | 512 | 2,623,687 | 2,624,199 |

To determine if Canadians are more or less likely than Americans to die as a result of falling from a bed, we calculate the relative risk ratio. A relative risk ratio represents the ratio of the risk of an event occurring across two groups. We can calculate the relative risk ratio as follows:

**Step 1:** The relative risk for Canada = the number of deaths due to falling from a bed (62) divided by the total number of deaths (226,584) = 0.0002736.

**Step 2:** The relative risk for the United States = the number of deaths due to falling from a bed (450) divided by the total number of deaths in the United States (2,397,615) = 0.0001877.

**Step 3:** We divide the relative risk for Canada (0.0002736) by the relative risk for the United States (0.000187) to get the relative risk ratio = 1.458.

The relative risk ratio is often used in the branch of statistics called epidemiology, which is the application of statistics to health related matters.

Consider the following example comparing pregnancy data from Statistics Canada for teenagers ($\leq$ 19 years of age) versus all others ($\geq$ 20 years of age).

| | 2005 Pregnancy Outcomes | | 2005 Total |
| --- | --- | --- | --- |
| Age | Live Births | Non-Live Births* | Pregnancies[6] |
| 19 and under | 14,013 | 16,935 | 30,948 |
| 20 and over | 328,163 | 88,374 | 416,537 |
| Total | 342,176 | 105,309 | 447,485 |

* Non-Live Births includes fetal loss and induced abortions from the Statistics Canada data definitions.

Using the relative risk ratio we can tell that those who are 20 years of age and older are 1.74 times more likely to have a live birth pregnancy outcome than those 19 years of age and under.

Several other interesting examples of relative risk ratio:

In 2004 . . .

- Canadians were 1.93 times more likely to die by falling from a cliff than those in the United States.

- Americans were 1.58 times more likely to die by a lightning strike than those in Canada.

- Canadians were 1.26 times more likely to die from an object that was either thrown at them or that fell on them than those in the United States.

- Americans were 14.42 times more likely to die from a handgun being discharged than those in Canada.

**Sources:** For points 1–4, all data requiring total number of deaths for Americans in 2004 came from the Center for Disease Control's *National Vital Statistics Report,* Minino AM, Heron MP, Murphy SL, Kochankek, KD. "Deaths: Final data for 2004." *National Vital Statistics Reports;* vol. 55 no. 19. Hyattsville, MD: National Center for Health Statistics. All data requiring total number of deaths for Canadians in 2004, is in part based on the Statistics Canada publication *The Daily,* Catalogue 11-001-XWE, December 20, 2006, http://www.statcan.gc.ca/daily-quotidien/061220b-eng.htm.

# Paired Sample *t*-Test of Two Means

**LO2** **LO7**

Now that we have covered how to test hypotheses for the difference in means when samples are independent of one another (independent sample *t*-test), we can examine the situation where samples are dependent on each other. As a refresher, two samples are considered to be dependent on one another if they are the same sample in each group or the selection of the sample for the first group influences the selection of the sample for the second group. When we have two samples that are dependent on each other and we want to compare the means of the two samples, we use a paired sample *t*-test. Consider the following research situations where a paired sample *t*-test for means would be used.

1. Did the mean number of drug overdose fatalities decrease after a safe injection site was opened in the community?
2. Does the level of social integration of new immigrants to Canada change between the first and second year after their arrival?
3. Did sense of belonging to a political party change after a new party leader was elected?
4. Does a parent's opinion of how his or her child is performing in school differ from the child's teacher's opinion?
5. Did the frequency of texting while driving decrease after the distracted driver legislation came into effect?

In all of the examples we have two samples. In some cases, the individuals in the first sample are the same individuals in the second sample. In these situations we are repeating the measurement of a variable across two different time periods. In other cases, the individuals in the first sample are not the same individuals in the second sample; however, they are considered dependent because they are rating the same person, place, or thing that they have in common.

To conduct the paired sample test we'll follow the same format as we did with the independent sample *t*-test. First we will discuss the test assumptions. Then we will cover the null and alternative hypotheses. Following that we will discuss the formula, and finally we will go through the hypothesis testing process with the use of an example.

**LO6**

## Assumptions for the Paired Sample *t*-Test

To conduct a paired sample *t*-test we must meet the following assumptions.

1. The variables must be measured at either the interval or ratio level of measurement (otherwise we can't calculate the mean, variance, and standard deviation).
2. The two groups (and more specifically the data) must be dependent on one another.
3. The differences between the two samples must be relatively normally distributed.

LO7

## Setting Up the Null and Alternative Hypotheses for a Paired Sample *t*-Test

Suppose you are conducting research for a political party regarding voter awareness of the party's platform. You randomly select 10 individuals to form the sample for your research. During week one of the election campaign you measure each individual's awareness of the party's platform using a scale ranging from 1 (unaware) to 10 (very aware). During the second week of the campaign the party runs a series of radio, television, and print advertisements promoting the party's platform. During week three of the election campaign you measure the same 10 individuals' awareness of the party's platform using the same scale as before. You now want to know if there is a difference between the participants' mean awareness rating before the advertisements were run and the mean awareness rating after the advertisements were run. The data are as follows:

| Participant | Awareness at Week One | Awareness at Week Three | Difference in Awareness |
|:---:|:---:|:---:|:---:|
| 1 | 3 | 5 | 2 |
| 2 | 4 | 4 | 0 |
| 3 | 2 | 6 | 4 |
| 4 | 6 | 6 | 0 |
| 5 | 3 | 5 | 2 |
| 6 | 4 | 5 | 1 |
| 7 | 7 | 6 | −1 |
| 8 | 1 | 3 | 2 |
| 9 | 3 | 5 | 2 |
| 10 | 4 | 4 | 0 |
| | $\bar{x}_1 = 3.70$ | $\bar{x}_2 = 4.90$ | $\Sigma d = 12$ |

In this situation, $\bar{x}_1$ represents the mean awareness score for time 1 (awareness at week 1) and $\bar{x}_2$ represents the mean awareness score for time 2 (awareness at week 3). By subtracting each individual score in time 1 from each individual score of time 2 we get the **difference between the paired scores** (*d*) for each individual (or pairs of individuals).

The **difference between the paired scores** is the difference between the first and second score for each individual or pairs of individuals.

Although we have dependent samples, we still consider the samples to come from two separate populations because they represent separate measurements and may have different population means. Therefore, the population mean for awareness at week 1 is $\mu_1$ and the population mean for awareness at week 3 is $\mu_2$. However, we're interested the difference between the two populations ($\mu_{\bar{D}}$), which is:

$$\mu_{\bar{D}} = \mu_2 - \mu_1 \qquad \textbf{(10.22)}$$

The symbol $\mu_{\bar{D}}$ represents the population mean difference between time 1 and time 2. Since a null hypothesis usually represents no difference or no change, we write our null hypothesis and consequently our alternative hypothesis as:

$$H_0: \mu_{\overline{D}} = 0$$

$$H_A: \mu_{\overline{D}} \neq 0$$

The null hypothesis states that there is no difference between the first and second measurement, whereas the alternative hypothesis states that there is a difference. Now that we have covered the null and alternative hypotheses, we can turn to the formula for the paired sample *t*-test.

## Formula for the Paired Sample *t*-Test

The paired sample *t*-test formula is:

$$t = \frac{\overline{D}}{s_{\overline{D}}} \tag{10.23}$$

where: $\overline{D}$ = the mean of the difference between the paired scores (the two samples)

$s_{\overline{D}}$ = the estimated standard error of the difference between the paired scores

You may notice some similarities between the formula for the paired sample *t*-test and other *t*-tests we have covered thus far. The numerator consists of a value calculated from our sample means and the denominator consists of the estimated standard error.

Before we can move on to the estimated standard error of the difference between the paired scores, we need to quickly cover how we calculate the mean of the difference between the paired scores $(\overline{D})$. The formula for calculating $\overline{D}$ is similar to the formula for calculating $\overline{x}$:

$$\overline{D} = \frac{\Sigma d}{n} \tag{10.24}$$

where: $d$ = is the individual differences between the paired scores

$n$ = is the sample size

While it seems obvious to mention that $n$ is the sample size in this formula, it is worth discussing, as some people question whether they should include both the sample size of the first sample plus the second (using the political campaign awareness example, it would be 20). The sample size in a paired sample *t*-test refers to the total number of matched or paired participants, subjects, or objects in the study. In the political campaign awareness example, we would have a sample size of 10 because we had 10 participants.

Using the political campaign awareness example, we find:

$$\overline{D} = \frac{\Sigma d}{n} = \frac{12}{10} = 1.20 \tag{10.25}$$

Therefore, the mean of the difference between the paired scores $(\overline{D})$ is 1.20.

## Take a Closer Look

Technically, the formula for the paired sample $t$-test includes the population difference value ($\mu_{\bar{D}}$):

$$t = \frac{\bar{D} - \mu_{\bar{D}}}{s_{\bar{D}}}$$

However, since we are testing the null hypothesis where $\mu_{\bar{D}} = 0$, we set the term ($\mu_{\bar{D}}$) to zero. As such, we often leave the term ($\mu_{\bar{D}}$) out of the equation.

*The Estimated Standard Error of the Difference Between the Paired Scores*

The formula for the estimated standard error of the difference between the paired scores is:

$$s_{\bar{D}} = \frac{s_d}{\sqrt{n}} \qquad (10.26)$$

where: $s_d$ = the sample standard deviation of the difference between the paired scores

$n$ = the sample size

We haven't yet calculated a sample standard deviation for difference between the paired scores ($s_d$), so this symbol is likely new to you. The formula for calculating $s_d$ is similar to calculating the regular sample standard deviation. However, instead of using individual scores ($x$) and the mean score ($\bar{x}$), we use the difference of individual scores ($d$) and the mean of the difference between the paired scores ($\bar{D}$). Therefore, the formula for calculating the standard deviation of the difference between the paired scores ($s_d$) is:

$$s_d = \sqrt{\frac{\Sigma(d - \bar{D})^2}{n - 1}} \qquad (10.27)$$

Using the political campaign awareness example, we can calculate the $s_d$ as:

| Participant | Awareness at Week One ($A$) | Awareness at Week Three ($B$) | Difference ($d$) in Awareness ($B - A$) | ($d - \bar{D}$) | ($d - \bar{D}$)$^2$ |
|---|---|---|---|---|---|
| 1 | 3 | 5 | 2 | 0.80 | 0.64 |
| 2 | 4 | 4 | 0 | −1.20 | 1.44 |
| 3 | 2 | 6 | 4 | 2.80 | 7.84 |
| 4 | 6 | 6 | 0 | −1.20 | 1.44 |
| 5 | 3 | 5 | 2 | 0.80 | 0.64 |
| 6 | 4 | 5 | 1 | −0.20 | 0.04 |
| 7 | 7 | 6 | −1 | −2.20 | 4.84 |
| 8 | 1 | 3 | 2 | 0.80 | 0.64 |
| 9 | 3 | 5 | 2 | 0.80 | 0.64 |
| 10 | 4 | 4 | 0 | −1.20 | 1.44 |
| $n = 10$ | | $\Sigma d = 12$ | $\Sigma(d - \bar{D}) = 0$ | | $\Sigma(d - \bar{D})^2$ = 19.60 |

$$\bar{D} = \frac{\Sigma d}{n} = \frac{12}{10} = 1.20$$

Therefore, the standard deviation of the difference between the paired scores ($s_d$) is:

$$s_d = \sqrt{\frac{\Sigma(d - \overline{D})^2}{n - 1}} = \sqrt{\frac{19.60}{10 - 1}} = \sqrt{2.18} = 1.476 = 1.48 \quad \textbf{(10.28)}$$

It is worth pointing out here that you also have the variance of the difference between the paired scores ($s_d^2$), which is 2.18.

### *The Expanded Formula for the Paired Sample* t-*Test*

Now that we understand the estimated standard error of the difference between the paired scores, our formula for the paired sample *t*-test can be expanded to:

$$t = \frac{\overline{D}}{\left(\dfrac{s_d}{\sqrt{n}}\right)} \quad \textbf{(10.29)}$$

**LO7**

## Example of a Paired Sample *t*-Test

We'll use the following scenario and our five steps for hypothesis testing to work through hypothesis testing using a paired sample *t*-test. Again we will focus on the two-tailed hypothesis test.

## Scenario:

In 2011, Matthew Ruby and his colleagues at the University of British Columbia published the paper "The Invisible Benefits of Exercise" in the journal *Health Psychology*. The researchers were interested in knowing whether individuals underestimated the enjoyment that they would receive from exercising. Prior to exercising, 32 participants were asked to rate on a scale of 1 (not at all) to 10 (very much) the extent to which they believed they would enjoy their workout.[7]

The summary data is as follows:

|  | Sample Means | Sample Size | Mean of the Difference between the Paired Scores | Standard Deviation of the Difference between the Paired Scores |
|---|---|---|---|---|
| Pre-Exercise Rating of Enjoyment | $\overline{x}_1 = 6.94$ |  |  |  |
|  |  | $n = 32$ | $\overline{D} = .75$ | $s_d = 1.40$ |
| Post-Exercise Rating of Enjoyment | $\overline{x}_2 = 7.69$ |  |  |  |

*Note: This is not the actual data from this study or paper. This summary data is simulated based on the summary data provided in the paper.

Let's test the alternative hypothesis that the post-exercise enjoyment rating will be different than the pre-exercise enjoyment rating. For this test we will use an alpha value ($\alpha$) of 0.01.

**Step 1:** Define the null and alternative hypotheses.

$$H_0: \mu_{\bar{D}} = 0$$
$$H_A: \mu_{\bar{D}} \neq 0$$

**Step 2:** Define the sampling distribution and critical values.
Using the formula for the estimated standard error of the difference between the paired scores we get:

$$s_{\bar{D}} = \frac{s_d}{\sqrt{n}} = \frac{1.40}{\sqrt{32}} = \frac{1.40}{5.66} = 0.247 \qquad \textbf{(10.30)}$$

Again, seeing a graphical representation of the sampling distribution (as in Figure 10.3) is helpful in understanding what is happening within the hypothesis test. Since we are using the *t*-distribution, we need to know the number of degrees of freedom (*df*) in order to draw the distribution and determine the critical values. For a paired sample *t*-test, the *df* are calculated as:

$$df = n - 1 = 32 - 1 = 31 \qquad \textbf{(10.31)}$$

Looking up our critical value of *t* in the *t*-distribution table, we find that with 31 *df* and a two-tailed alpha value ($\alpha$) of 0.01, our critical value of $t_{(\alpha = 0.01)}$ is $\pm 2.744$.

**FIGURE 10.3**
**Sampling Distribution for the $\mu_{\bar{D}} = 0$**

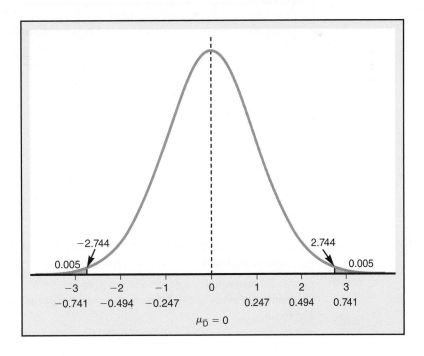

**Step 3:** Calculate the test statistic using the sample data.
Using the paired sample *t*-test formula we get:

$$t = \frac{\overline{D}}{s_{\overline{D}}} = \frac{0.75}{0.247} = 3.04 \qquad\qquad (10.32)$$

We can see in Figure 10.4 that the *t*-statistic of 3.04 is within the shaded area of the right tale of the distribution.

**FIGURE 10.4**
**Sampling Distribution and the *t*-test Statistic**

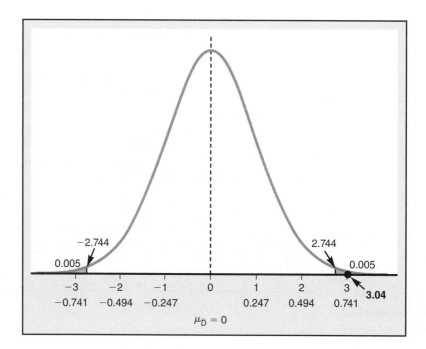

**Step 4:** Make the decision regarding the hypothesis.
Our *t*-statistic is 3.04, and the two-tailed critical value for an alpha value ($\alpha$) of 0.01 is $\pm2.744$. Given that our *t*-statistics is past the critical value (3.04 > 2.744) we can reject the null hypothesis.

**Step 5:** Interpret the results.
Based on our sample, we can say that there appears to be a statistically significant difference ($\overline{D} = 0.75$) between the pre-exercise enjoyment rating ($\overline{x}_1 = 6.94$) and the post-exercise enjoyment rating ($\overline{x}_2 = 7.69$).

**LO8**

## Confidence Intervals for the Mean of the Difference Between Paired Scores in the Population

As was the case with the independent sample *t*-test, we can use confidence intervals to estimate the mean of the difference between the paired scores in the population. The formula is:

$$CI = \text{Point Estimate} \pm t_{(\alpha)}(s_{\overline{D}}) \qquad\qquad (10.33)$$

For paired sample *t*-test, the point estimate is the mean of the difference between the paired scores. Therefore, the formula becomes:

$$CI = \overline{D} \pm t_{(\alpha)}(s_{\overline{D}}) \qquad (10.34)$$

Using our pre- and post-exercise enjoyment example, the point estimate is 0.75. With an alpha value ($\alpha$) of 0.01, the critical value of *t* was $\pm2.744$ and our estimated standard error (of the difference between the paired scores) was 0.247.

Therefore, our confidence interval for the mean of the difference between the paired scores:

$$CI = 0.75 \pm 2.744(0.247) \qquad (10.35)$$

$$CI = 0.75 \pm 0.68$$

Therefore:

$$\text{The lower limit of the } CI = 0.75 - 0.68 = 0.07$$

$$\text{The upper limit of the } CI = 1.31 + 0.84 = 1.43$$

Therefore, we can say that we are 95 percent confident that the mean of the difference between the paired scores for the population is between 0.07 and 1.43.

Now that we have the confidence intervals, we can revisit steps 4 and 5 from our previous results to incorporate the confidence intervals.

**Step 4:** Make the decision regarding the hypothesis.
Our *t*-statistic is 3.04, and the two-tailed critical value for an alpha value ($\alpha$) of 0.01 is $\pm2.744$. Given that our *t*-statistic is past the critical value (3.04 > 2.744) we can reject the null hypothesis. The 95 percent confidence interval for the mean of the difference between the paired scores for the population is [0.07, 1.43].

**Step 5:** Interpret the results.
Based on our sample, we can say that there appears to be a statistically significant difference ($\overline{D} = 0.75$) between the pre-exercise enjoyment rating ($\overline{x}_1 = 6.94$) and the post-exercise enjoyment rating ($\overline{x}_2 = 7.69$). Furthermore, we are 95 percent confident that the mean of the difference between the paired scores for the population is between 0.07 and 1.43.

---

**EXERCISE 10.2**   To complete your honours political science degree, you decide to write an undergraduate thesis on the rating of political orientation of friends. For your research you decide to collect data from groups of three friends. Two of the friends (called Friend 1 and Friend 2) will rate the political orientation of the third friend (called Target Friend). You have a theory that the two friends will differ in how they rate the target friend. Using a five point political orientation scale ranging from 1 (very liberal) to 5 (very conservative) you collect data from 125 dependent samples. The samples consist of the ratings the two friends provided with respect to the third friend's (the target friend) political orientation. The summary data is as follows:

| | Sample Means | Sample Size | Mean of the Difference between the Paired Scores | Standard Deviation of the Difference between the Paired Scores |
|---|---|---|---|---|
| Friend 1 Political Orientation Rating | $\bar{x}_1 = 2.40$ | $n = 125$ | $\bar{D} = .20$ | $s_d = 1.20$ |
| Friend 2 Political Orientation Rating | $\bar{x}_2 = 2.80$ | | | |

Test the alternative hypothesis that the two friends will differ in their rating of the political orientation of the third friend using a two-tailed hypothesis test and alpha value ($\alpha$) of 0.05. Include the confidence intervals of the difference in your answer.

## Take a Closer Look

We can use the independent sample *t*-test and the paired sample *t*-test (and their confidence intervals) to test the difference between two proportions.

More discussion about testing the difference between the two proportions can be found in the supplemental material on Connect. ▤ **connect**

## Conclusion

The independent sample *t*-test and the paired sample *t*-test are useful methods for testing hypotheses with two sample means. When we test hypotheses with two sample means and those samples are considered independent, then we use the independent sample *t*-test. When we want to test two sample means from dependent samples then we use the paired sample *t*-test.

While both of these test are useful, our research questions often involve comparing more than two groups of individuals. For example, suppose we want to know if access to government-sponsored student funding for post-secondary education differed by three groupings of social economic status (low, medium, and high). The independent sample *t*-test can only handle two groups and so it is not appropriate for situations where we want to compare the means of three or more groups. For that situation, we need to use what is called an analysis of variance. Analysis of variance, or ANOVA for short, is the topic of the next chapter.

## Key Chapter Concepts and Terms

## Frequently Asked Questions

1. Other resources or textbooks use the *t*-test for small samples and the *z*-test for large samples. Why are we not using the *z*-test for the independent sample and paired sample tests?

   Consider the *t*-distribution. As the sample size [and the associated degrees of freedom (*df*)] increases, the distribution of *t*, meaning its curve, becomes narrower and taller. Once the sample size is greater than 120, the *t*-distribution looks similar to the normal distribution. In fact, if you look at the critical value of *t* with over 120 *df*, the critical values are the same for *t* and *z*. For example, with over 120 *df*, the critical value of *t* when alpha ($\alpha$) is 0.05 is $\pm 1.96$, which is the same as the critical value for *z*. Therefore, technically the *t*-test is a *z*-test once you have larger sample sizes. The trend in software programs and most fields of research is to just report the *t*-value rather than having to switch between *t* and *z*.

2. Why can I only test two samples with the independent sample *t*-test and the paired sample *t*-test?

   Both formulas are based on having one difference score in the numerator. If you had more than two variables, you would have multiple difference scores. For example, if you have three groups you would have three difference scores—the difference between groups 1 and 2, groups 1 and 3, and groups 2 and 3.

3. If I have three groups of independent samples, can I not just run three different independent sample *t*-tests?

   This question does come up quite frequently and unfortunately the answer is quite technical. When you run multiple independent *t*-tests you actually increase the chance of committing a Type I error. That means that you are increasing the chances that you will reject a null hypothesis when in fact you should fail to reject it. Other tests, such as the analysis of variance (ANOVA), are designed to handle situations where you have more than three groups.

4. Is it possible to use proportions in independent sample *t*-tests and paired sample *t*-tests?

   Yes, you can test hypotheses with two sample proportions. However, you would use the normal distribution instead of the *t*-distribution. Therefore, the formulas would be the independent sample *z*-test for proportions and the

paired sample *z*-test for proportions. These tests can be found in the supplemental material on Connect. ▣ **connect**

5.   What exactly is the assumption of homogeneity again?

The assumption of homogeneity is that the variance in group 1 is equal
(statistically speaking) to the variance in group 2. Sometimes it is easier to
think of this in standard deviation language. Suppose you find that the
standard deviation of group 1 is 1.5, and the standard deviation is 1.25.
What the assumption of homogeneity of variance is stating is the standard
deviations squared ($s^2$) should not be statistically different from one
another.

**Research
Example:**

The 2006 Statistics Canada report "The Internet: Is it Changing the Way Canadians
Spend Their Time?" reported on how Canadians spend their time relative to their
daily Internet usage. 19,600 respondents were divided into one of three groups:

(i)   Non-users of the Internet,

(ii)   Moderate users of the Internet (between 5 minutes and 1 hour per day), and

(iii)   Heavy users of the Internet (more than 1 hour per day).

The following table represents some of the findings outlined in the report for
the moderate and heavy user groups.[8]

|  | Mean Time per Activity in Minutes | |
| --- | --- | --- |
| Time spent . . . | Moderate Users | Heavy Users |
| At work | 199.6 | 117.6 |
| Housekeeping | 31.7 | 28.3 |
| Talking on the phone | 6.7 | 7.3 |
| With friends | 99.6 | 92.3 |

**Research
Example
Questions:**

**Question 1:**  Are the two samples (moderate users and heavy users) considered
independent or dependent samples?

**Question 2:**  Suppose that for moderate users the standard deviation for
time spent talking on the telephone is 2.7 and the sample size is 8,428.
Furthermore, for heavy users the standard deviation for time spent talking
on the telephone is 3.2 and the sample size is 8,428. Is there a significant
difference between the mean times spent talking on the telephone with an
alpha value ($\alpha$) is 0.05?

**Question 3:**  With 95 percent confidence, what can we expect to be the
population value of the difference between the means for the time spent talking
on the phone?

**Research Example Answers:**

**Question 1:**  Are the two samples (moderate users and heavy users) considered independent or dependent samples?

The samples are independent samples because they represent two groups that are independent of one another. An individual in the moderate Internet usage group cannot be in the heavy Internet usage group and vice-versa. Similarly, the selection of the sample for one group does not influence the selection of the sample for the other.

**Question 2:**  Suppose that for moderate users the standard deviation for time spent talking on the telephone is 2.7 and the sample size is 8,428. Furthermore, for heavy users the standard deviation for time spent talking on the telephone is 3.2 and the sample size is 8,428. Is there a significant difference between the mean times spent talking on the telephone with an alpha value ($\alpha$) is 0.05?

To determine if there is a difference in the mean time spent talking on the telephone, we need to conduct an independent sample $t$-test. The formula is:

$$ t = \frac{\bar{x}_1 - \bar{x}_2}{\sqrt{\frac{(n_1 - 1)s_1^2 + (n_2 - 1)s_2^2}{(n_1 + n_2 - 2)} \times \left(\frac{1}{n_1} + \frac{1}{n_2}\right)}} $$

Therefore:

$$ t = \frac{6.7 - 7.3}{\sqrt{\frac{(8{,}428 - 1)2.7^2 + (8{,}428 - 1)3.2^2}{(8{,}428 + 8{,}428 - 2)} \times \left(\frac{1}{8{,}428} + \frac{1}{8{,}428}\right)}} $$

$$ t = \frac{-0.60}{\sqrt{\frac{(8{,}427)7.29 + (8{,}427)10.24}{(16854)} \times (0.00024)}} $$

$$ t = \frac{-0.60}{\sqrt{\frac{61432.83 + 86292.48}{(16854)} \times (0.00024)}} $$

$$ t = \frac{-0.60}{\sqrt{8.765 \times (0.00024)}} = \frac{-.60}{0.046} = -13.04 $$

The degrees of freedom is:

$$ n_1 + n_2 - 2 = 16854 $$

The critical value for $t$ with an alpha ($\alpha$) of 0.05 is $\pm 1.96$.

Since the $t$-value of $-13.04$ passes the critical value of $\pm 1.96$, we reject the null of no difference and accept the alternative hypothesis that there is a difference.

**Question 3:** With 95 percent confidence, what can we expect to be the population value of the difference between the means for the time spent talking on the phone?

The 95 percent confidence interval is:

$$CI = (\bar{x}_1 - \bar{x}_2) \pm t_{(\alpha)}(s_{\bar{x}})$$
$$CI = -.60 \pm 1.96(0.046)$$
$$CI = -.60 \pm 0.09$$

Therefore, the confidence interval is $[-0.51, -0.69]$.

---

**ANSWER TO EXERCISE 10.1**

**Step 1:** Define the null and alternative hypotheses.

$$H_0: \mu_1 = \mu_2$$
$$H_A: \mu_1 \neq \mu_2$$

**Step 2:** Define the sampling distribution and critical values.
The mean of the sampling distribution is zero because it represents the null hypothesis where $\mu_1 - \mu_2 = 0$. Using pooled variance, the estimated standard error of the difference of the means is equal to:

$$s_{\bar{x}_1 - \bar{x}_2} = \sqrt{\frac{(n_1 - 1)s_1^2 + (n_2 - 1)s_2^2}{(n_1 + n_2 - 2)} \times \left(\frac{1}{n_1} + \frac{1}{n_2}\right)}$$

$$s_{\bar{x}_1 - \bar{x}_2} = \sqrt{\frac{(220 - 1)0.4624 + (230 - 1)0.5625}{(220 + 230 - 2)} \times \left(\frac{1}{220} + \frac{1}{230}\right)}$$

**Note:** You were provided with the standard deviations for both groups. Therefore, you need to first square the standard deviations to get the variances for this calculation.

$$s_{\bar{x}_1 - \bar{x}_2} = \sqrt{\frac{101.27 + 128.81}{448} \times 0.009} = \sqrt{0.005} = 0.071$$

The degrees of freedom ($df$) are:

$$df = n_1 + n_2 - 2 = 220 + 230 - 2 = 448$$

Looking up our critical value of $t$ in the $t$-distribution table, we find that with 448 $df$ and a two-tailed alpha ($\alpha$) of 0.01, our critical value of $t$ is $\pm 2.576$.

Notice that we haven't included the $\pm 3$ estimated standard errors here. As mentioned in the examples, you only need to calculate the estimated standard error, you do not have to go out to $\pm 3$ standard errors or draw the distribution. However, it is handy to do so when you are learning how the process works.

**Step 3:** Calculate the test statistic using the sample data.
Using the formula for an independent sample *t*-test our test statistic is:

$$t = \frac{\bar{x}_1 - \bar{x}_2}{s_{\bar{x}_1 - \bar{x}_2}} = \frac{3.05 - 2.85}{0.071} = \frac{0.20}{0.071} = 2.817$$

**Step 4:** Make the decision regarding the hypothesis.
Our *t*-statistic is 2.817, and the two-tailed critical value for an alpha value ($\alpha$) of 0.01 is $\pm 2.576$. Given that our t-statistic is past the critical value we can reject the null hypothesis. The difference between the two mean grade point averages was 0.20. Therefore, the 99 percent confidence interval (because $\alpha = 0.01$ you should stay consistent) is:

$$CI = (\bar{x}_1 - \bar{x}_2) \pm t_{(\alpha)}(s_{\bar{x}})$$
$$CI = 0.20 \pm 2.576(0.071)$$
$$CI = 0.20 \pm 0.18$$

Therefore, the confidence interval is [0.02, 0.38].

**Step 5:** Interpret the results.
Based on the sample, there appears to be a difference in the grade point average between male teenagers with high self-esteem and male teenagers with low self-esteem. The 99 percent confidence interval for the difference is [0.02, 0.38], which means we are 99 percent confident that the difference in the means for the population is between 0.02 and 0.38. Given that the interval does not contain a zero value, 99 out of 100 times we can expect to find a difference in the means.

**Note:** Given that the lower level of the confidence interval is close to zero, you might want to point that out to your readers. It doesn't change your confidence level but it does provide readers with the knowledge that if they go beyond 99 percent, say to 99.9 percent, the confidence interval would include a zero. In fact, at 99.9 percent confidence the interval would be [−0.03, 0.43].

---

**ANSWER TO EXERCISE 10.2**

**Step 1:** Define the null and alternative hypotheses.

$$H_0: \mu_{\bar{D}} = 0$$
$$H_A: \mu_{\bar{D}} \neq 0$$

**Step 2:** Define the sampling distribution and critical values.
Using the formula for the estimated standard error of the difference between the paired scores we get:

$$s_{\bar{D}} = \frac{s_d}{\sqrt{n}} = \frac{1.20}{\sqrt{125}} = \frac{1.20}{11.18} = 0.107$$

The degrees of freedom (*df*) are:

$$df = n - 1 = 125 - 1 = 124$$

Looking up our critical value of *t* in the *t*-distribution table, we find that with 124 *df* and a two-tailed alpha value ($\alpha$) of 0.05, our critical value of *t* is ±1.960.

**Step 3:** Calculate the test statistic using the sample data.
Using the paired sample t-test formula we get:

$$t = \frac{\overline{D}}{s_{\overline{D}}} = \frac{0.20}{0.107} = 1.87$$

**Step 4:** Make the decision regarding the hypothesis.
Our t-statistic is 1.87, and the two-tailed critical value for an alpha ($\alpha$) of 0.05 is ±1.960. Given that our *t*-statistic does not pass the critical value (1.87 < 1.96) we fail to reject the null hypothesis. The confidence interval for the mean of the difference between the paired scores is:

$$CI = D \pm t_{(\alpha)}(s_{\overline{D}})$$
$$CI = 0.20 \pm 1.96(0.107)$$
$$CI = 0.20 \pm 0.21$$

Therefore:

$$\text{The lower limit of the } CI = 0.20 - 0.21 = -.01$$
$$\text{The upper limit of the } CI = 0.20 + 0.21 = 0.41$$

Therefore, we can say that we are 95 percent confident that the mean of the difference between the paired scores for the population is between −0.01 and 0.41.

**Step 5:** Interpret the results.
Based on the sample, there is no difference between the two friends' ratings of the third friend's political orientation. The mean difference ($\overline{D} = .20$) was not statistically significant. Furthermore, the 95 percent confidence interval [−.01, 0.41] included the value of zero, which further supports the finding of no difference.

## Problems

1. Is there a difference in nicotine level? Cools were compared to Camels with the following results drawn from independent samples.

| Cools | Camels |
|---|---|
| Mean = 25.5 mg | Mean = 26.6 mg |
| $S_1$ = 5.2 mg | $S_2$ = 4.3 mg |
| $n_1 = 11$ | $n_2 = 11$ |

a) Provide a 99 percent confidence interval for the difference between the means.

b) Is there evidence, with alpha = 0.01, to show that the average amount of nicotine is different for each of these cigarette brands?

c) What *p*-value would you report for your test statistic?

2. The Scholastic Achievement Test (SAT) is used as a guide for entrance into a specialized private school. The test examines oral and written communication with a maximum score of 800. The following information was drawn from two independent local high schools: Trinity Prep and Brantford Academy.

| Trinity | Brantford |
|---|---|
| Mean = 649 | Mean = 625 |
| $s^2 =$ 11.2 | $s^2 =$ 9.3 |
| = 16 | $n =$ 14 |

a) Provide a 95 percent confidence interval for the difference between the means of the two schools.

b) If alpha = 0.05, is there evidence to show that the average score on the SAT is different for each school?

c) What $p$-value would you report for your test statistic?

3. The Duramax company claims that by taking their "special" vitamin supplement, an athlete can improve his strength and recovery time. Eight test athletes were used and given a strength test using a standard bench press. After two weeks of taking the vitamin with training, the athletes were tested again with the following results being the maximum amount each individual can bench press.

| Subject | 1 | 2 | 3 | 4 | 5 | 6 | 7 | 8 |
|---|---|---|---|---|---|---|---|---|
| Before vitamin ($x_1$) | 210 | 228 | 180 | 206 | 260 | 255 | 215 | 216 |
| After vitamin ($x_2$) | 220 | 235 | 185 | 205 | 273 | 252 | 225 | 218 |

a) Provide a 95 percent confidence interval for the difference between the means.

b) Is there evidence to show that the drug is effective on average? (Hint: Test the difference between the means for a dependent sample)

c) What $p$-value would you report for your test statistic?

# Estimation and Hypothesis Testing III: One-Way Analysis of Variance

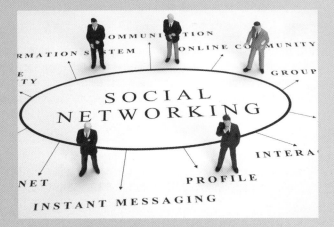

**Learning Objectives:**

By the end of this chapter you should be able to:

1. Describe when to use a one-way analysis of variance ANOVA test.
2. Describe the concept of the ANOVA test.
3. Describe the assumptions of the ANOVA test.
4. Manually calculate the formulas for the test and populate the ANOVA table.
5. Describe the $F$-ratio and the $F$-distribution.
6. Test hypotheses using the one-way ANOVA test.
7. Briefly discuss the purpose of post-hoc tests.

**George W. Snedecor** (1882–1974)

George W. Snedecor studied physics and mathematics as a graduate student, before joining Iowa State University as a professor of mathematics. While there he founded the first statistics department in the United States. His books on analysis of variance and statistical methods have been a standard in classrooms around the world. In fact, he calculated the *f*-distribution, which he named in honour of Sir Ronald A. Fisher.[1]

# Introduction

**LO1**

In the last chapter we looked at the independent sample *t*-test and the paired sample *t*-test. Both tests are useful when you want to compare the means of two independent or dependent samples (or groups). Often, researchers collect data from complex experiments and surveys where there are more than two groups involved. Consider the following examples, which use the three minority group classifications as defined by the Statistics Canada classification of visible minority:

1. A sociologist is interested in determining if access to health care differs across three specific minority group classifications of South Asian, Black, Not a Visible Minority.
2. An economist is interested in the level of income inequality across the minority group classifications of South Asian, Black, Not a Visible Minority.
3. A political scientist is interested in understanding how political involvement differs across the minority group classifications of South Asian, Black, Not a Visible Minority.
4. A criminologist wants to determine if the number of community service hours young offenders are sentenced to for property crime offences differs by the minority group classifications of South Asian, Black, Not a Visible Minority.
5. A social psychologist is interested in how citizens' trust in local police forces differs across the minority group classifications of South Asian, Black, Not a Visible Minority.

## Take a Closer Look

A Type I error occurs when we reject a null hypothesis that we should have failed to reject. We can control for Type I errors by setting the alpha value ($\alpha$). For example, an alpha value ($\alpha$) of 0.05 means that we have a 5 percent chance of committing a Type I error. However, we can inadvertently increase our Type I error rate by conducting multiple *t*-tests when we should be using an ANOVA test.

For example, suppose you are comparing the mean level of math ability of three groups of students (grades 10, 11, and 12) and rather than conducting an ANOVA test, you conduct three separate independent sample *t*-tests comparing those in grade 10 and 11, grade 10 and 12, and grade 11 and 12. Running three multiple comparisons rather than one ANOVA increases the Type I error rate. We refer to this as the familywise error rate. With three comparisons instead of one, our Type I error rate could be 14.26 percent rather than 5 percent.[2]

In each of these examples we have three independent samples—South Asian, Black, and Not a Visible Minority. If the variable that we wish to compare across groups (e.g., access to health care) is either interval or ratio, a researcher might be tempted to run three separate independent sample *t*-tests comparing South Asian to Black and then South Asian to Not a Visible Minority, and finally Black to Not a Visible Minority. While running separate independent sample *t*-tests would tell you if there are significant differences in the dependent variable (also referred to as the response variable), it would also increase your probability of rejecting the null hypothesis when in fact you should fail to reject it (Type I error).

Therefore, when we have three or more groups and we want to compare the means of those groups we use the analysis of variance method, or ANOVA for short. We will get into more detail about the test shortly, but at this point it important to stress the following points that define what an analysis of variance is. An ANOVA:

- is meant for simultaneous comparisons of three or more group means,
- attempts to attribute the variability in the observations to their underlying sources,
- only tells us whether there is a difference between at least one of the means and another group, it does not tell us which group means differ, and
- requires additional tests (such as post-hoc tests) to determine exactly which groups differ.

Although we refer to this test as an ANOVA, there are quite a few different types of ANOVA tests. In this chapter we deal specifically with the one-way ANOVA (also referred to as a single factor ANOVA). To grasp what we mean by one-way, suppose you collected data from nine students, three of which attended high school A, three of which attended high school B, and three of which attended high school C. You record their first year university grade average and want to determine if there is a difference in the mean first year university grade across the three groups of high schools. Your data might look as follows:

| Respondent | Factor School | Dependent Variable First Year University Grade |
|---|---|---|
| 1 | A | 67% |
| 2 | A | 82% |
| 3 | A | 75% |
| 4 | B | 72% |
| 5 | B | 78% |
| 6 | B | 79% |
| 7 | C | 61% |
| 8 | C | 92% |
| 9 | C | 74% |

In ANOVA, a **factor** is the independent variable that the researcher manipulates.

In an ANOVA test, we often refer to the independent variable ("school" in this example) as a **factor**. A factor is simply an independent variable that the researcher manipulates. We controlled this factor by deciding which high schools were involved. Since we have only one factor in this analysis, we call it a one-way ANOVA (or single factor ANOVA). If we had two factors (such as school and social economic status) we would call it a two-way ANOVA.

Now that you know what a one-way ANOVA is and when to use it, we can get into the details. For simplicity, we will continue to refer to the one-way ANOVA as just ANOVA for the remainder of this chapter. To start, we'll cover the concept of ANOVA in more detail. Following that, we will consider how to set up the null and alternative hypotheses and discuss the assumptions of the test. Then we will discuss the formulas and the $F$-distribution, followed by an example of a hypothesis test.

**Note:** Technically, you can use an ANOVA to test the difference in two independent sample means. This results in what is called Hotelling's $T^2$.

# The Concept of ANOVA: Between Group and Within Group Variance

**LO2**

In order to discuss the concept of an ANOVA, let's consider the following question:

"Did the number of tweets posted by the leaders of the Conservative Party, Liberal Party, and the New Democrat Party (NDP) differ for the last four months of 2010?"

# Take A Closer Look

| | Matching the Research Situation to the Type of Analysis | | |
|---|---|---|---|
| Situation | Example | Statistical Test | Refer to... |
| I need to estimate the population parameter based on my sample statistic. The variable is measured at the interval or ratio level. | You calculate the mean score of the Law School Admission Test (LSAT) for a random sample of students who did not study criminology during their undergraduate education, and you want to estimate what the mean LSAT score might be in the population of students who did not study criminology during their undergraduate education. | Confidence Intervals: Use confidence intervals when you need to make an inference about a population mean or proportion and you have a sample mean or proportion. | Chapter 8 |
| I calculated a mean based on data from one sample of respondents and want to compare it to a known mean such as the one I found in a published report. Both my variable and the one in the report are measured at the interval or ratio level. | You calculate the mean LSAT score of students in your university who just took the test. You want to test the alternative hypothesis that the mean score from your sample is higher than the mean LSAT score for all of Canada as published by the Law School Admission Council. | Single Sample Mean (or Proportion): Use a single sample test for a mean (or proportions when you have proportions) when you need to compare your sample mean to a known mean value. | Chapter 9 |
| I have two means from two independent samples and need to determine if they differ from one another. The variable is measured at the interval or ratio level. | Based on a random sample you have calculated the mean LSAT score for students from your university and the mean LSAT score for students from another university. You want to test the hypothesis that the mean score from your university is higher than the mean score of the other university. | Independent Sample *t*-Test: Use an independent sample *t*-test when you are comparing the means from two samples that are independent of each other. | Chapter 10 |
| I have two means from a paired sample and need to determine if they differ from one another. The variable is measured at the interval or ratio level. | Ten students took the LSAT exam last year and again this year. You want to test the hypothesis that the mean LSAT score from last year is lower than the mean LSAT score from this year. | Paired Sample *t*-Test: Use a paired sample *t*-test when you are comparing the means samples that are not independent of one another. | Chapter 10 |
| I have three or more means from an independent sample and need to determine if they differ from one another. The variable is measured at the interval or ratio level. | Thirty students took the LSAT exam. Ten had studied political science in university, 10 had studied sociology, and 10 had studied management economics. You want to test the hypothesis that the mean LSAT score is different in at least one of the three groups. | One-way ANOVA: Use a one-way analysis of variance when you are comparing the means of three or more groups. | Chapter 11 |

Data from TweetStats reveals the following:

**TABLE 11.1**
**Four Month Twitter Statistics for Party Leaders**

Source: http://tweetstats.com

Note: The October 2010 tweets for the Conservative Leader was changed from 6 to 5 for the purpose of this example. The November 2010 tweets for the NDP Leader was changed from 19 to 18 for the purpose of this example.

| | Political Group Leader | | |
| --- | --- | --- | --- |
| | Conservative Leader "@pmharper" | Liberal Leader "@M_Ignatieff" | NDP Leader "@jacklayton" |
| September, 2010 | 8 | 15 | 19 |
| October, 2010 | 5 | 14 | 14 |
| November, 2010 | 6 | 13 | 18 |
| December, 2010 | 3 | 9 | 8 |
| Mean | $\bar{x}_1 = 5.50$ | $\bar{x}_2 = 12.75$ | $\bar{x}_3 = 14.75$ |
| Variance | $s_1^2 = 4.33$ | $s_2^2 = 6.92$ | $s_3^2 = 24.92$ |
| Sample Size | $n_1 = 4$ | $n_2 = 4$ | $n_2 = 4$ |
| Grand Mean | $\bar{\bar{x}} = 11.00$ | | |

In this scenario we have three groups each with their own mean ($\bar{x}_1, \bar{x}_2, \bar{x}_3$), variance ($s_1^2, s_2^2, s_3^2$), and sample size ($n_1, n_2, n_3$). We could have included more than three groups and more than four observations per group, but limiting the number of groups and observations makes it easier to understand at this point.

Suppose we were to plot the individual observations by group from the data in Table 11.1. Figure 11.1 represents individual observations (each dot), whereas the solid line going through each dot represents the mean for that group. We can see how the data for each group varies from its mean. For example, we can see that

**FIGURE 11.1**
**Plot of Individual Observations by Group**

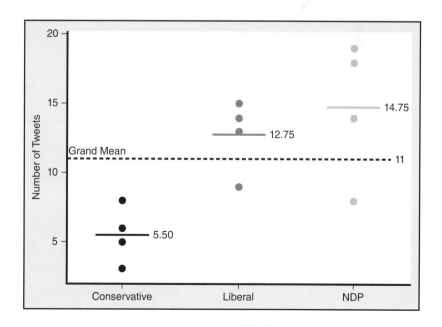

the data for the NDP leader seems to have more variation from the mean than the other two. Looking at Table 11.1 we can confirm that this is true. The variance for the NDP leader ($s_3^2 = 24.92$) is greater than the variance for the Conservative leader ($s_1^2 = 4.33$) and the Liberal leader ($s_2^2 = 6.92$). Notice the thick dotted line marked "Grand Mean." The **Grand Mean** ($\bar{\bar{x}}$) represents the mean of all of the observations (12 in this case) in the data.

> The **Grand Mean** is the total of all observations divided by the total sample size. The notation for the grand mean is $\bar{\bar{x}}$ (pronounced "*x*-double-bar").

**Note:** When the sample sizes are equal in each group, you can calculate $\bar{\bar{x}}$ by taking the mean of the sampling means. However, this does not work if the sample sizes are different in each group.

We previously stated that an ANOVA compares multiple groups simultaneously and in doing so tries to attribute the variability in the observations to the underlying sources. We refer to the underlying sources of variability as Between Group Variance and Within Group Variance. When thinking about between versus within group variance, it is helpful to remember what the basic definition of variance is. Recall that variance is a measure of the extent to which the data varies from its mean. **Between Group Variance** is the total amount that the group means ($\bar{x}_1, \bar{x}_2, \bar{x}_3$) vary from the grand mean ($\bar{\bar{x}}$). **Within Group Variance** is the total amount that all individual observations vary from their group mean. When we add the between group and within group variability the result is the total variability. Therefore:

> **Between Group Variance** is the total amount the group means vary from the Grand Mean. This is also referred to as between group variability.

> **Within Group Variance** is the total amount that all individual observations vary from their group mean. This is also referred to as within group variability.

Total Variance = Between Group Variance + Within Group Variance

So when we say that an ANOVA compares groups simultaneously and attempts to attribute the variability in the observations to the underlying sources what we are saying is:

1. In the population, the scores on a given variable differ from one another.
2. The sum of all of the variability is called the total variance.
3. Total variance is made up of two parts: between group variance and within group variance.
4. Between group variance is the variability that is attributed to the difference between groups.
5. Within group variance is the variability that is attributed to the difference within the groups.

**Note:** Some disciplines refer to between group and within group variance as between subject and within subject variance. The meaning is the same.

# Setting up the Null and Alternative Hypotheses

Now that we understand conceptually what an ANOVA is, we can focus on the null and alternative hypotheses. The null and alternative hypotheses for an ANOVA are:

$$H_0 = \mu_1 = \mu_2 = \mu_3 \ldots \mu_K$$
$$H_A \neq \mu_1 \neq \mu_2 \neq \mu_3 \ldots \mu_K$$

where: $\mu$ refers to the population mean and the subscript refers to the group number.

Therefore, $\mu_1$ refers to the population mean for group 1 and $\mu_k$ refers to the population mean for the last group. So, if we have 10 groups, then $k = 10$.

Recall that for the independent sample *t*-test the null hypothesis was that the population mean for the first group was equal to the population mean for the second group. The same is true for an ANOVA, only this time we have more groups. We test the difference between groups to determine whether they are from the same population. For example, when we divide groups by social economic status we are testing if the population means of those groups are equal. If they are equal, then they are likely from the same population. If they are not equal then they are likely from a different population with a different population mean ($\mu$). Figure 11.2 provides a graphical representation of this concept.

**FIGURE 11.2**
**Groups Within a Population**

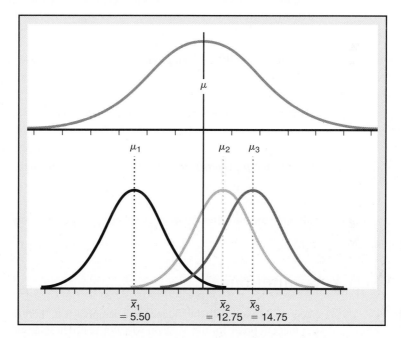

The null hypothesis is that groups come from the sample population. If that is the case, then there won't be a significant difference in the means. If there isn't a difference, then the population ($\mu_1$) for $\bar{x}_1$ is equal to the population ($\mu_2$) for $\bar{x}_2$, which is equal to the population ($\mu_3$) for $\bar{x}_3$, and so on. Although we write this as…

$$H_0: \mu_1 = \mu_2 = \mu_3$$

…what this means is:

$$\mu_1 = \mu_2$$
$$\mu_1 = \mu_3$$
$$\mu_2 = \mu_3$$

**Note:** As you add more groups to your hypothesis, you increase the number of $\mu$s in your null and alternative hypotheses. So a null hypothesis with five groups would be $H_0$: $\mu_1 = \mu_2 = \mu_3 = \mu_4 = \mu_5$.

Considering the null hypothesis, the alternative hypothesis is that the groups did not come from the same population and therefore the population means are not equal:

$$H_A: \mu_1 \neq \mu_2 \neq \mu_3$$

This format for writing the null hypothesis is standard in the social sciences. However, it is a little deceiving or at least confusing because you could have the situation where two groups are equal but a third is not. Remember, an ANOVA only tests whether at least one of the groups differs from the others. A post-hoc test (discussed later in the chapter) is required to determine which groups actually differ from one another. Therefore, what this alternative hypothesis is saying is:

$\mu_1 = \mu_2$ but $\mu_3$ differs from $\mu_1$ and $\mu_2$ ... which is to say ... $\mu_1 = \mu_2$ but $\mu_3 \neq \mu_1$
$$\mu_1 = \mu_2 \text{ but } \mu_3 \neq \mu_2$$

or

$\mu_1 = \mu_3$ but $\mu_2$ differs from $\mu_1$ and $\mu_3$ ... which is to say ... $\mu_1 = \mu_3$ but $\mu_2 \neq \mu_1$
$$\mu_1 = \mu_3 \text{ but } \mu_2 \neq \mu_3$$

or

$\mu_2 = \mu_3$ but $\mu_1$ differs from $\mu_2$ and $\mu_3$ ... which is to say ... $\mu_2 = \mu_3$ but $\mu_1 \neq \mu_2$
$$\mu_2 = \mu_3 \text{ but } \mu_1 \neq \mu_3$$

or

all three means differ from one another ... which is to say ... $\mu_1 \neq \mu_2 \neq \mu_3$

# The ANOVA Assumptions

**LO3**

As was the case with the independent sample *t*-test, there are assumptions we need to meet in order for us to use an ANOVA test. These assumptions are:

1. The dependent variable must be measured at either the interval or ratio level of measurement.

2. The groups (and more specifically the data) must be independent of one another.

3. The data must be relatively normally distributed.

4. The variance in the population must be equal for all groups ($\sigma_1^2 = \sigma_2^2 = \sigma_n^2$). This is the assumption of homogeneity of variance that we covered in our discussion of the independent sample *t*-test. The difference here is that there is more than two groups.

## Take A Closer Look

Assumption number two often requires some clarification. In our Twitter example, we are attempting to determine if there is a difference in the mean number of tweets across the three leaders. This is different than asking if the mean number of tweets for the Conservative Leader differed over the four month period.

In our one-way ANOVA scenario, we are not interested in whether the mean number of tweets per month per leader is different, but rather whether the mean number of tweets differed across the three leaders. If we were looking at the difference in number of tweets for a specific leader across the

number of months, we would need to conduct a repeated measures ANOVA. The repeated measures ANOVA is similar to the paired sample *t*-test, only it's used when we have more than two time periods or dependent samples. In that case, the four months would be analyzed as Time 1 through Time 4. We often refer to a one-way ANOVA as a between-subjects design because the analysis is focussed on comparing means between groups. Similarly, we often refer to a repeated measures ANOVA as a within-subjects design because the analysis is focussed on the comparison of means within groups.

## Formulas for the Analysis of Variance Test

**LO4**

There are several different formulas that we need to use to conduct an ANOVA. When we conduct an ANOVA, we summarize the results in what we commonly refer to as the ANOVA table. Most statistical packages generate the results of an ANOVA in a similar looking table, so we will use this common format to go through the formulas. Figure 11.3 provides an ANOVA table for our tweeting example. Although it may seem a little backwards, we find that starting with the last calculation, the *F*-Ratio, first makes the concept of an ANOVA easier to grasp. So we will work our way through the formulas, starting with the *F*-Ratio.

**FIGURE 11.3**
**ANOVA Table of Results for Tweeting Example**

| Source | Sum of Squares | df | Mean Sum of Squares | F-Ratio |
|---|---|---|---|---|
| Between Groups | 189.500 | 2 | 94.750 | 7.859 |
| Within Groups | 108.500 | 9 | 12.056 | |
| Total | 298.000 | 11 | | |

**LO5**

An **F-Ratio** is the ratio of the between group variance to within group variance.

## The *F*-Ratio and the *F*-Distribution

### The F-Ratio

The basic purpose of an ANOVA is to compare the two sources of variability: between group variability and within group variability. Once we have that information, we can calculate a ratio of the two. This ratio is called the **F-Ratio**.

**Note:** Other resources may refer to the *F*-Ratio as the *F*-Statistic or the *F*-Value. The meaning is the same.

The *F*-Ratio is a ratio that compares the between group variance to the within group variance. In a general sense the formula is:

$$F\text{-Ratio} = \frac{\text{Between Group Variance}}{\text{Within Group Variance}} \qquad (11.1)$$

By comparing the two sources of variance, the *F*-Ratio tells us how far apart the group means are from one another. It may seem strange to use variances to determine if there is a difference in group means, so let's explore the idea further. Consider Figure 11.4. Suppose we randomly select five individuals for each of three groups called Blue, Purple, and Green. Now consider the top plot in Figure 11.4, which shows the distributions for the three groups. The mean for Blue is 13, the mean for Purple is 20, and the mean for Green is 27; they all have a variance of 1. We can see that there is variation in the group means (the dotted lines) in that they differ from one another. However, since taking a random sample from a population can result in many different sample means (think back to the

**FIGURE 11.4** **Comparison of Within and Between Group Variation**

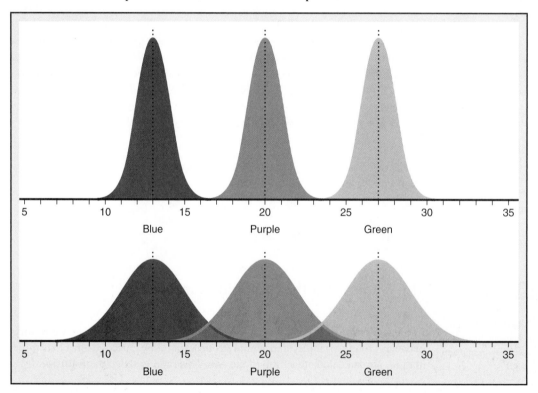

sampling distribution) what is the probability that, if we drew another random sample of 15 individuals, the means of the three groups would be different from one another? After all, the differences in the means could just be due to sampling error. Again, looking only the top plot in Figure 11.4, since individual scores from each sample do not vary much from their group means and the curves don't seem to overlap with one another, it is likely that those in Blue are from a different population than those in Purple, and so on.

Now look at the bottom plot in Figure 11.4. Each group has the same mean as before but now the variance of each group is 2 instead of 1. Now we can see that individuals in each group vary a fair bit more from their mean than they previously did. In fact, the curves from the three groups overlap, meaning there is enough individual variation that those in the far right tail of the Blue distribution have the same values as those individuals in the far left Purple distribution. The same could also be said of the right tail of the Purple distribution and the left tail of the Green distribution. Since the individual scores from each sample varies a fair bit from their group means and the curves seem to overlap with one another, it is possible that those in the Blue group are not from a different population than those in the Purple group, and so on.

Within group variation is just as important in determining the difference between the group means as between group variation when determining whether multiple groups differ from one another. Furthermore, the *F*-Ratio tells us how different the group means are in relation to the variability of their individual observations.

As the group means come closer together, the between group variance gets smaller in relation to the within group variance. As that happens, the *F*-Ratio also gets smaller. Similarly, as the within group variance gets larger in relation to the between group variance, the *F*-Ratio gets smaller. The *F*-Ratio gets larger as the between group variance gets larger in comparison to the within group variance. The larger the *F*-ratio, the more variation we have due to between group differences than within group differences.

**Note:** An *F*-ratio of 0 indicates no difference between the means. An *F*-ratio of 1 indicates that there is an equal amount of between and within group variance.

### The F-Distribution

The *F*-Ratio is our test statistic for testing the equality of three or more means. Similar to how the *t*-value follows the *t*-distribution, the *F*-Ratio follows its own distribution called the *F*-distribution. Unlike the *t*-distribution, which can have both positive and negative values, the values of the *F*-distribution range from 0 to positive infinity because variances can only be zero or positive. Furthermore, like the *t*-distribution, the *F*-distribution is a family of distributions with a separate distribution (and shape) based on degrees of freedom (*df*). However, since we are dealing with between group and within group variances, we will have two numbers for the *df*. The first number represents the *df* for between group variance, whereas the second represents the *df* for the within group variance.

We calculate the between group *df* as:

Between Group Degrees of Freedom = Number of Groups − 1

We calculate the within group *df* as:

Within Group Degrees of Freedom = Total Sample Size − Number of Groups

Therefore, if we had three groups (often represented as *k*) and a sample size (*n*) of 15, then our between group degrees of freedom would be:

Between Group Degrees of Freedom = 3 − 1 = 2

while our within group *df* would be:

Within Group Degrees of Freedom = 12 − 3 = 12

We use the *df* to determine the *F*-Distribution and the critical values. If you consider the formula for the *F*-Ratio, you will see that the between group variance is the numerator and the within group variance is the denominator. When we communicate our *df* for *F* we start with numerator *df* and then the denominator. So we would state that we want the critical value of *F* for 2 and 12 *df*.

**Note:** You will often find that the *df* for *F* are written as $F(2,12)$ where the first number is the numerator *df* and the second is the denominator *df*.

---

**EXERCISE 11.1**   Calculate the degrees of freedom for the following *k* groups and *n* sample size. State your results as $F(\_,\_)$.

$$k = 5, n = 60$$
$$k = 8, n = 25$$
$$k = 4, n = 102$$
$$k = 3, n = 22$$
$$k = 7, n = 126$$

---

The *F*-Distribution is a positively-skewed distribution, and therefore we use the right tail for the critical values. To determine the critical values we look up the degrees of freedom (*df*) in the table of critical values for the *F*-Distribution at the desired significance level found in Appendix B and C. Separate tables are provided for an alpha (*α*) of 0.01 (or 1%) and an alpha (*α*) of 0.05 (or 5%). Once you have the table for the correct alpha (*α*), you look across the top for the numerator *df* and then go down the left-hand side for the denominator *df*. For example, for $F(2,12)$ the critical value for an alpha (*α*) of 0.01 is 6.93 and for an alpha (*α*) of 0.05 is 3.88. Figure 11.5 provides the *F*-Distribution for $F(2,12)$ with an alpha (*α*) of 0.05.

**FIGURE 11.5**
*F*-**Distribution for**
*F*(2,12) **with an**
**Alpha (α) of 0.05**

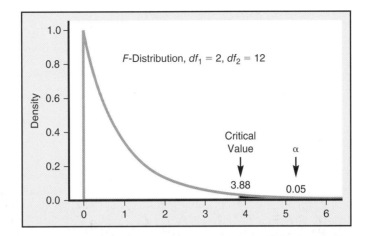

As with the other tests, the critical value determines the point at which we fail to reject or reject the null. Recall that our *F*-Ratio increases as the between group variance gets larger in relation to the within group variance. When the *F*-Ratio is larger than the critical value of *F*, we reject the null hypothesis of no difference between the groups. Similarly, when the *F*-Ratio is smaller than the critical value of *F*, we fail to reject the null hypothesis of no difference between the groups. The shaded area in Figure 11.5 shows the region where we reject the null hypothesis.

## Calculating the Between Group Sum of Squares (*SS_B*)

If you look back to the ANOVA table in Figure 11.3 you will notice the column titled Sum of Squares. Think back to our discussion about the calculation for variance in chapter 3. In calculating the variance, we subtracted the mean from each individual score, squared the difference to get the individual squared deviation, and the summed the individual squared deviations to get the sum of squares. That is what we are doing here for the **between group sum of squares** (written using the notation *SS_B*).

The **between group sum of squares** is the sum of the squared deviations of each group mean from the grand mean.

The formula for the between group sum of squares is:

$$SS_B = \Sigma n_i (\bar{x}_i - \bar{\bar{x}})^2 \qquad (11.2)$$

where: $n_i$ = the sample size (*n*) for each group

$\bar{x}_i$ = the mean for each group

$\bar{\bar{x}}$ = grand mean

This equation tells us to subtract the grand mean $(\bar{\bar{x}})$ from the mean $(\bar{x}_i)$ of each group $(\bar{x}_i - \bar{\bar{x}})$. The subscript *i* on the group mean $(\bar{x}_i)$ represents each group. Square the result $(\bar{x}_i - \bar{\bar{x}})^2$ and then multiply it by the sample size $(n_i)$ of each group. The result is as many of $n_i (\bar{x}_i - \bar{\bar{x}})^2$ as there are groups. Finally, the summation sign (Σ) tells us to add each of the group values of $n_i (\bar{x}_i - \bar{\bar{x}})^2$ together to get the total *SS_B*.

In the ANOVA table for our tweeting example (Figure 11.3) the value of the between group sum of squares ($SS_B$) was 189.500. That is the value that we are going to calculate here. Looking at our twitter data from Table 11.1, we have:

Group 1 (Conservative Leader): $\bar{x}_1 = 5.50$ with $n_1 = 4$

Group 2 (Liberal Leader): $\bar{x}_2 = 12.75$ with $n_2 = 4$

Group 3 (NDP Leader): $\bar{x}_3 = 14.75$ with $n_3 = 4$

The Grand Mean: $\bar{\bar{x}} = 11.00$

Therefore, our calculation of the $SS_B$ is:

$$SS_B = \Sigma n_i (\bar{x}_i - \bar{\bar{x}})^2 \qquad\qquad (11.3)$$

$$SS_B = 4(5.50 - 11.00)^2 + 4(12.75 - 11.00)^2$$
$$+ 4(14.75 - 11.00)^2$$
$$SS_B = 121.00 + 12.25 + 56.25 = 189.500$$

Looking at the ANOVA table in Figure 11.3, we can see we have calculated the $SS_B$ correctly and can now look at the within group sums of square calculation ($SS_W$).

**Note:** Most statistical software packages round numbers to three decimal places for an ANOVA; therefore, we are following that convention.

## Calculating the Within Group Sum of Squares ($SS_W$)

The **within groups sum of squares** is the sum of the squared deviations of each observation from its group mean.

The calculation for the **within group sum of squares** ($SS_W$) resembles the calculation of the sum of squares for estimating a variance (chapter 3). Referring back to the ANOVA table for our tweeting example (Figure 11.3), we want to calculate the $SS_W$ value, which was 108.500.

The formula for calculating the within group sums of squares is ($SS_W$):

$$SS_w = \Sigma(x_i - \bar{x}_i)^2 \qquad\qquad (11.4)$$

where: $x_i$ = the individual observation for each group

$\bar{x}_i$ = the mean for each group

You'll notice that this formula looks almost exactly the same as the formula for the sum of squares in chapter 3. The only difference is the subscript $i$ on $x_i$ and $\bar{x}_i$. The subscript refers to the individual groups and the observations in each group. Therefore, we subtract each individual score within a group ($x_i$) from its group mean ($\bar{x}_i$) and square the result for each observation ($x_i - \bar{x}_i)^2$. Then we sum ($\Sigma$) those values to get the total $SS_W$.

In the ANOVA table for our tweeting example (Figure 11.3) the value of the within group sum of squares ($SS_W$) was 108.500. This is the value that we are going to calculate here. The relevant pieces of information from Table 11.1 are repeated in Table 11.2 to make it easier to follow along with the equations for the next two calculations.

**TABLE 11.2**
**Four Month Twitter Statistics for Party Leaders**

| | Political Group Leader | | |
|---|---|---|---|
| | Conservative Leader "@pmharper" | Liberal Leader "@M_Ignatieff" | NDP Leader "@jacklayton" |
| September, 2010 | 8 | 15 | 19 |
| October, 2010 | 5 | 14 | 14 |
| November, 2010 | 6 | 13 | 18 |
| December, 2010 | 3 | 9 | 8 |
| Mean | $\bar{x}_1 = 5.50$ | $\bar{x}_2 = 12.75$ | $\bar{x}_3 = 14.75$ |
| Grand Mean | $\bar{\bar{x}} = 11.00$ | | |

Our calculation of the $SS_W$ is:

$$SS_w = \Sigma(x_i - \bar{x}_i)^2 \tag{11.5}$$

$$\begin{aligned} SS_w = &(8 - 5.50)^2 + (5 - 5.50)^2 + (6 - 5.50)^2 + (3 - 5.50)^2 \\ &+ (15 - 12.75)^2 + (14 - 12.75)^2 + (13 - 12.75)^2 + (9 - 12.75)^2 \\ &+ (19 - 14.75)^2 + (14 - 14.75)^2 + (18 - 14.75)^2 + (8 - 14.75)^2 \end{aligned}$$

$$\begin{aligned} SS_w = &(2.50)^2 + (-0.50)^2 + (0.50)^2 + (-2.50)^2 + (2.25)^2 + (1.25)^2 \\ &+ (0.25)^2 + (-3.75)^2 + (4.25)^2 + (-0.75)^2 + (3.25)^2 + (-6.75)^2 \end{aligned}$$

$$\begin{aligned} SS_w = &6.25 + 0.25 + 0.25 + 6.25 + 5.0625 + 1.5625 + 0.0625 + 14.0625 \\ &+ 18.0625 + 0.5625 + 10.5625 + 45.5625 \end{aligned}$$

$$SS_w = 108.50$$

Looking at the ANOVA table in Figure 11.3, we can see we have calculated the $SS_B$ correctly and can now calculate the total sum of squares.

## Calculating the Total Sum of Squares ($SS_T$)

Since we already know that the total sum of squares is:

Total Variance = Between Group Variance + Within Group Variance

We could simply add the $SS_B$ of 189.500 to the $SS_W$ of 108.500 to get our $SS_T$ of 298.000. Looking at the ANOVA table in Figure 11.3, we can confirm that this is correct. However, there is another way to calculate the total sum of squares ($SS_T$). Since the **total sum of squares** represents the total of the squared deviations of each case ($x_i$) from the grand mean ($\bar{\bar{x}}$) our formula is:

The **total sum of squares** is the sum of the squared deviations of each observation from the grand mean.

$$SS_T = \Sigma(x_i - \bar{\bar{x}}_i)^2 \tag{11.6}$$

where: $x_i$ = the individual observation for each group
$\bar{\bar{x}}_i$ = the grand mean

Therefore, with a grand mean $(\bar{\bar{x}})$ of 11.00 we get:

$$SS_T = \Sigma(x_i - \bar{\bar{x}}_i)^2 \qquad\qquad \textbf{(11.7)}$$

$$\begin{aligned} SS_T = \;&(8 - 11)^2 + (5 - 11)^2 + (6 - 11)^2 + (3 - 11)^2 + (15 - 11)^2 \\ &+ (14 - 11)^2 + (13 - 11)^2 + (9 - 11)^2 + (19 - 11)^2 + (14 - 11)^2 \\ &+ (18 - 11)^2 + (8 - 11)^2 \end{aligned}$$

$$\begin{aligned} SS_T = \;&(-3)^2 + (-6)^2 + (-5)^2 + (-8)^2 + (4)^2 + (3)^2 + (2)^2 \\ &+ (-2)^2 + (8)^2 + (3)^2 + (7)^2 + (-3)^2 \end{aligned}$$

$$SS_T = 9 + 36 + 25 + 64 + 16 + 9 + 4 + 4 + 64 + 9 + 49 + 9$$

$$SS_T = 298.000$$

Again, looking at the ANOVA table in Figure 11.3, we can see we have calculated the $SS_T$ correctly. The reason why we show both ways to calculate the $SS_T$ is that some people find it easier to calculate the $SS_T$ and the $SS_B$ and then subtract the $SS_B$ from the $SS_T$ to get the value for $SS_W$. But, since $SS_T = SS_B + SS_W$ you can now select any two calculations that you find the easiest and then add or subtract those two values as necessary to get the third value.

## Calculating the Degrees of Freedom

We have already covered the calculation for the degrees of freedom $(df)$, but in order to remain consistent with our replication of the ANOVA table in Figure 11.3, we will recalculate it. Looking at the table we see that the $df$ for the between groups is 2, the $df$ for the within groups is 9, and the total $df$ is 11. These are the values that we need to calculate. We also know that we have three groups and a sample size of 12.

We calculate the between group $df$ as:

$$\text{Between Groups Degrees of Freedom } (df_B) = k - 1 \quad \textbf{(11.8)}$$

where: $k$ = the number of groups

Therefore, our between groups $df$ is:

$$df_B = k - 1 = 3 - 1 = 2 \qquad\qquad \textbf{(11.9)}$$

We calculate the within groups $df$ as:

$$\text{Within Group Degrees of Freedom } (df_W) = n - k \quad \textbf{(11.10)}$$

where: $n$ = the total sample size
$k$ = the number of groups

Therefore, our within groups $df$ equals

$$df_W = n - k = 12 - 3 = 9 \qquad\qquad \textbf{(11.11)}$$

Since the total $df$ is equal to the between groups $df$ plus the within groups $df$, our total $df$ is 11 (2 + 9). Recall that our sample size is 12. It is not a coincidence that the total $df$ is 1 less than our sample size. In fact, you can also calculate the total $df$ using $n - 1$.

When you see the degrees of freedom for an ANOVA reported in a research paper, you can calculate the number of groups and sample size from that information. For example, if you read F(3,30), you know that they had four groups ($k - 1$) and a sample size of 34 ($n - k$).

## Calculating the Mean Sum of Squares

Before we start working with the formulas for the mean sum of squares for the between groups ($MS_B$) and the within groups ($MS_W$), it is worth spending a bit of time discussing the concept.

Recall from chapter 3 that we calculate the sample variance as…

$$s^2 = \frac{\Sigma(x - \bar{x})^2}{n - 1} = \frac{\text{Sum of the squares}}{n - 1} \qquad \textbf{(11.12)}$$

… and that by dividing the sum of squares by $n - 1$ we get an estimate of the average variability (variance) within the data. Now recall that we said the *F*-Ratio is the ratio of between group variance to within group variance.

The **mean sum of squares for between groups** ($MS_B$) is the estimated variance for the between groups and the **mean sum of squares for within groups** ($MS_W$) is the estimated variance for the within groups. This creates two important definitions that are key to understanding an ANOVA:

The **mean sum of squares for between groups** represents the between group variance.

1. The mean sum of squares for between groups ($MS_B$) is an estimate of the average variability between the groups. Therefore, it represents the between group variance.

The **mean sum of squares for within groups** represents the within group variance.

2. The mean sum of squares for the within groups ($MS_W$) is an estimate of the average variability within the groups. Therefore, it represents the within group variance.

Now that you know what the mean sum of squares is, how do you calculate it for both the between groups and within groups?

### *Calculating the Mean Sum of Squares for Between Groups (MS_B )*

Think back again to the formula for variance. The sum of squares is in the numerator and the sample size ($n$) $-1$ is in the denominator. It is the denominator that gives us the average variance. The same is true for the $MS_B$ except that $k - 1$ [the degrees of freedom for the between group ($df_B$)] is in the denominator rather than $n - 1$.

$$\frac{\text{Mean Squares for}}{\text{Between Groups}} = \frac{\text{Sum of Squares for Between Groups}}{\text{Degrees of Freedom for Between Groups}} \qquad \textbf{(11.13)}$$

More formally, we write it as:

$$MS_B = \frac{SS_B}{df_B} \quad \text{or} \quad MS_B = \frac{SS_B}{(k - 1)} \qquad \textbf{(11.14)}$$

Looking at the ANOVA table in Figure 11.3, our mean sum of squares for the between groups is 94.750. Using the formula and our previous results we get...

$$MS_B = \frac{SS_B}{df_B} = \frac{189.500}{2} = 94.750 \qquad \textbf{(11.15)}$$

...which is correct.

### *Calculating the Mean Sum of Squares for Within Groups ($MS_w$)*

The same logic behind the $MS_B$ applies to the mean sum of squares for the within groups ($MS_W$). This time, since we are dealing with the within groups, we use the degrees of freedom for the within group ($df_W$) in the denominator:

$$\frac{\text{Mean Squares for}}{\text{Within Groups}} = \frac{\text{Sum of Squares for Within Groups}}{\text{Degrees of Freedom for Within Groups}} \qquad \textbf{(11.16)}$$

More formally, we write it as:

$$MS_W = \frac{SS_W}{df_W} \quad \text{or} \quad MS_W = \frac{SS_W}{(n - k)} \qquad \textbf{(11.17)}$$

Looking at the ANOVA table in Figure 11.3, our mean sum of squares for the within groups is 12.056. Using the formula and our previous results we get...

$$MS_W = \frac{SS_W}{df_W} = \frac{108.500}{9} = 12.056 \qquad \textbf{(11.18)}$$

...which is correct.

## Calculating and Interpreting the *F*-Ratio

### *Calculating the F-Ratio*

Now we are ready to return to where we started, the *F*-Ratio. We have discussed the meaning of the *F*-Ratio and how to interpret it, but we haven't calculated it. Earlier we said that the *F*-Ratio is:

$$F\text{-Ratio} = \frac{\text{Between Group Variance}}{\text{Within Group Variance}} \qquad \textbf{(11.19)}$$

Now that we know what the between group variance and the within group variance are, we can be more specific with the formula. The *F*-Ratio is calculated as:

$$F\text{-Ratio} = \frac{\text{Mean Sum of Squares Between}}{\text{Mean Sum of Squares Within}} \quad \text{or} \quad F\text{-Ratio} = \frac{MS_B}{MS_W} \qquad \textbf{(11.20)}$$

Looking at the ANOVA table in Figure 11.3, the *F*-Ratio is 7.859. Using the formula we get...

$$F\text{-Ratio} = \frac{MS_B}{MS_W} = \frac{94.750}{12.056} = 7.859 \qquad \textbf{(11.21)}$$

...which is correct.

*Interpreting the F-Ratio*

We previously stated that the *F*-Ratio tested our null hypothesis of no difference. Using our tweeting example, our null and alternative hypotheses were:

$$H_0: \mu_1 = \mu_2 = \mu_3$$
$$H_A: \mu_1 \neq \mu_2 \neq \mu_3$$

Looking at the table of critical values for the *f*-distribution with an alpha ($\alpha$) of 0.05 (Appendix C), we find that the critical value of *f* for 2 and 9 *df* is 4.26. Given that our *F*-ratio ($F = 7.859$) is greater than the critical value ($7.859 > 4.26$), we can reject the null hypothesis of no difference. More specifically, we can state: "Based on our data, there is evidence to suggest that at least one of the groups is different from the others. Our *F*-ratio is $F(2,9) = 7.859$."

It is important to note that our findings suggest that there is a difference in the group means, but they don't tell us which groups differ. It could be that there is a difference between the mean number of tweets between the Conservative and Liberal leaders, and the Conservative and NDP leaders, but not the Liberal and NDP leaders. Basically, we just don't know. An ANOVA test only tells us if there is a difference between at least one of the group means and the others. In order for us to determine which groups differ from one another we need to perform a post-hoc test, which we will briefly discuss at the end of this chapter.

What would happen to our results if we had chosen an alpha ($\alpha$) of 0.01 instead of 0.05? To determine this, we need to look up the critical value for $F(2,9)$ when alpha ($\alpha$) is 0.01 and then make the decision regarding the null hypothesis. To help you in making the fail to reject or reject decision, consider Figure 11.6, which

**FIGURE 11.6**
**The Fail to Reject and Reject Regions of the *F*-Distribution**

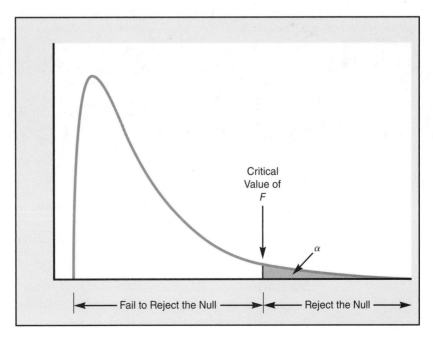

Critical Value of *F*

$\alpha$

Fail to Reject the Null          Reject the Null

shows the fail to reject and reject regions of the $F$-Distribution. Looking up the critical value of $F(2,9)$ with an alpha ($\alpha$) of 0.01 (Appendix B), the critical value of $F$ is 8.02. In this case, we would fail to reject the null hypothesis. More specifically we can state: "Based on our data, there is no evidence to suggest that at least one of the groups is different from the others. Our $F$-ratio is $F(2,9) = 7.859$."

**Note:** When we report the $F$-ratio, we usually write it as $F(2,9) = 7.859$, although some disciplines subscript the degrees of freedom ($df$) value so that it reads $F_{(2,9)} = 7.859$.

## Did You Know?

Imagine you are on the third floor of a 10-story building and you want to go to the seventh floor. You push the up button and wait for an elevator to arrive. What usually happens when the first elevator arrives? You'll probably find that the first one that arrives is almost always going the wrong way, and you'll hesitate in front of the elevator door while trying to decide whether to get in. This phenomenon, referred to as the Elevator Paradox, was first described by physicists Gamow and Stern in their 1958 book called *Puzzle Math*.

Why does this happen? Imagine that the graphic below represents the number of floors in a

building with only one elevator (it gets messy otherwise).

If you are on the third floor, then there are nine remaining floors, seven of which are above you. Therefore, approximately 78 percent ($7 \div 9$) of the time the elevator is more likely to be going down. As such, it will seem like the first elevator to arrive is always going the wrong way.

**Sources:** (1) Donald D. Spencer, *Game Playing with Computers* (New York: Spartan Books, 1968, p. 237); (2) Weisstein, Eric. W. "Elevator Paradox." From MathWorld—A Wolfram Web Resource, http://mathworld.wolfram.com/ElevatorParadox.html.

| Floors: | 1 | 2 | 3 | 4 | 5 | 6 | 7 | 8 | 9 | 10 |

---

**LO6**

## Example of an ANOVA Test

We'll use the following example and our five steps for hypothesis testing to work through hypothesis testing using an ANOVA test.

To make it easier to find the formulas, Table 11.3 compiles them in to a single ANOVA table.

## Scenario:

Suppose you are interested in determining if automobile drivers who have had their drivers' licenses revoked for drinking and driving differ by age group in the

**TABLE 11.3**
**ANOVA Formulas**

| Source | Sum of Squares | df | Mean Sum of Squares | F-Ratio |
|---|---|---|---|---|
| Between Groups | $\Sigma n_i (\bar{x}_i - \bar{\bar{x}})^2$ | $k - 1$ | $\dfrac{SS_B}{df_B}$ | $\dfrac{MS_B}{MS_W}$ |
| Within Groups | $\Sigma (x_i - \bar{x}_i)^2$ | $n - k$ | $\dfrac{SS_W}{df_W}$ | |
| Total | $\Sigma (x_i - \bar{\bar{x}}_i)^2$ or $SS_B + SS_W$ | $n - 1$ or $df_B + df_W$ | | |

number of non-alcohol related traffic violations they received prior to losing their licenses. Our age groups are 18 to 22, 23 to 27, and 28 to 32. From a database, we randomly select five individuals for each age group. Our data is as follows:

**TABLE 11.4**
**Age Groups and Number of Violations**

| 18 to 22 | 23 to 27 | 28 to 32 |
|---|---|---|
| 2 | 4 | 4 |
| 4 | 4 | 6 |
| 4 | 5 | 6 |
| 5 | 6 | 6 |
| 5 | 6 | 8 |
| $\bar{x}_1 = 4$ | $\bar{x}_1 = 5$ | $\bar{x}_1 = 6$ |
| $s_2^2 = 1.5$ | $s_1^2 = 1.0$ | $s_1^2 = 2.0$ |
| $n_1 = 5$ | $n_1 = 5$ | $n_1 = 5$ |

The grand mean is

$$\left( \bar{\bar{x}} = \frac{2 + 4 + 4 + 5 + 5 + 4 + 4 + 5 + 6 + 6 + 4 + 6 + 6 + 6 + 8}{15} = 5 \right) \quad \textbf{(11.22)}$$

For this scenario we will test the alternative hypothesis that there is a significant difference in at least one of these groups. For this test we will use an alpha ($\alpha$) of 0.05.

**Step 1:** Define the null and alternative hypotheses.

$$H_0: \mu_1 = \mu_2 = \mu_3$$
$$H_A: \mu_1 \neq \mu_2 \neq \mu_3$$

**Step 2:** Define the sampling distribution and critical values.
Unlike the independent sample *t*-test, the ANOVA test does not have a mean difference that represents a point estimate. However, it still has a sampling

distribution: the *F*-distribution. We use the *F*-distribution to determine the critical value. Since you need the degrees of freedom (*df* ) to obtain the critical value of *F*, it is helpful to create the ANOVA table at this point:

| Source | Sum of Squares | df | Mean Sum of Squares | F-Ratio |
|---|---|---|---|---|
| Between Groups | | 2 | | |
| Within Groups | | 12 | | |
| Total | | 14 | | |

Our between groups *df* is calculated as:

$$df_B = k - 1 = 3 - 1 = 2 \qquad (11.23)$$

Our within groups *df* is calculated as:

$$df_W = n - k = 15 - 3 = 12 \qquad (11.24)$$

Using Appendix C, our critical value for an alpha ($\alpha$) of 0.05 with $F(2,12) = 3.88$. This means that we will reject the null hypothesis if we observe an *F*-value greater than the critical value of 3.88.

**Step 3:** Calculate the test statistic using the sample data.
First we need to calculate the squared deviations for each observation as shown below.

| Group | 18 to 22 | | | 23 to 27 | | | 28 to 32 | | |
|---|---|---|---|---|---|---|---|---|---|
| | $x$ | $(x - \bar{x}_1)$ | $(x - \bar{x}_1)^2$ | $x$ | $(x - \bar{x}_2)$ | $(x - \bar{x}_2)^2$ | $x$ | $(x - \bar{x}_3)$ | $(x - \bar{x}_3)^2$ |
| | 2 | −2 | 4 | 4 | −1 | 1 | 4 | −2 | 4 |
| | 4 | 0 | 0 | 4 | −1 | 1 | 6 | 0 | 0 |
| | 4 | 0 | 0 | 5 | 0 | 0 | 6 | 0 | 0 |
| | 5 | 1 | 1 | 6 | 1 | 1 | 6 | 0 | 0 |
| | 5 | 1 | 1 | 6 | 1 | 1 | 8 | 2 | 4 |
| Totals | 20 | 0 | 6 | 25 | 0 | 4 | 30 | 0 | 8 |
| sample sizes ($n_i$) | 5 | | | 5 | | | 5 | | |
| means ($\bar{x}_i$) | 4 | | | 5 | | | 6 | | |

The Grand Mean ($\bar{\bar{x}}$) is: 5 (calculated in equation 11.22).

In the interest of space we have included only a portion of the calculation:

$$SS_B = \Sigma n_i(\bar{x}_i - \bar{\bar{x}})^2 = 5(4-5)^2 + 5(5-5)^2 + 5(6-5)^2 = 10.000 \textbf{ (11.25)}$$

$$SS_W = \Sigma(x_i - \bar{x}_i)^2 = (2-4)^2 + (4-4)^2 + \cdots$$
$$+ (6-6)^2 + (8-6)^2 = 18.000$$

$$SS_T = SS_B + SS_W = 10 + 18 = 28.000$$

$$MS_B = \frac{SS_B}{df_B} = \frac{10}{2} = 5$$

$$MS_W = \frac{SS_W}{df_W} = \frac{18}{12} = 1.5$$

$$F\text{-Ratio} = \frac{MS_B}{MS_W} = \frac{5}{1.5} = 3.33$$

We can now finish our ANOVA table:

| Source | Sum of Squares | df | Mean Sum of Squares | F-Ratio |
|---|---|---|---|---|
| Between Groups | 10.000 | 2 | 5 | 3.33 |
| Within Groups | 18.000 | 12 | 1.5 | |
| Total | 28.000 | 14 | | |

**Step 4:** Make the decision regarding the hypothesis.
Our *F*-Ratio was 3.33. The critical value for $F(2,12)$ for an alpha ($\alpha$) of 0.05 is 3.88. Since we observed an *F*-value of 3.33, which is less than 3.88, we conclude that we fail to reject the null hypothesis.

**Step 5:** Interpret the results.
Based on our sample, we fail to reject the null hypothesis. We did not find evidence to suggest that the means differ from one another. Our $F(2,12) = 3.33$. An important note to make here is that we have not proven that the group means are equal, only that they do not differ significantly. This is a subtle but important point.

---

**EXERCISE 11.2**

As an education researcher you are interested in understanding if student grades differ by the method in which the course is taught. You randomly select 20 students from one of four separate methods of delivering an introductory statistics course. These are (1) the course is taught by mail in distance education; (2) the course is taught by electronic distance education; (3) the course is taught in class with lectures only; and (4) the course is taught in class with lectures and labs. Final grades are calculated and recorded for each method (which is the group). The data is as follows.

| Group | 1 | | 2 | | 3 | | 4 | |
|---|---|---|---|---|---|---|---|---|
| | $x$ | $(x - \bar{x}_1)^2$ | $x$ | $(x - \bar{x}_2)^2$ | $x$ | $(x - \bar{x}_3)^2$ | $x$ | $(x - \bar{x}_4)^2$ |
| | 70 | 29.16 | 65 | 10.24 | 74 | 12.96 | 78 | 7.84 |
| | 74 | 1.96 | 66 | 4.84 | 77 | 0.36 | 79 | 3.24 |
| | 76 | 0.36 | 69 | 0.64 | 78 | 0.16 | 81 | 0.04 |
| | 78 | 6.76 | 70 | 3.24 | 79 | 1.96 | 82 | 1.44 |
| | 79 | 12.96 | 71 | 7.84 | 80 | 5.76 | 84 | 10.24 |
| Totals | 377 | 51.2 | 341 | 26.80 | 388 | 21.2 | 404 | 22.80 |
| Sample size ($n_i$) | 5 | | 5 | | 5 | | 5 | |
| Means ($\bar{x}_i$) | 75.4 | | 68.2 | | 77.6 | | 80.8 | |

GRAND MEAN ($\bar{\bar{x}}$) is 75.5

Conduct a one-way ANOVA and test the null hypothesis that there is no difference in the group means. Use an alpha ($\alpha$) of 0.05.

# Advanced Issues Relating to the ANOVA Test

**LO7**

One of the assumptions of a one-way ANOVA is that the population variances are equal across the groups (the assumption of homogeneity of variance). In this chapter, we assumed that this assumption was met. However, we can test whether we have met that assumption. One of the most widely-used tests for the assumption of homogeneity of variances is called the Levene's Test for Equal Variances. The Levene's test examines the null hypothesis that there is no difference in the population variances across the groups. The Levene's test is a separate ANOVA test (using residuals), which produces an $F$-ratio. If the $F$-ratio is less than the critical value of $F$ for the Levene's test, then we fail to reject the null hypothesis and assume that the variances are equal. If the $F$-ratio is greater than the critical value of $F$ for the Levene's test, then we reject the null hypothesis that the variances are equal and we assume that they are not equal. If the variances are not equal, we need to consider other methods for our data.[3] We will cover some of these alternative tests in chapter 13.

*More information about the Levene's test can be found in the supplemental material on Connect* ▓ connect

Another important issue regarding an ANOVA is the concept of post-hoc tests. As you have seen, an ANOVA can only determine if at least one of the group means differs from the others. It does not tell us which groups actually differ from each other. In our example of the political party leaders and their number of tweets, we found that there is a difference in the group means, but we also noted that we do not know which means are significantly different from one another. When we reject the null hypothesis using an ANOVA test, all we can say is that at least one of the group means differs from the others.

In order to determine which group means actually differ from one another, we need to perform a post-hoc test. The term "post-hoc" is Latin for "after this" and we use it to describe a test that we perform after the ANOVA test in order to look at actual group differences in means. There are several different post-hoc tests that can be done; however, the most common are Tukey's Honestly Significant Difference Test (or Tukey's HSD), Bonferroni's test, and the Scheffe test. Each of these tests performs a comparison of the group means and provides test statistics that allow us to determine which groups, if any, differ from each other.

*More information about Tukey's HSD, Bonferroni's test, and the Scheffe test can be found in the supplemental material on Connect*

## Conclusion

In this chapter we discussed the one-way analysis of variance test, ANOVA. The ANOVA test is useful for comparing group means and is widely used in the statistical analysis of experiments and surveys across many academic disciplines. More advanced versions of ANOVA allow us to analyze complex experimental designs including allowing for repeated measures across different groups. These more advanced topics unfortunately must be left for another textbook to cover.

All of the statistical tests we have dealt with so far have involved the comparison of means. But what if we are interested in measuring the association of two interval or ratio level variables? For example, is there an association between the number of police in a community and its level of crime? Or, what if we want to predict one interval or ratio level variable with another interval or ratio level variable? For example, can we predict a community's crime rate based on the number of police officers assigned to that community? These types of questions involve correlation and regression analysis, which is the subject of chapter 12.

## Key Chapter Concepts and Terms

ANOVA factor, 301
Grand mean, 304
Between Group
    Variance, 304
Within Group
    Variance, 304

*F*-Ratio, 307
Between group sum of
    squares, 311
Within groups sum of
    squares, 312
Total sum of squares, 313

Mean sum of squares for
    between groups, 315
Mean sum of squares for
    within groups, 315

**Frequently Asked Questions**

1. Can an ANOVA be used if we only have two groups?

   Yes. And in fact, it will give you the same results as an independent sample *t*-test.

2. How do we get the degrees of freedom (*df*) values?

   The between group degrees of freedom are calculated as the number of groups you have minus 1 or $(k - 1)$. The within group degrees of freedom are calculated as the total sample size minus the number of groups you have or $(n - k)$.

3. What is a post-hoc procedure?

   When we know ahead of time that we just want to compare two groups of interest, then we perform a *t*-test. But if we have no idea what the hypothesis will be until we look at the data, then we perform a post-hoc test (meaning after the data is collected).

4. I have seen other resources refer to between groups and within groups as between subjects and within subjects. Are they the same thing?

   Some disciplines, such as psychology and sometimes biology, will refer to the groups as subjects. This is really just a terminology difference. With respect to an ANOVA, the terms between groups and between subjects refer to the same thing. Similarly, within groups and within subjects refer to the same thing.

5. Is there an ANOVA equivalent to the paired sample *t*-test?

   Yes. It is called a repeated measures ANOVA. It allows you to have more than two dependent samples such as various time periods. So, for example, whereas the paired sample *t*-test can handle only two time periods, the repeated measures ANOVA can handle three or more time periods.

**Research Example:**

In their 2011 study, Montgomery and colleagues examined individual, social, health, and quality of life differences among women who had been diagnosed with mental health issues.[4] Of particular interest to the researchers was identifying the difference between women who either had young children, adult children, or no children. For the purposes of this example, we will examine whether there is a difference in "age of first contact with the mental health system" between these three groups. The data is as follows:

| Groups | With Young Children | With Adult Children | With No Children |
|---|---|---|---|
| Sample sizes | 68 | 58 | 108 |
| Means | 19.57 | 23.13 | 21.40 |
| Variances | 76.39 | 113.00 | 102.40 |

**Research Example Questions:**

**Question 1:** Why is this a one-way ANOVA?

**Question 2:** What is the grand mean?

**Question 3:** What is the mean sum of squares for the between groups ($MS_B$)?

**Question 4:** Assuming that the within group sum of squares ($SS_W$) equals 22,515.57, what is the sum of squares for the within group ($MS_W$)?

**Question 5:** Is there a significant difference between the groups at an alpha ($\alpha$) level of 0.05?

**Research Example Answers:**

**Question 1:** Why is this a one-way ANOVA?

This is a one-way ANOVA because you are comparing three means that come from independent samples and the means are being compared across the groups.

**Question 2:** What is the grand mean?

Since we have the group means and not individual values, we first need to convert the mean values to the sum of the individual values. Since the mean is equal to the sum of the numbers divided by the sample size, we can get the sum of the numbers by multiplying the mean for each group by its sample size. Therefore, the sum of the numbers for each group is:

With Young Children group is $19.57 \times 68 = 1,330.76$

With Adult Children group is $23.13 \times 58 = 1,341.54$

With No Children group is $21.40 \times 108 = 2,311.20$

The total sample size is $68 + 58 + 108 = 234$. So the grand mean is:

$$\bar{\bar{x}} = \frac{1,330.76 + 1,341.54 + 2,311.20}{234} = 21.29 \approx 21.30$$

**Question 3:** What is the mean sum of squares for the between groups ($MS_B$)? The between group sum of squares ($SS_B$) is:

$$
\begin{aligned}
SS_B &= \Sigma n_i(\bar{x}_i - \bar{\bar{x}})^2 \\
&= 68(19.57 - 21.30)^2 + 58(23.13 - 21.30)^2 + 108(21.40 - 21.30)^2 \\
&= 398.83
\end{aligned}
$$

With $k - 1 = 2$ $df$, the mean sum of squares for the between groups ($MS_B$) is:

$$MS_B = \frac{SS_B}{df_B} = \frac{398.83}{2} = 199.42$$

**Question 4:** Assuming that the within group sum of squares ($SS_W$) equals 22,515.57, what is the sum of squares for the within group ($MS_W$)?

With $n - k = 231$ $df$, the mean sum of squares for the within group ($MS_W$) is:

$$MS_W = \frac{SS_W}{df_W} = \frac{22,515.57}{231} = 97.47$$

**Question 5:** Is there a significant difference between the groups at an alpha level ($\alpha$) of 0.05?

The $F$-ratio is:

$$F\text{-Ratio} = \frac{MS_B}{MS_W} = \frac{199.42}{97.50} = 2.05$$

Given an alpha ($\alpha$) of 0.05, the critical value of $F(2,231)$ is approximately 3.07. As our $F$-ratio is less than the critical value ($2.05 < 3.07$), we fail to reject the null hypothesis of equal means. Therefore, the mean age of the first visit to the mental health system did not depend on the groups having young, adult, or no children.

---

**ANSWERS TO EXERCISE 11.1**

$F(4,55)$
$F(7,17)$
$F(3,98)$
$F(2,19)$
$F(6,119)$

---

**ANSWER TO EXERCISE 11.2**

**Step 1:** Define the null and alternative hypotheses.

$$H_0: \mu_1 = \mu_2 = \mu_3$$
$$H_A: \mu_1 \neq \mu_2 \neq \mu_3$$

**Step 2:** Define the sampling distribution and critical values.
Using an $F$-ratio with $(k - 1)$ and $(n - k)$ degrees of freedom, where $k = 4$ and $n = 20$, and an alpha ($\alpha$) of 0.05, we look up the critical $F$-value with 3 and 16 degrees of freedom. With $F(3,16)$ the critical value is 3.24. Therefore, we will reject the null hypothesis of equal means if we observe an $F$-ratio of more than 3.24.

**Step 3:** Calculate the test statistic using the sample data.

$$SS_B = \Sigma n_i (\bar{x}_i - \bar{\bar{x}})^2 = 5(75.4 - 75.5)^2 + 5(68.2 - 75.5)^2$$
$$+ 5(77.6 - 75.5)^2 + 5(80.8 - 75.5)^2$$
$$= 429.000$$

$$SS_T = \Sigma(x_i - \bar{\bar{x}}_i)^2 = (70 - 75.5)^2 + (74 - 75.5)^2 + \cdots + (84 - 75.5)^2 = 551.000$$

$$SS_W = \Sigma(x_i - \bar{x}_i)^2 \text{ or } SS_W = SS_T - SS_B = 122.000$$

$$MS_B = \frac{SS_B}{df_B} = \frac{429.000}{3} = 143.000$$

$$MS_W = \frac{SS_W}{df_W} = \frac{122.000}{16} = 7.625$$

$$F\text{-Ratio} = \frac{MS_B}{MS_W} = \frac{143.000}{7.625} = 18.75$$

Our calculations produce:

| Source | Sum of Squares | df | Mean Sum of Squares | F-Ratio |
|---|---|---|---|---|
| Between Groups | 429.000 | 3 | 143.000 | 18.754 |
| Within Groups | 122.000 | 16 | 7.625 | |
| Total | 551.000 | 19 | | |

**Step 4:** Make the decision regarding the hypothesis.
As the observed *F*-ratio of 18.75 is greater than the critical value of 3.24, we reject the null hypothesis of equal means.

**Step 5:** Interpret the results.
Based on our sample, we reject the null hypothesis. We can state that at least one of the group means differs from the others. Our result is $F(3,16) = 18.754$.

## Problems

1. Calculate the degrees of freedom (*df*) for the following *k* groups and *n* sample size. State your results as $F(\ ,\ )$ and provide the critical value for $F(\ ,\ )$ at the 5 percent level.

   a) $k = 5, n = 30$
   b) $k = 8, n = 15$
   c) $k = 4, n = 24$

2. Provincial employees in Ontario would like to know if there is a significant difference in the average number of employees answering calls at three government call centres. The data for the offices is given below. Answer the questions that follow relative to the data provided.

| York Centre | Dundas Centre | Dundee Centre |
|---|---|---|
| 7 | 10 | 1 |
| 14 | 1 | 12 |
| 32 | 1 | 1 |
| 19 | 0 | 9 |
| 10 | 11 | 1 |
| 11 | 1 | 11 |

   a) What are the null and alternative hypotheses for the test?
   b) What are the degrees of freedom (*df*) for the numerator and denominator?
   c) What are the between group sum of squares and within group sum of squares?
   d) What are the mean between group sum of squares and mean within group sum of squares?

e) Based on this information, what is the *F*-statistic and conclusion at the 5 percent level?

f) Fill in the table below with the information from a) through e).

| Source | Sum of Squares | df | Mean Sum of Squares | F-Ratio |
|---|---|---|---|---|
| Between Groups | | | | |
| Within Groups | | | | |
| Total | | | | |

3. A researcher would like to know if there is a difference between the type of food eaten and the time it takes to eat it. Individuals are asked to eat one of three types of food randomly and the length of time it takes to eat, in minutes, is recorded. The information for the subjects is shown below.

| Chicken | Beef | Pork |
|---|---|---|
| 3 | 10 | 8 |
| 6 | 12 | 3 |
| 7 | 11 | 2 |
| 4 | 14 | 5 |
| | 8 | |
| | 6 | |

a) Fill in the table below using the above data.

b) At the 5 percent level, is there enough evidence to conclude that individuals take the same time to eat all types of foods?

| Source | Sum of Squares | df | Mean Sum of Squares | F-Ratio |
|---|---|---|---|---|
| Between Groups | | | | |
| Within Groups | | | | |
| Total | | | | |

# Estimation and Hypothesis Testing IV: Bivariate Correlation and Regression

# 12

## Learning Objectives:

By the end of this chapter you should be able to:

1. Describe the association between two interval or ratio level variables.
2. Interpret a scatterplot.
3. Calculate and interpret Pearson's correlation coefficient ($r$).
4. Test hypotheses using Pearson's $r$.
5. Explain linear regression between two interval or ratio level variables.
6. Explain the least-squares regression criterion.
7. Calculate and interpret unstandardized and standardized beta coefficients.
8. Write and interpret a least-squares regression equation.
9. Test hypotheses using bivariate linear regression.

### Karl Pearson (1857–1936)

Born in England, Karl Pearson is known as one of the greatest contributors to the field of statistics. Deeply interested in the application of statistics to biological research and in particular evolution, he was the founder of biometrics (the statistical analysis of biological phenomena) and co-founder of the prestigious journal *Biometrika*.

During his time as a professor of statistics at University College London, Pearson coined the term "standard deviation" and developed some of the most common statistical methods, such as the

Pearson correlation coefficient and the Pearson chi-square goodness of fit test.[1]

## Introduction

In the last two chapters, we have concentrated on analyzing group differences in the means of an interval or ratio level dependent variable. In this chapter we will focus on what is referred to as association and prediction. This involves analyzing two variables, rather than just one, both of which are measured at the interval or ratio level. Analytical methods that include two variables are often referred to as bivariate methods. The term 'bivariate' simply means two variables. There are two types of bivariate analysis we will explore in this chapter: correlation and regression. Using correlation, we can measure the linear association between two interval or ratio level variables. Using regression, we can use one variable to try to predict the value of the other variable.

Correlation and regression have two different analytical purposes. If we are interested in determining if one variable is related to another, but we are not concerned with whether one predicts the other, then we are interested in bivariate correlation analysis. If we want to know if one variable can predict the value in the other, then we are interested in bivariate regression analysis. In both cases, we are asserting that there is a linear association between the two variables. Since this is a concept we have not explored yet, we'll start by explaining what is meant by linear association.

## Understanding Linear Association

**LO1**

Often, researchers are interested in understanding the degree to which two or more variables co-vary. For example, suppose you were interested in investigating how hours spent playing video games is related to academic performance. You might hypothesize that the more hours a person spends playing video

# Take A Closer Look

## Matching the Research Situation to the Type of Analysis

| Situation | Example | Statistical Test | Refer to... |
|-----------|---------|------------------|-------------|
| I need to estimate the population parameter based on my sample statistic. The variable is measured at the interval or ratio level. | You calculate the mean score of the Law School Admission Test (LSAT) for a random sample of students who did not study criminology during their undergraduate education, and you want to estimate what the mean LSAT score might be in the population of students who did not study criminology during their undergraduate education. | Confidence Intervals: Use confidence intervals when you need to make an inference about a population mean or proportion and you have a sample mean or proportion. | Chapter 8 |
| I calculated a mean based on data from one sample of respondents and want to compare it to a known mean such as the one I found in a published report. Both my variable and the one in the report are measured at the interval or ratio level. | You calculate the mean LSAT score of students in your university who just took the test. You want to test the alternative hypothesis that the mean score from your sample is higher than the mean LSAT score for all of Canada as published by the Law School Admission Council. | Single Sample Mean (or Proportion): Use a single sample test for a mean (or proportions when you have proportions) when you need to compare your sample mean to a known mean value. | Chapter 9 |
| I have two means from two independent samples and need to determine if they differ from one another. The variable is measured at the interval or ratio level. | Based on a random sample you have calculated the mean LSAT score for students from your university and the mean LSAT score for students from another university. You want to test the hypothesis that the mean score from your university is higher than the mean score of the other university. | Independent Sample *t*-Test: Use an independent sample *t*-test when you are comparing the means from two samples that are independent of each other. | Chapter 10 |
| I have two means from a paired sample and need to determine if they differ from one another. The variable is measured at the interval or ratio level. | Ten students took the LSAT exam last year and again this year. You want to test the hypothesis that the mean LSAT score from last year is lower than the mean LSAT score from this year. | Paired Sample *t*-Test: Use a paired sample *t*-test when you are comparing the means of samples that are not independent of one another. | Chapter 10 |
| I have three or more means from an independent sample and need to determine if they differ from one another. The variable is measured at the interval or ratio level. | Thirty students took the LSAT exam. Ten had studied political science in university, 10 had studied sociology, and 10 had studied management economics. You want to test the hypothesis that the mean LSAT score is different in at least one of the three groups. | One-way ANOVA: Use a one-way analysis of variance when you are comparing the means of three or more groups. | Chapter 11 |

| I have two variables and I want to see if there is an association between them. The variables are measured at the interval or ratio level. | Thirty students from your university took the LSAT preparation course prior to taking the LSAT exam. You want to test if the hours spent studying during the LSAT preparation course is associated with the scores on the LSAT exam. | Pearson's Correlation: Use Pearson's correlation (*r*) when you want to measure the association between two interval or ratio level variables. | Chapter 12 |
|---|---|---|---|
| I have two variables—independent and dependent—and I want to know if the independent variable predicts the dependent variable. The variables are measured at the interval or ratio level. | Twenty-five individuals wrote the LSAT exam today. You record their age and their LSAT score. You want to know if a person's age predicts his or her score on the LSAT exam. | Linear Regression: Use linear regression when you want to test if the scores in one variable predict the scores in a second variable. | Chapter 12 |

games, the lower his or her academic performance will be. Here we are saying that the variable "hours spent playing video games" is associated with the variable "academic performance," in that they vary in relation to one another. When two (or more) variables co-vary—that is, they vary together—we say that there is an **association** between them. That is, the variables have some sort of relationship between them that cause them to co-vary. For the time being we'll leave out why we call it "linear association" so that we can first understand the idea of association.

**Association** is the relationship between two or more variables that co-vary with one another.

**Note:** The terms "relationship" and "association" are often used interchangeably. We are doing the same here.

## LO2

A **scatterplot** is a graph that displays individual respondent (or subject) scores on two variables. One variable is represented on the *x*-axis and the other on the *y*-axis.

It is useful to use a **scatterplot** to visually inspect the association between two variables. For example, suppose we randomly selected 15 second year sociology students and recorded their final grade in their last high school math course and their final grade in their first year university math course. A scatterplot of the data (Table 12.1) is provided in Figure 12.1. Looking at the table you can see that the 7th respondent's final grades in her high school and university math courses respectively were 84.74 and 80.92. Similarly, we can see that the 14th respondent's final grades in his high school and university math courses respectively were 87.73 and 73.60.

An observation of two variables does not, by itself, show an association between two variables. You need a number of observations (scores for individuals on both variables) to help determine the association. However, by looking at the scatterplot in Figure 12.1, you can see that lower grades in a high school math course appear to be associated with lower grades in a university math course. Similarly,

**FIGURE 12.1** **Scatterplot of High School and University Math Grades**

**TABLE 12.1**
**Math Grade Data***

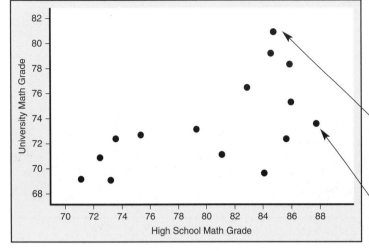

| | High School Math Grade(x) | University Math Grade(y) |
|---|---|---|
| 1 | 84.56 | 79.21 |
| 2 | 85.86 | 78.34 |
| 3 | 73.56 | 72.40 |
| 4 | 71.11 | 69.17 |
| 5 | 72.45 | 70.88 |
| 6 | 84.09 | 69.64 |
| 7 | 84.74 | 80.92 |
| 8 | 81.09 | 71.12 |
| 9 | 85.62 | 72.38 |
| 10 | 75.33 | 72.70 |
| 11 | 85.95 | 75.31 |
| 12 | 73.20 | 69.09 |
| 13 | 79.28 | 73.15 |
| 14 | 87.73 | 73.60 |
| 15 | 82.88 | 76.47 |

*This is fictitious data.

higher grades in a high school math course seem to be associated with higher grades in a university math course.

We can interpret the scatterplot by looking for a pattern that might suggest a direction that the plots of the data are following. The pattern and its direction tell us something about the relationship between the two variables. For example, in Figure 12.1 we see that the plot slopes upwards from the bottom of the *y*-axis. This suggests that as the value of the *x*-axis increases, the value of the *y*-axis also increases. When an increase in the first variable is associated with an increase in the second variable (or a decrease in the first variable is associated with a decrease in the second variable), we say that they are **positively associated**. More specifically, drawing on our example we can state that there appears to be a positive relationship (or positive association) between the two variables. As high school math grades increase so do the university math grades.

Two variables are considered **positively associated** when lower values of the first variable are found with lower values of the second variable, or higher values of the first variable with higher values of the second variable.

Figure 12.2 provides another example of two variables that are positively associated. In 2009, Statistics Canada reported the violent crime severity index for the 10 provinces. This is a police-reported index of the severity of violent crimes, with higher values indicating more violent crimes. Statistics Canada also reported the number of police officers per 100,000 people in each of the 10 provinces. The scatterplot in Figure 12.2 shows the relationship between severity of violent crimes (*x*-variable) and the number of police officers per 100,000 people (*y*-variable). By looking at the pattern of the data we can see that it slopes upwards from low values of *x* and *y* to high values of *x* and *y*. This suggests that there are fewer police officers in provinces with lower violent crime severity and more police officers in provinces with higher violent crime severity. In interpreting this information we might say that violent crime severity is positively related to the number of police officers per 100,000 people.

**FIGURE 12.2**
**Scatterplot of Crime Severity and Number of Police Officers**

Data Source: Statistics Canada, CANSIM, table 254-0002 and Statistics Canada, CANSIM table 252-0052.

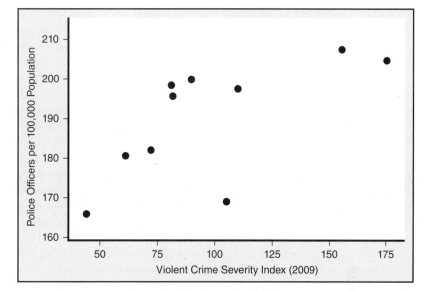

Before looking at Figure 12.3, imagine what the scatterplot might look like if the patterned indicated a negative relationship between the *x* and *y* variables. The pattern would show that lower values of the *x* variable coincide with higher values of the *y* variable, and higher values of the *x* variable with lower values of the *y* variable. In 2009, Aryn Karpinksi, a doctoral student at Ohio State University, found a negative relationship between the numbers of hours students spend on Facebook

**FIGURE 12.3**   **Scatterplot of Hours Studying and Spent on Facebook**

**TABLE 12.2**
**Study and Facebook Data***

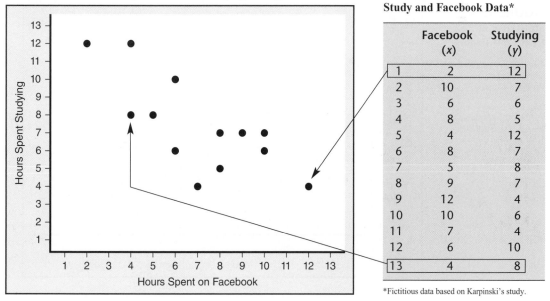

|  | Facebook (x) | Studying (y) |
|---|---|---|
| 1 | 2 | 12 |
| 2 | 10 | 7 |
| 3 | 6 | 6 |
| 4 | 8 | 5 |
| 5 | 4 | 12 |
| 6 | 8 | 7 |
| 7 | 5 | 8 |
| 8 | 9 | 7 |
| 9 | 12 | 4 |
| 10 | 10 | 6 |
| 11 | 7 | 4 |
| 12 | 6 | 10 |
| 13 | 4 | 8 |

*Fictitious data based on Karpinski's study.

and the number of hours they spend studying. Figure 12.3 represents fictitious data, created based on Karpinski's findings, that express the association between the two variables "hours spent on Facebook" and "hours spent studying."

Looking at the scatterplot in Figure 12.3, you can see that fewer hours spent on Facebook seems to be associated with more hours spent studying, whereas more hours spent on Facebook seems to be associated with fewer hours spent studying. As a result, we say that these two variables are **negatively associated** because an increase in the first variable is associated with a decrease in the second variable (or a decrease in the first variable is associated with an increase in the second variable).

We've now discussed the situations where two variables can be either negatively or positively associated, but what if there is no association between the two? Picturing the no-relationship case as a scatterplot is a little less intuitive than our previous examples. However, if you recall that patterns reveal that a relationship exists then lack of a pattern would suggest that no relationship exists. As such, changes in the *x*-value would not appear to be related to changes in the *y*-value. This is what we refer to as **no association** or no relationship.

Consider the scatterplot in Figure 12.4 of Statistics Canada's 2009 Charitable Donors data. Here the *x*-variable consists of the median income of those who donate to charities (separated into the 10 provinces) whereas the *y*-variable represents the median charitable donation amount (separated into the 10 provinces). The data point at the lowest median income (with just under a median donation of $350) is Newfoundland and Labrador, whereas the data point at the highest median income (a median donation between $350 and $400) is Alberta. Looking at the data point pattern we can see that lower median incomes seem to coincide with a level of median donation amounts similar to those with higher median

> Two variables are considered **negatively associated** when lower values of the first variable are found with higher values of the second variable, and vice versa.

> Two variables are considered to have **no association** when a change in the first variable does not coincide with a change in the second variable.

**FIGURE 12.4**
**Scatterplot of Charitable Donors**

Adapted from Statistics Canada publication *Family Violence in Canada: A Statistical Profile,* Catalogue 85-224-XIE2010000, http://www.statcan.gc.ca/pub/85-224-x2010000-eng.pdf. The values were pulled from Table 4.1 Homicides by sex and accused-victim relationship, Canada, 2000 to 2009.

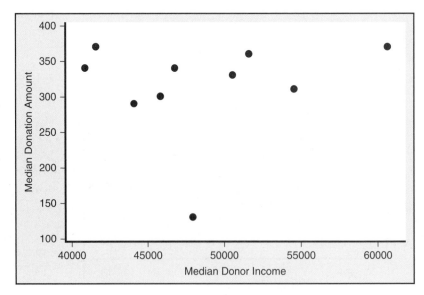

incomes. In other words, given that a change in median donor income does not seem to be associated with a change in median donation amount, we can state that it appears that the variables "median donor income" and "median donation amount" are not related.

## Linear versus Curvilinear Association

At the beginning of our discussion we decided to ignore the word "linear" in the term linear association so that we could focus on first understanding what we mean by association. As you have seen in the examples, we examined the pattern of the data in the scatterplot to determine the direction of the relationship (negative, positive, or none). As the association between two variables becomes stronger the data points come closer to forming a straight line. As such, we are interested in determining if the two variables follow a straight line such that their relationship has a constant proportionate amount of change between the two. That is to say, we want to know if the association (or relationship) between two variables is linear (meaning straight line). It is important that we distinguish the difference between a linear relationship and a curvilinear relationship. Consider Figure 12.5. Both scatterplots show a form of curvilinear relationship called a quadratic relationship. In a curvilinear relationship, the direction of the association between the two variables may change as the value of the *x*-variable increases.

**FIGURE 12.5**
**Scatterplot of a Curvilinear Relationship**

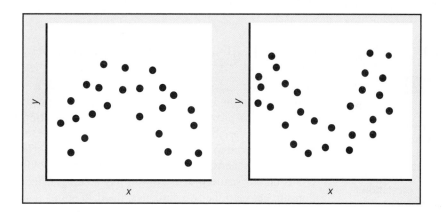

For example, Figure 12.6 provides a scatterplot of the relationship between adult literacy and the under-five-years-old mortality rate for 33 countries within the Sub-Sahara Africa region in 2008. As you can see, the relationship between the two variables is curvilinear. With literacy rates between 30 percent and 50 percent, the relationship seems to be almost non-existent. However, after literacy rates surpass 50 percent, the mortality rate seems to decrease at a much greater pace. Analyzing curvilinear relationships is out of the scope of this textbook but it is still important to be able to recognize the difference between linear and curvilinear relationships.

**FIGURE 12.6** **Scatterplot of Adult Literacy and Child Mortality**

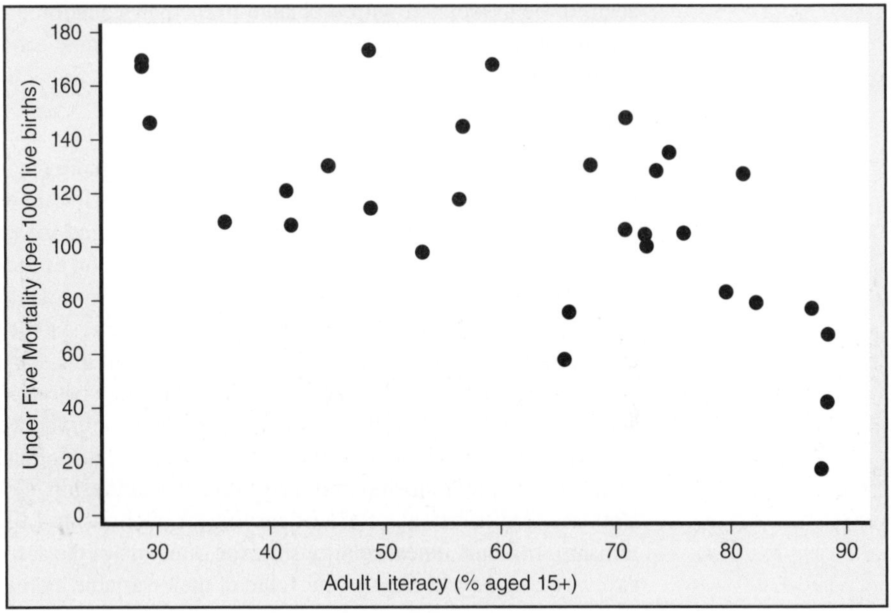

Source: United Nations Development Programme (UNDP) Human Development Reports Database 2008 Data

# Measuring the Strength of a Linear Association

**LO3**

The **strength of an association** is the degree to which two variables are associated.

The **correlation coefficient** is a numerical value representing the strength and direction of a linear association between two variables.

**Pearson's correlation coefficient** is the correlation coefficient most commonly used for measuring the association between two interval or ratio level variables.

So far we've covered two different characteristics of association: direction (negative, positive, and none) and type (linear and curvilinear). While these two characteristics provide us with important information about the relationship between two variables, they don't tell us the degree to which they are related. For this, we need to discuss the strength of a linear association. One way we can describe the **strength of an association** is by looking at how close the data points on our scatterplot are to forming a straight line. When there is no relationship between the two variables, the data points tend to be scattered widely across the plot. As the relationship between two variables strengthens, the pattern of the data points moves from being scattered to a more elliptical shape. When the data points form a perfect line we say that there is a "perfect" linear association between the two variables.

The problem with making a judgment about the strength of an association based on visual inspection is that our eyes can be fooled and so we can't necessarily rely on our visual perception. In order to more accurately describe the strength of an association we use a numeric value called the **correlation coefficient**. For interval and/or ratio level variables the most common correlation coefficient used by social scientists is the Pearson Product Moment Coefficient or **Pearson's correlation coefficient** for short. When estimating the correlation of two variables in the population we refer to Pearson's *rho* (with *rho* written using the Greek letter $\rho$), whereas when referring to the correlation in a sample we refer to it as Pearson's *r*. Since we are usually dealing with sample data as opposed to population data, we'll focus on Pearson's *r*.

## Estimating the Correlation Coefficient Using Pearson's *r*

There are a number of different ways to write the formula for estimating Pearson's *r*. Furthermore, how you estimate the coefficient depends on whether you are dealing with raw data scores or *z*-scores. When dealing with raw data the formula is often written as:

$$r = \frac{\Sigma xy - \left(\frac{\Sigma x \Sigma y}{n}\right)}{\sqrt{\left(\Sigma x^2 - \frac{(\Sigma x)^2}{n}\right)\left(\Sigma y^2 - \frac{(\Sigma y)^2}{n}\right)}} \qquad (12.1)$$

While this looks like a complicated formula, calculating it in steps makes it much easier to follow. For example, suppose we wanted to estimate Pearson's *r* for the high school and university math grade data that we introduced earlier. First, we calculate the values, as indicated in Table 12.3:

**TABLE 12.3** Calculating the Values Required to Estimate Pearson's *r*

| Participant | High School Math Grade<br>*x* | University Math Grade<br>*y* | *xy* | $x^2$ | $y^2$ |
|---|---|---|---|---|---|
| 1 | 84.56 | 79.21 | 6698.00 | 7150.39 | 6274.22 |
| 2 | 85.86 | 78.34 | 6726.27 | 7371.94 | 6137.16 |
| 3 | 73.56 | 72.40 | 5325.74 | 5411.07 | 5241.76 |
| 4 | 71.11 | 69.17 | 4918.68 | 5056.63 | 4784.49 |
| 5 | 72.45 | 70.88 | 5135.26 | 5249.00 | 5023.97 |
| 6 | 84.09 | 69.64 | 5856.03 | 7071.13 | 4849.73 |
| 7 | 84.74 | 80.92 | 6857.16 | 7180.87 | 6548.05 |
| 8 | 81.09 | 71.12 | 5767.12 | 6575.59 | 5058.05 |
| 9 | 85.62 | 72.38 | 6197.18 | 7330.78 | 5238.86 |
| 10 | 75.33 | 72.70 | 5476.49 | 5674.61 | 5285.29 |
| 11 | 85.95 | 75.31 | 6472.89 | 7387.40 | 5671.60 |
| 12 | 73.20 | 69.09 | 5057.39 | 5358.24 | 4773.43 |
| 13 | 79.28 | 73.15 | 5799.33 | 6285.32 | 5350.92 |
| 14 | 87.73 | 73.60 | 6456.93 | 7696.55 | 5416.96 |
| 15 | 82.88 | 76.47 | 6337.83 | 6869.09 | 5847.66 |
| $\Sigma$ | 1207.45 | 1104.38 | 89082.30 | 97668.63 | 81502.16 |
| Mean | 80.50 | 73.63 | | | |
| Standard deviation | 5.81 | 3.70 | | | |

Then, using the values from Table 12.2, our calculation becomes:

$$r = \frac{89082.3 - \left(\dfrac{1207.45 \times 1104.38}{15}\right)}{\sqrt{\left(97{,}668.63 - \dfrac{(1207.45)^2}{15}\right)\left(81502.16 - \dfrac{(1104.38)^2}{15}\right)}} \quad \textbf{(12.2)}$$

$$= \frac{183.39}{\sqrt{477.93 \times 191.81}} = 0.609$$

Pearson's correlation coefficient (both $\rho$ and $r$) have a range of $-1.00$ to $+1.00$, where $-1.00$ equates to a perfect negative linear relationship, $0.00$ represents no relationship, and $+1.00$ represents a perfect positive linear relationship. While there are no definitive rules stating when Pearson's $r$ value represents a strong versus weak relationship, Table 12.4 provides a rough guide for interpreting the coefficient. By examining Figure 12.7, you can also see how Pearson's $r$ and the

**TABLE 12.4**
**Interpretation of Pearson's $r$**

Source: This table is based on De Vaus (2002, p. 259 Box 14.6).

| Value (+ and −) | Description |
|---|---|
| 0.00 | No relationship |
| 0.01–0.10 | Very weak |
| 0.11–0.25 | Weak to moderate |
| 0.26–0.50 | Moderate to strong |
| 0.51–0.75 | Strong |
| 0.76–0.85 | Very strong |
| 0.85+ | Almost perfect |

**FIGURE 12.7**   **Scatterplots and Pearson's $r$**

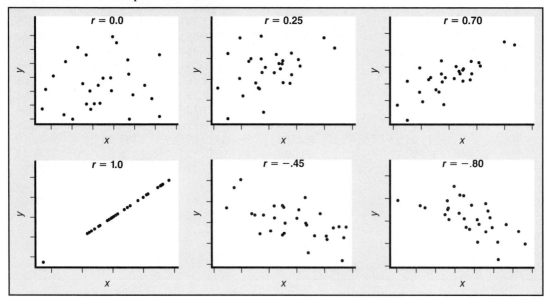

## Take a Closer Look

**Estimating Pearson's r using z-scores**
Equation 12.1 represents how we calculate Pearson's r when using raw scores. If we are working with data
that has been converted to z-scores, the formula is as shown in equation 12.3.

$$r = \frac{\sum z_X z_Y}{n} \qquad \textbf{(12.3)}$$

scatterplot are connected. Notice how stronger relationships have data points that
are closer to forming a straight line. Using our high school and university math
grade examples, we found that the two variables were positively related with a
Pearson's r of 0.609; that's a strong correlation.

LO4

## Hypothesis Testing Using Pearson's r

Using Pearson's r, we can test hypotheses about the relationship between two or
more variables. Suppose we want to test a hypothesis about the relationship between
our high school and university math grades. We can use our Five Steps of Hypothesis Testing (from chapter 7 to accomplish this).

**Step 1:** Define the null and alternative hypotheses.

$$H_0: \rho = 0$$
$$H_A: \rho \neq 0$$

Note that we are using *rho* ($\rho$) in our hypotheses. This is because we are hypothesizing ($H_A$) that in the population from which our sample came, the population
correlation ($\rho$) between high school math grades and university math grades is
not zero. Similarly, the null hypothesis is that there is no relationship, meaning
that *rho* ($\rho$) is zero.

**Step 2:** Define the sampling distribution and critical values.
When defining the sampling distribution for r, we use the t-distribution. To determine the standard error for r, we use the following formula:

$$s_r = \sqrt{\frac{1 - r^2}{n - 2}} \qquad \textbf{(12.4)}$$

Based on our sample, the standard error of r is:

$$s_r = \sqrt{\frac{1 - r^2}{n - 2}} = \sqrt{\frac{1 - (0.609)^2}{15 - 2}} = \sqrt{\frac{0.629}{13}} = 0.220 \quad \textbf{(12.5)}$$

With an alpha ($\alpha$) of 0.05 and the hypothesis being two-tailed, the critical value
of $t_{(\alpha = 0.05)}$ is $\pm 2.160$ with 13 degrees of freedom (*df*). For a refresher on degrees

of freedom, refer back to chapter 8. In this case we have two variables, so our degrees of freedom are:

$$n - 2 = 15 - 2 = 13 \qquad (12.6)$$

**Step 3:** Calculate the test statistic using the sample data.

To calculate the test statistic ($t$-value), we divide our sample $r$ value by the standard error of $r$ as follows:

$$t = \frac{r}{\sqrt{\dfrac{1 - r^2}{n - 2}}} = \frac{0.609}{0.220} = 2.77 \qquad (12.7)$$

**Step 4:** Make the decision regarding the hypothesis.

The test statistic of $t = 2.77$ is past the critical value $t_{(\alpha = 0.05)} = \pm 2.160 (2.77 > 2.160)$; therefore, you reject the null hypothesis and state that the correlation is significantly different from zero.

**Step 5:** Interpret the results.

The correlation (using Pearson's $r$) between high school math grades and university math grades is positive and statistically significant ($r = 0.609$). Therefore, we can say that, based on this sample, there is positive association between the high school math grade and the university math grade.

## Summarizing Pearson's *r*

In summarizing our discussion on association and correlation there are a few points worth reiterating. First, when we want to know if there is a relationship between two variables, what we are asking is if there is an association between the two. While we can visually inspect the scatterplot to determine the type, direction, and strength of an association, we will get a much more accurate understanding of the relationship by using Pearson's $r$. When dealing with association and the correlation coefficient ($r$) we are not concerned about which variable is the dependent versus independent. It is important to remember that when we use correlation as an analysis method we are not attempting to determine if one variable predicts another, we are simply trying to establish whether a relationship exists. If we want to test hypotheses that specify prediction—where an independent variable predicts the change in a dependent variable—then we need to move beyond correlation and into regression.

**EXERCISE 12.1**

For the *x*- and *y*-variable, shown below, compute the correlation coefficient *r*, and test that the population correlation is significantly different from 0.

| *x* | 1 | 3 | 4 | 4 | 5 | 8 |
|-----|---|---|---|---|----|----|
| *y* | 2 | 5 | 9 | 8 | 13 | 18 |

# Linear Regression

**LO5**

With correlation analysis we are not concerned about distinguishing between the independent and dependent variables because we are simply trying to establish if the variables co-vary with one another. However, if we know that two variables have a linear relationship we can use linear regression to try to predict the value of one variable by knowing the value of a second variable.

Suppose we were to hypothesize that a person's high school math grade (the independent variable $x$) is a predictor of the university math grade (the dependent variable $y$). We could create a scatterplot of the data, and determine the value of Pearson's $r$ ($r = 0.609$), as we did in the previous section. However, as seen in Figure 12.8, we could also add a regression line that represents the linear association between the independent and dependent variable. The problem in drawing the **regression line** is that we need to create a line that best represents the association between the two variables. As you can see (in Figure 12.8), unless there is a perfect relationship between $x$ (independent variable) and $y$ (dependent variable), there is no way we can draw a straight line that goes through each data point in the scatterplot.

Therefore, in establishing our regression line, what we need to do is draw the line such that it minimizes the vertical distances between the data points and our regression line. Here's how we do that:

We want our regression line to represent our prediction of the value of $y$ (written as $\hat{y}$ and pronounced "$y$-hat") based on knowing the value of $x$. Formally, we refer to

A **regression line** is a line of best fit that describes the linear association between an independent and dependent variable.

**FIGURE 12.8**
**Scatterplot and Regression Line**

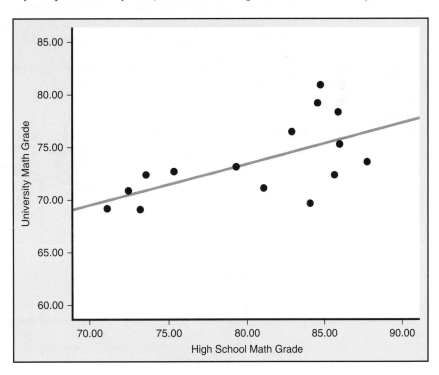

**FIGURE 12.9**
**Predicting University Math Grade Using High School Math Grade**

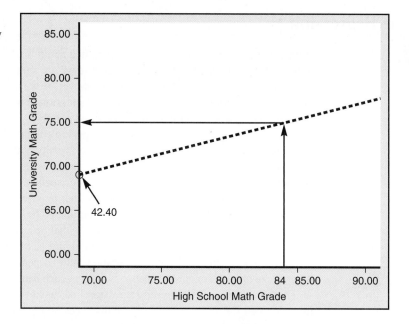

this as regressing $y$ on $x$ or, in our example, regressing university math grade on high school math grade. For example, looking at Figure 12.9, based on our regression line we predict that an individual who received an 84 ($x$-value) in his high school math course would achieve a grade of 75 ($\hat{y}$-value) in his first year university math course. However, as you can see in Figure 12.10, sometimes we accurately predict

**FIGURE 12.10**
**Predicting University Math Grade Using High School Math Grade**

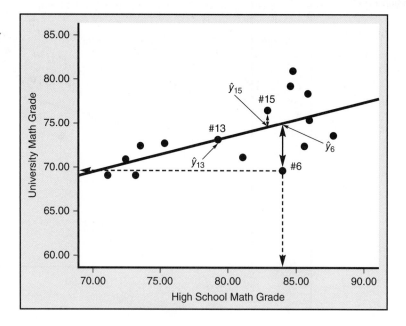

the value of the university math grade ($\hat{y}_{13}$ for participant #13), sometimes we over-predict the value ($\hat{y}_6$ for participant #6), and sometimes we under-predict the value ($\hat{y}_{15}$ for participant #15). Therefore, try as we might, our prediction of $\hat{y}$ contains errors and thus does not always equal the actual value of $y$.

## LO6  LO7

## Least-Squares Regression Criterion

A **least-squares regression line** is a regression line that minimizes the sum of the squared distances between the observations and the line itself.

We can minimize the amount of error in our prediction by drawing our regression line using the **least-squares regression** criterion. To picture how this works, imagine measuring the vertical distance between each observed value and the regression line, squaring each of those distances, and then adding them up to one number called the sum of the squares. In least-squares regression we draw the line in such a way that we get the lowest (or least) sum of the squares value.

We can describe this line (drawn using the least-squares criterion) using the following equation:

$$\hat{y} = \alpha + bx \qquad\qquad \textbf{(12.8)}$$

where: $\hat{y}$ = the predicted value of the dependent $y$-variable

$\quad\alpha$ = the intercept, meaning the value of $y$ when $x$ equals 0

$\quad b$ = the slope of the regression line, representing the change in $y$ due to the change in $x$

$\quad x$ = observed value of the independent variable.

We read this equation as follows: Our predicted value equals the intercept plus the slope of the regression line times the observed value of $x$.

An **intercept ($\alpha$)** is the constant in the regression equation. It represents the value of $y$ when $x$ equals 0.

The **intercept** is a constant in the equation. It tells us that no matter what the value of $bx$ is, we need to add the value of the intercept in order to predict the value of $y$. This is because (as in Figure 12.9) the location where our regression line intercepts the $y$-axis is the location where $x = 0$ but $y$ still has a value. In our example, the intercept is 42.40, meaning that based on our prediction, if an individual received a grade of 0 in high school math, he or she would receive a grade of 42.40 in university math. To calculate the intercept, we need the beta value ($b$), so we'll start there first.

**Beta ($b$)** represents the slope of the regression line. It tells us how the value of $y$ changes in relation to a one-unit change in the value of $x$.

**Beta** represents the slope of the regression line. This tells us how the $y$-value changes in relation to a one-unit change in the $x$-value. If $b$ is positive, we know that when $x$ increases, $y$ increases by the value of the slope times the value of $x$, plus the intercept. If $b$ is negative, then as $x$ increases, $y$ decreases by the value of the slope times the value of $x$, plus the intercept. If $b = 0$, then the line is flat, indicating no relationship between $x$ and $y$. When working with raw data scores for $x$ and $y$, we can estimate $b$ using the following equation:

$$b = \frac{\Sigma xy - \dfrac{(\Sigma x)(\Sigma y)}{n}}{\Sigma x^2 - \dfrac{(\Sigma x)^2}{n}} \qquad\qquad \textbf{(12.9)}$$

First, we calculate the values, as indicated in Table 12.5:

**TABLE 12.5** Calculating the Values Required to Estimate Beta ($b$)

| Participant | High School Math Grade $x$ | University Math Grade $y$ | $xy$ | $x^2$ | $y^2$ |
|---|---|---|---|---|---|
| 1 | 84.56 | 79.21 | 6698.00 | 7150.39 | 6274.22 |
| 2 | 85.86 | 78.34 | 6726.27 | 7371.94 | 6137.16 |
| 3 | 73.56 | 72.4 | 5325.74 | 5411.07 | 5241.76 |
| 4 | 71.11 | 69.17 | 4918.68 | 5056.63 | 4784.49 |
| 5 | 72.45 | 70.88 | 5135.26 | 5249.00 | 5023.97 |
| 6 | 84.09 | 69.64 | 5856.03 | 7071.13 | 4849.73 |
| 7 | 84.74 | 80.92 | 6857.16 | 7180.87 | 6548.05 |
| 8 | 81.09 | 71.12 | 5767.12 | 6575.59 | 5058.05 |
| 9 | 85.62 | 72.38 | 6197.18 | 7330.78 | 5238.86 |
| 10 | 75.33 | 72.7 | 5476.49 | 5674.61 | 5285.29 |
| 11 | 85.95 | 75.31 | 6472.89 | 7387.40 | 5671.60 |
| 12 | 73.2 | 69.09 | 5057.39 | 5358.24 | 4773.43 |
| 13 | 79.28 | 73.15 | 5799.33 | 6285.32 | 5350.92 |
| 14 | 87.73 | 73.6 | 6456.93 | 7696.55 | 5416.96 |
| 15 | 82.88 | 76.47 | 6337.83 | 6869.09 | 5847.66 |
| $\Sigma$ | 1207.45 | 1104.38 | 89082.3 | 97668.63 | 81502.16 |
| Mean | 80.5 | 73.63 | | | |
| Standard deviation | 5.81 | 3.70 | | | |

Then, using those values we get:

$$b = \frac{\Sigma xy - \frac{(\Sigma x)(\Sigma y)}{n}}{\Sigma x^2 - \frac{(\Sigma x)^2}{n}} = \frac{89082.30 - \frac{1207.45 \times 1104.38}{15}}{97668.63 - \frac{1207.45^2}{15}} \quad \textbf{(12.10)}$$

$$= \frac{183.39}{472.93} = 0.388$$

The **unstandardized beta coefficient ($b$)** is the value of the slope of the regression line in the raw score values (units).

Since we used raw scores in this calculation, as opposed to standardized scores ($z$-scores), we call this beta value ($b$) the **unstandardized beta coefficient**. We interpret this unstandardized $b$ as follows. A one-unit increase in the independent variable corresponds to a 0.388 unit increase in the dependent variable. So a one-unit (1 grade percent) increase in a high school math score corresponds to a 0.388 unit (0.388 of 1 grade percent) increase in a university math score. It often makes more sense to calculate the slope using standardized scores. This not only allows for better comparisons across studies where the units of measurement may be different, but also makes it easier to interpret the slope of the regression line if the units of measurement differ between the independent and dependent variables. When calculating the slope using standardized scores (creating the **standardized beta coefficient**, which is often written as $\beta$) we use a different formula:

The **standardized beta coefficient ($\beta$)** is the value of the slope of the regression line in standardized values (standard deviations).

$$\beta = b\frac{s_x}{s_y} \qquad \textbf{(12.11)}$$

where:  $\beta$ = standardized beta coefficient

$b$ = unstandardized beta coefficient

$s_x$ = standard deviation of $x$

$s_y$ = standard deviation of $y$

Knowing the value of $b$ and the values for the standard deviations of $y$ and $x$, we can calculate the standardized beta coefficient:

$$\beta = b\frac{s_x}{s_y} = 0.388 \times \frac{5.81}{3.70} = 0.609 \qquad \textbf{(12.12)}$$

Now that we are using standardized scores, our interpretation of the slope needs to be in reference to standard deviations. We interpret this value as follows: A one-standard deviation increase in the independent variable ($x$) is associated with an increase of 0.609 standard deviations in the dependent variable ($y$). Of course, if the coefficient were negative, then the increase in $x$ would result in a decrease in $y$. So, in the context of our example, a one-standard deviation increase in a high school math score is associated with an increase of 0.609 standard deviations in a university math score.

When we introduced this example we said that the correlation ($r$) between high school and university math scores was 0.609. As you can see, the standardized beta coefficient is also 0.609. This is not a coincidence. In the bivariate regression case, since both the standardized beta coefficient and the correlation coefficient use standardized scores in their calculation, they will always be the same. However, this is not the case if we have more than one independent variable (which is beyond the scope of this textbook).

Now that we have the beta coefficient for our least-squares regression equation, we can estimate the intercept ($\alpha$). The formula for calculating the intercept is:

$$\alpha = \bar{y} - b\bar{x} \qquad \textbf{(12.13)}$$

where:  $\bar{y}$ = the mean value of $y$

$\bar{x}$ = the mean value of $x$

$b$ = the unstandardized beta coefficient

Substituting our values in the equation we get:

$$\alpha = \bar{y} - b\bar{x} = 73.63 - .388 \times 80.50 = 42.40 \quad \textbf{(12.14)}$$

As noted previously, the intercept represents the point where the regression line crosses the $y$-axis, which in turn represents the value of $y$ when $x$ equals 0.

## Putting the Least-Squares Regression Equation Together

Now that we have calculated the values needed for our least-squares regression equation, we can put the equation to use. Based on the values we calculated previously, our equation . . .

$$\hat{y} = a + bx \qquad (12.15)$$

becomes . . .

$$\hat{y} = 42.40 + 0.388x \qquad (12.16)$$

By substituting each *x*-value (high school math grade) in our equation, we get our predicted $\hat{y}$-value (university math grade). For example, for participant #1:

$$42.40 + 0.388(84.56) = 75.21 \qquad (12.17)$$

Recall that earlier we said that our predicted value of $\hat{y}$ will not always equal the actual value of *y* because of error in our prediction. As you can see in Table 12.6, we can estimate the amount of error in our prediction for each observation. We call this error the residual and often write it using the Greek letter epsilon ($\varepsilon$). The residual is simply the difference between the actual *y*-value and our estimated value of $\hat{y}$. Formally, we calculate the residual using the formula:

$$\text{Residual} = y - \hat{y} \qquad (12.18)$$

Although our prediction is not perfect, we can at least be assured that by using the least-squares regression criterion that we have minimized the residuals.

**TABLE 12.6**  Calculating the Residual Values

| Participant | High School Math Grade<br>*x* | Predicted University Math Grade<br>$\hat{y}$ | Actual University Math Grade<br>*y* | Residual $(y - \hat{y})$<br>$\varepsilon$ |
|---|---|---|---|---|
| 1 | 84.56 | 75.21 | 79.21 | 4.00 |
| 2 | 85.86 | 75.71 | 78.34 | 2.63 |
| 3 | 73.56 | 70.94 | 72.4 | 1.46 |
| 4 | 72.11 | 69.99 | 69.17 | −0.82 |
| 5 | 72.45 | 70.51 | 70.88 | 0.37 |
| 6 | 84.09 | 75.03 | 69.64 | −5.39 |
| 7 | 84.74 | 75.28 | 80.92 | 5.64 |
| 8 | 81.09 | 73.86 | 71.12 | −2.74 |
| 9 | 85.62 | 75.62 | 72.38 | −3.24 |
| 10 | 75.33 | 71.63 | 72.7 | 1.71 |
| 11 | 85.95 | 75.75 | 75.31 | −0.44 |
| 12 | 73.2 | 70.80 | 69.09 | −1.71 |
| 13 | 79.28 | 73.16 | 73.15 | −0.01 |
| 14 | 87.73 | 76.44 | 73.6 | −2.84 |
| 15 | 82.88 | 74.56 | 76.47 | 1.91 |

## The Coefficient of Determination ($r^2$)

When interpreting the results of a linear regression, our ability to report how a change in our independent variable corresponds to a change in our dependent variable is important. However, we still need to take into consideration that our regression line has some error. In that respect, unless the correlation between the independent and dependent variables is perfect (i.e., $\pm 1.00$) we can't explain all the variability in the dependent variable just from our independent variable. So we need a way to be able to explain how much of the variability in the dependent variable can be explained by the independent variable. To do this, we use the **coefficient of determination**, often referred to as $r$-square ($r^2$).

The **coefficient of determination ($r^2$)** is the percentage of the variance in the dependent variable that is explained by the independent variable.

Looking back at our example we know that there is variability in university math scores because individual students get different grades. There are likely many different variables that can explain the variability of these grades. For example, students might take extra courses during the summer, receive tutoring, or at the other end of the spectrum, not go to their university math class. In our example, we used one independent variable (high school math scores) to try to predict some of the variability in university math scores (the dependent variable). To determine how much of the variability (in the dependent variable) our independent variable explains, we use the coefficient of determination.

To calculate the coefficient of determination ($r^2$), you use the square of the Pearson's correlation coefficient ($r$). In our example, we found that the correlation between our two variables was 0.609. So, the coefficient of determination is $0.609^2 = 0.371$. We interpret this value as follows: The independent variable (high school math grade) explains approximately 37.1 percent of the variance in the dependent variable (university math grade). This means that there is still an additional 62.9 percent of the variance in the university math grade that is not accounted for in our regression equation.

LO9

## Hypothesis Testing with Linear Regression

Now that we understand bivariate linear regression, we can test hypotheses about predictions between interval or ratio level independent and dependent variables. Let's use our Five Steps of Hypothesis Testing to work through an example of hypothesis testing using our math grade example.

**Step 1:** Define the null and alternative hypotheses.

$$H_0: b = 0$$

$$H_A: b \neq 0$$

Our null hypothesis is that there is no relationship between the independent and dependent variable. To put this in regression terms, we say that the slope ($b$) of the regression line is zero, or $b = 0$. Since the alternative hypothesis is that there is a relationship between the independent and dependent variables, we state that the slope ($b$) of the regression line will not be zero, or $b \neq 0$ (meaning it could be positive or negative).

**Step 2:** Define the sampling distribution and critical values.

We generally use the $t$-distribution for defining the sampling distribution and critical values for regression. To estimate the standard error of the slope we using the following formula:

$$s_b = \frac{\sqrt{\dfrac{\Sigma(\text{residuals})^2}{n-2}}}{\sqrt{\Sigma(x-\bar{x})^2}} = \frac{\sqrt{\dfrac{120.694}{13}}}{\sqrt{472.93}} = \frac{3.047}{21.747} = 0.140 \quad \textbf{(12.19)}$$

The numerator is the square root of the sum of the squared residuals divided by the degrees of freedom, and the denominator is the square root of the sum of the squared deviations of $x$ from its mean. With an alpha ($\alpha$) of 0.05 and a two-tailed hypothesis, the critical value $t_{(\alpha = 0.05)}$ is $\pm 2.160$ with 13 degrees of freedom ($df$). As with correlation, since we have two variables, our degrees of freedom ($df$) are calculated as $df = n - 2$.

**Step 3:** Calculate the test statistic using the sample data.

To calculate the test statistic ($t$-value), we divide our unstandardized beta value ($b$) by the standard error of the slope ($s_b$) as follows:

$$t = \frac{b}{s_b} = \frac{.388}{.140} = 2.77 \quad \textbf{(12.20)}$$

Note that we obtain exactly the same $t$-value as the $t$-test for a linear correlation.

**Step 4:** Make the decision regarding the hypothesis.

The test statistic of $t = 2.77$ is past the critical value $t_{(\alpha = 0.05)} = \pm 2.160$ ($2.77 > 2.160$); therefore, you reject the null hypothesis and state that the slope is significantly different from zero.

**Step 5:** Interpret the results.

Based on our sample, the high school math grade is a positive predictor of the university math grade. A one-unit (1 grade percent) increase in the high school math score corresponds to a 0.388 unit (0.388 of 1 grade percent) increase in the university math score. Furthermore, the high school math grade explains approximately 37.1 percent of the variance in the university math grade.

---

**EXERCISE 12.2**

Using the data in the table below, estimate the best fitting (least squares) regression line and test the alternative hypothesis that the slope is significantly different from 0.

| $x$ | 1 | 3 | 4 | 4 | 5 | 8 | 12 |
|-----|----|----|----|----|----|---|----|
| $y$ | 22 | 18 | 15 | 16 | 10 | 6 | 4 |

# Take a Closer Look

In chapter 10 we looked at the analysis of variance (ANOVA). We can approach regression analysis in the same way. We start with a y-variable and compute the total variability in the data as the sums of squares total:

$$SS(Total) = \Sigma(y - \bar{y})^2$$

We then try to explain why the values of the y-variable are not all the same. While university math grades (y) vary for many reasons we can try to explain some of this variability with high school math grades (x). Therefore, we place a straight line through the data to get predicted values of:

$$\hat{y} = a + bx$$

The unexplained variation in the y-variable is the difference between the observed y-values and the predicted values ($\hat{y}$) on the line. The unexplained variability is called the sum of squares due to error and is represented by:

$$SS(Error) = \Sigma(y - \hat{y})^2$$

The difference in the sum of squares total and the sum of squares due to error represents the variability accounted by the explanatory x-variable.

$$SS(Regression) = SS(Total) - SS(Error).$$

We can create an ANOVA table to summarize the results.

We reject the null hypothesis that the slope is 0 if the F-test statistic is greater than the f-table value on 1 and $n - 2$ df. The f-test in this case is the square of the t-test and gives the same conclusions. Many computer packages use the ANOVA table to summarize the results of the analysis.

| Source | Degrees of Freedom (df) | Sum of Squares (SS) | Mean Sum of Squares (MS) | F |
|---|---|---|---|---|
| Regression (slope) | 1 | SS(Regression) | MS(Regression) | $F = \dfrac{MS\,(Regression)}{MSE}$ |
| Error | $(n - 2)$ | SS(Error) | MSE | |
| Total (corrected) | $n - 1$ | SS(Total) | | |

# Did You Know?

Sabremetrics (from the Society for American Baseball Research) is the study of baseball statistics. Bill James, in his annual baseball handbook, discusses the relationship between the proportion of wins by a team and a variable based on the Pythagorean law. We define the x-variable as:

$$x = \frac{(runs\ for)^2}{(runs\ for)^2 + (runs\ against)^2}$$

where: runs for = total runs the team scored in the season
runs against = total runs they allowed the other team to score

A scatterplot of y versus x results in a straight line through the origin with a slope of 1.

Let's use the example of the 2010 final standings for the American League East.

The regression line takes the form of:

$$\hat{y} = a + bx = 90.103 + 0.807x$$

If we look at a scatter plot of y versus x we see a very strong relationship.

The correlation coefficient for this small sample is 0.998, a very strong relationship.

| Team | Proportion Wins (Y) | Runs For | Runs Against | x |
|------|---------------------|----------|--------------|---|
| Tampa | 0.593 | 802 | 649 | 0.60429 |
| Yankees | 0.586 | 859 | 693 | 0.60575 |
| Boston | 0.549 | 818 | 744 | 0.54727 |
| Toronto | 0.525 | 755 | 728 | 0.51820 |
| Orioles | 0.407 | 613 | 785 | 0.37880 |

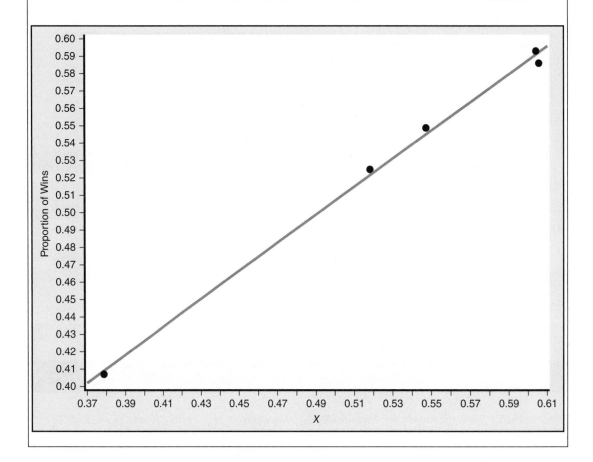

# Conclusion

In this chapter we found that we can use the Pearson's correlation coefficient to estimate the direction and strength of association between two variables. We also found that using linear regression, we can test hypotheses regarding the prediction of an independent and dependent variable. Both of these tests focussed on interval or ratio level variables. If we find that there are other variables that explain some of the variability in the response variable $y$, or if the relationship between $x$ and $y$ is not linear, we can use other more advanced regression techniques. However, we will have to leave that for another course.

In the final chapter, we will look at measures of association with nominal and/or ordinal variables.

## Key Chapter Concepts and Terms

Association, 333
Scatterplot, 333
Positively associated, 334
Negatively
  associated, 336
No association, 336
Strength of an
  association, 338

Correlation
  coefficient, 338
Pearson's correlation
  coefficient, 338
Regression line, 343
Least-squares
  regression line, 345
Intercept, 345

Beta, 345
Unstandardized beta
  coeffecient, 346
Standardized beta
  coeffecient, 347
Coeffecient of
  determination, 349

## Frequently Asked Questions

1. What do the correlation coefficient and the slope represent?

   The correlation coefficient is a measure of the strength of the relationship between the variables $x$ and $y$. The slope of the regression line represents the change in the $y$-variable given a change in the $x$-variable. If we regress the time spent studying ($y$) on the time spent on Facebook ($x$), then the slope represents the amount of time we study for each hour we spend on Facebook. The slope also shows the steepness of the line placed through the data points.

2. If the variables $x$ and $y$ have a significant correlation, does that mean that the $x$ variable causes $y$ to change?

   No, correlation does not mean causation. There could be other factors that cause both $x$ and $y$ to co-vary. Unless we perform controlled experiments where we keep everything fixed and vary $x$ to see what happens to $y$, we can only conclude that they are related.

3. When looking at a regression analysis, should we have our $x$ values close together or far apart?

   The standard error of the mean is smaller when the variability in the $x$-values is larger. So we should keep our $x$ values as far apart as possible. If we have a controlled experiment we can choose our $x$-values. But if we are doing surveys then we have to ensure variability in our subjects. If we are looking at an $x$-variable of age, sampling only 12-year-olds is not going to be very useful.

4. How do I plot the best fitting straight line through a scatterplot?

   Statistical packages can do it for you. However, as a rough estimate, you could pick two $x$-values (that are far apart) and their respective predicted values of $y$ ($\hat{y}$), plot them, and then connect the two data points to create the fitted line.

5. How do I get a predicted *y*-value from a given *x*-value?

Calculate the values of *a* and *b* and then substitute these values into the equation. Then you can calculate $\hat{y}$ for any value of *x*:

$$\hat{y} = a + bx$$

**Research Example:**

In 2008, Dr. Christopher O'Connor (University of Calgary) published his study "Citizen attitudes toward the police in Canada" in the journal *Policing: An International Journal of Policing Strategies and Management*. His research focussed on Canadians' attitudes toward police and predictors of positive or negative attitudes. One of the hypotheses in his paper stated that individuals who are satisfied with their level of personal safety will have more favourable opinions of the police. His results found that the unstandardized beta coefficient was positive (0.259) and significant.[2]

**Research Example Questions:**

**Question 1:** Explain the direction of the association between the dependent and independent variables.

**Question 2:** Interpret the unstandardized regression coefficient.

**Question 3:** How could the standardized regression coefficient be useful in this study?

**Research Example Answers:**

**Question 1:** Explain the direction of the association between the dependent and independent variable.

The dependent variable is public perception of the police and the independent variable is satisfaction with personal safety. Since the unstandardized beta coefficient is positive and significant, this indicates that there is a positive association (relationship) between satisfaction with personal safety and perception of the police. Meaning that low satisfaction is associated with unfavourable opinions of the police, and high satisfaction is associated with favourable opinions of the police.

**Question 2:** Interpret the unstandardized regression coefficient.

A one-unit increase in the independent variable (satisfaction with personal safety) corresponds to a 0.259 unit increase in the dependent variable (perception of the police).

**Question 3:** How could the standardized regression coefficient be useful in this study?

If the measurement for satisfaction with personal safety has a different unit of measurement than the measurement for perception of the police, then using the standardized regression coefficient allows a researcher to discuss the relationship in terms of standard deviations. For example, if the standardized beta coefficient were 0.500 then the results could be interpreted as a 1 standard deviation increase in satisfaction with personal safety corresponds to a 0.500 standard deviation (half of one standard deviation) increase in perception of the police.

**ANSWERS TO EXERCISE 12.1**

Summary statistics yield the following:

| $x$ | $y$ | $xy$ | $x^2$ | $y^2$ |
|-----|-----|------|-------|-------|
| 1 | 2 | 2 | 1 | 4 |
| 3 | 5 | 15 | 9 | 25 |
| 4 | 9 | 36 | 16 | 81 |
| 4 | 8 | 32 | 16 | 64 |
| 5 | 13 | 65 | 25 | 169 |
| 8 | 18 | 144 | 64 | 324 |
| $\Sigma = 25$ | 55 | 294 | 131 | 667 |

The correlation coefficient is:

$$r = \frac{\Sigma xy - \left(\dfrac{\Sigma x \Sigma y}{n}\right)}{\sqrt{\left(\Sigma x^2 - \dfrac{(\Sigma x)^2}{n}\right)\left(\Sigma y^2 - \dfrac{(\Sigma y)^2}{n}\right)}}$$

$$r = \frac{294 - \left(\dfrac{25 \times 55}{6}\right)}{\sqrt{\left(131 - \dfrac{(25)^2}{6}\right)\left(667 - \dfrac{(55)^2}{6}\right)}} = \frac{64.83}{\sqrt{26.83 \times 162.83}} = 0.980$$

To see if the correlation is significantly different from 0 follow the Five Steps of Hypothesis Testing.

**Step 1:** Define the null and alternative hypotheses.

$$H_0: \rho = 0$$
$$H_A: \rho \neq 0$$

The null hypothesis is that there is no linear relationship between $x$ and $y$. The alternative hypothesis is that there is a linear relationship.

**Step 2:** Define the sampling distribution and critical values.
We use the $t$-distribution with a standard error defined by:

$$s_r = \sqrt{\frac{1 - r^2}{n - 2}} = \sqrt{\frac{1 - (0.980)^2}{6 - 2}} = \sqrt{\frac{0.0396}{4}} = 0.0995$$

With an alpha value ($\alpha$) of 0.05, the two-tailed critical value is $\pm 2.201$ with 11 degrees of freedom. Since we have two variables, our degrees of freedom are $n - 2 = 13 - 2 = 11$.

**Step 3:** Calculate the test statistic using the sample data.

To calculate the test statistic ($t$-value), we divide our sample $r$-value by the standard error of $r$ as follows:

$$t = \frac{r}{\sqrt{\dfrac{1 - r^2}{n - 2}}} = \frac{0.98}{0.0995} = 9.85$$

**Step 4:** Make the decision regarding the hypothesis.

The critical value of $t$ with 4 $df$ is 2.775. Since we observed a $t$-value of 9.85, which is greater than our critical value ($9.85 > 2.775$), we reject the null hypothesis.

**Step 5:** Interpret the results.

We conclude that there is a statistically significant correlation between the two variables $x$ and $y$.

---

**ANSWERS TO EXERCISE 12.2**

Summary statistics yield the following:

| $x$ | $y$ | $xy$ | $x^2$ | $y^2$ |
|-----|-----|------|-------|-------|
| 1 | 22 | 22 | 1 | 484 |
| 3 | 18 | 54 | 9 | 324 |
| 4 | 15 | 60 | 16 | 225 |
| 4 | 16 | 64 | 16 | 256 |
| 5 | 10 | 50 | 25 | 100 |
| 8 | 6 | 48 | 64 | 36 |
| 12 | 4 | 48 | 144 | 16 |
| $\Sigma = 37$ | 91 | 346 | 275 | 1441 |

To calculate the slope:

$$b = \frac{\Sigma xy - \dfrac{(\Sigma x)(\Sigma y)}{n}}{\Sigma x^2 - \dfrac{(\Sigma x)^2}{n}} = \frac{346 - \dfrac{37 \times 91}{7}}{275 - \dfrac{37^2}{7}} = \frac{-135}{79.43} = -1.70$$

Since the sample means of the two variables are $\bar{y} = 13.0$ and $\bar{x} = 5.286$, the intercept is:

$$a = \hat{y} - b\bar{x} = 13.0 - (-1.70) \times 5.286 = 21.99$$

The estimated regression line is expressed as:

$$\hat{y} = 21.99 - 1.70x$$

Note that two negatives make a positive, so be careful with calculations in the formulas. We then substitute the x-values into the equation above to obtain the values of $\hat{y}$.

| x | y | $\hat{y}$ | $y - \hat{y}$ | $(y - \hat{y})^2$ |
|---|---|---|---|---|
| 1 | 22 | 20.29 | 1.71 | 2.924 |
| 3 | 18 | 16.89 | 1.11 | 1.232 |
| 4 | 15 | 15.19 | −0.19 | 0.036 |
| 4 | 16 | 15.19 | 0.81 | 0.656 |
| 5 | 10 | 13.49 | −3.49 | 12.180 |
| 8 | 6 | 8.39 | −2.39 | 5.712 |
| 12 | 4 | 1.59 | 2.41 | 5.808 |
| | | | | $\Sigma = 28.548$ |

**Step 1:** Define the null and alternative hypotheses.

$$H_0: b = 0$$
$$H_A: b \neq 0$$

The null hypothesis is that the slope of the line is 0. That is, as x changes y does not change. This is equivalent to no relationship between the variables.

**Step 2:** Define the sampling distribution and critical values.
We generally follow the t-distribution for defining the sampling distribution and critical values for regression. With an alpha ($\alpha$) of 0.05 and a two-tailed hypothesis, the critical value ($t_\alpha$) is ±2.571 with 5 degrees of freedom (where degrees of freedom = $n - 2$).

The standard error of the slope is:

$$s_b = \frac{\sqrt{\dfrac{\Sigma(residuals)^2}{n - 2}}}{\sqrt{\Sigma(x - \bar{x})^2}} = \frac{\sqrt{\dfrac{28.548}{7}}}{8.912} = \frac{2.39}{8.912} = 0.268$$

**Step 3:** Calculate the test statistic using the sample data.
To calculate the test statistic (t-value), we divide our unstandardized beta value (b) by the standard error of the slope.

$$t = \frac{b}{s_b} = \frac{-1.70}{0.268} = -6.34$$

**Step 4:** Make the decision regarding the hypothesis.
The test statistic of $t = -6.34$ is past the critical value ($t_\alpha$) of $\pm 2.571$, based on 5 degrees of freedom. Therefore, we reject the null hypothesis and state that the slope is significantly different from zero.

**Step 5:** Interpret the results.
We conclude that there is a statistically significant negative slope of $-1.70$. For each one unit increase in $x$, there is a decrease in $y$ by 1.70 units.

## Problems

1. The following data are the ages and the asking prices for 10 used foreign cars:

| Age ($x$)<br>in Years | Price ($y$)<br>($\times \$100$) |
|:---:|:---:|
| 3 | 68 |
| 5 | 52 |
| 3 | 63 |
| 6 | 24 |
| 4 | 60 |
| 4 | 60 |
| 6 | 28 |
| 7 | 36 |
| 2 | 68 |
| 2 | 64 |

a) Draw a scatterplot of the data.

b) Calculate $r$.

c) Is the correlation coefficient statistically different from 0 at the 5 percent level?

d) Calculate the least-squares regression line using the appropriate formulas.

e) Does $r^2$ indicate a good or poor fit? What about a $t$-test for regression? In each case, assume alpha is 5 percent.

2. You are given the following information for two variables $x$ and $y$ (independent and dependent variables respectively).

| $x$ | 2 | 12 | 4 | 6 | 9 | 4 | 11 | 3 | 10 | 11 | 3 | 1 | 13 | 12 | 14 | 7 | 2 | 8 |
|---|---|---|---|---|---|---|---|---|---|---|---|---|---|---|---|---|---|---|
| $y$ | 4 | 8 | 10 | 9 | 10 | 8 | 8 | 5 | 10 | 9 | 8 | 3 | 9 | 8 | 8 | 11 | 6 | 9 |

a) Draw a scatterplot for the data points. Does there appear to be a positive or negative association?

b) Calculate $r$. Is the result statistically different from 0?

c) Calculate the least-squares regression line using the appropriate equation. Is *b* statistically different from 0 at the 5 percent level? (Hint: Use the *t*-test)

d) Do you believe that there is a good fit or poor fit, and why if alpha is 5 percent?

e) Do your results support what you see on the scatterplot?

3. A college professor would like to know if there is a relationship between hours worked outside of school at a part-time job and the grades received in college, using the following data.

| Hours Worked (*x*) | Grade |
|---|---|
| 0 | 84 |
| 7 | 60 |
| 6 | 56 |
| 12 | 73 |
| 8 | 63 |
| 14 | 49 |
| 10 | 68 |
| 13 | 49 |
| 11 | 69 |
| 5 | 53 |

a) Calculate *r*. Is the result statistically different from 0 at the 5 percent level?

b) Calculate the least-squares regression line using the appropriate equation. Is *b* statistically different from 0 at the 5 percent level? (Hint: Use the *t*-test)

c) Do you believe that there is a good fit or poor fit based on the coefficient of determination and the *t*-test for regression? Assume alpha = 5 percent.

# Estimation and Hypothesis Testing V: Chi-square and Correlation for Nominal and Ordinal Data

# 13

**Learning Objectives:**

By the end of this chapter you should be able to:

1. Analyze data consisting of two nominal variables.

2. Measure the strength of an association between nominal variables using the Phi coefficient or Cramér's V coefficient.

3. Analyze data consisting of one dichotomous variable and one interval or ratio variable using the point-biserial correlation coefficient.

4. Understand the similarity between the point-biserial correlation coefficient and Pearson's correlation coefficient.

5. Analyze data consisting of two rank ordered ordinal variables using Spearman's correlation coefficient.

## Charles Edward Spearman (1863–1945)

Charles Spearman was a British psychologist well known for his contributions to the fields of statistics and intelligence testing. Born in England, Spearman spent a great deal of his life as an officer in the British Army and didn't enter academia until the age of 41. Spearman completed his PhD in experimental psychology in Leipzig, Germany. He was a Professor at the University College London, was elected to the Royal Society in 1924, and retired from his position as Professor of Psychology in 1931.

Aside from the significant contribution he made in the areas of intelligence and intelligence testing, Spearman is also well known for two major contributions to the field of statistics. His first contribution was an analytical method called factor analysis and his second was an adaptation of Pearson's Correlation Coefficient to rank ordered ordinal data. This test is called Spearman's correlation coefficient, also known as Spearman's *rho*.[1]

# Introduction

In chapter 12, we examined correlation and regression as methods of testing of association and prediction. Specifically, we focussed on Pearson's correlation co-efficient and least-squares regression. Both of those analytical methods require that we have two (or more) variables that are measured at either the interval or ratio level. But what do we do if we have nominal or ordinal data? For example, we might be interested in:

- the association between gender (nominal) and type of program studied at university (nominal),
- the association between categories of social economic status (ordinal) and categories of likelihood to commit a crime (ordinal),
- the association between the ranking of cities by homicide and poverty rates, or
- a mix of nominal and interval variables such as gender and number of cigarettes smoked per day.

All of the analytical procedures we have covered so far rely on the mean, standard deviation, and variance of the variables. However, nominal and ordinal data are categorical not continuous, and therefore estimating values such as the mean are not appropriate. For example, you can't calculate the mean value of the variable "religious affiliation" when it is measured in categories representing different forms of religion. Therefore, when we need to analyze data that is either nominal or ordinal, we must use a different grouping of analysis called non-parametric statistics. These analytical methods do not have the same type of mean and variance assumptions as the other tests we have covered so far. In this chapter, we will concentrate on testing the association between nominal or ordinal variables and the circumstance where we may have a mix of continuous (interval and ratio) and nominal variables. We will focus specifically on the measure of association and will not cover regression with these cases. Although there are a number of interesting analytical techniques for regression analysis with nominal and ordinal data, that topic is beyond the scope of this textbook.

There are many different types of measures of association for various different scenarios and combinations of variable types. In this chapter we will focus specifically on four different situations that researchers commonly face. These are measures of association when (1) both variables are nominal, (2) one variable is

## Take A Closer Look

| | Matching the Research Situation to the Type of Analysis | | |
|---|---|---|---|
| **Situation** | **Example** | **Statistical Test** | **Refer to...** |
| I need to estimate the population parameter based on my sample statistic. The variable is measured at the interval or ratio level. | You calculate the mean score of the Law School Admission Test (LSAT) for a random sample of students who did not study criminology during their undergraduate education, and you want to estimate what the mean LSAT score might be in the population of students who did not study criminology during their undergraduate education. | Confidence Intervals: Use confidence intervals when you need to make an inference about a population mean or proportion and you have a sample mean or proportion. | Chapter 8 |
| I calculated a mean based on data from one sample of respondents and want to compare it to a known mean such as the one I found in a published report. Both my variable and the one in the report are measured at the interval or ratio level. | You calculate the mean LSAT score of students in your university who just took the test. You want to test the alternative hypothesis that the mean score from your sample is higher than the mean LSAT score for all of Canada as published by the Law School Admission Council. | Single Sample Mean (or Proportion): Use a single sample test for a mean (or proportions when you have proportions) when you need to compare your sample mean to a known mean (or proportion) value. | Chapter 9 |
| I have two means from two independent samples and need to determine if they differ from one another. The variable is measured at the interval or ratio level. | Based on a random sample you have calculated the mean LSAT score for students from your university and the mean LSAT score for students from another university. You want to test the hypothesis that the mean score from your university is higher than the mean score of the other university. | Independent Sample *t*-Test: Use an independent sample *t*-test when you are comparing the means from two samples that are independent of each other. | Chapter 10 |
| I have two means from a paired sample and need to determine if they differ from one another. The variable is measured at the interval or ratio level. | Ten students took the LSAT exam last year and again this year. You want to test the hypothesis that the mean LSAT score from last year is lower than the mean LSAT score from this year. | Paired Sample *t*-Test: Use a paired sample *t*-test when you are comparing the means of samples that are not independent of one another. | Chapter 10 |

| | | | |
|---|---|---|---|
| I have three or more means from an independent sample and need to determine if they differ from one another. The variable is measured at the interval or ratio level. | Thirty students took the LSAT exam. Ten had studied political science in university, 10 had studied sociology, and 10 had studied management economics. You want to test the hypothesis that the mean LSAT score is different in at least one of the three groups. | One-way ANOVA: Use a one-way analysis of variance when you are comparing the means of three or more groups. | Chapter 11 |
| I have two variables and I want to see if there is an association between them. The variables are measured at the interval or ratio level. | Thirty students from your university took the LSAT preparation course prior to taking the LSAT exam. You want to test if the hours spent studying during the LSAT preparation course is associated with the scores on the LSAT exam. | Pearson's Correlation: Use Pearson's Correlation ($r$) when you want to measure the association between two interval or ratio level variables. | Chapter 12 |
| I have a dependent and an independent variable and I want to know if the independent variable predicts the dependent variable. The variables are measured at the interval or ratio level. | Twenty-five individuals wrote the LSAT exam today. You record their age and their LSAT score. You want to know if a person's age predicts his or her score on the LSAT exam. | Linear Regression: Use linear regression when you want to test if the scores in one variable predict the scores in a second variable. | Chapter 12 |
| I have two nominal variables and I want to see if they are related. | I sample a class of students learning Spanish. I measure if they are doing well or not, and I ask if they feel sympathetic towards Castro and his reforms in Cuba. | Chi-Square Test of Independence: We use a chi-square test of independence between two nominal (categorical) variables. The variables are good/poor performance in Spanish and for/against Castro. | Chapter 13 |
| I have one variable that represents the number (frequency) of votes that each of the three political party leaders received in an election. I want to see if the number of votes is equal across the three leaders. | I sample 1,000 voters and ask them for which of the three candidates they voted. | Chi-Square Test of Fit: We use a chi-square test of fit when we want to know if the frequency in each of the categories differs. In this case, we want to know if it differs from a frequency where each leader received one-third of the total votes. | Chapter 13 |
| I have two rank ordered ordinal variables and I want to test if there is an association between them. | I sampled 25 schools and have rank ordered them on two variables: social economic status of the surrounding area, and percentage of students admitted to a post-secondary education institution. | Spearman's correlation coefficient: We use Spearman's correlation coefficient (Spearman's *rho*) to measure the association between two rank ordered ordinal variables. | Chapter 13 |

**Note:** Although we cover more tests in this chapter, the three listed in this table tend to be the most commonly used.

nominal (and dichotomous) and the other is interval or ratio, (3) both variables are rank ordered ordinal (where the rank matters), and (4) both variables are ordinal but the ranking doesn't matter.

# Two Nominal Variables

**LO1**

**Contingency tables** compare two (or more) categorical variables by cross tabulating the categories of each variable.

As stated in chapter 1, nominal data consists of named categories such as gender (male/female), school type (private/public), and relationship (sibling/friend/acquaintance). When we want to investigate the relationship between two nominal variables—for example, the relationship between gender and whether an individual is a smoker—we are asking if one variable is contingent on the other. That is to say, does one variable (smoker) depend on the other (gender)? To analyze this, we start by creating a **contingency table** (often referred to as a crosstab) that allows us to compare categories of the first variable with the categories of the second. Within the cells of the table are the frequencies with which each cross tabulated category occurs. Table 13.1

**TABLE 13.1**
**Contingency Table**

|  |  | Gender | | Total |
|---|---|---|---|---|
|  |  | Male | Female |  |
| Smoker | Yes | A | B | A + B |
|  | No | C | D | C + D |
|  | Total | A + C | B + D | A + B + C + D |

## Take a Closer Look

### The Chi-Square Distribution

Recall that we use the *t*-distribution for *t*-tests and the *F*-distribution for an ANOVA. The chi-square test relies on its own distribution with 1 degree of freedom. The shape of the distribution changes based on the number of degrees of freedom.

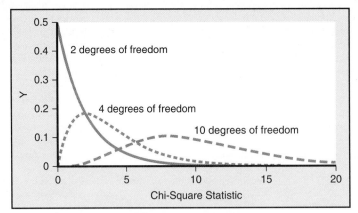

**Note:** Chi-square is pronounced "ki-square," where ki rhymes with tie.

is an example of a two (row) by two (column) contingency table representing the relationship between Gender (Male/Female) and Smoker (Yes/No). Cell A represents the frequency of male smokers, cell B the frequency of female smokers, and so on for cells C and D. The Total row and column are the sum of the respective cells.

## The Pearson's Chi-Square Test of Independence

In January of 2011, Statistics Canada released the twelfth annual *Family Violence in Canada* report, which is created by the Canadian Centre for Justice Statistics. Table 13.2 represents the contingency table of reported homicides (from 2000 to 2009) by gender where the individual accused of committing the homicide was either the victim's friend or neighbour. As you can see, a total of 441 homicides were committed by either a friend or neighbour, with the highest frequency being male victims murdered by friends. Now suppose we wanted to know if there was a relationship between these two nominal variables. What we are actually asking is if the relationship of the accused is independent of the gender of the victim.

**TABLE 13.2**   **Reported Homicides by Gender and Relationship to Accused**

| Relationship of Accused | Gender of Victim | | Total | Row Percent |
|---|---|---|---|---|
| | Male | Female | | |
| Friend | 277 | 39 | 316 | 71.66% |
| Neighbour | 98 | 27 | 125 | 28.34% |
| Total | 375 | 66 | 441 | 100.00% |
| Column Percent | 85.03% | 14.97% | 100.00% | |

Source: Adapted from Statistics Canada publication *Family Violence in Canada: A Statistical Profile,* Catalogue 85-224-XIE2010000, http://www.statcan.gc.ca/pub/85-224-x/85-224-x2010000-eng.pdf. The values were pulled from "Table 4.1 Homicides by sex and accused-victim relationship, Canada, 2000 to 2009."

In this scenario, our null and alternative hypotheses would be:

$H_0$: The two variables are independent (no relationship) of one another

$H_A$: The two variables are dependent (is a relationship) on one another

*Calculating Pearson's Chi-Square Test of Independence*

In order to analyze the data and test the hypotheses, we need to use the Pearson's chi-square test of independence, the formula for which is:

$$\chi^2 = \Sigma \frac{(O - E)^2}{E} \qquad \textbf{(13.1)}$$

where: $\chi^2$ = the chi-square statistic

$O$ = the observed frequencies from the contingency table

$E$ = the expected frequencies based on the null hypothesis

An **observed frequency** is the values we found in our sample data.

An **expected frequency** is the values we would expect to occur by chance or other expected values as set by the researcher.

This formula compares the **observed frequencies**, those values that we found in our sample data, to the **expected frequencies**, which are the values that we would expect to find if the null hypothesis were true. To estimate the observed frequencies we use the formula:

$$E_{ij} = \frac{Row_i \times Column_j}{N}$$   (13.2)

where: $E_{ij}$ = the expected value for the cell in row $i$, column $j$

$Row_i$ = the total value of row $i$

$Column_j$ = the total value of column $j$

$N$ = the grand total

As shown in Table 13.3, the expected frequencies are often shown in parentheses next to or below their respective observed values. For Female (Gender of Victim) and Friend (Relationship of Accused), we can see that if the null hypothesis were true, we would expect to observe 47.29 female victims whose friend is accused of their homicide.

**TABLE 13.3   Reported Homicides by Gender and Relationship to Accused with Expected Frequencies**

| Relationship of Accused | Gender of Victim | | Total | Row Percent |
|---|---|---|---|---|
| | Male | Female | | |
| Friend | 277 (268.71) | 39 (47.29) | 316 | 71.66% |
| Neighbour | 98 (106.29) | 27 (18.71) | 125 | 28.34% |
| Total | 375 | 66 | 441 | 100.00% |
| Column Percent | 85.03% | 14.97% | 100.00% | |

Source: Adapted from Statistics Canada publication *Family Violence in Canada: A Statistical Profile,* Catalogue 85-224-XIE2010000, http://www.statcan.gc.ca/pub/85-224-x/85-224-x2010000-eng.pdf. The values were pulled from Table 4.1 Homicides by sex and accused-victim relationship, Canada, 2000 to 2009.

The column and row totals and percentages remain the same for expected and observed values.

Using the formula for equation 13.2, the expected frequencies are calculated as follows:

For male and friend: $\dfrac{316 \times 375}{441} = 268.71$   (13.3)

For male and neighbour: $\dfrac{125 \times 375}{441} = 106.29$

For female and friend: $\dfrac{316 \times 66}{441} = 47.29$

For female and neighbour: $\dfrac{125 \times 66}{441} = 18.71$

Now that we have both the observed and expected frequencies, our chi-square value is calculated as:

$$\chi^2 = \Sigma\frac{(O - E)^2}{E} = \frac{(277 - 268.71)^2}{268.71} + \frac{(39 - 47.29)^2}{47.29} \quad \text{(13.4)}$$
$$+ \frac{(98 - 106.29)^2}{106.29} + \frac{(27 - 18.71)^2}{18.71} = 6.03$$

**Note:** Due to rounding, this calculation may be off slightly from that done by a statistical package.

In order to determine if our chi-square value is significant we first need to estimate the number degrees of freedom (*df*). For the chi-square test of independence, *df* is calculated as:

$$df = (R - 1)(C - 1) \quad \text{(13.5)}$$

where: *df* = degrees of freedom

  *R* = number of rows in the contingency table

  *C* = number of columns in the contingency table

Since we have two rows and two columns our *df* equals:

$$df = (2 - 1)(2 - 1) = 1 \quad \text{(13.6)}$$

Now that we have now our chi-square value (5.81) and *df* (1)—often written as $\chi^2_{(1)} = 5.81$—we can now find the critical value for chi-square at 1 *df* in the table of critical values for the chi-square distribution (see Appendix D). At 1 *df* with an alpha ($\alpha$) of 0.05 the critical value is 3.84. Therefore, since our chi-square value (5.81) is greater than our critical value (3.84), we reject the null hypothesis and conclude that based on our sample, the victim's gender and relationship to the accused are dependent on one another.

---

**EXERCISE 13.1**

The following table, which is based on Matthews and Farewell (1996), represents the amount of prenatal health care delivered to an expectant mother versus infant mortality. Using a chi-square test for independence and an alpha ($\alpha$) value of 0.05, test the null hypothesis that there is no relationship between the amount of prenatal care delivered and infant mortality (meaning the two variables are independent of one another).

| Infant Mortality | Amount of Prenatal Care Delivered | |
|---|---|---|
| | Less Care | More Care |
| Died | 12 | 16 |
| Survived | 176 | 309 |

**Source:** Matthews, D.E. and Farewll, V.Y. (1996). *Using and Understanding Medical Statistics*. Third Edition, Karger, Basel Switzerland.

## Take a Closer Look

Odds ratios are a useful way of explaining the results of a two by two cross-tab (contingency table). They allow us to take the data from two variables, such as Student Type (attentive vs. inattentive) and Course Outcome (pass vs. failed), and make statements, such as "the odds of attentive students passing the course are three times greater than the odds of inattentive students passing the course." Consider the following table, which shows the association between the variables Smoker (No/Yes) and Lung Cancer (No/Yes). This data and the scenario were adapted from Breslowe and Day (1990).

| Lung Cancer | Smoker | | Total | Row Percent |
|---|---|---|---|---|
| | No | Yes | | |
| No | 260 | 148 | 408 | 59.82% |
| Yes | 25 | 249 | 274 | 40.18% |
| Total | 285 | 397 | 682 | 100.00% |
| Column Percent | 41.79% | 58.21% | 100.00% | |

We can see that of those who smoke, 249 currently have lung cancer compared to 148 who do not have lung cancer. Of the non-smokers, 25 currently have lung cancer compared to 260 who do not have lung cancer. We can calculate the odds ratio as follows:

$$\text{Odds Ratio} = \frac{\text{smoker with cancer} \div \text{smoker without cancer}}{\text{non-smoker with cancer} \div \text{non-smoker without cancer}}$$

$$\text{Odds Radio} = \frac{(249 \div 148)}{25 \div 260} = 17.5$$

Therefore, the odds of smokers getting lung cancer is 17.5 times higher than the odds of non-smokers getting lung cancer.

**Source:** Breslowe N.E. and Day N.E. (1980). *Statistical Methods in Cancer Research,* Vol 1. "The analysis of case = control studies." IARC publications No 32. Lyon France.

---

**Example 1**

What If You Have More Than Two Categories?

Suppose we have more than two categories of relationship of accused, as in the contingency table below.

| Relationship of Accused | Gender of Victim | | Total | Row Percent |
|---|---|---|---|---|
| | Male | Female | | |
| Friend | 277 (184.30) | 39 (131.70) | 316 | 44.95% |
| Neighbour | 98 (72.90) | 27 (52.10) | 125 | 17.78% |
| Spouse | 35 (152.80) | 227 (109.20) | 262 | 37.27% |
| Total | 410 | 293 | 703 | 100.00% |
| Column Percent | 58.32% | 41.68% | 100.00% | |

We can use the exact same formula and method for investigating the association between two nominal variables, where there are categories in either or both variables.

Using the formula for the Pearson's chi-square test of independence, we find the expected values as indicated in parentheses in the table, and a $\chi^2_{(2)} = 350.52$. With an alpha ($\alpha$) of 0.05 and 2 *df*, the critical value for this test is 5.99. Given that the test value exceeds the critical value (350.52 > 5.99), there is evidence to suggest that there is a significant association between the two variables.

**LO2**

*Measuring the Strength of the Association*

The chi-square test of independence tells us whether there is an association between two nominal variables and whether that association is significant. However, it doesn't tell us the strength of the association. To determine the strength of an association we need to use either the **Phi Coefficient ($\phi$)** or **Cramér's V Coefficient**. Which one you use depends on the size of your contingency table. When you have 2 × 2 contingency table (rows × columns), such as with two nominal variables that are both dichotomous, use the phi coefficient ($\phi$). When you have a contingency table that is larger than 2 × 2—for example, one nominal variable that is dichotomous (e.g., male vs. female) and one nominal variable that has three categories (e.g., school 1 vs. school 2 vs. school 3)—use Cramér's V.

The formula for the phi coefficient ($\phi$) is:

The **phi coefficient ($\phi$)** is appropriate for nominal variables in a two by two (rows × columns) contingency table.

$$\phi = \sqrt{\frac{x^2}{N}} \qquad \textbf{(13.7)}$$

where: $x^2$ = chi-square value

$N$ = sample size

The formula for Cramér's V coefficient is:

**Cramér's V coefficient** is used for nominal variables in a contingency table that is larger than two by two.

$$V = \sqrt{\frac{x^2}{N(k-1)}} \qquad \textbf{(13.8)}$$

where: $x^2$ = chi-square value

$N$ = sample size

$k$ = lesser value of the number of rows and columns

Using our example of the homicide victim's gender and the relationship of the accused variables from Table 13.3, we would calculate $\phi$ because we have a 2 × 2 contingency table. The result is:

$$\phi = \sqrt{\frac{x^2}{N}} = \sqrt{\frac{6.03}{441}} = 0.117 \qquad \textbf{(13.9)}$$

An important note about $\phi$ is that it differs from Pearson's *r* (correlation coefficient), which we discussed in chapter 12, in that it has a range of 0 (indicating no relationship) to +1 (indicating a perfect relationship). Similar to Pearson's *r* there appear to be no written rules regarding what constitutes a weak versus strong relationship. However, many consider anything below 0.30 to be a weak relationship, anything between 0.30 and 0.50 to be a moderate relationship, and anything above 0.50 to be a strong relationship. With a $\phi = 0.117$, we would likely classify this as a weak relationship.

Now let's consider an example where the variable relationship of the accused consisted of three categories rather than two, resulting in a $3 \times 2$ contingency table. In this case, we would use Cramér's V coefficient to estimate the strength of the association. Using the formula previously noted we get:

$$V = \sqrt{\frac{\chi^2}{N(k-1)}} = \sqrt{\frac{350.52}{703(2-1)}} = .706 \quad \textbf{(13.10)}$$

Interpreting Cramér's V coefficient is the same as that of $\phi$ and also ranges from 0 (indicating no relationship) to $+1$ (indicating a perfect relationship). Using the same criteria as $\phi$ for interpreting the values of $V$, we would say that this is a very strong relationship.

## Interpreting the Test of Independence and Measure of Association

We can combine the chi-square test of independence with the measure of the strength of the association into one interpretation. Using our $2 \times 2$ homicide example, we can say that we conducted a chi-square test of independence with the two nominal variables and found a significant association between the victim's gender and his or her relationship to the accused because our $\chi^2_{(1)} = 5.81$. Furthermore, using the $\phi$ as a test of the strength of the association we found that, although the relationship is significant, it appears to be a weak one ($\phi = 0.115$).

Looking at the $3 \times 2$ example, we can say that we found that an association exists between the victim's gender and his or her relationship to the accused because our $\chi^2_{(1)} = 350.52$. Furthermore, our test of the strength of the association found a very strong association between the two (Cramér's V $= 0.706$).

## The Pearson Chi-Square Goodness of Fit

At this point it is worth looking at another application of the chi-square test. Suppose you run an experiment whereby you present 30 respondents with three different political television advertisements (A, B, and C). After watching the advertisements, the respondents are to select the advertisement they feel motivates them the most. You want to know if people select one advertisement more than others. In this case you have one nominal variable with three categories, and you want to know if the observed results deviate significantly from what we might expect to occur by chance.

Table 13.4 provides the frequency of the specific choices as well as the values that we would expect to see (expected frequencies) if the choices were evenly distributed. In this case, the expected value becomes the probability of randomly selecting one of the three advertisements. Given that there are three possible outcomes from which to choose, they each have a one third chance of being selected. We know from our discussions regarding probability that it is highly unlikely that the observed frequency (based on the responses of our 30 participants) will equal the expected

**TABLE 13.4**
**Advertising Format**
**Frequencies**

|       | Observed | Expected |
|-------|----------|----------|
| A     | 8        | 10       |
| B     | 5        | 10       |
| C     | 17       | 10       |
| Total | 30       |          |

frequency. So the question is, does the observed frequency differ from the expected frequency more than what we might expect to happen by chance? In this situation we can still use Pearson's chi-square test. In fact, the formula for the Pearson's chi-square test of independence is also used in the Pearson's chi-square goodness of fit. However, instead of using it as a test of independence it becomes a test of the goodness of fit. It is referred to as "goodness of fit" of because it is testing if the observed data fits a known distribution, which is the expected value. So in short, the **Pearson chi-square goodness of fit** tests the null hypothesis that there is no significant difference between the observed frequency and the expected frequency.

The **Pearson chi-square goodness of fit** tests the null hypothesis that there is no significant difference between the observed and expected frequencies.

Using our Pearson's chi-square formula we get:

$$\chi^2 = \Sigma \frac{(O - E)^2}{E} = \frac{(8 - 10)^2}{10} + \frac{(5 - 10)^2}{10} + \frac{(17 - 10)^2}{10} = 7.8 \quad \textbf{(13.11)}$$

With $k - 1$ $(3 - 1 = 2)$ degrees of freedom $(df)$, where $k$ represents the number of categories in the variable, we can now look up the critical chi-square value in the table of critical values for the chi-square distribution. With 2 $df$ and an alpha $(\alpha)$ of 0.05, the critical value is 5.99. Since $\chi^2_{(2)} = 7.80$ exceeds the critical value of 5.99, we can reject the null hypothesis and state that the frequency of the observed values differs significantly (more than can be expected by chance) from the frequency of the expected values.

---

**EXERCISE 13.2**

Ninety people were asked to state which party leader they would prefer to have as the next Prime Minister ($A$, $B$, or $C$). The following represents the results:

| $A$ | $B$ | $C$ |
|-----|-----|-----|
| 20  | 40  | 30  |

Using an alpha $(\alpha)$ value of 0.05, test the null hypothesis that all three leaders were equally preferred.

---

## One Nominal and One Interval or Ratio Variable

**LO3**

The **point-biserial correlation ($r_{pb}$)** measures the assoication between a dichotomous nominal variable and an interval or ratio variable.

Table 13.5 provides a fictitious data set of the total number of text messages sent, separated into two groups of people—those who are technically savvy (Yes) and those who are not technically savvy (No).

Here we have one dichotomous nominal variable and one ratio level variable. To test the association between these two variables, we need to use the **Point-Biserial Correlation ($r_{pb}$)**. The point-biserial correlation coefficient can measure the association between two groups (dichotomies) and an interval or ratio level

**TABLE 13.5**
**Users With and Without Technical Savvy**

| Participant | Group (0 = Yes, 1 = No) | Number of Text Messages |
|:-----------:|:-----------------------:|:-----------------------:|
| 1  | 0 | 19 |
| 2  | 0 | 29 |
| 3  | 0 | 25 |
| 4  | 0 | 17 |
| 5  | 0 | 22 |
| 6  | 0 | 16 |
| 7  | 0 | 23 |
| 8  | 1 | 12 |
| 9  | 1 | 15 |
| 10 | 1 | 18 |
| 11 | 1 | 16 |
| 12 | 1 | 12 |
| 13 | 1 | 12 |
| 14 | 1 | 22 |

variable. The outcome will essentially tell us if one group scores higher or lower than the other. To visualize this concept, look at the scatterplot of the data in Figure 13.1. You should be able to see how the two groups (along the $x$-axis) differ on the variable number of text messages sent.

The point-biserial correlation coefficient ranges from $+1$, representing a perfectly positive relationship, to $-1$, representing a perfectly negative relationship, with 0 representing no relationship. Interpreting the sign for this coefficient is a little less intuitive given that one variable is dichotomous; however, Table 13.6 should help you in its interpretation.

**FIGURE 13.1**
**Scatterplot of Technical Savvy and Sent Text Messages**

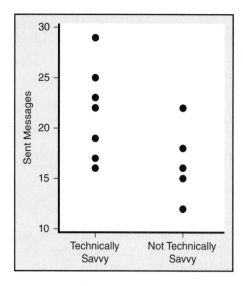

**TABLE 13.6**
**Point-Biserial**
**Correlation**
**Coefficient**
**Interpretations**

| | | **Interpretation of the Results** |
|---|---|---|
| **Point-biserial** | Negative | Scores in Group 1 are higher than Group 2 |
| **Correlation** | Zero | Scores in Group 1 are no different than Group 2 |
| | Positive | Scores in Group 1 are lower than 2 |

**Note:** You may be curious about why we would use a point-biserial correlation rather than an indpendent sample *t*-test. The former is used when you want to understand the association between the two variables, whereas the latter is used when you want to understand the difference between the means of the two variables.

## Calculating the Point-Biserial Correlation Coefficient ($r_{pb}$)

To calculate the $r_{pb}$ we use the following formula:

$$r_{pb} = \frac{(\bar{Y}_1 - \bar{Y}_0)\sqrt{p(1-p)}}{\sqrt{\dfrac{\sum Y^2 - \dfrac{(\sum Y)^2}{N}}{N}}} \tag{13.12}$$

where: $\bar{Y}_0$ = the mean value of $Y$ (interval/ratio variable) when $X$ (nominal variable) = 0

$\bar{Y}_1$ = the mean value of $Y$ (interval/ratio variable) when $X$ (nominal variable) = 1

$p$ = the portion of values where $X$ (nominal variable) = 1

$\sum Y^2$ = the sum of all values of $Y$ after they have been squared

$(\sum Y)^2$ = the square of the sum of all values of $Y$

$N$ = the total sample size

Calculating the means and standard deviations we get:

$\bar{Y}_0 = 21.57$ (mean number of text messages sent by the tech savvy group)

$\bar{Y}_1 = 15.29$ (mean number of text messages sent by the non-tech savvy group)

$p = 0.50$ (the portion of case in the tech savvy group)

$\sum Y^2 = 5,106$

$(\sum Y)^2 = (258)^2$

$N = 14$

Entering these values in our equation we get:

$$r_{pb} = \frac{(15.29 - 21.57)\sqrt{0.50(1-0.50)}}{\sqrt{\dfrac{5106 - \dfrac{(258)^2}{14}}{14}}} = \frac{-3.14}{\sqrt{\dfrac{351.429}{14}}} \tag{13.13}$$

$$= \frac{-3.14}{5.0102} = -0.627$$

**LO4**

Algebraically, the formula for the point-biserial correlation is the same as the Pearson correlation coefficient, so $r_{pb} = r$. This is because the point-biserial correlation is a special case of Pearson's correlation coefficient. By now you're probably wondering why we took you through the pain of calculating it manually if it is the same as $r$. The reason is that many people don't realize that this is the case and struggle to figure out how to run point-biserial in their software packages. Now that you know, you can do it simply by using Pearson's $r$.

To test how significant the correlation is, we can conduct a $t$-test using the following formula:

$$t = \frac{r_{pb}\sqrt{N - 2}}{\sqrt{1 - r_{pb}^2}} \qquad (13.14)$$

where: $r_{pb}$ = the point-biserial correlation coefficient

$\quad\quad\quad N$ = the sample size

Using the values we just calculated, we get a $t$-value of:

$$t = \frac{-0.627\sqrt{14 - 2}}{\sqrt{1 - (-0.627)^2}} = \frac{-2.172}{0.779} = -2.788 \quad (13.15)$$

We can then determine the critical value of $t$ with $n - 2$ degrees of freedom $(df)$ $(14 - 2 = 12)$ by using the $t$-distribution of critical values. With an alpha ($\alpha$) of 0.05 and 12 $df$, the critical value is $\pm 2.179$. Given that our $t$-value falls past the critical value $(-2.788 < -2.179)$, we can reject the null hypothesis of no relationship. Just as the point-biserial correlation coefficient is the same as the Pearson correlation coefficient, the significance value will also be the same. Again, if you need to run a point-biserial correlation using a statistical software package, you can simply use Pearson's $r$ to obtain the result.

### Interpreting the Point-Biserial Correlation Coefficient ($r_{pb}$)

Using our previous example, we can reject the null hypothesis of no relationship and state that there appears to be a significant negative relationship between groups and the number of text messages sent ($r_{pb} = -0.627, t = -2.788$). Those in Group 1 (technically savvy group) have significantly higher numbers of text messages sent than those in Group 2 (non-technically savvy group).

## Two Rank Ordered Ordinal Variables

**LO5**

In their 1972 paper regarding adolescent drug use, Johnson et al. investigated the association between drug use and social and environmental factors. While this example may be somewhat dated it provides a very good example of association between rank ordered ordinal variables. Table 13.7 provides two rank ordered ordinal variables: drug use rank, and broken families rank. The variable "drug use rank" was measured based on the use of particular types of drugs. The variable "broken families rank" was measured as the percentage of the population in that area who

**TABLE 13.7**
**Survey of Adolescent Drug Use and Broken Families**

Source: "Survey of Adolescent Drug Use," *American Journal of Public Health,* Johnson, Abbey, Scheble, and Weitman, 62(2), Feb. 1972, p. 166.

| School Area | Drug Use Rank of School Area | Broken Families Rank | D | $D^2$ |
|---|---|---|---|---|
| A | 1 | 2 | −1 | 1 |
| B | 2 | 1 | 1 | 1 |
| C | 3 | 5 | −2 | 4 |
| D | 4 | 7 | −3 | 9 |
| E | 5 | 4 | 1 | 1 |
| F | 6 | 3 | 3 | 9 |
| G | 7 | 6 | 1 | 1 |
| H | 8 | 8 | 0 | 0 |
| | | | $\Sigma = 0$ | $\Sigma = 26$ |

were separated, divorced, or widowed. Each school area was then ranked by variable in comparison with the others. For example, school area A was ranked the highest in drug use and the second highest in broken families.

For measuring the association between ranked ordinal variables, we use **Spearman's correlation coefficient**, or Spearman's *rho* for short, in order to ensure that the ranking is taken into consideration. We use the symbol $\rho$ when estimating *rho* in the population and $r_s$ when estimating *rho* for a sample. To estimate the correlation coefficient we use the following formula:

**Spearman's correlation coefficient** (Spearman's rho) is used to measure the association between two ranked ordered variables.

$$r_s = 1 - \frac{6\Sigma D^2}{N(N^2 - 1)} \qquad \textbf{(13.16)}$$

where: $D$ = the difference between the ranks of the two variables for each respondent (school in this case)

$N$ = the total sample size

Using the information in Table 13.7, we can calculate Spearman's *rho* as follows:

$$r_s = 1 - \frac{6 \times 26}{8(8^2 - 1)} = 1 - \frac{156}{504} = 1 - 0.310 = 0.690 \quad \textbf{(13.17)}$$

Spearman's *rho* has the same range as Pearson's *r*, from −1 to +1. However, given that it is an association of rank, the interpretation is slightly different. If the two variables are perfectly correlated (+1) this indicates that the rank on the first variable is the same on the second. Conversely, if there is a perfectly negative correlation (−1) then the two variables have the opposite rankings (e.g., ranked first on the first variable and last on the second).

The significance of *rho* can be estimated using a *t*-test, calculated as follows:

$$t = r_s\sqrt{\frac{N - 2}{1 - r_s^2}} = 0.690 \times \sqrt{\frac{6}{.5239}} = 2.34 \quad \textbf{(13.18)}$$

We can then determine the critical value of *t* with $n - 2$ degrees of freedom (*df*) ($8 - 2 = 6$) by using the *t*-distribution of critical values. With an alpha ($\alpha$) of 0.05 and 6 *df*, the critical value is ±2.447. Since our *t*-value does not exceed the critical value (2.34 < 2.447), we would fail to reject the null hypothesis of no relationship.

## Interpreting the Spearman Correlation Coefficient (*rho*)

In our previous example, we failed to reject the null hypothesis of no relationship. While the association is positive it is not significant at an alpha ($\alpha$) of 0.05 using a two-tailed test. For an additional comparison of one-tailed versus two-tailed tests, had we used a one-tailed test the critical value would be $\pm 1.943$ and we would have concluded that there was a significant relationship between the two variables ($r_s = 0.690$, $t = 2.34$). Meaning, those areas ranked higher in drug use are also ranked higher in broken families.

# Did You Know?

Have you ever been at a bus stop and felt like you were waiting longer than normal for the bus. This is called the "Bus Paradox" and it is actually true. Consider four buses arriving over a 60 minute period. They arrive at intervals of 10, 20, 5, and 25 minutes. On average, you would expect that for a 10 minute interval you would wait 5 minutes, or half the total time between buses. Sometimes you arrive at the beginning of the interval and sometimes at the end but on average it will be the middle of the interval. So the waiting times will be 5, 10, 2.5, and 12.5 minutes. The average waiting time is then:

$$(5 + 10 + 2.5 + 12.5) \div 4$$
$$= 30 \div 4$$
$$= 6.5 \text{ minutes}$$

However, if you think of an hour as 60 minutes and you randomly arrive at the bus stop in one of those minutes, then there are only 10 minutes in the first interval but 20 in the second. So you have twice the chance of picking the second interval than the first. Therefore, we look at the probability of arriving in each interval, calculated as the number of minutes in the interval divided by 60. We now calculate a weighted average using the probabilities as weights, and the average wait time becomes:

$$(10 \div 60) \times 5 + (20 \div 60) \times 20 + (5 \div 60)$$
$$\times 2.5 + (25 \div 60) \times 12.5 = 9.58 \text{ minutes.}$$

So although the average waiting time between buses is 6.5 minutes, because there is a much greater chance of arriving in a long interval than a short interval, the actual waiting time is 9.58 minutes. So you really do wait longer than expected.

| Interval Length | 10 | 20 | 5 | 25 |
|---|---|---|---|---|
| Probability | 10 ÷ 60 | 20 ÷ 60 | 5 ÷ 60 | 25 ÷ 60 |
| Wait time | 5 | 10 | 2.5 | 12.5 |

# Conclusion

In many situations, social scientists need to collect data that isn't interval or ratio in nature. For example, we often measure the variables such as smoking marijuana as a dichotomous variable (yes, no) or degree of political engagement as low, medium, and high. In this chapter we found that we can use a number of different methods to analyze nominal and ordinal level variables. While these methods are not as common as the methods explained in previous chapters, they are still very useful.

**Key Chapter Concepts and Terms**

| | | |
|---|---|---|
| Contingency tables, 364 | Cramér's | Point-biserial correlation |
| Observed frequency, 365 | V coefficient, 369 | ($r_{pb}$), 371 |
| Expected frequency, 365 | Pearson chi-square | Spearman's correlation |
| Phi coefficient, 369 | goodness of fit, 371 | coefficient, 375 |

**Frequently Asked Questions**

1. How important is it for students to know how to use $2 \times 2$ tables?

   Along with the *t*-test, the analysis of $2 \times 2$ tables is one of the most important topics in statistics. You can break down almost all data into categories and analyze their relationships. For example, even if we measure reaction times we can always summarize them as slow or fast. So independence in $2 \times 2$ tables is widely used in research.

2. Does it matter in what order I place the nominal variables?

   No, the chi-square test gives the same value even if you rearrange the order of the categories as long as you are rearranging the order of rows and columns.

3. Why is the Phi coefficient of association never negative?

   The measure of association is based on a chi-square value. As the chi-square test does not depend on the order of the categories, the measure of association is not looking for a direction, just a relationship. If there is a relationship between happy or sad and the colours of the room being black, red, and green, then what would a positive or negative relationship actually mean?

4. Does it matter how many people we sample in our surveys and experiments?

   Yes. The test statistics for count type data are based on large sample approximations. We really do need expected cell counts to be at least 5. There are other exact methods for the analysis of small sample data, but we leave those methods to a more advanced text.

**Research Example:**

In 2010, Dr. Jason Ulsperger and colleagues published their study "Pirates on the Plank: Neutralization Theory and the Criminal Downloading of Music Among Generation Y in the Era of Late Modernity" in the *Journal of Criminal Justice and Popular Culture*.

Their research focussed on the prevalence of illegal music downloading via the Internet. Furthermore, they focussed on understanding how individuals rationalize illegal downloading. Their study involved 800 students across four universities in the United States. The following tables have been reproduced, based on their study.[2]

| Downloading Behaviour by Gender | | |
|---|---|---|
| **Music Downloading** | **Gender** | |
| | Female | Male |
| **Illegally** | 398 | 275 |
| **Legally** | 40 | 65 |

### Downloading Behaviour by Age

| Music Downloading | Age | |
|---|---|---|
| | <25 | ≥25 |
| Illegally | 601 | 72 |
| Legally | 69 | 36 |

**Research Example Questions:**

**Question 1:** What type of analysis should you run to measure the association between gender (female vs. male) and music downloading (illegal vs. legal)?

**Question 2:** Test the hypothesis that there is an association between gender and music downloading.

**Question 3:** Interpret the results from question 2.

**Research Example Answers:**

**Question 1:** What type of analysis should you run to measure the association between gender (female vs. male) and music downloading (illegal vs. legal)?

Since both variables are nominal, you need to run a Pearson's chi-square test of independence in order to measure the association.

**Question 2:** Test the hypothesis that there is an association between gender and music downloading.

### Downloading Behaviour by Gender

| Music Downloading | Gender | | Total | Row Percent |
|---|---|---|---|---|
| | Female | Male | | |
| Illegally | 398 (378.90) | 275 (294.10) | 673 | 85.50% |
| Legally | 40 (59.10) | 65 (45.90) | 105 | 14.50% |
| Total | 438 | 340 | 778 | 100.00% |
| Column Percent | 56.30% | 43.70% | 100.00% | |

Expected frequencies

For female and illegally: $673 \times \dfrac{438}{778} = 378.9$

For female and legally: $105 \times \dfrac{438}{778} = 59.1$

For male and illegally: $673 \times \dfrac{340}{778} = 294.1$

For male and legally: $105 \times \dfrac{340}{778} = 45.9$

$$\chi^2 = \Sigma \frac{(0-E)^2}{E} = \frac{(398-378.9)^2}{378.9} + \frac{(275-294.1)^2}{294.1}$$
$$+ \frac{(40-59.1)^2}{59.1} + \frac{(65-45.9)^2}{45.9} = 16.32$$

$$df = (R-1)(C-1) = (2-1)(2-1) = 1$$

$$\phi = \sqrt{\frac{\chi^2}{N}} = \sqrt{\frac{16.32}{778}} = .145$$

**Question 3:** Interpret the results from question 2.

The null and alternative hypotheses are:

$H_0$: There is no association between gender and music downloading

$H_A$: There is an association between gender and music downloading

The critical value for chi-square with 1 *df* is 3.84. Our result shows that $\chi^2_{(1)} = 16.32$. Therefore, we reject the null hypothesis and state that based on our sample there appears to be a relationship between gender and music downloading. To assess the strength of the relationship the Phi ($\phi$) coefficient was calculated. With $\phi = 0.145$, we know that although the relationship is significant, it is a fairly weak one.

**ANSWERS TO EXERCISE 13.1**

First, calculate the row and column totals:

| Level of Care | Less | More | Total | Row Percent |
|---|---|---|---|---|
| Died | 12 | 16 | 28 | 5.46% |
| Survived | 176 | 309 | 485 | 94.54% |
| Total | 188 | 315 | 513 | 100.00% |
| Column Percent | 36.65% | 63.35% | 100.00% | |

Then, calculate the expected cell counts:

$$E_{ij} = \frac{Row_i \times Column_j}{N}$$

So for the cell Died/Less (care), the expected count is $(28 \times 188) \div 513 = 10.261$. Completing the table in a similar fashion gives the observed counts (expected counts) as:

| | Level of Care | | Total | Row Percent |
|---|---|---|---|---|
| | Less | More | | |
| Died | 12 (10.261) | 16 (17.739) | 28 | 5.46% |
| Survived | 176 (177.74) | 309 (307.26) | 485 | 94.54% |
| Total | 188 | 315 | 513 | 100.00% |
| Column Percent | 36.65% | 63.35% | 100.00% | |

$$\chi^2 = \Sigma\frac{(O - E)^2}{E}$$

where: $\chi^2$ = the chi-square statistic

$O$ = the observed frequencies from the contingency table

$E$ = the expected frequencies based on the null hypothesis

The $\chi^2$ value is 0.4919. With 1 *df* and an alpha ($\alpha$) of 0.05, the critical value for the chi-squared distribution is 3.84. As the observed chi-square value of 0.4919 is less than the critical value, we fail to reject the null hypothesis of independence and claim there is no significant relationship between level of care and mortality.

**ANSWERS TO EXERCISE 13.2**

$H_0$: Leaders equally preferred
$H_A$: Leaders not equally preferred

If all three leaders were equally preferred then we would expect one third of the sample to favour each of the three leaders. So, the expected counts for each cell with 90 people sampled is:

$$(1 \div 3) \times 90 = 30$$

| A | Observed | Expected |
|---|---|---|
| A | 20 | 30 |
| B | 40 | 30 |
| C | 30 | 30 |
| Total | 90 | 90 |

$$\chi^2 = \Sigma\frac{(O - E)^2}{E}$$
$$= (20 - 30)^2 \div 30 + (40 - 30)^2 \div 30 + (30 - 30)^2 \div 30$$
$$= 100 \div 30 + 100 \div 30 + 0$$
$$= 200 \div 30$$
$$= 6.67$$

As we have three cells, we use $3 - 1 = 2$ *df* for our goodness of fit test. Using an alpha ($\alpha$) of 0.05, the critical $\chi^2$ value on 2 *df* is 5.99. As the observed chi-square value 6.67 is greater than 5.99 we reject the null hypothesis of independence and claim there is a difference in the preference for Prime Minister.

**Problems**

1. Students use many kinds of criteria when selecting courses. "Teacher is a very easy grader" is often one such criterion. Three teachers are scheduled to teach statistics in the winter term. A sample of the grade distributions for each of these three teachers follows.

| Grades | James | Jackson | Julian | Total |
|---|---|---|---|---|
| $80 \leq$ grade $\leq 100$ (*A*) | 12 | 11 | 27 | |
| $70 \leq$ grade $\leq 79$ (*B*) | 16 | 29 | 25 | |
| $60 \leq$ grade $\leq 69$ (*C*) | 35 | 30 | 15 | |
| $0 \leq$ grade $\leq 59$ (*F*) | 27 | 40 | 23 | |
| Total | | | | |

   a) Test the null hypothesis that grade received is independent of the professor at the 5 percent level.

   b) Does the result indicate a strong or weak relationship?

2. Two teachers were asked to rate a series of books on a scale from 1 to 20 as per the likelihood they would use it as a text in their class. The data are shown in the table below.

| Textbook | Teacher 1 | Teacher 2 |
|---|---|---|
| 1 | 4 | 4 |
| 2 | 10 | 6 |
| 3 | 18 | 20 |
| 4 | 20 | 14 |
| 5 | 12 | 16 |
| 6 | 2 | 8 |
| 7 | 5 | 11 |
| 8 | 9 | 7 |

   a) Calculate Spearman's $\rho - r_s$.

   b) Do you believe there is a relationship between the two at the 5 percent level (Hint: Is the result statistically different from 0 at the 5 percent level)?

3. The following table is from the National Institute on Aging. The individuals in the following table have only one of the three mentioned types of irritations.

| | Age (years) | | | | |
|---|---|---|---|---|---|
| | 18–29 | 30–44 | 45–64 | 65 | Total |
| Eye | 440 | 567 | 349 | 59 | |
| Nose | 924 | 1311 | 794 | 102 | |
| Throat | 253 | 311 | 157 | 19 | |
| Total | | | | | |

a) Test the null hypothesis that age is independent of type of irritation at the 5 percent level.

b) Does the result indicate a strong or weak relationship?

c) How would your answer change if alpha ($\alpha$) were 1 percent instead?

  McGraw-Hill Connect provides you with a powerful tool for improving academic performance and truly mastering course material. You can diagnose your knowledge with pre- and post-tests, identify the areas where you need help, search the entire learning package, including the eBook, for content specific to the topic you're studying, and add these resources to your personalized study plan. Visit **connect** to register.

# Appendix A

## Area Under the Normal Curve

| z-value | Area between mean and z | Area Past z | z-value | Area between mean and z | Area Past z | z-value | Area between mean and z | Area Past z |
|---|---|---|---|---|---|---|---|---|
| 0.00 | 0.0000 | 0.5000 | 0.60 | 0.2258 | 0.2743 | 1.20 | 0.3849 | 0.1151 |
| 0.01 | 0.0040 | 0.4960 | 0.61 | 0.2291 | 0.2709 | 1.21 | 0.3869 | 0.1131 |
| 0.02 | 0.0080 | 0.4920 | 0.62 | 0.2324 | 0.2676 | 1.22 | 0.3888 | 0.1112 |
| 0.03 | 0.0120 | 0.4880 | 0.63 | 0.2357 | 0.2644 | 1.23 | 0.3907 | 0.1094 |
| 0.04 | 0.0160 | 0.4841 | 0.64 | 0.2389 | 0.2611 | 1.24 | 0.3925 | 0.1075 |
| 0.05 | 0.0199 | 0.4801 | 0.65 | 0.2422 | 0.2579 | 1.25 | 0.3944 | 0.1057 |
| 0.06 | 0.0239 | 0.4761 | 0.66 | 0.2454 | 0.2546 | 1.26 | 0.3962 | 0.1038 |
| 0.07 | 0.0279 | 0.4721 | 0.67 | 0.2486 | 0.2514 | 1.27 | 0.3980 | 0.1020 |
| 0.08 | 0.0319 | 0.4681 | 0.68 | 0.2518 | 0.2483 | 1.28 | 0.3997 | 0.1003 |
| 0.09 | 0.0359 | 0.4641 | 0.69 | 0.2549 | 0.2451 | 1.29 | 0.4015 | 0.0985 |
| 0.10 | 0.0398 | 0.4602 | 0.70 | 0.2580 | 0.2420 | 1.30 | 0.4032 | 0.0968 |
| 0.11 | 0.0438 | 0.4562 | 0.71 | 0.2612 | 0.2389 | 1.31 | 0.4049 | 0.0951 |
| 0.12 | 0.0478 | 0.4522 | 0.72 | 0.2642 | 0.2358 | 1.32 | 0.4066 | 0.0934 |
| 0.13 | 0.0517 | 0.4483 | 0.73 | 0.2673 | 0.2327 | 1.33 | 0.4082 | 0.0918 |
| 0.14 | 0.0557 | 0.4443 | 0.74 | 0.2704 | 0.2297 | 1.34 | 0.4099 | 0.0901 |
| 0.15 | 0.0596 | 0.4404 | 0.75 | 0.2734 | 0.2266 | 1.35 | 0.4115 | 0.0885 |
| 0.16 | 0.0636 | 0.4364 | 0.76 | 0.2764 | 0.2236 | 1.36 | 0.4131 | 0.0869 |
| 0.17 | 0.0675 | 0.4325 | 0.77 | 0.2794 | 0.2207 | 1.37 | 0.4147 | 0.0853 |
| 0.18 | 0.0714 | 0.4286 | 0.78 | 0.2823 | 0.2177 | 1.38 | 0.4162 | 0.0838 |
| 0.19 | 0.0754 | 0.4247 | 0.79 | 0.2852 | 0.2148 | 1.39 | 0.4177 | 0.0823 |
| 0.20 | 0.0793 | 0.4207 | 0.80 | 0.2881 | 0.2119 | 1.40 | 0.4192 | 0.0808 |
| 0.21 | 0.0832 | 0.4168 | 0.81 | 0.2910 | 0.2090 | 1.41 | 0.4207 | 0.0793 |
| 0.22 | 0.0871 | 0.4129 | 0.82 | 0.2939 | 0.2061 | 1.42 | 0.4222 | 0.0778 |
| 0.23 | 0.0910 | 0.4091 | 0.83 | 0.2967 | 0.2033 | 1.43 | 0.4236 | 0.0764 |
| 0.24 | 0.0948 | 0.4052 | 0.84 | 0.2996 | 0.2005 | 1.44 | 0.4251 | 0.0749 |
| 0.25 | 0.0987 | 0.4013 | 0.85 | 0.3023 | 0.1977 | 1.45 | 0.4265 | 0.0735 |
| 0.26 | 0.1026 | 0.3974 | 0.86 | 0.3051 | 0.1949 | 1.46 | 0.4279 | 0.0722 |
| 0.27 | 0.1064 | 0.3936 | 0.87 | 0.3079 | 0.1922 | 1.47 | 0.4292 | 0.0708 |
| 0.28 | 0.1103 | 0.3897 | 0.88 | 0.3106 | 0.1894 | 1.48 | 0.4306 | 0.0694 |
| 0.29 | 0.1141 | 0.3859 | 0.89 | 0.3133 | 0.1867 | 1.49 | 0.4319 | 0.0681 |
| 0.30 | 0.1179 | 0.3821 | 0.90 | 0.3159 | 0.1841 | 1.50 | 0.4332 | 0.0668 |
| 0.31 | 0.1217 | 0.3783 | 0.91 | 0.3186 | 0.1814 | 1.51 | 0.4345 | 0.0655 |
| 0.32 | 0.1255 | 0.3745 | 0.92 | 0.3212 | 0.1788 | 1.52 | 0.4357 | 0.0643 |
| 0.33 | 0.1293 | 0.3707 | 0.93 | 0.3238 | 0.1762 | 1.53 | 0.4370 | 0.0630 |
| 0.34 | 0.1331 | 0.3669 | 0.94 | 0.3264 | 0.1736 | 1.54 | 0.4382 | 0.0618 |
| 0.35 | 0.1368 | 0.3632 | 0.95 | 0.3289 | 0.1711 | 1.55 | 0.4394 | 0.0606 |
| 0.36 | 0.1406 | 0.3594 | 0.96 | 0.3315 | 0.1685 | 1.56 | 0.4406 | 0.0594 |
| 0.37 | 0.1443 | 0.3557 | 0.97 | 0.3340 | 0.1660 | 1.57 | 0.4418 | 0.0582 |
| 0.38 | 0.1480 | 0.3520 | 0.98 | 0.3365 | 0.1635 | 1.58 | 0.4430 | 0.0571 |
| 0.39 | 0.1517 | 0.3483 | 0.99 | 0.3389 | 0.1611 | 1.59 | 0.4441 | 0.0559 |
| 0.40 | 0.1554 | 0.3446 | 1.00 | 0.3413 | 0.1587 | 1.60 | 0.4452 | 0.0548 |
| 0.41 | 0.1591 | 0.3409 | 1.01 | 0.3438 | 0.1563 | 1.61 | 0.4463 | 0.0537 |
| 0.42 | 0.1628 | 0.3372 | 1.02 | 0.3461 | 0.1539 | 1.62 | 0.4474 | 0.0526 |
| 0.43 | 0.1664 | 0.3336 | 1.03 | 0.3485 | 0.1515 | 1.63 | 0.4485 | 0.0516 |
| 0.44 | 0.1700 | 0.3300 | 1.04 | 0.3508 | 0.1492 | 1.64 | 0.4495 | 0.0505 |
| 0.45 | 0.1736 | 0.3264 | 1.05 | 0.3531 | 0.1469 | 1.645 | 0.4500 | 0.0500 |
| 0.46 | 0.1772 | 0.3228 | 1.06 | 0.3554 | 0.1446 | 1.654 | 0.4505 | 0.0495 |
| 0.47 | 0.1808 | 0.3192 | 1.07 | 0.3577 | 0.1423 | 1.66 | 0.4515 | 0.0485 |
| 0.48 | 0.1844 | 0.3156 | 1.08 | 0.3599 | 0.1401 | 1.67 | 0.4525 | 0.0475 |
| 0.49 | 0.1879 | 0.3121 | 1.09 | 0.3621 | 0.1379 | 1.68 | 0.4535 | 0.0465 |
| 0.50 | 0.1915 | 0.3085 | 1.10 | 0.3643 | 0.1357 | 1.69 | 0.4545 | 0.0455 |
| 0.51 | 0.1950 | 0.3050 | 1.11 | 0.3665 | 0.1335 | 1.70 | 0.4554 | 0.0446 |
| 0.52 | 0.1985 | 0.3015 | 1.12 | 0.3686 | 0.1314 | 1.71 | 0.4564 | 0.0436 |
| 0.53 | 0.2019 | 0.2981 | 1.13 | 0.3708 | 0.1292 | 1.72 | 0.4573 | 0.0427 |
| 0.54 | 0.2054 | 0.2946 | 1.14 | 0.3729 | 0.1271 | 1.73 | 0.4582 | 0.0418 |
| 0.55 | 0.2088 | 0.2912 | 1.15 | 0.3749 | 0.1251 | 1.74 | 0.4591 | 0.0409 |
| 0.56 | 0.2123 | 0.2877 | 1.16 | 0.3770 | 0.1230 | 1.75 | 0.4599 | 0.0401 |
| 0.57 | 0.2157 | 0.2843 | 1.17 | 0.3790 | 0.1210 | 1.76 | 0.4608 | 0.0392 |
| 0.58 | 0.2190 | 0.2810 | 1.18 | 0.3810 | 0.1190 | 1.77 | 0.4616 | 0.0384 |
| 0.59 | 0.2224 | 0.2776 | 1.19 | 0.3830 | 0.1170 | 1.78 | 0.4625 | 0.0375 |

| z-value | Area between mean and z | Area Past z | z-value | Area between mean and z | Area Past z | z-value | Area between mean and z | Area Past z |
|---|---|---|---|---|---|---|---|---|
| 1.79 | 0.4633 | 0.0367 | 2.50 | 0.4938 | 0.0062 | 3.20 | 0.4993 | 0.0007 |
| 1.80 | 0.4641 | 0.0359 | 2.51 | 0.4940 | 0.0060 | 3.21 | 0.4993 | 0.0007 |
| 1.81 | 0.4649 | 0.0352 | 2.52 | 0.4941 | 0.0059 | 3.22 | 0.4994 | 0.0006 |
| 1.82 | 0.4656 | 0.0344 | 2.53 | 0.4943 | 0.0057 | 3.23 | 0.4994 | 0.0006 |
| 1.83 | 0.4664 | 0.0336 | 2.54 | 0.4945 | 0.0055 | 3.24 | 0.4994 | 0.0006 |
| 1.84 | 0.4671 | 0.0329 | 2.55 | 0.4946 | 0.0054 | 3.25 | 0.4994 | 0.0006 |
| 1.85 | 0.4678 | 0.0322 | 2.56 | 0.4948 | 0.0052 | 3.26 | 0.4994 | 0.0006 |
| 1.86 | 0.4686 | 0.0314 | 2.57 | 0.4949 | 0.0051 | 3.27 | 0.4995 | 0.0005 |
| 1.87 | 0.4693 | 0.0307 | 2.576 | 0.4950 | 0.0050 | 3.28 | 0.4995 | 0.0005 |
| 1.88 | 0.4700 | 0.0301 | 2.58 | 0.4951 | 0.0049 | 3.29 | 0.4995 | 0.0005 |
| 1.89 | 0.4706 | 0.0294 | 2.59 | 0.4952 | 0.0048 | 3.30 | 0.4995 | 0.0005 |
| 1.90 | 0.4713 | 0.0287 | 2.60 | 0.4953 | 0.0047 | 3.31 | 0.4995 | 0.0005 |
| 1.91 | 0.4719 | 0.0281 | 2.61 | 0.4955 | 0.0045 | 3.32 | 0.4996 | 0.0004 |
| 1.92 | 0.4726 | 0.0274 | 2.62 | 0.4956 | 0.0044 | 3.33 | 0.4996 | 0.0004 |
| 1.93 | 0.4732 | 0.0268 | 2.63 | 0.4957 | 0.0043 | 3.34 | 0.4996 | 0.0004 |
| 1.94 | 0.4738 | 0.0262 | 2.64 | 0.4959 | 0.0041 | 3.35 | 0.4996 | 0.0004 |
| 1.95 | 0.4744 | 0.0256 | 2.65 | 0.4960 | 0.0040 | 3.36 | 0.4996 | 0.0004 |
| 1.96 | 0.4750 | 0.0250 | 2.66 | 0.4961 | 0.0039 | 3.37 | 0.4996 | 0.0004 |
| 1.97 | 0.4756 | 0.0244 | 2.67 | 0.4962 | 0.0038 | 3.38 | 0.4996 | 0.0004 |
| 1.98 | 0.4762 | 0.0239 | 2.68 | 0.4963 | 0.0037 | 3.39 | 0.4997 | 0.0003 |
| 1.99 | 0.4767 | 0.0233 | 2.69 | 0.4964 | 0.0036 | 3.40 | 0.4997 | 0.0003 |
| 2.00 | 0.4773 | 0.0228 | 2.70 | 0.4965 | 0.0035 | 3.41 | 0.4997 | 0.0003 |
| 2.01 | 0.4778 | 0.0222 | 2.71 | 0.4966 | 0.0034 | 3.42 | 0.4997 | 0.0003 |
| 2.02 | 0.4783 | 0.0217 | 2.72 | 0.4967 | 0.0033 | 3.43 | 0.4997 | 0.0003 |
| 2.03 | 0.4788 | 0.0212 | 2.73 | 0.4968 | 0.0032 | 3.44 | 0.4997 | 0.0003 |
| 2.04 | 0.4793 | 0.0207 | 2.74 | 0.4969 | 0.0031 | 3.45 | 0.4997 | 0.0003 |
| 2.05 | 0.4798 | 0.0202 | 2.75 | 0.4970 | 0.0030 | 3.46 | 0.4997 | 0.0003 |
| 2.06 | 0.4803 | 0.0197 | 2.76 | 0.4971 | 0.0029 | 3.47 | 0.4997 | 0.0003 |
| 2.07 | 0.4808 | 0.0192 | 2.77 | 0.4972 | 0.0028 | 3.48 | 0.4998 | 0.0002 |
| 2.08 | 0.4812 | 0.0188 | 2.78 | 0.4973 | 0.0027 | 3.49 | 0.4998 | 0.0002 |
| 2.09 | 0.4817 | 0.0183 | 2.79 | 0.4974 | 0.0026 | 3.50 | 0.4998 | 0.0002 |
| 2.10 | 0.4821 | 0.0179 | 2.80 | 0.4974 | 0.0026 | 3.51 | 0.4998 | 0.0002 |
| 2.11 | 0.4826 | 0.0174 | 2.81 | 0.4975 | 0.0025 | 3.52 | 0.4998 | 0.0002 |
| 2.12 | 0.4830 | 0.0170 | 2.82 | 0.4976 | 0.0024 | 3.53 | 0.4998 | 0.0002 |
| 2.13 | 0.4834 | 0.0166 | 2.83 | 0.4977 | 0.0023 | 3.54 | 0.4998 | 0.0002 |
| 2.14 | 0.4838 | 0.0162 | 2.84 | 0.4977 | 0.0023 | 3.55 | 0.4998 | 0.0002 |
| 2.15 | 0.4842 | 0.0158 | 2.85 | 0.4978 | 0.0022 | 3.56 | 0.4998 | 0.0002 |
| 2.16 | 0.4846 | 0.0154 | 2.86 | 0.4979 | 0.0021 | 3.57 | 0.4998 | 0.0002 |
| 2.17 | 0.4850 | 0.0150 | 2.87 | 0.4980 | 0.0021 | 3.58 | 0.4998 | 0.0002 |
| 2.18 | 0.4854 | 0.0146 | 2.88 | 0.4980 | 0.0020 | 3.59 | 0.4998 | 0.0002 |
| 2.19 | 0.4857 | 0.0143 | 2.89 | 0.4981 | 0.0019 | 3.60 | 0.4998 | 0.0002 |
| 2.20 | 0.4861 | 0.0139 | 2.90 | 0.4981 | 0.0019 | 3.61 | 0.4999 | 0.0001 |
| 2.21 | 0.4865 | 0.0136 | 2.91 | 0.4982 | 0.0018 | 3.62 | 0.4999 | 0.0001 |
| 2.22 | 0.4868 | 0.0132 | 2.92 | 0.4983 | 0.0018 | 3.63 | 0.4999 | 0.0001 |
| 2.23 | 0.4871 | 0.0129 | 2.93 | 0.4983 | 0.0017 | 3.64 | 0.4999 | 0.0001 |
| 2.24 | 0.4875 | 0.0126 | 2.94 | 0.4984 | 0.0016 | 3.65 | 0.4999 | 0.0001 |
| 2.25 | 0.4878 | 0.0122 | 2.95 | 0.4984 | 0.0016 | 3.66 | 0.4999 | 0.0001 |
| 2.26 | 0.4881 | 0.0119 | 2.96 | 0.4985 | 0.0015 | 3.67 | 0.4999 | 0.0001 |
| 2.27 | 0.4884 | 0.0116 | 2.97 | 0.4985 | 0.0015 | 3.68 | 0.4999 | 0.0001 |
| 2.28 | 0.4887 | 0.0113 | 2.98 | 0.4986 | 0.0014 | 3.69 | 0.4999 | 0.0001 |
| 2.29 | 0.4890 | 0.0110 | 2.99 | 0.4986 | 0.0014 | 3.70 | 0.4999 | 0.0001 |
| 2.30 | 0.4893 | 0.0107 | 3.00 | 0.4987 | 0.0013 | 3.71 | 0.4999 | 0.0001 |
| 2.31 | 0.4896 | 0.0104 | 3.01 | 0.4987 | 0.0013 | 3.72 | 0.4999 | 0.0001 |
| 2.32 | 0.4898 | 0.0102 | 3.02 | 0.4987 | 0.0013 | 3.73 | 0.4999 | 0.0001 |
| 2.33 | 0.4901 | 0.0099 | 3.03 | 0.4988 | 0.0012 | 3.74 | 0.4999 | 0.0001 |
| 2.34 | 0.4904 | 0.0096 | 3.04 | 0.4988 | 0.0012 | 3.75 | 0.4999 | 0.0001 |
| 2.35 | 0.4906 | 0.0094 | 3.05 | 0.4989 | 0.0011 | 3.76 | 0.4999 | 0.0001 |
| 2.36 | 0.4909 | 0.0091 | 3.06 | 0.4989 | 0.0011 | 3.77 | 0.4999 | 0.0001 |
| 2.37 | 0.4911 | 0.0089 | 3.07 | 0.4989 | 0.0011 | 3.78 | 0.4999 | 0.0001 |
| 2.38 | 0.4913 | 0.0087 | 3.08 | 0.4990 | 0.0010 | 3.79 | 0.4999 | 0.0001 |
| 2.39 | 0.4916 | 0.0084 | 3.09 | 0.4990 | 0.0010 | 3.80 | 0.4999 | 0.0001 |
| 2.40 | 0.4918 | 0.0082 | 3.10 | 0.4990 | 0.0010 | 3.81 | 0.4999 | 0.0001 |
| 2.41 | 0.4920 | 0.0080 | 3.11 | 0.4991 | 0.0009 | 3.82 | 0.4999 | 0.0001 |
| 2.42 | 0.4922 | 0.0078 | 3.12 | 0.4991 | 0.0009 | 3.83 | 0.4999 | 0.0001 |
| 2.43 | 0.4925 | 0.0075 | 3.13 | 0.4991 | 0.0009 | 3.84 | 0.4999 | 0.0001 |
| 2.44 | 0.4927 | 0.0073 | 3.14 | 0.4992 | 0.0008 | 3.85 | 0.4999 | 0.0001 |
| 2.45 | 0.4929 | 0.0071 | 3.15 | 0.4992 | 0.0008 | 3.86 | 0.4999 | 0.0001 |
| 2.46 | 0.4931 | 0.0070 | 3.16 | 0.4992 | 0.0008 | 3.87 | 0.5000 | 0.0000 |
| 2.47 | 0.4932 | 0.0068 | 3.17 | 0.4992 | 0.0008 | 3.88 | 0.5000 | 0.0000 |
| 2.48 | 0.4934 | 0.0066 | 3.18 | 0.4993 | 0.0007 | 3.89 | 0.5000 | 0.0000 |
| 2.49 | 0.4936 | 0.0064 | 3.19 | 0.4993 | 0.0007 | 3.90 | 0.5000 | 0.0000 |

# Appendix B

Critical Values for the F-distribution at the 1% Significance Level

| Degrees of Freedom Denominator | Degrees of Freedom Numerator | | | | | | | |
|---|---|---|---|---|---|---|---|---|
| | 1 | 2 | 3 | 4 | 5 | 6 | 7 | 8 |
| 1 | 4052.18 | 4999.50 | 5403.35 | 5624.58 | 5763.65 | 5858.99 | 5928.36 | 5981.07 |
| 2 | 98.50 | 99.00 | 99.17 | 99.25 | 99.30 | 99.33 | 99.36 | 99.37 |
| 3 | 34.12 | 30.82 | 29.46 | 28.71 | 28.24 | 27.91 | 27.67 | 27.49 |
| 4 | 21.20 | 18.00 | 16.69 | 15.98 | 15.52 | 15.21 | 14.98 | 14.80 |
| 5 | 16.26 | 13.27 | 12.06 | 11.39 | 10.97 | 10.67 | 10.46 | 10.29 |
| 6 | 13.75 | 10.92 | 9.78 | 9.15 | 8.75 | 8.47 | 8.26 | 8.10 |
| 7 | 12.25 | 9.55 | 8.45 | 7.85 | 7.46 | 7.19 | 6.99 | 6.84 |
| 8 | 11.26 | 8.65 | 7.59 | 7.01 | 6.63 | 6.37 | 6.18 | 6.03 |
| 9 | 10.56 | 8.02 | 6.99 | 6.42 | 6.06 | 5.80 | 5.61 | 5.47 |
| 10 | 10.04 | 7.56 | 6.55 | 5.99 | 5.64 | 5.39 | 5.20 | 5.06 |
| 11 | 9.65 | 7.21 | 6.22 | 5.67 | 5.32 | 5.07 | 4.89 | 4.74 |
| 12 | 9.33 | 6.93 | 5.95 | 5.41 | 5.06 | 4.82 | 4.64 | 4.50 |
| 13 | 9.07 | 6.70 | 5.74 | 5.21 | 4.86 | 4.62 | 4.44 | 4.30 |
| 14 | 8.86 | 6.51 | 5.56 | 5.04 | 4.69 | 4.46 | 4.28 | 4.14 |
| 15 | 8.68 | 6.36 | 5.42 | 4.89 | 4.56 | 4.32 | 4.14 | 4.00 |
| 16 | 8.53 | 6.23 | 5.29 | 4.77 | 4.44 | 4.20 | 4.03 | 3.89 |
| 17 | 8.40 | 6.11 | 5.18 | 4.67 | 4.34 | 4.10 | 3.93 | 3.79 |
| 18 | 8.29 | 6.01 | 5.09 | 4.58 | 4.25 | 4.01 | 3.84 | 3.71 |
| 19 | 8.18 | 5.93 | 5.01 | 4.50 | 4.17 | 3.94 | 3.77 | 3.63 |
| 20 | 8.10 | 5.85 | 4.94 | 4.43 | 4.10 | 3.87 | 3.70 | 3.56 |
| 21 | 8.02 | 5.78 | 4.87 | 4.37 | 4.04 | 3.81 | 3.64 | 3.51 |
| 22 | 7.95 | 5.72 | 4.82 | 4.31 | 3.99 | 3.76 | 3.59 | 3.45 |
| 23 | 7.88 | 5.66 | 4.76 | 4.26 | 3.94 | 3.71 | 3.54 | 3.41 |
| 24 | 7.82 | 5.61 | 4.72 | 4.22 | 3.90 | 3.67 | 3.50 | 3.36 |
| 25 | 7.77 | 5.57 | 4.68 | 4.18 | 3.85 | 3.63 | 3.46 | 3.32 |
| 26 | 7.72 | 5.53 | 4.64 | 4.14 | 3.82 | 3.59 | 3.42 | 3.29 |
| 27 | 7.68 | 5.49 | 4.60 | 4.11 | 3.78 | 3.56 | 3.39 | 3.26 |
| 28 | 7.64 | 5.45 | 4.57 | 4.07 | 3.75 | 3.53 | 3.36 | 3.23 |
| 29 | 7.60 | 5.42 | 4.54 | 4.04 | 3.73 | 3.50 | 3.33 | 3.20 |
| 30 | 7.56 | 5.39 | 4.51 | 4.02 | 3.70 | 3.47 | 3.30 | 3.17 |
| 40 | 7.31 | 5.18 | 4.31 | 3.83 | 3.51 | 3.29 | 3.12 | 2.99 |
| 60 | 7.08 | 4.98 | 4.13 | 3.65 | 3.34 | 3.12 | 2.95 | 2.82 |
| 120 | 6.85 | 4.79 | 3.95 | 3.48 | 3.17 | 2.96 | 2.79 | 2.66 |
| ∞ | 6.64 | 4.61 | 3.78 | 3.32 | 3.02 | 2.80 | 2.64 | 2.51 |

# Appendix C

## Critical Values for the F-distribution at the 5% Significance Level

| Degrees of Freedom Denominator | Degrees of Freedom Numerator | | | | | | | |
|---|---|---|---|---|---|---|---|---|
| | 1 | 2 | 3 | 4 | 5 | 6 | 7 | 8 |
| 1 | 161.45 | 199.50 | 215.71 | 224.58 | 230.16 | 233.99 | 236.77 | 238.88 |
| 2 | 18.51 | 19.00 | 19.16 | 19.25 | 19.30 | 19.33 | 19.35 | 19.37 |
| 3 | 10.13 | 9.55 | 9.28 | 9.12 | 9.01 | 8.94 | 8.89 | 8.85 |
| 4 | 7.71 | 6.94 | 6.59 | 6.39 | 6.26 | 6.16 | 6.09 | 6.04 |
| 5 | 6.61 | 5.79 | 5.41 | 5.19 | 5.05 | 4.95 | 4.88 | 4.82 |
| 6 | 5.99 | 5.14 | 4.76 | 4.53 | 4.39 | 4.28 | 4.21 | 4.15 |
| 7 | 5.59 | 4.74 | 4.35 | 4.12 | 3.97 | 3.87 | 3.79 | 3.73 |
| 8 | 5.32 | 4.46 | 4.07 | 3.84 | 3.69 | 3.58 | 3.50 | 3.44 |
| 9 | 5.12 | 4.26 | 3.86 | 3.63 | 3.48 | 3.37 | 3.29 | 3.23 |
| 10 | 4.96 | 4.10 | 3.71 | 3.48 | 3.33 | 3.22 | 3.14 | 3.07 |
| 11 | 4.84 | 3.98 | 3.59 | 3.36 | 3.20 | 3.09 | 3.01 | 2.95 |
| 12 | 4.75 | 3.89 | 3.49 | 3.26 | 3.11 | 3.00 | 2.91 | 2.85 |
| 13 | 4.67 | 3.81 | 3.41 | 3.18 | 3.03 | 2.92 | 2.83 | 2.77 |
| 14 | 4.60 | 3.74 | 3.34 | 3.11 | 2.96 | 2.85 | 2.76 | 2.70 |
| 15 | 4.54 | 3.68 | 3.29 | 3.06 | 2.90 | 2.79 | 2.71 | 2.64 |
| 16 | 4.49 | 3.63 | 3.24 | 3.01 | 2.85 | 2.74 | 2.66 | 2.59 |
| 17 | 4.45 | 3.59 | 3.20 | 2.96 | 2.81 | 2.70 | 2.61 | 2.55 |
| 18 | 4.41 | 3.55 | 3.16 | 2.93 | 2.77 | 2.66 | 2.58 | 2.51 |
| 19 | 4.38 | 3.52 | 3.13 | 2.90 | 2.74 | 2.63 | 2.54 | 2.48 |
| 20 | 4.35 | 3.49 | 3.10 | 2.87 | 2.71 | 2.60 | 2.51 | 2.45 |
| 21 | 4.32 | 3.47 | 3.07 | 2.84 | 2.68 | 2.57 | 2.49 | 2.42 |
| 22 | 4.30 | 3.44 | 3.05 | 2.82 | 2.66 | 2.55 | 2.46 | 2.40 |
| 23 | 4.28 | 3.42 | 3.03 | 2.80 | 2.64 | 2.53 | 2.44 | 2.37 |
| 24 | 4.26 | 3.40 | 3.01 | 2.78 | 2.62 | 2.51 | 2.42 | 2.36 |
| 25 | 4.24 | 3.39 | 2.99 | 2.76 | 2.60 | 2.49 | 2.40 | 2.34 |
| 26 | 4.23 | 3.37 | 2.98 | 2.74 | 2.59 | 2.47 | 2.39 | 2.32 |
| 27 | 4.21 | 3.35 | 2.96 | 2.73 | 2.57 | 2.46 | 2.37 | 2.31 |
| 28 | 4.20 | 3.34 | 2.95 | 2.71 | 2.56 | 2.45 | 2.36 | 2.29 |
| 29 | 4.18 | 3.33 | 2.93 | 2.70 | 2.55 | 2.43 | 2.35 | 2.28 |
| 30 | 4.17 | 3.32 | 2.92 | 2.69 | 2.53 | 2.42 | 2.33 | 2.27 |
| 40 | 4.08 | 3.23 | 2.84 | 2.61 | 2.45 | 2.34 | 2.25 | 2.18 |
| 60 | 4.00 | 3.15 | 2.76 | 2.53 | 2.37 | 2.25 | 2.17 | 2.10 |
| 120 | 3.92 | 3.07 | 2.68 | 2.45 | 2.29 | 2.18 | 2.09 | 2.02 |
| ∞ | 3.84 | 3.00 | 2.61 | 2.37 | 2.21 | 2.10 | 2.01 | 1.94 |

# Appendix D

## Critical Values for the Chi Square Distribution

| Degrees of Freedom | Level of Significance ($\alpha$) | | | | | | | | | |
|---|---|---|---|---|---|---|---|---|---|---|
| | 0.99 | 0.95 | 0.90 | 0.75 | 0.50 | 0.25 | 0.10 | 0.05 | 0.01 | 0.001 |
| 1 | 0.000 | 0.004 | 0.016 | 0.102 | 0.455 | 1.323 | 2.706 | 3.841 | 6.635 | 10.828 |
| 2 | 0.020 | 0.103 | 0.211 | 0.575 | 1.386 | 2.773 | 4.605 | 5.991 | 9.210 | 13.816 |
| 3 | 0.115 | 0.352 | 0.584 | 1.213 | 2.366 | 4.108 | 6.251 | 7.815 | 11.345 | 16.266 |
| 4 | 0.297 | 0.711 | 1.064 | 1.923 | 3.357 | 5.385 | 7.779 | 9.488 | 13.277 | 18.467 |
| 5 | 0.554 | 1.145 | 1.610 | 2.675 | 4.351 | 6.626 | 9.236 | 11.070 | 15.086 | 20.515 |
| 6 | 0.872 | 1.635 | 2.204 | 3.455 | 5.348 | 7.841 | 10.645 | 12.592 | 16.812 | 22.458 |
| 7 | 1.239 | 2.167 | 2.833 | 4.255 | 6.346 | 9.037 | 12.017 | 14.067 | 18.475 | 24.322 |
| 8 | 1.646 | 2.733 | 3.490 | 5.071 | 7.344 | 10.219 | 13.362 | 15.507 | 20.090 | 26.124 |
| 9 | 2.088 | 3.325 | 4.168 | 5.899 | 8.343 | 11.389 | 14.684 | 16.919 | 21.666 | 27.877 |
| 10 | 2.558 | 3.940 | 4.865 | 6.737 | 9.342 | 12.549 | 15.987 | 18.307 | 23.209 | 29.588 |
| 11 | 3.053 | 4.575 | 5.578 | 7.584 | 10.341 | 13.701 | 17.275 | 19.675 | 24.725 | 31.264 |
| 12 | 3.571 | 5.226 | 6.304 | 8.438 | 11.340 | 14.845 | 18.549 | 21.026 | 26.217 | 32.909 |
| 13 | 4.107 | 5.892 | 7.042 | 9.299 | 12.340 | 15.984 | 19.812 | 22.362 | 27.688 | 34.528 |
| 14 | 4.660 | 6.571 | 7.790 | 10.165 | 13.339 | 17.117 | 21.064 | 23.685 | 29.141 | 36.123 |
| 15 | 5.229 | 7.261 | 8.547 | 11.037 | 14.339 | 18.245 | 22.307 | 24.996 | 30.578 | 37.697 |
| 16 | 5.812 | 7.962 | 9.312 | 11.912 | 15.338 | 19.369 | 23.542 | 26.296 | 32.000 | 39.252 |
| 17 | 6.408 | 8.672 | 10.085 | 12.792 | 16.338 | 20.489 | 24.769 | 27.587 | 33.409 | 40.790 |
| 18 | 7.015 | 9.390 | 10.865 | 13.675 | 17.338 | 21.605 | 25.989 | 28.869 | 34.805 | 42.312 |
| 19 | 7.633 | 10.117 | 11.651 | 14.562 | 18.338 | 22.718 | 27.204 | 30.144 | 36.191 | 43.820 |
| 20 | 8.260 | 10.851 | 12.443 | 15.452 | 19.337 | 23.828 | 28.412 | 31.410 | 37.566 | 45.315 |
| 21 | 8.897 | 11.591 | 13.240 | 16.344 | 20.337 | 24.935 | 29.615 | 32.671 | 38.932 | 46.797 |
| 22 | 9.542 | 12.338 | 14.041 | 17.240 | 21.337 | 26.039 | 30.813 | 33.924 | 40.289 | 48.268 |
| 23 | 10.196 | 13.091 | 14.848 | 18.137 | 22.337 | 27.141 | 32.007 | 35.172 | 41.638 | 49.728 |
| 24 | 10.856 | 13.848 | 15.659 | 19.037 | 23.337 | 28.241 | 33.196 | 36.415 | 42.980 | 51.179 |
| 25 | 11.524 | 14.611 | 16.473 | 19.939 | 24.337 | 29.339 | 34.382 | 37.652 | 44.314 | 52.620 |
| 26 | 12.198 | 15.379 | 17.292 | 20.843 | 25.336 | 30.435 | 35.563 | 38.885 | 45.642 | 54.052 |
| 27 | 12.879 | 16.151 | 18.114 | 21.749 | 26.336 | 31.528 | 36.741 | 40.113 | 46.963 | 55.476 |
| 28 | 13.565 | 16.928 | 18.939 | 22.657 | 27.336 | 32.620 | 37.916 | 41.337 | 48.278 | 56.892 |
| 29 | 14.256 | 17.708 | 19.768 | 23.567 | 28.336 | 33.711 | 39.087 | 42.557 | 49.588 | 58.301 |
| 30 | 14.953 | 18.493 | 20.599 | 24.478 | 29.336 | 34.800 | 40.256 | 43.773 | 50.892 | 59.703 |
| 40 | 22.164 | 26.509 | 29.051 | 33.660 | 39.335 | 45.616 | 51.805 | 55.758 | 63.691 | 73.402 |
| 50 | 29.707 | 34.764 | 37.689 | 42.942 | 49.335 | 56.334 | 63.167 | 67.505 | 76.154 | 86.661 |
| 60 | 37.485 | 43.188 | 46.459 | 52.294 | 59.335 | 66.981 | 74.397 | 79.082 | 88.379 | 99.607 |

# Glossary

**alternative hypothesis:** states that the result was not due to chance and represents a real difference or effect or relationship.

**applied statistics:** the practice of developing knowledge by using statistical methods to analyze data and make inferences about the population from which the data came.

**association:** is the relationship between two or more variables that co-vary with one another.

**assumption of homogeneity of variances:** is the assumption that the variances are equal across the groups under investigation. In the case of an independent sample $t$-test this means the variance of group 1 equals the variance of group 2.

**asymmetric distribution:** occurs when the left and right sides are not the same shape in reverse.

**bar chart:** displays the frequency of a variable with the variable categories along the $x$-axis and the variable frequencies on the $y$-axis.

**beta ($b$):** represents the slope of the regression line. It tells us how the value of y changes in relation to a one-unit change in the value of x.

**between group sum of squares:** is the sum of the squared deviations of each group mean from the grand mean.

**between group variance:** is the total amount the group means vary from the Grand Mean. This is also referred to as between group variability.

**boxplot:** is a graphical summary of the data based on percentiles. Also known as a box-and-whisker plot.

**central tendency:** is the value at the middle point of a distribution.

**class interval:** is a set of values that are combined into a single group for a frequency table.

**class limits:** are actual values in the data that are used as starting and ending values in each class interval.

**class width:** is the range of each class interval.

**coefficient of determination ($r^2$):** is the percentage of the variance in the dependent variable that is explained by the independent variable.

**complement of an event:** refers to all of the possible outcomes within a sample space except for the event of interest.

**confidence interval:** is a range of values that we expect will contain the true population parameter.

**contingency tables:** compare two (or more) categorical variables by cross tabulating the categories of each variable.

**correlation coefficient:** is a numerical value representing the strength and direction of a linear association between two variables.

**Cramér's V coefficient:** is used for nominal variables in a contingency table that is larger than two by two.

**critical value:** is the corresponding value to the significance level that determines the boundary for rejecting or failing to reject the null hypothesis.

**cumulative frequency polygon:** is a frequency polygon that graphs the cumulative percentage frequency column in a frequency table.

**cumulative percentage frequency:** gives the percentage of observations up to the end of a specific value.

**degrees of freedom:** are the number of independent observations/pieces of information used in estimating a parameter. For single sample confidence intervals, degrees of freedom is calculated as $n - 1$.

**dependent samples:** are considered to be dependent of one another if they consist of the same individuals and/or the selection of the individuals in the first group determines the selection of the second group.

**dependent variable:** is a variable that changes as a result of the change in an independent variable.

**descriptive statistics:** explains how frequently something of interest occurs in the observations you have made.

**deviation:** is the distance of an observed score from its mean.

**difference between the paired scores:** the difference between the first and second score for each individual or pairs of individuals.

**distribution:** is the arrangement of any values based on the frequencies with which they occur.

**empirical data:** is gathered from objects or participants for a research study.

**estimated standard error of the mean:** is the estimate of the standard error of the mean based on the sample standard deviation ($s$).

**estimated standard error of the proportion:**   is the estimate of the standard error of the proportion based on the sample proportion.

**event:**   a set of outcomes that we are interested in.

**expected frequency:**   is the values we would expect to occur by chance or other expected values as set by the researcher.

**experiment:**   a procedure or process that allows us to control specific conditions while observing a specific outcome.

***F*-Ratio:**   is the ratio of the between group variance to within group variance.

**factor:**   In ANOVA, a factor is the independent variable that the researcher controls or manipulates.

**frequency:**   refers to the number of observations of a specific value within a variable. Some textbooks call this absolute frequency but the meaning is the same.

**frequency distribution:**   is the summary of the values of a variable based on the frequencies with which they occur.

**frequency polygon:**   is a line graph of the frequency of interval or ratio data.

**generalize:**   to generalize the sample results to the population means to apply information from the sample to the population. We say that our findings are generalizable if the conclusions from the sample can be applied to the population of interest.

**grand mean:**   is the total of all observations divided by the total sample size.

**histogram:**   is a plot of the frequency of interval or ratio data.

**hypothesis testing with a single sample mean:**   is the statistical evaluation of a hypothesis whereby we compare a single sample mean to a known mean which is often, but not always, the population mean.

**hypothesis testing with a single sample proportion:**   is statistical evaluation of a hypothesis whereby we compare a single sample proportion to a known proportion which is often, but not always, the population proportion.

**independent samples:**   samples are considered to be independent of one another if they consist of different individuals and the selection of the individuals in the first group does not influence the selection of the second group.

**independent variable:**   is a variable that is hypothesized to influence the dependent variable.

**inferential statistics:**   are used to help generalize the results found in a sample to the entire population of interest.

**intercept ($\alpha$):**   the constant in the regression equation. It represents the value of *y* when *x* equals 0.

**interquartile range:**   considers only the middle 50 percent of the data in estimating a range.

**interval:**   a level of measurement in which there is an equal and meaningful difference between the levels of the variable but the variable itself does not have a meaningful absolute zero value.

**kurtosis:**   is the measure of the "peakedness" of a distribution.

**least-squares regression line:**   is a regression line that minimizes the sum of the squared distances between the observations and the line itself.

**leptokurtic:**   refers to the shape of a distribution when scores are clustered around the centre point.

**level of confidence:**   is the estimated probability that the true value of the population parameter falls within the stated confidence interval.

**mathematical statistics:**   the study of how to create the statistical methods using mathematical principles.

**mean:**   is the average score in a distribution.

**mean of the sampling distribution means:**   is the average of all of the means in the sampling distribution. It is the mean value of the sampling distribution means.

**mean sum of squares for between groups:**   represents the between group variance.

**mean sum of squares for within groups:**   represents the within group variance.

**measures of central tendency:**   are methods to calculate the centre or middle point of a distribution. The most common measures are mean, median, and mode.

**measures of dispersion:**   describe the variability in the data.

**median:**   is the middle point in the distribution that separates the upper and lower 50 percent of the data.

**mode:**   is the value that occurs with the greatest frequency.

**negatively associated:**   occurs when lower values of the first variable are found with higher values of the second variable, and vice versa.

**no association:**   occurs when a change in the first variable does not coincide with a change in the second variable.

**nominal:**   a level of measurement in which the difference within the variable is just a name or symbol.

**non-probability sampling:**   is a method of creating a sample that does not use a random method of sampling.

**normal curve:**   is a theoretical probability distribution that has a symmetrical bell shape.

**null hypothesis:** states that the result was due to chance (from sampling error) and as such is not a true difference.

**observed frequency:** the values we find in our sample data.

**one-tailed hypothesis:** states a predicted direction (directional).

**ordinal:** a level of measurement in which the answers to the qualitative categories, or attributes, have some order to them.

**Pearson's correlation coefficient:** is the correlation coefficient most commonly used for measuring the association between two interval or ratio level variables.

**percentage change:** is a fraction out of 100 that indicates the relative change in a variable from one time period to another.

**percentage frequency:** is the relative frequency expressed as a percentage value.

**percentiles:** are percentage frequencies indicating the percentage of scores that fall within a given area.

**phi coefficient:** is appropriate for nominal variables with a two by two (rows $\times$ columns) contingency table.

**pie chart:** displays the distribution of a variable out of 100 percent, where 100 percent represents the entire pie.

**platykurtic:** refers to the shape of a distribution when scores are fairly evenly spread out across the possible range of values.

**point-biserial correlation ($r_{pb}$):** measures the association between a dichotomous nominal variable and an interval or ratio variable.

**point estimate:** is a statistic that is used to estimate a parameter.

**pooled estimated standard error of the difference in the means:** is the estimated standard error used when the assumption of homogeneity of variances has been met.

**pooled sample variance:** an unbiased estimator of the variance that both groups have in common.

**population:** the total number of individuals, objects, or items that you are interested in.

**population mean:** uses the symbol $\mu$, which is pronounced "mu."

**population parameter:** is a numeric value in the population.

**population parameter estimation:** is the analytical method for calculating the expected population parameter based on a sample statistic.

**population standard deviation:** uses the symbol $\sigma$, which is pronounced "sigma."

**population variance:** uses the symbol $\sigma^2$, which is pronounced "sigma squared."

**positively associated:** occurs when lower values of the first variable are found with lower values of the second variable, or higher values of the first variable with higher values of the second variable.

**probability:** is a measure of the proportion of times that the event would occur if the experiment were repeated many times, under the same conditions.

**probability distribution:** is a theoretical frequency distribution with an infinite number of trials.

**probability sampling:** is a method of creating a sample by using some form of random method for selecting the participants from the population.

**random experiment:** any experiment that can be repeated, under the exact same conditions, and where the outcomes cannot be predicted with certainty.

**random outcome:** what an experiment has if the outcome cannot be predicted with certainty.

**range:** is the value of the largest observation minus the value of the smallest observation.

**rate:** is the frequency with which a phenomenon occurs relative to a population size or time unit.

**ratio:** a level of measurement in which the intervals between the values are equal and comparable and the zero value means the absence of something; a comparison of two values of a variable based on their frequency.

**raw score:** is the natural unit of measurement for a variable.

**regression line:** is a line of best fit that describes the linear association between an independent and dependent variable.

**relative frequency:** is a comparative measure of the proportion of observed values to the total number of responses within a variable.

**representative of the population:** a sample in which those in the sample have been randomly selected from the population such that each individual has an equal chance of being in the sample.

**respondent:** is the person being observed in the research study. For example, someone who is completing a survey on his or her political views is a respondent in the study. Often, in experimental research, we refer to respondents as subjects but the meaning is the same.

**sample:** a subset of the population.

**sample space:** refers to all of the possible outcomes of a random experiment.

**sample statistic:** is a numeric value in sample.

**sampling distribution:** is a theoretical distribution of all the potential values of a sample statistic that you would find if you could draw all possible combinations of random samples.

**sampling distribution of means:** is a theoretical distribution of all potential values of a sample mean that you would find if you could draw all possible combinations of random samples.

**sampling error:** the difference between the sample mean ($\bar{x}$) and the population mean ($\mu$). This occurs as a result of only sampling a portion of the population.

**scatterplot:** a graph that displays individual respondent (or subject) scores on two variables. One variable is represented on the $x$-axis and the other on the $y$-axis.

**scientific method:** is a process by which we investigate phenomena whether natural or social in nature.

**significance level ($\alpha$):** this value is used to determine whether to reject or fail to reject the null hypothesis.

**single sample $t$-test of a mean:** involves the comparison of a single sample mean ($\bar{x}$) to a known (or desired) population mean ($\mu$) when the standard population deviation ($\sigma$) is unknown.

**single sample $z$-test of a mean:** involves the comparison of a single sample mean ($\bar{x}$) to a known (or desired) population mean ($\mu$) when the standard population deviation ($\sigma$) is known.

**single sample $z$-test of a proportion:** involves the comparison of a single sample proportion to a known (or desired) population proportion.

**skewness:** is a measure of the amount to which a distribution departs from a symmetric shape. Skewed distributions are asymmetric.

**Spearman's correlation coefficient:** (Spearman's rho) is used to measure the association between two ranked ordinal variables.

**standard deviation:** is the average amount, measured in standard units, in which the data scores vary (positively and negatively) from its mean.

**standard error of mean:** is the standard deviation of the sampling means.

**standardized beta coefficient ($\beta$):** is the value of the slope of the regression line in standardized values (standard deviations).

**standardized score ($z$-score):** is a raw score that has been converted into the number of standard deviations that score is from its mean.

**statistical hypothesis testing:** is the use of statistical methods to test a hypothesis.

**statistical inference:** is the process for making statements about the broader population based on the use of sample data from that population.

**statistically significant:** results are considered statistically significant when it is unlikely that they occurred by chance.

**statistics:** the science and practice of developing human knowledge through the use of empirical data. It is based on statistical theory that uses probability theory to estimate population values.

**stem-and-leaf plot:** is a plot of the frequency of interval or ratio data similar to the histogram but more informative since it provides actual data values.

**strength of an association:** is the degree to which two variables are associated.

**sum of squares:** represents the total of the squared distance from one end of the range to the other.

**symmetric distribution:** occurs if the left and right sides of the distribution are the same shape, only reversed.

**test statistic:** is a summary value (statistic), based on our sample data, that indicates how far our sample estimate (such as $\bar{x}$) differs from zero under the null hypothesis distribution.

**total sum of squares:** is the sum of the squared deviations of each observation from the grand mean.

**two-tailed hypothesis:** does not state a predicted direction (non-directional).

**unbiased error:** a statistic is an unbiased estimator if its value equals the value of the parameter being estimated.

**unstandardized beta coefficient ($b$):** is the value of the slope of the regression line in the raw score values (units).

**variability:** is the extent to which the data varies from its mean.

**variable:** is a phenomenon of interest that can take on different values and can be measured.

**variance:** is a measure of the extent to which the data varies from its mean. When referring to a sample, it is called sample variance. When referring to the population it is called the population variance.

**violating an assumption:** is the situation where our data has not met one of the assumptions of a test.

**within group variance:** is the total amount that all individual observations vary from their group mean. This is also referred to as within group variability.

**within groups sum of squares:** is the sum of the squared deviations of each observation from its group mean.

# References

## Chapter 1

1. James R. Thompson, Richard A. Tapia, "Nonparametric function estimation, modeling, and simulation." *Society for Industrial Mathematics:* January 1, 1987; http://www.enotes.com/public-health-encyclopedia/graunt-john; "Biography of John Graunt," http://encyclopedia.stochastikon.com/; http://www.cs.xu.edu/math/Sources/Graunt/graunt.html.

2. Statistics Canada, Table 102-0563, Leading causes of death, total population, by sex, Canada, provinces and territories, annual, CANSIM (database). http://cansim2.statcan.gc.ca/cgi-win/cnsmcgi.exe?Lang=E&CNSM-Fi=CII/CII_1-eng.htm (accessed: August 18, 2009).

3. Based on numbers provided in J.S. Rosenthal (2005). *Struck by Lightning. The Curious World of Probabilities.* Harper Perennial: Toronto.

4. Katherine Marshall and Harold Wynne (Summer 2004). "Against the odds: A profile of at-risk and problem gamblers." *Canada Social Trends.* Statistics Canada—Catalogue No. 11-008.

5. Statistical Society of Canada, Code of Ethical Statistical Practice, www.ssc.ca.

6. Lance Lochner (2008), "Education and Crime," in B. McGraw, P. Peterson and E. Baker (editors), International Encyclopedia of Education, 3rd Edition, Amsterdam: Elsevier.

7. Ida Ferrara and Paul Missios (2005). "Recycling and Waste Diversion Effectiveness: Evidence from Canada," *Environmental and Resource Economics,* 30(2), 221–238.

8. Johnson, G.M. (2005). "Student Alienation, Academic Achievement, and WebCT Use." *Educational Technology & Society,* 8(2), 179–189.

9. Harvey Krahn and Leslie Kennedy (1985). "Producing Personal Safety: The Effects of Crime Rates, Police Force Size, and Fear of Crime." *Criminology* 23(4) 697–710.

10. Judith W. Tansky, Daniel G. Gallagher, and Kurt W. Wetzel (1997). "The Effect of Demographics, Work Status, and Relative Equity on Organizational Commitment: Looking Among Part-Time Workers." *Canadian Journal of Administrative Sciences,* 14(3), 315–326.

11. Allison Harell (2010). "The Limits of Tolerance in Diverse Societies: Hate Speech and Political Tolerance Norms Among Youth." *Canadian Journal of Political Science* 43(2), 407–432.

12. H. Wesley Perkins (2007). "Misperceptions of peer drinking norms in Canada: Another look at the 'reign of error' and its consequences among college students," *Addictive Behaviours* 32, 2645–2656.

13. Reutter, L., Veenstra, G., Stewart, M.J., Raphael, D., Love, R., Makwarimba, E. and McMurray, S. (2006). "Public attributions for poverty in Canada." *Canadian Review of Sociology and Anthropology,* 43(1), 1–22.

## Chapter 2

1. Cohen, I.B. "Florence Nightingale." *Scientific American,* 250 (March 1984), 128–137; Kopf, E.W. "Florence Nightingale as a Statistician," J. Amer. Statisti. Assoc., 15 (1916), 388–404.

2. Statistics Canada, 2004 Canadian Addiction Survey Data.

## Chapter 3

1. Mathworld: http://mathworld.wolfram.com/GaltonBoard.html; http://galton.org/; Nicholas W. Gillham, "Sir Francis Galton: From African Exploration to the Birth of Eugenics," New York: Oxford University Press, 2001.

2. Ezra W. Zukerman and John T. Jost (2001). "What makes you think you're so popular? Self-Evaluation Maintenance and the Subjective Side of the Friendship Paradox." *Social Psychology Quarterly,* 64(3), 207–223.

3. Scott L. Feld (1991). "Why your friends have more friends than you do." *American Journal of Sociology,* 96(6), 1464–1477.

## Chapter 4

1. Ivo Schneider (2001). "Abraham de Moivre." In C.C. Heyde and E. Seneta (eds), *Statisticians of the*

*Centuries.* Springer: New York; Ted Goertzel and Joseph Fashing (1981), "The Myth of the Normal Curve: A Theoretical Critique and Examination of its Role in Teaching and Research." *Humanity and Society,* 5, pp. 14–31.

2. E. Seneta (2001). "Abraham de Moivre." In C.C Heyde and E. Seneta (eds), *Statisticians of the Centuries.* Springer: New York.

3. Trenchard More, Jr. (1959). "On the Construction of Venn Diagrams." *The Journal of Symbolic Logic,* pp. 303–304.

4. Elections Canada. Refer to printout 4.2.pdf

5. Margot Shields (2006). "Stress and Depression in the Employed Population." Health Reports, Vol. 17, No. 4, October. See Printout 4.3.pdf

6. Statistics Canada report "Measured adult body mass index (BMI)." See Printout 4.4.pdf

7. C. Montmarquette, S. Mahseredjian, and R. Houle (2001). "The determinants of university dropouts: A bivariate probability model with sample selection." *Economics of Education Review,* 20, 475–484.

## Chapter 5

1. http://www-history.mcs.st-and.ac.uk/Mathematicians/Gauss.html; Waterhouse, W. (1990), Gauss's first argument for least squares, Arch. Hist. Exact Sci. 41 41–52.

2. Statistics Canada. *Health Indicators.* Ottawa, Statistics Canada, 2007 (Cat. No. 82-221-XIE) See print-out 4.5b.pdf

## Chapter 6

1. http://bayesian.org/bayes; Thomas Bayes: http://encyclopedia.stochastikon.com/; Encyclopedia Britannica: http://www.britannica.com/EBchecked/topic/56807/Thomas-Bayes; http://www.maa.org/devlin/devlin_2_00.html.

## Chapter 7

1. S.L. Zabell (2001). "Robert Aylmer Fisher." In C.C Heyde and E. Seneta (eds), *Statisticians of the Centuries.* Springer: New York. p. 389; Robert A. Fisher (1935). *The Design of Experiments.* Edinburgh: Oliver and Boyd; Joan Fisher Box (1978). *R.A. Fisher, The Life of a Scientist.* New York: Wiley.

2. Robin Wright, Lindsay John, Anne-Marie Livingstone, Nicole Shepherd, and Eric Duku (2007), "Effects of School-Based Interventions on Secondary School Students with High and Low Risks for Antisocial Behaviour." *Canadian Journal of School Psychology,* 22(1), June 2007 32–49.

## Chapter 8

1. Reid, Constance, *Jerzy Neyman—From Life.* Springer Verlag, (1982); Neyman, Jerzy (1937). "Outline of a Theory of Statistical Estimation Based on the Classical Theory of Probability." Philosophical Transactions of the Royal Society of London. Series A, Mathematical and Physical Sciences, 236(767): pp. 333–380; Lehmann, E.L. (1994). *Jerzy Neyman 1894–1981.* National Academy of Sciences, Washington D.C.

2. "Canadians Decisively Pro-Choice on Abortion: No Change Over the Decade" April 1, 2010 press release from http://www.ekos.com/media/default.asp.

3. LSAT Performance with Regional, Gender, and Racial/Ethnic Breakdowns: 2001–2002 through 2009–2010 Testing Years, Dalessandro, Sitwell, Lawlor, and Reese, October 2010.

4. Published by authority of the Minister responsible for Statistics Canada © Minister of Industry, 2002. May 2002, Catalogue no. 85-403-XIE ISSN 1488-5611.

5. Hovsepian, S.L, Blais, M, Manseau, H, Otis, J. and Girard, M. (2010). Prior Victimization and Sexual and Contraceptive Self-Efficacy among Adolescent Females under Child Protective Services Care. *Health Education and Behavior,* 37, 65–83.

## Chapter 9

1. Student (1908). The probable error of a mean. Biometrika 6(1): 1–252; Zabell, S.L. (2008). On Student's 1908 Article "The Probable Error of a Mean." *Journal of the American Statistical Association* 103 1–7.

2. Canadian Tobacco Use Monitoring Survey (CTUMS) 2009. Health Canada: http://www.hc-sc.gc.ca/hc-ps/tobac-tabac/research-recherche/stat/ctums-esutc_2009_graph-eng.php.

## Chapter 10

1. David J, Bartholomew (2001). "Egon Sharpe Pearson." In C.C Heyde and E. Seneta (eds), *Statisticians of the Centuries.* Springer: New York. pp. 373–376; C. Scott and R. Nowak, "A Neyman-Pearson approach to statistical learning," IEEE Trans. Inform. Theory, vol. 51, no. 8, pp. 3806–3819, 2005; October 2003, MacTutor History of Mathematics, School of Mathematics and Statistics, University of St Andrews, Scotland [http://www-history.mcs.st-andrews.ac.uk/Biographies/Pearson_Egon.html].

2. Veronica Stinson, Marc W. Patry, Steven M. Smith (2007), "The CSI Effect: Reflections from Police and Forensic Investigators," *Canadian Journal of Police and Security Services,* Vol. 5, No. 3, pp. 125–133.

3. The databases at http://www.nationmaster.com/statistics this source is used in other books such as Rosenthal's "Struck by lightning" published by Harper Perennial.

4. For Canada the data came from Statistics Canada's "The Daily" Wenesday, December 20, 2006 at http://www.statcan.gc.ca/daily-quotidien/061220/dq061220b-eng.htm.

5. For the United States the data came from the Center for Disease Control report "National Vital Statistics Report" Volume 55, Number 19, August 21, 2007. DHHS Publication No. (PHS) 2007–1120 US Department of Health and Human Services by Minino, Heron, Murphy, and Kochanek.

6. Statistics Canada—Pregnancy Outcomes by Birth http://www40.statcan.ca/l01/cst01/hlth65b-eng.htm.

7. Matthew B. Ruby, Elizabeth W. Dunn, Andrea Perrino, Randall Gillis, and Sasha Viel (2011), "The invisible benefits of exercise," *Health Psychology,* Vol. 30, No. 1, pp. 67–74.

8. Statistics Canada, The Internet: Is it changing the way Canadians spend their time? By B. Veenhof. Catalogue no. 56F0004MIE—no. 013, ISSN: 1492-7918, ISBN: 0-662-43693-8, August 2006.

## Chapter 11

1. Kempthorne, O. (1974). "George W. Snedecor," *International Statistical Review,* 42, 319–321;

2. Snedecor, G, W. (1934). *Calculation and Interpretation of Analysis of Variance and Covariance.* Collegiate Press, Ames Iowa.

2. Ullrich Munzel and Ajit Tamhane (2002) "Nonparametric multiple comparisons in repeated measure designs for data with ties. *Biometrical Journal,* 6, 762–779.

3. Levene, H. (1960), "Robust Tests for the Equality of Variance," in I. Olkin, ed., *Contributions to Probability and Statistics,* 278–292, Palo Alto, CA: Stanford University Press

4. Montgomery et al (2011). A comparison of individual and social vulnerabilities, health and quality of life among Canadian women with mental diagnoses and young children. Women's Health Issues 21-1, pp. 48–56.

## Chapter 12

1. http://statprob.com/encyclopedia/KarlPEARSON.html; http://www.gap-system.org/~history/Biographies/Pearson.html; M. Eileen Magnello, "Karl Pearson and the Origins of Modern Statistics: An Elastician becomes a Statistician," http://www.rutherfordjournal.org/article010107.html

2. Christopher D. O'Connor (2009). "Citizen attitudes toward the police in Canada." In *Policing: An International Journal of Policing Strategies and Management* 31(4) pp. 578–579.

## Chapter 13

1. Williams, Zimmerman, Zumbo, and Ross. "Charles Spearman: British Behavioral Scientist." In *The Human Nature Review* Volume 3, 2003, pp. 114–118.

2. Ulsperger, Hodges, and Paul (2010). "Pirates on the Plank: Neutralization Theory and the Criminal Downloading of Music Among Generation Y in the Era of Late Modernity." In the *Journal of Criminal Justice and Popular Culture* 17(1), pp. 124–151.

# Photo Credits

*All A Brief History Of . . . box sketches courtesy of Rhiana Sneyd.*

## Chapter 1
Page 2: Photo courtesy of Andresr/Dreamstime/GetStock.

## Chapter 2
Page 36: Photo courtesy of Sellingpix/Dreamstime/ GetStock; page 37: Photo courtesy of http://www. florence-nightingale-avenging-angel.co.uk/ Coxcomb.htm.

## Chapter 3
Page 74: Photo Courtesy of Markogt/Dreamstime/ GetStock; page 75: Wikimedia: http://en.wikipedia.org/ wiki/File:Quincunx_(Galton_Box)_-_Galton_1889_ diagram.png.

## Chapter 4
Page 104: Photo courtesy of Georgeman/Dreamstime/ GetStock; page 105: Wikimedia: http://en.wikipedia. org/wiki/File:Abraham_de_Moivre_-_Doctrine_of_ Chance_-_1718.gif.

## Chapter 5
Page 132: Photo of courtesy of Marekuliasz/ Dreamstime/GetStock.

## Chapter 6
Page 160: Photo courtesy of Miluxian/Dreamstime/GetStock.

## Chapter 7
Page 186: Photo courtesy of Mikle15/Dreamstime/ GetStock.

## Chapter 8
Page 212: Photo courtesy of Seriga/Dreamstime/ GetStock.

## Chapter 9
Page 242: Photo courtesy of Davidgarry/Dreamstime/GetStock.

## Chapter 10
Page 264: Photo courtesy of Todd Bigelow/ GetStock.

## Chapter 11
Page 298: Photo courtesy of Icefields/Dreamstime/ GetStock.

## Chapter 12
Page 330: Photo courtesy of Fastexposure/ Dreamstime/GetStock.

## Chapter 13
Page 360: Photo courtesy of Richard Lautens/ GetStock.

# Index

# Appendix G

## Frequently Used Equations

ANOVA formulas

| Source | Sum of Squares | df | Mean Sum of Squares | F-Ratio |
|---|---|---|---|---|
| Between Groups | $\Sigma n_i(\bar{x}_i - \bar{\bar{x}})^2$ | $k - 1$ | $\dfrac{SS_B}{df_B}$ | $\dfrac{MS_B}{MS_W}$ |
| Within Groups | $\Sigma(x_i - \bar{x}_i)^2$ | $n - k$ | $\dfrac{SS_W}{df_W}$ | |
| Total | $\Sigma(x_i - \bar{\bar{x}}_i)^2$ or $SS_B + SS_W$ | $n - 1$ or $df_B + df_W$ | | |

Confidence interval of a proportion with $p_0$ is unknown

$$CI = \hat{p} \pm z_{(\alpha)}\left(\sqrt{\frac{\hat{p}(1 - \hat{p})}{n}}\right)$$

Confidence interval of the mean when $\sigma$ is known (8.8)*

$$CI = \bar{x} \pm z_{(\alpha)}\left(\sqrt{\frac{\sigma}{\sqrt{n}}}\right)$$

Confidence interval of the mean when $\sigma$ is unknown (8.17)*

$$CI = \bar{x} \pm t_{(\alpha)}\left(\sqrt{\frac{s}{\sqrt{n}}}\right)$$

Estimated standard error of the mean

$$s_{\bar{x}} = \frac{s}{\sqrt{n}}$$

Estimated standard error of the proportion

$$s_{\hat{p}} = \sqrt{\frac{\hat{p}(1 - \hat{p})}{n}}$$

Goodman and Kruskal's Gamma

$$Gamma = \frac{Na - Ni}{Na + Ni}$$

Independent sample $t$-test

$$t = \frac{x_1 - \bar{x}_2}{\sqrt{\dfrac{(n_1 - 1)s_1^2 + (n_2 - 1)s_2^2}{(n_1 + n_2 - 2)} \times \left(\dfrac{1}{n_1} + \dfrac{1}{n_2}\right)}}$$

Least squares regression line

$$\hat{y} = a + bx$$

Mutually-exclusive probability

$$P(A \text{ or } B) = P(A) + P(B)$$

Non-mutually-exclusive probability

$$P(A \text{ or } B) = P(A) + P(B) - P(A \text{ and } B)$$

Paired sample $t$-test

$$t = \frac{\bar{D}}{\left(\dfrac{s_d}{\sqrt{n}}\right)}$$

Pearson's chi-square

$$\chi^2 = \Sigma\frac{(0 - E)^2}{E}$$

Pearson's correlation coefficient ($r$)

$$r = \frac{\Sigma xy - \left(\dfrac{\Sigma x \Sigma y}{n}\right)}{\sqrt{\left(\Sigma x^2 - \dfrac{(\Sigma x)^2}{n}\right)\left(\Sigma y^2 - \dfrac{(\Sigma y)^2}{n}\right)}}$$

Percentage change

$$p = \frac{f_{time2} - f_{time1}}{f_{time1}} \times 100$$

Percentage frequency

$$\%f = \frac{f}{n} \times 100$$

Point-biserial correlation coefficient

$$r_{pb} = \frac{(\bar{Y}_1 - \bar{Y}_0)\sqrt{p(1 - p)}}{\sqrt{\Sigma Y^2 - \dfrac{(\Sigma Y)^2}{N}}}$$